D0934187

Mediated Women

Representations in Popular Culture

The Hampton Press Communication Series
Political Communication
David L. Paletz, Editor

Eastern European Journalism
*Jerome Aumente, Peter Gross, Ray Hiebert, Owen Johnson,
and Dean Mills*

The In/Outsiders: The Mass Media in Israel
Dan Caspi and Yehiel Limor

Media Entrepreneurs and the Media Enterprise in the United States
Congress: Influencing Policy in the Washington Community
Karen M. Kedrowski

The Politics of Disenchantment: Bush, Clinton, Perot, and the Press
*James Lemert, William R. Elliot, William L. Rosenberg, and
James M. Bernstein*

Mediated Women: Representations in Popular Culture
Marian Meyers (ed.)

Political Communication in Action: States, Institutions,
Movements, Audiences
David L. Paletz (ed.)

Glasnost and After: Media and Change in Central and Eastern Europe
David L. Paletz, Karol Jakubowicz, and Pavao Novosel (eds.)

Germany's "Unity Election": Voters and the Media
Holli A. Semetko and Klaus Schoenbach

Strategic Failures in the Modern Presidency
Mary E. Stuckey

forthcoming

Eden Online: Re-inventing Humanity in a Technological Universe
Kerric Harvey

Business as Usual: Continuity and Change in Central and
Eastern European Media
David L. Paletz and Karol Jakubowicz (eds.)

Global Communication, Local Cultures, and Intimate Coerseduction
René Jean Ravault

Gender, Politics and Communication
Annabelle Sreberny and Liesbet van Zoonen (eds.)

War in the Media Age
A. Trevor Thrall

Mediated Women

Representations in Popular Culture

edited by

Marian Meyers
Georgia State University

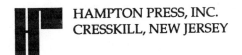

HAMPTON PRESS, INC.
CRESSKILL, NEW JERSEY

Copyright © 1999 by Hampton Press, Inc.

All rights reserved. No part of this publication may be reproduced, stored in a retrieval system, or transmitted in any form or by any means, electronic, mechanical, photocopying, microfilming, recording, or otherwise, without permission of the publisher.

Printed in the United States of America

Library of Congress Cataloging-in-Publication Data

Mediated women : representations in popular culture / edited by
    Marian Meyers.
        p.   cm. -- (The Hampton Press communication series)
    Includes bibliographical references and index.
    ISBN 1-57273-239-3. -- ISBN 1-57273-240-7
    1. Women in popular culture--United States. 2. Women in mass
media--United States. 3. Women on television--United States.
4. Women in motion pictures--United States. I. Meyers, Marian,
1954-   . II. Series.
HQ1421.M43   1999
305.4'0973--dc21   99-29090
                                                                 CIP

Cover photo: © 1996 Ron L. Brown c/o MIRA.
Eclipse Fax ad © 1993. Reprinted with permission.
Time cover (1/20/92) © Time Life Syndication. Reprinted with permission.

Hampton Press.
23 Broadway
Cresskill, NJ 07626

HON

HQ
1421
M43
1999

Mediated
women :
represe

For Talia and Emma

Contents

Acknowledgments

I am indebted to a number of people who have played a part in shaping this book and bring it to fruition. Conversations with Carolyn Byerly and Elayne Rapping were extremely helpful in broadening my view—and the focus of this book—to include research that reflects the gains within representation made by feminism and the women's movement over the years. Their encouragement to expand the book beyond studies whose primary focus is the operation of patriarchy within the text helped make this anthology more complete, complex and, ultimately, more useful to its readers.

Thanks are due, also, to graduate students Carolyn Lea for her help in soliciting manuscripts, Noelle Pearce for her careful attention to the manuscript when entering editorial changes on the computer, and to Debbie George and Wesley Chenault, for their thorough proofreading. I am grateful, as well, to the Department of Communication and the Women's Studies Institute at Georgia State University for their support of this project, more specifically by providing course releases and graduate research assistants. In addition, Lisa Cuklanz deserves thanks for her work during the initial stages in the development of a book which ultimately served as a starting point for *Mediated Women*.

I am particularly indebted to the students in my "women and media" class who, over the years, have challenged and inspired me. They are the reason I saw the need for a book that broadly examined the mediated representation of women in popular culture; this book truly would not have been written without them.

Finally my husband, Danny, deserves my heartfelt gratitude for his unflagging support and encouragement in this and all my endeavors.

About the Contributors

Roger C. Aden is an associate professor in the School of Interpersonal Communication at Ohio University. He has published articles about popular culture issues involving identity, gender, and/or place. He is the author of the forthcoming book, *Popular Stories and Promised Lands: Fan Cultures and Symbolic Pilgrimages*.

Susan Alexander is an assistant professor of sociology at Lycoming College in Williamsport, Pennsylvania. She is co-author of *The Ambivalent Welcome: Print Media, Public Opinion, and Immigration*. She has published in the areas of social psychology, sociology of education, bilingual education, marriage and family, and popular culture.

Shawny Anderson is an associate professor in the Department of Communication at Saint Mary's College of California in Moraga, California. Her research interests include rhetorical theory and criticism, cultural studies, qualitative methods, and communication and social justice.

S. Elizabeth Bird is a professor of anthropology at the University of South Florida. She is the author of *For Enquiring Minds: A Cultural Study of Supermarket Tabloids*, editor of *Dressing in Feathers: The Construction of the Indian in American Popular Culture*, and the author of many articles and book chapters in media and cultural studies.

Cristina Bodinger-deUriarte is an associate chair and advisor in the department of sociology at California State University-Los Angeles. She spent more than a decade working in "think tanks" as an evaluator of multicultural and diversity issues and educational programs, and is the author of a book on hate crime. She has published in the areas of diversity, media analysis and popular culture.

Carolyn M. Byerly is an assistant professor of journalism and international communication at Ithaca College in New York, where she also serves on the women's studies program faculty. Her research interests include the effects of feminism and other liberation movements on news organizations and news coverage of those movements, the political economy of the media, and news coverage of sex crimes. Her current research examines women's relationship to the global media industries. She also has been a longtime political activist, particularly in the movement to stop violence against women.

Jane Caputi is a professor of women's studies at Florida Atlantic University in Boca Raton. She is the author of *The Age of Sex Crime* and *Gossips, Gorgons and Crones: The Fates of the Earth*. She also collaborated with Mary Daly on *Webster's First New Intergalactic Wickedary of the English Language*.

Meta G. Carstarphen is an assistant professor of journalism at the University of North Texas. A former magazine editor, she continues to write poetry and fiction, as well as non-fiction, and her work has appeared in a variety of publications. She was a research fellow at the Poynter Institute in 1997-98, and has conducted research on journalists' views of race and reporting. She is the co-editor of the forthcoming book, *Sexual Rhetoric: Media Perspectives on Sexuality, Gender and Identity*.

Charlene Dellinger-Pate is an assistant professor in the communication department at Southern Connecticut State University. Her research involves feminist critical inquiry.

Bettina Fabos is an Iowa Fellow in the College of Education at the University of Iowa. Her background is in journalism and video production, and she writes about the media and culture.

Lisa A. Flores is an assistant professor in Communication and Ethnic Studies at the University of Utah. Her teaching and research interests include feminism, rhetoric, culture and chicana/o studies.

Jocelyn Géliga Vargas was born and raised in Puerto Rico and came to the United States in her late teens. She teaches mass media and journalism at Lehman College in the Bronx, N.Y., and is involved with alternative media projects, including co-production of the documentary *Aquí en la Lucha*, created in collaboration with Las Luchadoras (Woman Warriors), a grassroots *puertorriqueña* organization in Holyoke, Mass.

Carmen Gillespie is an assistant professor of English at Mary Washington College in Virginia. Her recent scholarship includes articles on African American women writers, intercultural intertextuality within the African diaspora, and representations of African American women in contemporary media.

Jill Birnie Henke is an associate professor of communication at Millersville University in Pennsylvania. She has published in the areas of political communication and feminist studies, and she is currently conducting research concerning learning outcomes of undergraduate students in a collaborative learning environment vs. the traditional lecture course. She also consults in the areas of diversity and conflict mediation.

Michelle A. Holling is a doctoral candidate in the Department of Communication at Arizona State University. Her research interests include rhetoric, feminist theory, postmodernism, and Chicana/o scholarship.

Carolyn Lea is a doctoral candidate in American Studies at Bowling Green State University in Ohio. Her research interests include feminist theory and cultural practices.

Carolyn Lin is an associate professor in the Department of Communication at Cleveland State University. Her research interests include the economic and socio-cultural impact of advertising and communication technology. She is the co-author of *Patterns of Teletext Use in the U.K.* and has written more than 40 book chapters and journal articles. Her background includes work in both the advertising and marketing industries.

Charlene Melcher is an assistant professor in the communication and theatre department at Saginaw Valley State University in Michigan. Her primary research interest is the study of social effects of the media, especially as they affect the development and maintenance of people's health-related beliefs, attitudes and behaviors.

Marian Meyers is an associate professor of communication at Georgia State University, where she also serves on the faculty of the Women's Studies Institute. Her research interests include news coverage of violence against women, as well as the representation of women and other socially marginalized groups within mediated popular culture. She is the author of *News Coverage of Violence against Women: Engendering Blame.*

Anjali Ram is a doctoral candidate at Ohio University. Her dissertation is an audience ethnography that explores how Indian immigrant women actively engage with Indian cinema, which reflects her interest in how popular culture mediates the constitution of national and gendered identities in the Asian-Indian diaspora. She currently teaches as adjunct faculty at Clark University and Worcester State College in Massachusetts.

Elayne Rapping is a professor of Arts and Letters at the University of Buffalo/State University of New York, and the author of book and articles, including *MEDIA-TIONS: Forays into the Culture and Gender Wars*. Her main areas of work are media and gender studies.

Tom Reichert is an assistant professor of advertising in the Department of Journalism at the University of North Texas. His research interests include message and advertising effects, images of women and men in the media, and the impact of sexually oriented appeals on persuasion.

Linda Steiner is an associate professor in the Department of Journalism and Mass Media at Rutgers University in New Jersey, where she also is director of the undergraduate honors program. Her most recent publications have dealt with why women journalists have quit the newsroom, the use of public access cable television by feminists, and feminist approaches to mass media ethics.

Diane Zimmerman Umble is an associate professor and chair of the Department of Communication and Theatre at Millersville University in Pennsylvania. Her research interests include gender studies, technology and social history. She is the author of *Holding the Line: The Telephone in Old Order Mennonite and Amish Life*.

Amy Villarejo is an assistant professor of film and women's studies at Cornell University in Ithaca, New York. She is the co-author of *Queen Christina* and is co-editing a volume on cultural studies approaches to popular film.

Barbara Wilinsky is a visiting assistant professor in the Department of Media Arts at the University of Arizona-Tucson. She received her Ph.D. from Northwestern University's Department of Radio-Television-Film. Her work has appeared in *Film History, The Velvet Light Trap, Spectator* (USC), and *Quarterly Review of Film and Video*.

I

INTRODUCTION

1

Fracturing Women

Marian Meyers

The bus stop posters advertising Fox television's *Melrose Place* featured a huge photo of star Heather Locklear with the words "Mondays are a bitch" scrawled across her face. Monday, according to Fox publicists, had been designated "Bitch Night" in honor of Locklear's character.

The super-thin body of super-model Kate Moss has become a ubiquitous icon of beauty, her reed-like frame idealized in magazine fashion spreads as the perfect female form.

The song "Smack My Bitch Up," from a hit album by the British group Prodigy, was released as a single on Madonna's Maverick label, along with 3,000 promotional posters that feature the title as a slogan for display in record stores. The music video created to promote the song showed women being hit and injected with drugs.

Should we care about these words and images? Do the representations of women in popular media affect us and the ways we view the world, or are they primarily fleeting in duration and inconsequential in impact? Considerable research indicates that the images *do* affect us, that they work, cumulatively and unconsciously, to create and reinforce a particular world view or ideology that shapes our perspectives and beliefs about the world, our neighborhoods, and ourselves. Research, for example, has linked the glamorization of thinness by models and actresses on television, in newspapers, and in magazines to potentially deadly eating

3

disorders such as bulimia and anorexia (Kilbourne, 1993, 1994; Stice, Schupak-Neuberg, Shaw, & Stein, 1994).

Of course, concern about the media's depiction of women is not new. Twenty years ago, in the first book to look broadly at the representation of women in mediated popular culture, Tuchman (1978) concluded that the mass media engaged in the "symbolic annihilation" of women through the condemnation, trivialization, and absence of them:

> Consider the symbolic representation of women in the mass media. Relatively few women are portrayed there, although women are fifty-one percent of the population and are well over forty percent of the labor force. Those working women who are portrayed are condemned. Others are trivialized: they are symbolized as child-like adornments who need to be protected or they are dismissed to the protective confines of the home. In sum, they are subject to *symbolic annihilation*. (p. 8; emphasis in original)

Much has changed since that book, *Hearth and Home: Images of Women in the Mass Media* (Tuchman, Daniels, & Benét, 1978), examined the portrayal of women in television, women's magazines, and newspapers in the late 1970s:

- MTV—which first took to the airwaves August 1, 1981—has altered permanently the visual terrain of television, not simply in its introduction of music videos as combination art form, entertainment, and advertisement, but also in pioneering production techniques that have become standard in other televisual genres.
- More women now work outside the home—and have increased their presence within the media industries—although they continue to earn lower wages than men, remain largely excluded from top management positions, and still do the bulk of the housework and child care at home (Rhode, 1997).
- Niche marketing has reached new heights of specialization, from the new WB and UPN television networks' focus on programming for young audiences to the growing number of new magazines targeting highly specialized consumer groups, from Mac computer users to women athletes and working mothers.
- The women's movement is now said to be in its Third Wave—the First Wave having occurred during the Suffrage Movement of the late 19th and early 20th century, and the Second during the 1960s and 1970s.

Despite the social, political, economic, and cultural upheavals during the 20 years since *Hearth and Home* was published, no book since has attempted to broadly assess the state of the image of women in the media. Writers have, of course, explored the meaning behind the mediated images of specific women such as Madonna (Frank & Smith, 1993; Schwichtenberg, 1993), or they have attempted to chronicle the popular media's representation of women within specific themes such as femininity (Macdonald, 1995), or particular genres such as advertising (Barthel, 1988; Goffman, 1979). But a book that closely examined a wide range of mediated texts for the portrayal of women in popular culture remained to be written.

Thus was born the idea for this book. Given that *Hearth and Home* was long out of print, as well as dated given the social and cultural transformations of the intervening years, an obvious question was whether the book's conclusions were similarly dated. Were the popular media still guilty of the symbolic annihilation of women? Or was something else going on?

Mediated Women: Representations in Popular Culture attempts to answer these questions with original research into the popular media's portrayal of women. Its goals are to provide a current look at the images of women, to examine their mediated representations as they appear at this historical point in time, and to demonstrate how media texts[1] promote particular understandings of women's lives and roles.

Of course, it would be impossible for any one book—or series—to adequately portray the vast array of mediated images of women. A quantitative approach could provide greater breadth by offering a summary of findings over a wider range of images. Indeed, such an approach is extremely useful in providing an overview of the representation of women as they appear in specific media programs or genres. The reports of the Women, Men and Media Project (1991, 1993, 1994, 1995, 1996), for example, have effectively documented the presence—or, more accurately, the absence—of women within print and broadcast news, both as sources and journalists. After concluding that women more often than not were "window dressing" in the world of news (1994), the project more recently found that the number of women in the news was actually beginning to decline (1995, 1996). Similarly, Nancy Signorielli's (1997) quantitative content analysis across six media[2] used heavily by teenage girls showed that the media play a dual role by presenting both positive and negative images of women, thus providing adolescent girls with conflicting messages about their own potential. Although many of the female characters in Signorielli's study were strong, independent, intelligent, and honest, physical appearance and relationships were of primary concern for them. By way of contrast, her analysis also found that jobs and careers were far more important for male characters. The overall message may be that girls and women can be strong, smart, and independent as long as they remain within the confines of their homes and relationships while also maintaining traditional standards of feminine beauty.

Although Signorielli's content analysis and others like it are of particular value in assessing the gains women have or have not made relative to a quantifiable standard, numbers by themselves do not tell the whole story. They do not, for instance, tell us how the representation of women's equality may be shaped by the media's primary allegiance to corporate interests (see Elayne Rapping's chapter on *Melrose Place*), or how media images collude with prevailing cultural notions of gender, race, and class to define and reinforce white, middle-class standards of feminine beauty and desirability (see Bettina Fabos's chapter on figure skating). Nor do they tell us how patriarchy may be reinscribed within the subtext of a television sitcom that *appears* to position its female lead as equal and authoritative (see Charlene Dellinger-Pate and Roger Aden's chapter on *Home Improvement*), or demonstrate how heterosexual anxiety and fear circumscribe the portrayal of the "acceptable" lesbian (see Amy Villarejo's chapter on the made-for-TV movie about a military officer discharged from service for being a lesbian), or show us how depictions of women of color may be made to resist racialized stereotyping (see chapters by Lisa Flores and Michelle Holling, Anjali Ram, and Meta Carstarphen). Quantitative studies cannot address nuance and underlying meanings as can qualitative, textual analyses.

This book, then, attempts to understand the meanings behind the representations of women in popular culture through primarily qualitative textual analyses[3] of films, television programs, the news, magazines, music videos, and advertising.[4] Although the term *popular culture* can be applied to such activities as shopping and going to the beach on a hot summer day, *mediated* popular culture refers to the mass produced commodities—television sitcoms and dramas, movies, books, newspapers, music CDS, and so on—created and disseminated by the media for wide consumption by various targeted segments of the population. Therefore, the crucial issues to be explored in this book are: what mediated popular culture says about women and their roles in contemporary society, whether and how the mediated representation of women addresses real women's goals and potential, how the popular media negotiate the tension between cultural constraint and social change within their portrayals of women, and whether women are still the victims of symbolic annihilation by the media.

This chapter situates the rest of this book within the broader context of research into the mediated representation of woman. It also addresses the role of the media in maintaining and, at times, challenging a patriarchal world view, and it argues that the representations of women in mediated popular culture are fractured, reflecting multiple and often contradictory images, so that "symbolic annihilation" may no longer be an appropriate term for describing the mass media's treatment and depiction of women. Finally, this chapter provides an overview of the rest of the book and its organization.

CREATING CONSENT

Culture is inherently political, for it is the process by which meanings of self, of social identity and social relations, are created within the context of a particular system of hierarchical social formations. In the case of U.S. and other Eurocentric cultures, that system is, as John Fiske (1989) states, "white, patriarchal capitalism" (p. 1). And the resources or products of popular culture within this capitalist formation "carry the interests of the ideologically dominant; they have lines of force within them that are hegemonic and that work in favor of the status quo" (p. 2).

Other cultural critics have also pointed out that the popular media help to shape a world view in their audiences which supports those in positions of power and authority (Althusser, 1971; Gitlin, 1980; Hall, 1982). By serving the interests of this ruling class, the popular media help to maintain its political, economic, and social dominance. Of course, patriarchy cannot do its job of supporting the status quo alone. It also must embrace and promote particular understandings of race, class, and sexuality—along with traditional gender stereotypes and beliefs—if the ideals, values, and opinions of white, heterosexual, middle- and upper class men are to remain the dominant ideology within society. Indeed, this prevailing ideology must appear natural, inevitable, commonsensical, and *consensual* to be effective.

The popular media play a key role in maintaining hegemonic consensus by helping those in power win the consent of the governed (Gramsci, 1971, 1983). Subordinated groups—women, people of color, the poor and working classes, lesbians and gay men, the elderly—are encouraged to "buy into" the dominant ideology which, in fact, maintains the status quo by keeping them subordinated. Thus, the ideological work of the media consists, in part, of presenting a reality[5] that appears more natural or real than the material circumstances of subordinated people's lives—even when those circumstances would appear to contradict the media's messages. Research conducted by Elizabeth Frazer (1987) illustrates the media's role in this process. In a study of how adolescent females "read" *Jackie*, a British teen magazine for girls, she found that when the media's version of reality conflicted with the girls' lived reality, the media's account was viewed as more credible and legitimate. Liesbet van Zoonen (1994) sums up the various studies in this area as follows:

> in research on stereotypes it is thought that children and adults learn their appropriate gender roles by a process of symbolic reinforcement and correction. . . . In research on ideology a process of familiarization with dominant ideology is assumed leading finally to its internalization and transformation into common sense. (p. 29)

Although media texts—that is, mediated cultural commodities—are molded by and are a product of the dominant ideology, their messages remain polysemic, open to various interpretations. Thus, although the "preferred reading" (Hall, 1980) of the text may be inscribed by and reflective of the dominant ideology, individuals may vary widely in their interpretation of the same text, depending on their backgrounds and who they are. Gender, race, class, ethnic background, age, and other signifiers of domination and exclusion, along with personal experience, become factors in determining how an individual subjectively creates meaning from and interprets or "decodes" a text (Morley, 1980). Celeste Condit (1989) has argued that this process may actually be more a function of "polyvalence" in which audience members may receive similar meanings from mediated messages but *evaluate* them differently, depending, again, on their individual decoding capabilities. Regardless of whether audience members construct meaning from or evaluate messages differently, what is clear is that individuals do different things with texts and come to different conclusions based on their individual experiences and background. For example, a moviegoer's decoding strategies and abilities will determine whether she or he finds pleasure in a pornographic film or is outraged by its degrading depiction of women. And although similarities in background and experience among a particular subcultural grouping such as white, middle-class, college-educated, young women may lead most members to interpret or read a text similarly, even within this seemingly homogenous subcultural formation, some variety and deviation is inevitable.

However, resistance to the dominant ideology is not limited to the subjectivity and decoding capabilities of the individual reader of cultural texts. It also exists within the texts themselves,[6] for they are fraught with the contradictions reflective of competing interest groups. Hegemony is never a given, but must be fought for, renewed, recreated, and defended on a continuous basis if it is to maintain its position of dominance. This struggle pits competing versions of reality against each other, with the prevailing ideology able to accommodate and incorporate some alternative meanings, values, opinions, attitudes, and beliefs within its periphery without changing its core (Williams, 1980). Few would deny, for example, that feminism has made considerable inroads into patriarchal ideology within the past 30 years, for women are no longer considered incapable of performing many of the jobs traditionally held by men. And yet, one need only look at the U.S. Congress or the boards of directors and chief executive officers of the nation's largest corporations to realize that relatively few women have achieved positions of significant economic and political power.

In a study of news coverage of the mass rape and murder of girls at the St. Kizito boarding school in Kenya,[7] H. Leslie Steeves (1997) has demonstrated how hegemony expands to accommodate ideological challenges within an overarching framework that maintains the patriarchal status quo. Steeves found that news reports of the St. Kizito massacre employed framing techniques or explanations that supported a patriarchal view by deflecting responsibility away from the boys "and the larger context of gender violence and oppression in society" (p. 97). Drawing on Chantal Mouffe's (1979) concept of expansive hegemony, Steeves noted that the news was "consistent with patterns and behaviors of expansive hegemony, which secures consent by incorporating small amounts of feminism while placing an overwhelming emphasis on reports favoring the dominant ideology" (p. 95).

As primary agents in the maintenance of the dominant ideology, the media do their work through the use of language and symbols, or signs, in discourse. According to Fiske (1994), discourse is:

> language in social use; language accented with its history of domination, subordination, and resistance; language marked by the social conditions of its use and its users: it is politicized, power-bearing language employed to extend or defend the interests of its discursive community. (p. 3)

Discourse is language linked to its "production and circulation" (Fiske, 1994, p. 3), as well. The discourse of television situation comedies, for example, is tied to the structure, codes, and function of the genre and the organizational imperatives and goals of the commercial television industry; it differs in content and kind from the discourses of television drama, slasher movies, or the news. Discourse also is the terrain on which the struggle over meaning is fought. The discourses of popular culture thus are primary sites in the battle over the articulation and rearticulation of "reality."

Because the creation of meaning is both the intent and work of representation, the control over representation is a key prize in this contest. Feminist and patriarchal/misogynistic visions of what "woman" means compete for dominance within the social arena, with the battle over the definition and articulation of what it is to be a woman being played out over the body of her representation. Myra Macdonald (1995) points out that representation "refers both to politics and culture," and the relationship between the two (p. 2). How women are represented within a specific historical juncture is a function of the political, social, cultural, and economic climate at that time.

REPRESENTING WOMEN

The academic study of the representation of women is rooted in the women's movement of the 1960s and 1970s, which influenced feminists in academia and spawned a feminist critique of the mass media that "deeply implicated (the media) in the patterns of discrimination operating against women in society" (Baehr & Gray, 1996, p. 1). Most of this early research into sex-role stereotyping, as well as much of the more recent academic work in this area, has involved quantitative or qualitative content analyses. These studies have concluded not only that women are underrepresented in the media in both content and production, but that "the women that do appear in media content tend to be young and conventionally pretty, defined in relation to their husband, father, son, boss and other men, and portrayed as passive, indecisive, submissive, dependent etc." (van Zoonen, 1994, p. 17).

Feminist scholars have been influenced by two theoretical positions in their examination of the representation of women in popular culture. The more historical view, although conceding the still very real problems and inequalities in the material existence and mediated representation of women, highlights—or at least acknowledges—that life for women, and the popular media's treatment of them, has dramatically improved since the Second Wave of feminism in the 1960s and 1970s forever changed the social and political landscape.[8] Media critic and scholar Elayne Rapping (1994) echoes the opinion of many who share this perspective in her critique of what she calls "backlash theory," which focuses on the fear that women's gains over the past 30 years are in danger of being swept away by a renewed and reinvigorated political conservativism. As explained by Rapping:

> The backlash model of media dynamics assumes an ahistoric, one-dimensional, either/or, them/us, then/now (in current academic jargon, "binary") playing field. According to backlash theorists, feminists made certain strides in the late 1960s and then, in the early 1980s, were pushed back to point zero by the monolithic, misogynistic forces of the backlash. (p. 9)

From this perspective, Rapping adds, "all movies, pulp fiction, television, and pop music could be easily 'read' as one-dimensional ideological messages from the centers of power, meant to confuse us all into buying their wares and doing their bidding" (pp. 9-10).

Although feminist media critics such as Rapping often choose to concentrate on the advances women have made thanks to earlier feminists and their social and political agendas,[9] the alternative perspective tends to view the job of cultural critic as that of ideological excavator, the goal being to uncover and expose the patriarchal myths, beliefs, and stereotypes that underlie mediated texts in the hope that this baring will lead to changes in both media content and social structure. Into this construct falls the vast majority of quantitative and qualitative research on gendered representation within the media. Much of this research has attempted to compare the media's portrayal of women's work status with women's reality in the workplace.[10] Van Zoonen (1994) notes that the "exemplary conclusion" of this research "is that media output fails to represent the actual numbers of women in the world (51 percent) and their contributions to the labour force" (p. 69).

Increasingly, feminist scholars are bridging this theoretical divide, acknowledging that single texts are rarely uniformly regressive or unvaryingly progressive. They are seeing media representation as less one-dimensional and more complex. Although their conclusions ultimately may appear to align them with one of these two positions, their readings of media texts are more likely to be concerned with the nuances and subtleties that carry various shades of meaning and prevent simplified and monolithic interpretations of the images. In addition, their examinations of the mediated portrayals of women utilize various theoretical and methodological perspectives to highlight the complexities and contradictions of textual representation.

These differences in perspective and approach are all needed. Studies that expose the workings of patriarchy within media texts can counter the media's limiting and damaging stereotypes and myths by assessing the current status of women within the media and within society so as to pinpoint areas in need of improvement. And studies that focus on the effects of feminism and the women's movement on the media remind us how far we have come and that change is possible—as well as emphasize the historical and continuing importance of the women's movement at a time when many see feminism as under siege by a reinvigorated political right. In addition, studies that emphasize the complexities, contradictions, and multiple meanings within media representation underscore the numerous possibilities of interpretation as well as the fractured nature of gendered images.

Although feminist scholars may take different tacks in their analysis of mediated images, the texts themselves are not uniformly stamped with the same ideological message. The media's prevailing viewpoint may be rooted in patriarchy, but the women's movement and feminism have provided countervailing influences which, in some instances, have undermined the misogynistic tendencies of society which are reflected by the media (see, e.g., Carolyn Byerly's chapter on feminism's influence on news coverage). The popular media do not always present images of women that reflect the dominant, patriarchal view of them as necessarily and deservedly subservient to men. Many media images bear the mark of feminists who have worked hard over the past 30 years to challenge and change what Tuchman et al. (1978) found to be the media's predominantly dismissive and demeaning depiction of women.

FRACTURED WOMEN

The chapters in this book indicate that symbolic annihilation is no longer an appropriate blanket description for the media's portrayal of women. Certainly, women continue to be trivialized, marginalized, and silenced by the media. However, over the past 20 years, feminism and the women's movement have, in many cases, made inroads in both society and the media, although not as much as the media would have us believe (Rhode, 1997). The overall result is not simply a few more positive, egalitarian models for women, but a complicated mix of images that may be more confusing than liberating. The representations of women just prior to the next millennium could more accurately be described as *fractured,* the images and messages inconsistent and contradictory, torn between traditional, misogynistic notions about women and their roles on the one hand, and feminist ideals of equality for women on the other. Mediated women appear both hypersexualized and asexual, passive and ruthlessly aggressive, nurturing and sadistic, independent and dependent, domestic and career-oriented, silent and shrill, conforming and deviant, and stereotypically racist and a departure from formulaic conventions of racial and ethnic representation. This should not be surprising: the contradictions of race, ethnicity, class, age, sexual orientation, and gender are writ large over the body of the mediated woman. The tug-of-war over representation reflects not simply the contested terrain over which the articulation and meaning of "woman" is being fought, it also mirrors real divisions among women of different backgrounds and social groupings and the prevailing social understandings of those divisions. Macdonald (1995) attributes the disparity of these "contradictory and conflicting images and ideas" to the postmodern age in which we live (p. 6). The result is that the representations of women are more contradictory and diverse than when Tuchman et al. described the status and mediated representations of women in 1978.

Some might argue that the current increased diversity of the available popular imagery is a positive development, presenting more options to women than did the model of hearth and home that was prevalent 20 years ago. Indeed, Tuchman (1978) was concerned then about the possible effects of the symbolic annihilation of women on girls and women. She suggested that:

> girls exposed to "television women" may hope to be homemakers when they are adults, but not workers outside the home. Indeed, as adults those girls may resist work outside the home unless necessary for the economic well-being of their families. (p. 6)

Although it is impossible to accurately or adequately predict media effects without benefit of audience studies, it nevertheless seems likely that the consequences of the proliferation of contradictory, fractured images of women may present new dangers and generate considerable confusion for women and girls. Macdonald (1995) rightly cautions that the optimism of those who would see these contradictions as indicative of resistance to the dominant ideology is misguided:

> Women, confronted with images of themselves as regular victims of crime, but also as superwomen with executive briefcases and designer suits, as gun-toting harpies or immaculate mothers, may find the mix confusing, but not necessarily ironic. In an era that multiplies forms of representation, but leaves balances of power fundamentally unaltered, we need to explore responses more carefully before leaping to the conclusion that contradictions in the representations of women (or any other marginalized group) will necessarily be a catalyst for social change. (p. 6)

As this book indicates, the contradictions of representation are rife with complication and potential pitfalls for girls and women. Mediated gender equality might appear both achievable and desirable, but it often is predicated on male values and/or a lack of integrity and sense of self. "Coming out" as a lesbian can be applauded as an act of honesty and integrity, but only if she is the "right kind" of lesbian. Although the possibilities presented within the media appear greater, so, too, do the rules, for those disparate images must be contained. And the rules can be deadly, as when they require slavish devotion to traditional standards of beauty that can lead to anorexia or bulimia and only be achieved by the vast majority of women through borderline starvation. Thus, the fractured representation of women may well cause the psychological and physiological fracturing of girls and women, as well.

THE BOOK

The following 21 chapters of original research in this book reflect this fractured view of mediated women in popular culture, as well as the current state of representational studies of women. The chapters examine the portrayal of women from a variety of discursive and feminist positions. Taken together, they paint a picture of mediated women as disjointed and fraught with contradictions.

In examining the representations of women across a variety of media and mediated genres, an attempt was made to be as inclusive as possible in terms of racial, ethnic, class, and sexual diversity.[11] The days when feminist scholars could talk about the representation of women and refer exclusively to white, middle-class, heterosexual women are, thankfully, gone. It is necessary to look at the portrayals of women of varied racial, ethnic, and class backgrounds, as well as sexual orientations and age, to more accurately understand how society views women and their roles. Clearly, the representation of women of color, white women, working class and middle-class women, and lesbians and heterosexual women are not the same, for the cultural myths and stereotypes ascribed to each are different and affect their portrayals within the media differently.

It is unlikely that all feminists would agree with the analyses in this book, for qualitative interpretative methodologies are admittedly subjective and depend on the decoding strategies and capabilities of the researcher—as they would with other readers of the texts—and the researcher's theoretical orientation and focus of study. In fact, in a few instances in the compiling of chapters for this anthology, more than one chapter on the same topic was submitted for consideration. In each case, the interpretations differed markedly. This should not be construed as a problem with the methodology of qualitative textual analysis so much as the inevitable result of the use of diverse and sometimes conflicting theoretical frameworks, as well as a variation in focus reflective of the researcher's unique interests. Indeed, this is amply demonstrated by two chapters in this book that utilize different perspectives and come to dissimilar conclusions about the lead character is the Disney animated film *Pocahontas*. S. Elizabeth Bird, whose chapter more broadly is about the mediated representations of American Indian women, finds the Disney caricature of Pocahontas a reinscription of the Indian princess stereotype that continues to hold sway within the white imagination. On the other hand, Jill Birnie Henke and Diane Zimmerman Umble, in their study of female Disney heroines, see the Pocahontas character as a welcome departure from other Disney heroines whose ultimate happiness is wholly dependent on a life with the man they love. As Bonnie Dow (1996) reminds those of us who do this kind of research:

> we should choose our approach to the objects we study because of what we want to find out, because of the problem(s) that we want to solve, rather than because we are convinced that one approach leads to truth and the other to conjecture. At the same time, we must always realize that we cannot solve *all* of the problems or explore *all* of the possibilities that the text (whether it is a television program or audience discourse *about* a television program) presents. (p. 16; emphasis in original)

The chapters in this book construct a continuum of the representation of women within popular culture. This continuum is defined, on the one hand, by the effects of feminism in shaping more positive images of women and, on the other, the continuing influences of a misogynistic and patriarchal society whose goal is to maintain the status quo's traditional gender role stereotypes and divisions. These opposing poles reflect the ideological influences that have shaped the portrayals of women. Indeed, it is impossible to make sense of the plethora of images without an understanding of the ideological roles both patriarchy and feminism have played in the contest over the meaning of women's representation.

The following sections contain chapters whose conclusions and findings reflect this continuum of mediated representations of women, from traditional, stereotypical depictions of women to portrayals indicative of ideological struggle—but not necessarily of a departure—from the stereotypic realm to images that are ripe with complexities, contradictions, and ambiguities to, finally, representations that offer more positive models and a more hopeful vision of what women are and can be.

Part II: Reinforcing Stereotypes contributes to our understanding of how popular culture continues to embrace patriarchal and racist stereotypes—updated a little here, reconfigured a bit there—in its depiction of women. As Susan Alexander contends in Chapter 2, women's magazines continue to promote traditional views of women and their expected roles in society, supporting the belief that a woman's place is—or should be—in the home. Shawny Anderson then demonstrates how *Readers' Digest*, with the second-largest magazine circulation in the United States (after *TV Guide*), constructs women's roles to serve its conservative, anti-feminist agenda. Jane Caputi, in looking at common-place

place mediated images of women in advertising and elsewhere, argues in Chapter 4 that these portrayals constitute a type of everyday pornography that reinforces traditional gender roles while objectifying and sexualizing women.

The next three chapters demonstrate how racial stereotypes continue to shape the popular representations of women of color. Carmen Gillespie illustrates how the portrayal of Molly, an African American seamstress in the soft-porn film *Showgirls*, is merely a modernized version of the racist Mammy image of old. S. Elizabeth Bird shows how the images of the Native American woman in popular culture are defined by stereotypes of the squaw and Indian princess—when they are visible at all. Jocelyn Géliga Vargas links Hollywood's portrayal of the Puertorriqueña to both the colonization of Puerto Rico and cultural stereotypes that marginalize the Puertorriqueña within an "us/them" dichotomy. Géliga Vargas maintains that independent, localized productions are the only hope for an alternative view of Puerto Rican women that speaks to their authentic cultural identity. In Chapter 8, Bettina Fabos looks at how the intersection of class and gender affects the world of figure skating in general, and the controversy over skaters Tonya Harding and Nancy Kerrigan in particular. She concludes that figure skating is defined by traditional notions of feminine behavior and athleticism, as well as classist notions that privilege middle-class status and aspirations.

Part III: Limit/ed/ing Challenges explores what can happen when the portrayals of women *appear* to press at the boundaries of what has been considered appropriate behavior for women but *in actuality* reinforce the norm of women's roles as mothers, daughters, wives, and sex objects. The chapters demonstrate how challenges to the patriarchal order are undercut and limited in representation while, at the same time, providing role models that are limiting to women and girls. Charlene Dellinger-Pate and Roger Aden provide a close look at *Home Improvement*'s Jill Taylor to show how that television show's premise of female equality is subverted by the text so that patriarchy remains triumphant. In her analysis of a made-for-television special about a military officer discharged on the basis of her sexual orientation, Amy Villarejo argues that a prime-time TV program about a lesbian is not necessarily a good thing. When that portrayal is circumscribed by traditional family values, the result is a limited, and limiting, view of the socially acceptable lesbian. In Chapter 11, Cristina Bodinger-deUriarte points out that when Latinas or African American women are stand-up comics, the humor is deafeningly silent when it comes to politics, feminism, or their lives. And although Madonna seems to have pushed aside many of the limitations of popular notions of female sexuality and power, she does so, according to Carolyn Lea, by reinscribing herself as the ultimate Boy Toy. Finally, Linda Steiner examines the *New York Times*'s coverage of the Congressional hearing into charges of sexual harassment brought by Anita Hill against Supreme Court nominee Clarence Thomas. She determines that news conventions, coupled with the tendency of journalists to uniquely position themselves as unaffected, objective observers, resulted in Hill being portrayed as a cipher, stripped of voice as well as identity.

Part IV: Complexities and Contradictions provides examples of how women's representations can contain ambiguities and contradictions that defy containment in traditional forms, although this lack of restriction cannot necessarily be read as a challenge to patriarchal values and beliefs. Carolyn Lin's study of the portrayal of women in television advertising is illustrative of a primary focus of much quantitative content analysis into the representation of women in that it points to the lag between advertising's images and women's realities, despite advertisers' professed desire to reach contemporary women.

The next two chapters indicate the dangers of representing women as fully equal to men when that equality is measured by their ability to be ruthless, violent, and predacious—and to use their sexuality as a weapon. Equality for women can be achieved, the media tell us, but only by using a debased standard by which women lose their humanity while making themselves over as the ultimate (dangerous) sex object. Elayne Rapping shows how the lessons of *Melrose Place* are that to get ahead women can and must be as vicious and vengeful as men at their worst. Tom Reichert and Charlene Melcher similarly illustrate how Hollywood created the independent, sexually liberated women in the body of the pornographic, psychopathic, hypersexualized—and (possibly) homicidal—female lead of *Basic Instinct*. And, in the case of the situation comedy *The Nanny*, Barbara Wilinsky concludes that even though Fran, the central character, breaks with the traditional stereotype of the passive, silent female, she does so at the expense of possibly reinforcing negative stereotypes of Jewish women.

Part V: Representing Progress presents five chapters that break with stereotypical portrayals and provide examples of the representation of women that are truly improvements over what has gone before. Jill Birnie Henke and Diane Zimmerman Umble examine the most recent crop of Disney films with a female lead character and conclude that the film *Pocahontas* provides a radical departure from other Disney films which tell little girls that their ultimate goal in life should be to marry a prince and live happily ever after in his world. Although Lisa Flores and Michelle Holling find that the film *The Perez Family* reflects one-dimensional stereotypes about Latinas, they find hope and indications of

10. Carolyn Lin's chapter on advertising's images of women is an example of this type of research.
11. Even though 11 of the 21 chapters deal with the representation of women within the context of race, ethnicity, sexual preference, and class, even more diversity would have been preferable and was sought.

REFERENCES

Althusser, L. (1971). *Ideology and ideological state apparatuses.* In *Lenin and philosophy and other essays* (pp. 127-186). New York: Monthly Review Press.

Baehr, H., & Gray, A. (1996). *Turning it on: A reader in women and media.* New York: Arnold.

Barthel, D. (1988). *Putting on appearances: Gender and advertising.* Philadelphia: Temple University Press.

Berger, P.L., & Luckmann, T. (1966). *The social construction of reality.* New York: Doubleday.

Collins, P.H. (1993). The sexual politics of black womanhood. In P. Bart & E. Moran (Eds.), *Violence against women: The bloody footprints* (pp. 85-104). Newbury Park, CA: Sage.

Condit, C. (1989). The rhetorical limits of polysemy. *Critical Studies in Mass Communication, 6,* 103-122.

Dow, B.J. (1996). *Prime-time feminism: Television, media culture, and the women's movement since 1970.* Philadelphia: University of Pennsylvania Press.

Fiske, J. (1987). *Television culture.* London: Routledge.

Fiske, J. (1989). *Reading the popular.* Boston: Unwin Hyman.

Fiske, J. (1994). *Media matters.* Minneapolis: University of Minnesota Press.

Frazer, E. (1987). Teenage girls reading "Jackie." *Media, Culture and Society, 9*(4), 407-425.

Frank, L., & Smith, F. (1993). *Madonnarama: Essays on sex and popular culture.* Pittsburgh: Cleis Press.

Gitlin, T. (1980). *The whole world is watching.* Berkeley: University of California Press.

Goffman, E. (1979). *Gender advertisements.* New York: Harper Colophon Books.

Gramsci. A. (1971). *Selections from the prison notebooks.* London: Lawrence and Wishart.

Gramsci, A. (1983). *The modern Prince and other writings.* New York: International Publishers.

Hall, S. (1980). Encoding/decoding. In S. Hall, D. Hobson, A. Lowe, & P. Willis (Eds.), *Culture, media, language* (pp. 128-138). London: Hutchinson.

Hall, S. (1982). The rediscovery of "ideology": Return of the repressed in media studies. In M. Gurevitch, T. Bennett, J. Curran, & J. Woollacott (Eds.), *Culture, society and the media* (pp. 56-90). London: Methuen.

Kilbourne, J. (1993, October). Killing us softly: Gender roles in advertising. *Adolescent Medicine: State of the Art Reviews*, 4(3), 635-649.

Kilbourne, J. (1994). Still killing us softly: Advertising and the obsession with thinness. In P. Fallon, M. A. Katzman, & S. C. Wooley (Eds.), *Feminist perspectives on eating disorders* (pp. 395-418). New York: Guilford Press.

Macdonald, M. (1995). *Representing women: Myths of femininity in the popular media*. New York: Edward Arnold.

Meyers, M. (1992). Reporters and beats: The making of oppositional news. *Critical Studies in Mass Communication, 9*, 75-90.

Morley, D. (1980). *The "nationwide" audience: Structure and decoding.* London: Methuen.

Mouffe, C. (1979). Hegemony and ideology in Gramsci. In C. Mouffe (Ed.), *Gramsci and Marxist theory* (pp.168-204). London: Routledge and Kegan Paul.

Rapping, E. (1994). *Media-tions: Forays into the culture and gender wars.* Boston: South End.

Rhode, D.L. (1997). *Speaking of sex: The denial of gender inequality.* Cambridge, MA: Harvard University Press.

Schwichtenberg, C. (1993). *The Madonna connection.* Boulder, CO: Westview.

Signorielli, N. (1997, April). *A content analysis: Reflections of girls in the media.* Menlo Park, CA: Children Now and the Kaiser Family Foundation.

Steeves, H. L. (1997). *Gender violence and the press: The St. Kizito Story.* Athens: Ohio University Center for International Studies.

Stice, E., Schupak-Neuberg, E., Shaw, H.E., & Stein, R.I. (1994). Relation of media exposure to eating disorder symptomatology: An examination of mediating mechanisms. *Journal of Abnormal Psychology, 103*(4), 836-840.

Tuchman, G. (1978). Introduction: The symbolic annihilation of women by the mass media. In G. Tuckman, A.K. Daniels, & J. Benét (Eds.), *Hearth and home: Images of women in the mass media* (pp. 3-38). New York: Oxford University Press.

Tuchman, G., Daniels, A.K., & Benét, J. (1978). *Hearth and home: Images of women in the mass media.* New York: Oxford University Press.

van Zoonen, L. (1994). *Feminist media studies.* London: Sage.

Williams, R. (1980). *Problems in materialism and culture.* London: Verso.

Women, Men and Media Project (1991). *The invisible majority: Women ignored by news magazines.* Alexandria, VA: Unabridged Communications.

Women, Men and Media Project. (1993). *The news: Looking like America? Not yet...* Alexandria, VA: Unabridged Communications.

Women, Men and Media Project. (1994). *Arriving on the scene: Women's growing presence in the news.* Alexandria, VA: Unabridged Communications.

Women, Men and Media Project. (1995). *Slipping from the scene: News coverage of females drops.* Alexandria, VA: Unabridged Communications.

Women, Men and Media Project. (1996). *Marginalizing women: Front-page news coverage of females declines in 1996.* Alexandria, VA: Unabridged Communications.

II

REINFORCING STEREOTYPES

2

Messages to Women on Love and Marriage From Women's Magazines

Susan H. Alexander

Since the 1960s, the American family has undergone a period of especially rapid social change that has resulted in an ambiguity of gender roles
for both males and females. Furthermore, there is the question of what
the future holds. Are we likely to see a reversal in egalitarian trends in
family life due to the influence of such movements as the "moral majority," "prolife," and "profamily," as well as an increasingly
traditional/conservative sociopolitical mood (Weeks & Botkin, 1987, p.
50)? Major in-depth studies concerning intimate relationships (e.g.,
Bellah, Madsen, Sullivan, Swidler, & Tipton, 1985; Cancian, 1987) do not
resolve this quandary but instead present contrasting viewpoints and
further demonstrate the inconsistencies in our knowledge about love
and marriage in the United States.

Only recently have some researchers asked questions about the
content of fiction and/or nonfiction as a mechanism contributing to gender-role socialization. Media messages about love and marriage may say
more about how women and men are socialized into their accepted roles
than can be discovered by simply examining role relationships and related values. Thus, I contend that media messages about love and marriage

are fundamental to our understanding of how women perceive themselves and are perceived by others.

The purpose of this research is to examine and compare messages concerning love and marriage directed to women in two different female-oriented magazines and to ascertain if and how these messages have changed over time.

Previous research has demonstrated that women have always been the ones to receive advice on love and marriage, and thus they were deemed responsible for their marital relationships. For example, Francesca Cancian (1987) stated that Dorothy Dix, in her syndicated newspaper column published in 1931, advised women on ways to help their husbands. However, there was no parallel column instructing men on how to help their wives. Moreover, the magazines of that period consistently told women it was their responsibility to create successful marriages.

Virginia Kidd (1975) also found when she examined interpersonal relations in nonfiction selections in popular magazines that the bulk of the magazines carrying these articles were female-oriented. Today, magazine articles on how to improve marriage are still directed primarily to women (Cancian, 1987).

This chapter synthesizes and presents the findings acquired from examining messages about love and marriage that have been communicated to American women through the medium of nonfiction articles in popular magazines. In addition, the chapter demonstrates how the media stereotypically represent gender roles and the present-day reality of the separate cultures of the feminine and masculine worlds.

METHODS

I conducted a systematic content analysis of nonfiction articles in two varieties of women's magazines for the period 1966-1994. The magazines included in the study are *Mademoiselle* and *Ladies' Home Journal*. Both are high-circulation magazines oriented to a middle-class readership. It has been documented that "those magazines with middle-class audiences have been more responsive to changes in women's roles" (Andersen, 1988/1993, p. 29). Moreover, Bellah et al. (1985) have stated that "for the past hundred years or so, the middle class, in the modern sense of the term, has so dominated our culture that neither a genuinely upper-class nor a genuinely working class culture has fully appeared" (p. viii). In addition, Bellah et al. believe that "everyone in the United States thinks largely in middle-class categories, even when they are inappropriate" (p. viii). Thus, this research investigates what can be considered the dominant cultural status quo regarding love and marriage as disseminated by female-oriented magazines.

Mademoiselle is a magazine directed to college-educated, unmarried working women aged 18-35 (Neff, 1988). It was established in 1935 and has a circulation of over 1 million readers (Gill & Boyden, 1988). *Mademoiselle*'s nonfiction content is composed of articles relating to personal relationships, health, careers, trends, and current social problems (Neff, 1988). The tone and content of the magazine is aimed at the mature, single, career woman. "Male-female relationships are examined on an adult level" (Katz & Katz, 1986, p. 991).

In contrast, *Ladies' Home Journal* is aimed at an older, more mature, settled readership. *Ladies' Home Journal* has one of the leading circulation figures (over 5 million) among family- oriented magazines (Gill & Boyden, 1988). Magazine content is directed to the white, middle-class woman with a husband and children. As its name attests, its appeal is to the homemaker. In contrast to *Mademoiselle*'s monthly feature, "What Every Single Girl Should Know," The *Journal* carries a monthly feature entitled "Can This Marriage Be Saved?". The *Journal* was the first women's magazine to reach a circulation of 1 million and is "credited with transforming the entire field of women's service magazines" (Geise, 1979, p. 53).

Nonfiction selections from these magazines were analyzed for the period January 1966 (the year the women's movement gained increasing national recognition and the onset of a period of lower fertility rates for women) until August 1994. Four issues of each of the magazines were randomly selected for each even-numbered year from 1966-1994. From these selected issues, the principal article having to do with advice on love and marriage was analyzed.

SUMMARY OF MAJOR RESEARCH FINDINGS

The main similarity between the messages published in the two female-oriented magazines is that they both contain a plethora of love and/or marriage messages. Also, the overwhelming "self-help" nature of such messages adds to and reinforces the stereotype of the "helpless, flawed woman." It appears as if:

> the women's magazines all seem to want to better you in some way, the assumption being that you are in need of improvement. Men's magazines tell you how to make more money and how to dress and how to fix your golf putt . . . but they work from the assumption that men don't need to look inward, that they're essentially OK. (Salamon, 1988, p. A18)

The self-help nature of the articles have been previously detailed by Ferguson (1983) and more recently emphasized by Henkin (1989), Salamon (1988), and Gordon (1989). The notion that women need "self-help" in all areas, but especially in the areas of love and family relationships, is accentuated in this study's analysis of women's magazines.

These messages disseminated to women can be understood by recognizing that gender-specific magazines appeal to the different cultures that make up the female and male worlds (Bernard, 1983; Winship, 1987). The culture of the female world is concerned with femininity, love and romance, motherhood and family life, and beauty and fashion. In contrast, the elements that comprise the male culture have to do with work and careers, sports and hobbies, politics, and sexual success. Woman are still expected to be the nurturing partner and the guardian and custodian of the relationship. Paradoxically, "the personal qualities necessary to survive in the world of work are exactly the opposite of the qualities needed for healthy relationships" (Henkin, 1989, p. 66). In fact, one professional woman complained that: "Once even my unreasoning boss criticized me by saying that I 'mothered' the staff. That comment said everything I need to know about how little value maternal feelings or skills had in the workplace" (*Ladies' Home Journal*, April 1994, p. 116).

In addition, it appears that the messages from the popular media have "given us a subtle twist on traditional sexism, accepting the fact that women have entered the workplace but playing on their fears that they'll be left alone as a result" (Henkin, 1989, p. 65).

Ladies' Home Journal and *Mademoiselle* contain many advice articles specifically pertaining to love and marriage. The issues most frequently discussed by both magazines have to do with role prescriptions and the women's movement. They both transmit much the same message, that is, men are dominant and women dependent in female-male unions. Although subservience in women is expected and demanded by men, it is more-or-less excused and accepted by women. According to *Mademoiselle*:

> Men are still expected to take the lead, but now women are asking them to. Women now have the right to make the first move. We all like to drive. And women like men to drive. Women are asking men to drive. (September, 1992, p. 127)

The pivotal difference between the two magazines' messages is most often in the realm of values recommended or criticized.

Both magazines are also in general agreement that the women's movement has not granted women true equality but has hindered the relationship between the sexes. All agree that women are still responsible for the well-being of the relationship and for the great majority of household and childcare tasks. The women's responsibility for the male-female relationship and for the lion's share of the household and childcare tasks has been detailed in previous studies (Cancian, 1987; Franzwa, 1974; Giele, 1988; Kidd, 1975; Loughlin, 1983). This study confirms the inequality of women's roles as reported in magazines and concurs with the results of previous research that show that the working woman is still responsible for most of the childcare and housework.

The women's magazines highlight good communication, counseling, interdependence, and individuality as being necessary for relationship happiness. The concept of "interdependency," which was first alluded to by the women's magazines of the early 1970s and later referred to by name throughout the 1980s, corresponds with Cancian's (1987) conclusion that greater freedom does not necessarily entail a weakening of close relationships. Instead, greater happiness in marriage can be achieved by a combination of individual self-development together with love, devotion, and commitment. Finally, both magazines agree that love, fidelity, loyalty, commitment, and a satisfying sexual relationship are all important ingredients in a happy relationship. These messages have not changed over the years.

As far as values are concerned, there is some difference of opinion between the two gender-oriented magazines, perhaps because *Ladies' Home Journal* is targeted to a more mature and settled readership than *Mademoiselle*. This difference is most evident in beliefs concerning premarital sex, cohabitation, marriage, and divorce.

The present study also confirms Bellah et al.'s (1985) thesis that there is a large quest for intimacy in America today. In fact, since the mid 1970s, all the sampled issues have wholeheartedly endorsed marriage. The positive sanction of marriage is a message that has changed over time. In the 1960s, even *Ladies' Home Journal* (the more traditional of the two magazines) wrote of the joys of the single culture, with its proliferation of singles' bars, apartment houses, and clubs. The 1960s and early 1970s also were times when an unmarried woman of 25 was not considered an oddity but simply single by choice (*Ladies' Home Journal*, January 1968, pp. 62-63).

The present study indicates that, according to the popular press, the glories of the single culture are past. It is no longer considered square to "tie the knot," and the sampled magazines laud the advantages of marriage.

In addition, both magazines adamantly denounce extramarital sexual relations. The magazines take the view that "although adultery is not routinely listed today as 'cause for action' on divorce papers, experts believe at least half of all breakups can be attributed to infidelity"

(Gazze, 1988, p. C5). As can be expected, The *Journal*—whose main concern is with the home and family generally—takes the more conservative stand on all issues, and *Mademoiselle*—which focuses on premarital fun and sexual fantasy—the more liberal.

ADDITIONAL COMPARISONS: MORE SPECIFIC DIFFERENCES BETWEEN THE TWO MAGAZINES

An analysis of the contents of *Ladies' Home Journal* and *Mademoiselle* affirm that these gender-specific magazines have different formats and contents, are targeted to distinct readerships, and consequently attract different audiences. *Ladies' Home Journal's* focus is on marriage and the family. It provides its readers with self-help remedies for solving familial problems. For the 28 years encompassed by the study, the number of regular features (six per issue) and the number of additional articles (approximately six in total for the four sampled issues) having to do with love and marriage have remained fairly constant. In contrast, *Mademoiselle* is targeted toward sophisticated, young, working women, and it dispenses information on how to be a well-rounded, accomplished, intelligent, up-to-date, competitive, and sought-after woman.

Unlike *Ladies' Home Journal*, which has remained stable in its focus, *Mademoiselle* has changed in format and focus throughout the years. In 1966, only one monthly feature in *Mademoiselle* had to do with male-female relationships. Likewise, the four issues sampled showed that there was a paucity of articles concerning love and/or marriage. In 1972, the number of monthly features and articles devoted to male-female relationships increased sharply. Additionally, in 1976, the large section of *Mademoiselle* devoted to "Colleges and Careers" was eliminated and a section on "Food and Home" was added. Since 1980, there also has been a substantial surge in the number of monthly features concerned with love and/or marriage. In 1982, the number of articles related to relationships increased greatly. The increase in the number of features, as well as the number of articles, has remained constant throughout the sampled issues of 1994. In fact, the February 1994 issue of *Mademoiselle* ran a special section on "Love." The next issue changed the "Love" section to one called "relationships" and subsequently made it a permanent feature. Additionally, the regular section entitled "Q & A and the Real World" became "Q & A about Love, Men, Sex, Friends, Work, and Money," and a new feature, "Self-Discovery," joined the magazine. "Self-Discovery" was primarily concerned with love and marriage.

This suggests that the content of the two female magazines has coincided rather than diverged over the years, and that it is *Mademoiselle*, rather than The *Journal*, that has gone through the transformation. For the 28 years of this study, *Ladies' Home Journal* has maintained consistent interest in preserving and improving marital relationships. *Mademoiselle*'s focus, on the other hand, has evolved from college and careers to female-male relationships. It now appears that "Miss" *Mademoiselle* craves intimacy as much as her sister "Mrs." *Ladies' Home Journal*. According to *Mademoiselle*:

> loneliness will disappear if you have a husband, even one you don't love . . . happiness is loving and being loved by your husband . . . the feminists are either rich or married so it's all very well for them to talk about doing without men. (December 1970)

In fact, a sampling of the most recently analyzed issues of *Mademoiselle* (1990-1994) reveals articles with such titles as: "Men and the M Word" (December 1990), "Marriage Lust: Only One of You Has It" (March 1992), "Is He a Bachelor For Now . . . or Forever" (April 1992), "Hooking Him: A Last-Ditch Guide—5 Ways to Get a Guy to Commit" (February 1994), "Where the Boys Are: 5 Ways to Meet Men" (April 1994), and so on. These articles demonstrate that the marriage mania is continuing and most likely increasing as far as women are concerned. However, as a male contributor writes in *Mademoiselle*:

> Few women understand the almost bottomless depths of male immaturity. We feel no need to rush into marriage for the sake of having children . . . our adolescent dreams of a lifetime of sowing our oats amongst all of you supposedly panting, eager females are difficult to give up . . . men think with their dicks and your dick is definitely against marriage . . .whether it's affecting their sex life or career, most single men seem to agree that marriage's greatest peril lies in it limiting of options. . . . No amount of tears and cajoling will get a truly unwilling man to commit. (December, 1990, p. 143)

Additionally, the content of the messages disseminated in these two female-oriented magazines are similar despite the fact that they are targeted to different female readerships. The most notable similarity is that both audiences are instructed that it is the woman's responsibility for maintaining and preserving the female-male relationship. *Mademoiselle* tells us that even though

> women are trained today for a greater variety of careers than ever before, they continue to ponder what precisely is required for a marriage to succeed, especially when one partner is a gifted woman and

desirous of making the most of her talents, yet pathetically eager to keep her marital status. (March 1968, p. 199)

In the March 1990 issue, *Ladies' Home Journal* wrote about "sequencing," a new name for an increasingly popular solution to the family-versus-career problem. This entails a woman putting her career on hold and staying at home. As one professional woman proclaimed:

> No more twelve-hour days for me. I want a job that will give me the flexibility I need to be with my children. I used to believe I needed work, marriage and motherhood at the same time to make my life complete. But what's the good of having it all if you can't enjoy any of it? (p. 164)

Four months later, *Ladies' Home Journal* featured a special section entitled "The LHJ Guide to Pregnancy." Additionally, the March 1992 issue reported that, according to the *Yankelovich Monitor*, more than half (57%) of those questioned agreed with the statement, "Having a child is an experience every woman should have. . . . Advances in fertility treatment make motherhood seem more and more like a goal that can—and must—be reached." As the March 1992 *Ladies Home Journal* reported:

> More and more women are not willing to put off parenthood until they reach some perfect stopping place in their profession. Thus, they are often thinking about cutting their career back to part-time. As one professional woman volunteered, "I want to be there raising my child. . . . It's just the most wonderful thing that could happen to any couple." (pp. 176, 190)

The article also acknowledged today's demographics of motherhood:

> By 1989, 32.5% of women giving birth to their first child were unmarried. About 14% are over 30. The stigma of unwed motherhood is fast fading. Usually it's not that the women don't want to get married . . . it's that they haven't found the right person and time is running out to have a baby. (p. 176)

Both magazines also agree that couples in America marry or live together because of romantic love, and modern-day women ultimately want to marry, in addition to developing their talents and having successful careers. Both magazines acknowledge that the modern-day woman is still subservient to the desires of her partner, and in order to maintain a good relationship she must not hold a more prestigious position or earn more money than he does. Being a successful married woman is still touted as a woman's only true accomplishment, and a woman's true fulfillment can be reached only through having a loving husband and children.

Both magazines also claim that the women's movement has obstructed female-male relationships. *Mademoiselle* succinctly states:

> The women's movement has managed to shake the foundations of traditional male-female relationships. It also has brought to the surface much of the hidden resentment women have for men. There is distrust, confusion and fear about men and about our sexual identities and, most of all, an absence of any sense of the possibilities of men and women together. (July 1972, p. 90)

And in a later issue of *Ladies Home Journal*, sociologist Michael Kimmel adds,

> In the past twenty years, there has been a revolution in gender roles—but only one gender is aware of it. . . . [However,] women want men to be strong, capable, paternal and at the same time compassionate, vulnerable, and yielding. Meanwhile, men are crying foul because [they've] changed the rules in the middle of the game and they're perplexed by our mixed signals. (August 1990, p. 86)

The article goes on to report that 90% of women queried in a Roper poll were married or wanted to be someday. As one interviewee stated, "We do love our husbands and want to give them what they need. We just wish they were more attuned to our needs."

But it is still the woman who suffers from role strain as she performs most of the household and childcare tasks. As one woman in a professional position admitted in a recent issue of *Ladies Home Journal*, "no one talks about the back-breaking burden of the woman who works in and out of the home" (April 1994, p. 109).

Messages about the sources of marital/relationship happiness and/or discord do not differ in the two magazines, nor have they been altered notably over the years. Good communication, intimacy, fidelity, and individuality and independence are lauded as necessary ingredients for a successful union.

In the domain of values and recommended behaviors, the two magazines diverge somewhat in the prescriptions and proscriptions they transmit to their readers. The divergence is apparently the result of the magazines being targeted to readers of different ages and marital statuses. For example, *Ladies' Home Journal* does not advocate or devote much space to cohabitation before marriage. Most of the *Journal*'s readers are married. *Mademoiselle*, on the other hand, endorsed cohabitation until fairly recently. An article in the May 1990 issue, "Living Together: The Truth and the Consequences," scrutinizes this type of relationship by citing an academic study of more than 500 couples conducted by social scientists:

> 40 percent of the couples broke up without getting married and half of the breakups occurred within 18 months . . . compared with married couples, people who lived together were almost twice as likely to say they had thought their relationship was in trouble . . . once they get married, couples who have lived together are more likely to get divorced than those who haven't cohabitated. (p. 201)

Also, the *Journal* does not endorse premarital sex, whereas *Mademoiselle* accepts it as the norm. In fact, an article entitled "Dizzy With Desire: Why Men Do—and Don't—Make Passes" provided pointers for women dealing with men who are not sexually forthcoming: "You can ask him about it or refuse to ask; you can be patient, not put any pressure on the man; or you can train yourself to like men who will put out" (*Mademoiselle*, September 1992, p. 127).

As can be expected, most articles concerning AIDS were in *Mademoiselle*. The March 1992 issue included a special feature, "Before You Make Love Again—A Special Section on AIDS." The next month, *Mademoiselle* ran an article on "The AIDS Monster," and in the June 1992 issue, *Mademoiselle* cautioned their readers that: "Guys over 30 started having sex before AIDS made daily headlines. Condom use is not necessarily automatic for them. Insist he use a condom."

Ladies' Home Journal also discussed AIDS, advising victims of acquaintance rape to get tested for the HIV virus as soon as possible (May 1994). The May issue also featured a woman who took in HIV-positive babies. Additionally, in the June issue, *Ladies' Home Journal* presented testimonials from married couples living with the AIDS virus.

Ladies' Home Journal discourages divorce and represents it as causing unimaginable pain for all involved. In an article entitled "Let's Not Forget the Children," readers were informed of the Family Support Act of 1988 and given information on where to go if they need help (July 1990). In contrast, *Mademoiselle* sees divorce as a way to relieve the misery of a bad marriage.

Nevertheless, both magazines emphatically disapprove of extramarital sexual relations. They also agree on the importance of a woman gaining self-fulfillment through outside employment. But both caution their readers that employment interferes with male-female relationships.

In sum, love, romance, and marriage have always been a prescription for happiness and fulfillment in *Ladies' Home Journal*. *Mademoiselle*, on the other hand, in the 1960s and early 1970s, recommended friendship between the sexes and cohabitation. By the mid-1970s, Mademoiselle expanded its prescription for womanly happiness to include marriage and motherhood.

An examination of the content of the messages concerning love and marriage disseminated by these magazines further clarifies their dissimilarity and illustrates the reasons for their different audience appeal. But both women's magazines proclaim that the woman is responsible for the female-male union.

DISCUSSION AND IMPLICATIONS OF THE FINDINGS

This study has found that what is printed in popular magazines represents not reality but only an idea of what the media think is appropriate behavior. The data fail to acknowledge the dramatic changes that have occurred in American family patterns. The nonfiction messages of the magazines present a more conservative view of appropriate behavior and values than what is actually exhibited by society in general. For example, a Roper Poll conducted in 1985 found that:

> 76 percent of American women and 75 percent of men believed women's roles would continue to change. Only 10 percent of women and 9 percent of men believed women would return to more traditional roles. . . . By 1985, 48 percent of women (compared with 64 percent in 1974) said that having a loving husband who was able to take care of them was more important than making it on one's own. And only 37 percent of women in 1985, compared with 50 percent in 1974, thought the most satisfying lifestyle was having a traditional marriage with the husband assuming responsibility for providing for the family and the wife being responsible for the house and taking care of children. (Andersen, 1988/1993, p. 9)

Labor force participation statistics also showed that by 1990, 57.5% of all women were in the paid labor force compared with 76.1% of men. Moreover, since 1960, married women with children have nearly tripled their labor-force participation (Andersen, 1988/1993). These increases in the number of working mothers mean that whether or not a woman has children is no longer an accurate predicator of whether she will be engaged in paid labor (Andersen, 1988/1993).

These facts are in direct contrast with the findings of the present study, which have shown that nonfiction selections from women's magazines impart the message that a woman's ultimate happiness and true fulfillment depend on possessing a loving husband and children. The magazines also say that men and women are happy in traditional gender roles, although they may wish to expand them a little.

In sum, the magazine messages do not recognize or acknowledge that "'traditional' families consisting of a breadwinner father, a housewife mother, and one or more dependent children account for less than 15 percent of the nation's households" (Mintz & Kellogg, 1988, p. 203). In addition, there are many arrangements that fulfill the definition of "family." For example, "now the census distinguishes between household, family, family household, householder, and related subfamily" (Andersen, 1988/1993, pp. 152-153). The popular magazines continue to direct their messages to all readers, when these messages are applicable only to a small portion of traditional households. They continue to bombard the public with stereotypical images of gender roles and family prescriptions, while still making a clear-cut distinction between the masculine and feminine worlds.

REFERENCES

Andersen, M. (1993). *Thinking about women: Sociological perspectives on sex and gender*. New York: Macmillan. (Original work published 1988)

Bellah, R.N., Madsen, R., Sullivan, W.M., Swidler, A., & Tipton, S.M. (1985). *Habits of the heart*. New York: Harper and Row.

Bernard, J. (1983). *The female world*. New York: Free Press.

Cancian, F. (1987). *Love in America*. New York: Cambridge University Press.

Ferguson, M. (1983). *Forever feminine*. London: Heinemann.

Franzwa, H. H. (1974). Working women in fact and fiction. *Journal of Communication, 24*, 104-109.

Gazze, N. (1988, November 29). Uncovering infidelity. *The Washington Post*, p. C5.

Geise, L. A. (1979). The female role in middle class women's magazines from 1955 to 1976: A content analysis of non-fiction selections. *Sex Roles, 5*, 51-61.

Giele, J. Z. (1988). Chapter 9—Gender and sex roles. In N.J. Smelser (Ed.), *Handbook of sociology* (pp. 291-323). Newbury Park: Sage.

Gill, K., & Boyden, D.P. (Eds.). (1988). *Gale directory of publications*. Michigan: Gale Research.

Gordon, S. (1989, January 24). From mother to daughter to society: Mixed messages on the road to reality. Review of *Perfect Women: Hidden Fears of Inadequacy and the Drive to Perform* by Collette Dowling. *The Washington Post*, "Book World," p. 21.

Henkin, J. (1989). Individualism unbound: Reconsidering modern-day romance. *Utne Reader, 32,* 64

Katz, B., & Katz, L. S. (Eds.). (1986). *Magazines for libraries.* New York: R. R. Bowker.

Kidd, V. (1975). Happily ever after and other relationship styles: Advice on interpersonal relations in popular magazines, 1951-1973. *Quarterly Journal of Speech, 61,* 31-39.

Loughlin, B. (1983). The women's magazine short-story heroine. *Journalism Quarterly, 60,* 139-142.

Mintz, S., & Kellogg, S. (1988). *Domestic revolutions.* New York: The Free Press.

Neff, G. T. (Ed.). (1988). *Writer's market.* Cincinnati: F & W Publications.

Salamon, J. (1988, December 13). Giving the sexes what they want at the newsstand. *The Wall Street Journal,* p. A18.

Weeks, M. O., & Botkin, D.R. (1987). A longitudinal study of the marriage role expectations of college women: 1961-1984. *Sex Roles, 17,* 49-58.

Winship, J. (1987). *Inside women's magazines.* London: Pandora.

3

Reader's Digest on Women: Antifeminist Articulations of "The Second Sex"

Shawny Anderson

> There was always the suspicion that, like the communist commissars who preached sacrifice to their comrades and then bought caviar at the party store, feminist leaders were publicly telling mothers it was great to leave their husbands and be independent—then secretly dressing in Frederick's of Hollywood lingerie for their guys. . . . [M]any women have come to see the movement as anti-male, anti-child, anti-family, and anti-feminine. And therefore it has nothing to do with us.
> —Sally Quinn (1992)

In 1992, *Washington Post* writer Sally Quinn provided *Reader's Digest* with an article that the *Digest's* editors may well have been dreaming about for over 20 years; that is, in Quinn's attack on feminism and its adherents, the *Digest* had found a potential reprint that would communicate clearly the antifeminist view that the *Digest* had been constructing since its very inception: there is a "natural order" of relations between the sexes, and that order should not be challenged but, instead, celebrated. Not only did

Quinn's essay contain the desired content, it also included two other enticing features: it was written by a woman, and it was originally printed in a "respected" "mainstream" newspaper. Until Quinn's article arrived on the scene, the *Digest* had consistently maintained its antifeminist position, but it often had to rely on its own male writers or on the narratives of relatively unknown women to defend its stand.

Reader's Digest was founded in 1922 as a general interest magazine that would condense and edit articles from other popular magazines, then reprint them in booklet form. The magazine eventually began to rely more and more on its own staff writers to provide original articles that more closely matched its ideological interests. It is important to note that *Reader's Digest* touts itself as the "world's most-read magazine"; although that declaration might be an overstatement, it is indeed the world's highest-circulation magazine, with a subscription list requiring 28 million copies per month and translation into at least 17 different languages. In fact, one *Digest* historian contends that "the magazine reaches into every fourth American home" and that "a hundred million people around the world read it" (Schreiner, 1974, p. 3). By way of comparison, *Reader's Digest*'s circulation exceeds that of *Time, Newsweek, U.S. News and World Report, Sports Illustrated,* and *McCall's* magazines combined (*Ulrich's International Periodical Directory*, 1991). Thus, it appears that the *Digest* is one of the fundamental print sources by which the world is introduced to American ideology.

All of this is of particular interest to communication scholars because—despite its clear-cut antifeminist ideology—*Reader's Digest* is often seen as ideologically neutral and relatively harmless by most U.S. Americans. However, careful analysis reveals that it consistently provides an inordinate number of negative depictions of the political, social, personal, and economic potential of contemporary women. Although it is difficult to judge the intention or the real impact of the messages of any medium on the general public, it is easy enough to recognize that the consistently recurring images of women in the *Digest* are, for the most part, simplistic, homogenous, and limited. In the case of *Reader's Digest*, these recurring images are disseminated (if Schreiner is correct) to nearly 100 million people all over the world. The persuasive potential of that circulation is therefore enormous, especially in light of the general reputation of the magazine as an objective and innocuous source of entertainment, information, and advice. For these reasons, this chapter endeavors to provide insights into the sets of images and assumptions through which the *Digest* constructs the "reality" of women and, further, explores alternate visions that might open up a different range of possibilities for women in the United States. I begin with a brief examination of the idea of antifeminism. From there I discuss the manifestations of antifeminism present in *Reader's Digest*. Finally, I present an overview of the potential implications of such messages on the magazine's readership.

ANTIFEMINISM

Attempting to define the concept "antifeminism" could easily provoke as many territorial disputes as most efforts to define "feminism." For my purposes, I find that Offen (1988) offers a useful list of criteria for what legitimately should be labeled "feminist:"

> . . . I would consider as feminists any persons, female or male, whose ideas and actions (insofar as they can be documented) show them to meet three criteria:
>
> 1) they recognize the validity of women's own interpretations of their lived experience and needs and acknowledge the values women claim publicly as their own (as distinct from an aesthetic ideal of womanhood invented by men). . . ; 2) they exhibit consciousness of, discomfort at, or even anger over institutionalized injustice (or inequity) toward women as a group by men as a group in a given society; and 3) they advocate the elimination of that injustice by challenging, through efforts to alter prevailing ideas and/or social institutions and practices, the coercive power, force, or authority that upholds male prerogatives in that particular culture. Thus, to be a feminist is necessarily to be at odds with male-dominated culture and society. (p. 121)

As will be seen in the following pages, Offen's criteria offer an ethical framework that *Reader's Digest* rarely approaches; that is, based on Offen's ideas of what feminist thinking should be, the representations presented in *Digest* depictions of women clearly do not qualify as such.

On the other hand, David and Levitas (1988) identify central antifeminist themes as those that: (a) see the patriarchal family as a "natural" human condition; (b) link this natural patriarchy to a parallel societal condition; (c) position women in a state of subordinate, but idealized, motherhood; (d) justify these choices through arguments of biology and social destiny; or (e) refuse to challenge existing institutions that maintain such patriarchal positions and practices. As will become obvious in the following pages, *Reader's Digest* provides consistent, classic examples of each of these characteristics in its coverage of women and women's roles.

I analyze a random sample of the issues of *Reader's Digest* published in the Reagan/Bush era from 1980 to 1992, totaling 56 issues.

Within each edition, only narrative forms—fictional, nonfictional, and biographical—that include a woman or women as primary characters were analyzed. Each issue contained at least one of these narrative forms, although some contained as many as five, thereby providing a total sample of more than 150 articles.

Special attention was given to the "naturalized" depictions of women promoted by the *Digest*; that is, certain "elements" were consistently connected within *Digest* narratives on women. These strategic representations provided access to an overarching set of expectations about "appropriate" female social roles, thereby allowing insight into the *Digest*'s view of the "rightful" place of women. In short, the *Digest*'s view requires that women gain their sense of identity not from their own personal accomplishments, but from their accomplishments in service of others, especially family members.

It is important to note here that over 70% of the narratives that featured women as main characters from 1980-1992 were written by male authors, many of whom were *Reader's Digest* staff members. These articles reflect a general position held by the magazine's writers and editors on what the status of women is and should be. The tendency for males in powerful media positions to interpret the experiences of women is a classic example of what feminist critics call "appropriation" (Opie, 1992; Shotter & Logan, 1988). Put simply, by deciding and controlling the ways that women should be defined publicly, male writers—like those of the *Digest* staff—appropriate women's experiences and therefore often place severe constraints on women's potential as social agents.

Indeed, images of women in *Reader's Digest* and other similar dominant media institutions seem to consistently place women at a status level that indicates their position as "the Second Sex." As Simone de Beauvoir (1949) has written, women have historically been treated as categorically inferior to men and have often been defined in reference to their relationship to others, particularly males. Citing various creation myths and explanations of sex differences, de Beauvoir explains:

> Thus humanity is male and man defines woman not in herself but as relative to him; she is not regarded as an autonomous being . . . she is simply what man decrees. . . . She is defined and differentiated with reference to man and not he with reference to her; she is the incidental, the inessential as opposed to the essential. He is the Subject, he is the Absolute—she is the Other. (p. xxviii)

De Beauvoir goes on to assert that women's entire identities are wrapped up in the roles they fulfill for others—as wives, mothers, and daughters. Women's identities, then, are always relative to men, to children, possibly to other women (especially female family members), and are rarely self-defined. This mindset serves as the core of the *Digest's* approach to defining women and women's roles. *The Digest's* continued representation of women as the Second Sex also provides a frame by which to organize a critique of the *Digest's* naturalized representations; in other words, by looking at the various "other-oriented" identities established as the "natural" condition of female existence (i.e., woman as wife, mother, daughter, etc.), the antifeminist ideology of *Reader's Digest* becomes increasingly apparent. The following sections identify some of the consistent representations that constitute the *Digest's* expectations concerning women and their roles while accounting for relevant information absent from the magazine's traditionalist view.

REPRESENTATIONS OF WOMEN IN READER'S DIGEST NARRATIVES

As noted earlier, *Reader's Digest* primarily identifies women as social "Others"; that is, women are not seen as independent social agents in and of themselves, but rather as social dependents who function only through their connections to other people within traditionally male-dominated families, relationships, or workspaces. In the following sections, I explore four of the most common characterizations that demonstrate the secondary status of *Digest* women: women's lives as family-centered, women as wives, women as mothers, and women in occupational roles.

WOMEN'S LIVES AS FAMILY-CENTERED

For female characters in the short stories and brief biographies of *Reader's Digest*, life is family-centered. Indeed, over 90% of the articles featuring female characters from 1980-1992 utilize references to family roles as primary identifiers for their female characters. My analysis indicates that women as seen by *Reader's Digest* are expected to fulfill traditionalist obligations as family members, and families are presumed to fulfill certain apparently "essential" needs for women.

One significant role filled by women family members is the maintenance of the household, as indicated by a plethora of references to the type of house in which a certain family interacts and the general condition of its upkeep. A representative example of an ideal living space is described in the story "Please Let Him Live to See the Baby" (January, 1980). Although the plot of the story revolves around the drama of an escaped convict holding a family hostage, the reader is given a peek at the family's living situation as the story begins: "Mary Ann parked in the driveway of her isolated split-level. . . . Neat and spotless just as Mary Ann had left it, the house seemed secure" (p. 139). Within this brief passage, the reader is introduced to a familiar setting that recurs often in *Digest* narratives—that is, most of the magazine's female-charactered dramas occur in similar "typical" neat and spotless U.S. American homes in which the woman of the household is responsible for its upkeep.

Other stories emphasize the apparently natural connection between women and particular parts of the home, as in "The Woman in the Kitchen" (September 1989), in which the male author relates his impressions of his mother by telling the "Tale of the Three Stoves." As he unfolds the story of his family of struggling Hungarian immigrants, he consistently correlates his mother with stoves and cooking, beginning with the toy stove she cherished—but was forced to abandon—as a child, moving on to the portable Coleman stove on which she "cooked for half a dozen lumberjacks" (along with her family) in a California logging camp, and finally to the "hot six burner stove" of a church kitchen on which she helped to prepare special dinners for an entire congregation. The narrative ends with an account of the mother's reunion with a childhood friend, who, as an adult, returns to her the previously mentioned toy stove she had cherished as a child. The toy represents motherhood to the author and his family: "My brother, Robert, has it now. It sits in a place of honor, on a shelf in the sun porch of his home in Oakland. It stands for simplicity, courage, grace and service. It stands for the woman in the kitchen" (p. 90). Thus, the woman in this story is represented by a kitchen appliance and characterized by her service in the kitchens she occupied in her lifetime. As is typical in the pages of the *Digest*, this woman—like others in similar stories—is not motivated to do domestic work or maintain a respectable household based on her own desires. Instead, she performs these tasks out of an unquestioned sense of natural obligation to the male-dominated family unit.

Besides creating and maintaining a clean and happy home for the benefit of the family, women in *Digest* narratives consistently seek to utilize their various personal accomplishments for the good of the family unit. One example is Bertha Lee Ingram, who conquered her adult illiteracy despite her husband's initial protests ("Bertha's triumph," August 1987). Ingram's decision to "disobey" her husband was offset by the fact that her newfound literacy could benefit him and their children: "As Bertha learned to read and write, Thomas gained a new appreciation for her. 'She helps me understand things better,' he says" (p. 58). Here again, we find the featured female character acting not as an agent on her own behalf, but as a servant of her family's (more specifically her husband's) needs.

The *Digest* extends its representation of women as family members beyond the realm of voluntary caretaking. Indeed, the importance of the family in the lives of *Digest* women is emphasized in stories indicating that without their families, women's lives would be either chaotic or empty. A clear example of the disastrous effects that loss of family can have on a woman's life appears in the article "Thank You, Rosie" (January 1980), in which a woman is driven to depression, the streets, and eventually prostitution after the death of her daughter. It is clear within the *Digest* worldview that the absence of family means the absence of a purpose for women's lives. In turn, women can find no happiness unless families are restored. Specific roles played by women in families extend these themes, particularly roles as marital partners.

WOMEN AS WIVES

Women's roles as wives in *Digest* narratives emphasize their complete devotion to that particular social role. Their status as spouses generally locates them as dependent on and subordinate to their husbands, with this dependence resulting from their essential fear of loneliness. For example, "In the Autumn of Life" (March 1982) presents the thoughts of an elderly wife as she and her husband miss connections at train stations:

> I was calm at first,
> Then panic mounted,
> And insight.
> I realized how much I counted on him
> To give meaning to my life.
>
> If he didn't come,
> I didn't want to go home,
> Didn't want to go anywhere,
> Didn't care about anything. (p. 91)

Again, the female's identity is completely entrenched in her role as a wife and her dependent connection to her husband; without him, she knows she will cease to exist. In the pages of *Reader's Digest*, however, a woman's dependence on her husband often runs deeper than just a fear of loneliness. Indeed, in many of the dramas, a husband's absence leads directly to danger or trouble for his wife or her family. The hostage crisis described in "Please Let Him Live to See the Baby" is portrayed as a direct result of Mary Ann Cossano's husband's overtime assignment at work, which leaves the pregnant 26-year-old temporarily alone to protect her family from the evil intruder. The implication here is that the husband's mere presence would have prevented the entire incident. Women, then, depend on their husbands not only for companionship but for protection as well.

Even in death, men are portrayed as protectors of women, as in "One Woman's Wilderness Odyssey" (September 1988). After a boating accident in a remote Arctic research site, an experienced outdoorswoman realizes that her fiancee [almost-husband] is dead. She overcomes her initial response—"My life has ended"—by forging onward toward survival through the urging of the deceased's voice in her mind: "During several hours of semi-conscious sleep, Lydia dreamed of Jean-Jacques, feeling his presence. 'Don't stop here!' she heard him say. 'Stick to the plan!'" (p. 79). Although she guides herself through 70 miles of Arctic terrain with merely a compass, the article attributes her survival to the inspiration of a man who himself had not survived.

Some narratives give biographical accounts of the lives of celebrities or other apparent "successes." Often, those who qualify as outstanding women also qualify as outstanding wives. Perhaps the most obvious representative of this category is First Lady Barbara Bush, featured in the April 1989 issue. The *Digest* lays out the criteria for a perfect First Lady, then identifies Bush as a worthy candidate:

> A First Lady should be gracious but not a doormat, strong but not a co-President. She must defend her husband and smile bravely when he says stupid things. She must look great, possess perfect children (though such critters do not exist in nature) and traipse around the world when she would rather be home with a good book. Hardest of all, she has to appear to love every minute of it.
>
> History may prove Barbara Bush to be the right woman in the right place. . . . Like many political wives, Barbara has devoted her life to her husband, with whom she has survived a wartime separation, 44 years of marriage, 29 moves, the death of a child and the rigors of three national campaigns. ("Barbara Bush: Down-to-Earth First Lady," pp. 83-84)

Bush is continually promoted as a wife rather than a public figure in her own right; although Bush may have willingly accepted that definition as descriptive of her identity, the article implies that a First Lady has no choice but to define herself solely through her connection and service to her husband. That same practice is applied to other, less public wives who have gained some noticeable measure of success.

To summarize, women as wives in *Reader's Digest* are likely to: (a) serve as keepers of the household; (b) depend on the homespace as a primary force in solidifying the family unit; (c) serve as caretakers of all family members through adversity; (d) depend on men as the most significant source of meaning in their lives; and (e) consider any other roles that they might play as secondary to those involved in maintaining the family unit. These representations acknowledge the patriarchal family as the "natural" order of human existence and make no attempt to question or challenge traditional expectations for women. The magazine's antifeminist stance is continued in its coverage of idealized motherhood.

WOMEN AS MOTHERS

Where there are wives in the pages of the *Digest*, one can also generally expect to see mothers and vice versa. Motherhood is depicted as another essential life motivator for women, again bringing with it a very rigid set of expectations. Besides performing their prescribed duties as wives, women are generally expected to deal with the children, as in the list of experiences outlined by the elderly wife of "In the Autumn of Life:"

> Of course, he can be a big help, too,
> But where was he when the house was piled high with toys
> And I got chicken pox along with the boys?
>
> Where was he when Jennifer was teething
> And Tim broke his hand
> And I had to drive somebody somewhere every day?
>
> I know. He had to go to the office.
> Had to travel on business. He didn't choose to,
> It was all he knew. (p. 89)

There is no bitterness expressed by the female, as she apparently accepts this division of labor as "the way things are." Such recognition and acceptance of their duties is another primary characteristic of *Digest* female characters. Thus, this woman's list of responsibilities does not stand out as unusual among the characters of *Digest* narratives (although her level of self-reflexiveness distinguishes her from most *Digest* mothers). More often, women in *Reader's Digest* gain joy and exhilaration from the previously mentioned tasks, which are represented as a "natural" part of what it means to be a woman.

Women's mothering responsibilities are particularly clear in the case of danger, risk, or emergency for their children, especially if those children are sick or debilitated in some way. "Which Baby Should I Save?" (May 1984) is a prime example of the expectation for the mother to provide constant, immediate, and expert care for ailing infants. The story is an account of newborn triplets at risk of developing Sudden Infant Death Syndrome who are constantly connected to heart and lung monitors. The story includes a series of episodes during which one or more monitors sound, indicating a need for immediate medical attention. The babies' mother is always the only character prepared to respond; in fact, the narrative describes the sound of a beeping monitor as "an urgent call to the baby's mother to race to the crib" (p. 134). Clearly, motherhood is seen to bear with it instinctual capacities for assessing and meeting children's needs, and the role is to be filled exclusively by one woman.

Another expectation is for mothers to overcome any personal difficulties in service of their children. "I Have To Save My Baby!" (April 1989) is an account of the near-drowning of an infant girl who was saved by the actions of her wheelchair-using mother. The heroic effort is portrayed as a mere requirement of motherhood: "Even with her handicap, she had done what any mother would have done to save her child. When she needed it most, she had found an extraordinary inner strength—a strength fueled by love" (p. 70).

As in the story described earlier, women's service usually involves sacrifice—another recurring theme in *Digest* motherhood. For example, famous moms Erma Bombeck and Meryl Streep, both featured in articles in the 1980s ("Erma Bombeck: Syndicated soul of suburbia," November 1984; "Magnetic, magnificent Meryl," March 1988), confess that their families' needs override their own personal and professional concerns. Bombeck guarantees that her writing always "stopped before the family came home, and the minute steaks and ketchup always hit the table on time" (p. 45). Streep expresses a desire to balance both career and family needs, but the story implies her real priorities: "With all these young children, I don't know how much longer I'll be able to make movies at all!" (p. 92). The stories make no mention of these privileged women's access to paid professional help. Instead, both accounts acknowledge that the sacrifices for motherhood might be great, but they exclude the possibility that career decisions might override the instinctual desire for family.

Where motherhood and marriage are not factors—a rare occurrence in *Digest* narratives—stories tend to focus on women's roles as daughters. Accounts of the rebellious daughter of President Theodore Roosevelt ("Irreverent recollections of a President's daughter," March 1982), the brave, firefighting daughter of an average Maryland family ("Please don't let me die!," May 1984), and a young, but wise and loving daughter who helped her father to appreciate small pleasures ("The Daddy prize," October 1989) all serve to underscore the importance of such family roles even in the lives of women whose existence cannot be explained through spouses and children.

WOMEN IN OCCUPATIONAL ROLES

Unquestionably, the bulk of descriptors for women in *Reader's Digest* narratives focus around the family. Often, those are the only terms by which a woman character is identified. Some, however, are additionally identified by occupation. As might be expected, though, the occupation of many of the women characters appears to be housekeeping. In fact, nearly 40% of the female characters fall under the category of "Housewife/Domestic/Full-Time Mother." Their activities include childrearing, housecleaning, gardening, cooking, and sewing.

In spite of the typical housewife's apparent contentment with her position, she is occasionally permitted to recognize the drudgery of her role, although she ultimately accepts the duller aspects of her life in exchange for the rewards of maintaining a secure and happy home. Erma Bombeck can be seen as the prototypical housewife in this sense. In a biographical narrative about her rise to popularity, the focus is on her apparent distaste for housework:

> The message [of Bombeck's early columns] was that housework, if it is done right, can kill you. It was that the women who kept house in suburbia were so lonely that they could have conversations with their tropical fish. It was that kids find you about as exciting as the food blender. They come in, look you in the eye and ask you if anybody's home. ("Erma Bombeck: Syndicated soul of suburbia," November 1984, p. 39)

Despite this somewhat negative description of life as a housewife, Bombeck reassures the reader by giving a "heartfelt 'Whew!'" and confessing that "family life was warm and normal, not a succession of Bombeck disasters" (p. 45).

One "deviant" housewife character appears in a fictional short story by Roald Dahl ("Lamb to the slaughter," July 1980). The story meets all of the standard criteria for a female character—from her cooking and sewing to her pregnancy. The twist toward deviance occurs when her husband apparently confesses his infidelity; her response is to murder him with a frozen leg of lamb, then feed the cooked evidence to the investigating officers. Even this unusual story can be said to fit the

mold to some degree, however, as it was the disruption of an ideal family that led to the woman's extreme act. Additionally, her actions match
another stereotypical view of women: females who are "done wrong"
will turn psychotic.

In addition to housewives, readers find many examples of
women performing other traditionally female occupational roles.
Teachers, waitresses, children's counselors, religious instructors, nursing
home attendants, telephone operators, and nurses all make appearances
as featured or minor characters in the narratives. As expected, the
women who maintain these traditional occupational roles are again represented as superhuman givers, as in the case of "Unforgettable
Maureen O'Donnell" (January 1990), an exceptional high school Latin
teacher:

> Other students were amazed that [her] pupils had her home phone
> number and were encouraged to call or visit anytime. And we did.
> The O'Donnells had a rule: anyone there at 4 p.m. on Sunday was
> invited to dinner, as long as there was room at the table. At
> Christmas the house was always filled with [her] students, home
> from college, eager to see her and one another again.
>
> Students came in droves with the usual problems of school, ado-
> lescence and career choices. We always felt better when she restored
> perspective with her question, "*Quid ad aeternum* (What is it in the
> light of eternity)?" She never mentioned her own problems, and her
> joy in life never flagged. For those with great needs, she offered
> much. (p. 66)

O'Donnell's "own problems" include her battle with terminal cancer, a
struggle that never interferes with the teacher's devotion to her students
and her occupational duties. Like a good wife or mother, she fulfills her
role as a needed "Other" until her death.

Another traditional character who turns deviant appears in "My
Baby Can't Be Dead!" (March 1982), in which the reader is introduced to
a seemingly helpful, conventional nurse. However, as the story's plot
unfolds, it is revealed that the nurse is masterminding an elaborate
baby-switching scheme whereby mothers who should have given birth
to healthy babies are convinced that complications caused the stillbirth
of their children. Again, however, this devious character can be said to
fit the mold, as her motivation is neither malice nor profit—she is controlled by her desire to adopt and raise the children as her own. Once
again, a woman's actions—though in this case somewhat irrational—are
motivated by longings for a stable family.

Other occupational roles less traditionally identified as "female"
also appear in some of the narratives. Most of those nontraditional

female characters are popular public figures, celebrities, or artists. One of the occupational roles that is presented in a positive light is women as writers. These articles include the aforementioned coverage of Erma Bombeck, along with reports about advice columnist Ann Landers ("The woman who gives Ann Landers advice," June 1985) and less-well-known writers such as the 100-year-old folk historian featured in "Centenarian Chronicler of Country Life" (May 1984). Despite the independent successes of these and other featured female writers, the stories that introduce them to Digest readers again use the family as a central focal point, either by discussing their writings about families or by addressing the impact of their careers on their personal family lives.

Similar approaches are taken in dealing with other personalities, such as actress Meryl Streep and artist Georgia O'Keefe ("Georgia O'Keefe: All-American artist," March 1988). In the latter story, early paragraphs seem to indicate that the focus of the narrative will be on an artist and her life and work: "O'Keefe has been perceived differently over the years: first as a chaste femme fatale; later as a desert recluse who painted the cliffs and hills, the bones and stones of northern New Mexico; and, most recently, as an early feminist, an independent, self-sufficient and liberated woman. In fact, she was all of them" (p. 182). The focus of the article becomes relatively clear in subsequent passages, however, as the bulk of the piece focuses on O'Keefe's somewhat mysterious relationship with her husband, fellow artist Alfred Stieglitz. Although the author seems to imply that the marriage was a relatively unorthodox arrangement, the article still maps the relationship in terms of "devotion" and "commitment" between the two artists. Thus, the individual personal achievements of O'Keefe are addressed within a context that discusses families and relationships, a pattern that holds true for most of the female celebrity subjects of Digest narratives.

Nontraditional occupational roles occasionally extend into the traditional domain of men as in an unrelated pair of stories about female firefighters ("Hey, lady, where's the fire?," July 1980; "Please don't let me die," May 1984). Even in these stories, however, readers are constantly reassured that the featured women are not shirking their duties as females. First, the female firefighters are shown to be emerging from traditionally feminine roles to show support for their communities. Then, the reader is assured that these women will strive to maintain norms in other social arenas:

> In beauty shops, grocery stores, and bridge clubs across the United States, curlers, carts, and cards are dropped at the sound of a fire alarm. No longer restricted to auxiliary roles, such as fund raising and coffee toting, these women—often wives, mothers, even grand-

mothers—have filled a distressing void in their communities, increased the protection of lives and property, and won the sometimes grudging respect of their male peers.

. . . "It had nothing to do with women's liberation," says [female firefighter Betty Lou] Dudley. "It's just that we are needed." ("Hey, lady, where's the fire?" p. 99)

Despite their hard work as members of their communities, they still find themselves running into problems that are not likely to affect men, such as Katherine Geiger's discovery that "fire helmets won't fit over curlers" and Thelma Rowe's realization that if she dies in an explosion, she cannot guess "who would cook supper tonight?" ("Hey, lady, where's the fire?" pp. 101-102). Apparently, readers are to recognize that these "unusual" women still know their places.

IMPLICATIONS

As the examples cited earlier demonstrate, in the pages of *Reader's Digest*, women possess virtually no subjectivity that empowers them to act in any way other than as the prescribed other—serving identities of the magazine's traditionalist ideal. One primary problem with this *Digest* version of life, however, is that, according to Luke (1989), this idealized "'traditional' domestic model" describes only 7% of families in the contemporary United States (p. 99).

Hazou (1990) refers to this staunch support of the idealized nuclear family as "the myth of the pedestal." Hazou explains the power of this myth as she discusses the contradictions between this idealized view and the lived experience of women in the United States during the 1980s:

There are women who genuinely feel that they would lose a favored status if they are treated equally in society. Perhaps those who claim they want to keep women on the pedestal are not aware of what statistics show are the real conditions of women's lives. They might not realize that in 1987 there were 47.8 divorces for every 100 marriages and the rate is increasing; that after divorce the average woman's standard of living decreases by 73 percent while her ex-husband's increases by 42 percent; that the average court-ordered child support is less than the cost of day care alone; and that in 1986, female heads of household and their children accounted for 52 percent of the country's poor. They also might not know that divorced and unmarried men are reluctant to take responsibility for children that they have sired, based on the fact that ten years after divorce, 87 percent of fathers were no longer meeting court-ordered payments, and in 1981 28.2 percent paid nothing; furthermore, less than half of those who paid did not pay the full amount. Because of the increased rate of divorce and unwed motherhood, 42 percent of white and 86 percent of black children must be raised by the mother alone for part or all of their lives. In addition, those who believe the women-on-a-pedestal myth seem not to be aware of the amount of violence perpetrated by men (with virtual impunity) against women, and that the FBI crime reports (which represent only the reported incidents) show that the number of wife batterings and rapes is on the increase. (p. 101)

This lengthy passage helps to contextualize the traditionalist claims and characterizations in *Digest* narratives featuring women and clearly demonstrates that the vision of women's lives represented in *Reader's Digest* is drastically out of touch with the lived experience of most women in contemporary U.S. society.

Within the limited prescription of the *Digest* family, the women themselves admit that their roles as family members are the only things that give meaning to their lives. Hence, *Digest* wives are wholeheartedly devoted to their husbands, with no regrets; they willingly serve as all-purpose mothers who expect no outside assistance in meeting all the needs of their children; and, when in occupational roles outside of the home, they recognize that their careers or vocations are secondary to their families. No possibility of lifestyle alternatives is present in the magazine's narratives, as women who violate the *Digest*'s regressive prescription are shown to be social outcasts or downright crazy people.

Despite apparent shifts in popular ideology, no such shifts occur in the representations of women and women's roles in *Digest* narratives. The magazine's decision to cling to traditionalist role expectations is problematic, for it seems obvious that depictions of women like those in the narratives of the *Digest* are contributing factors to the continuing oppression of women in U.S. society today. Indeed, by consistently presenting such regressive images to millions of readers worldwide, the magazine constructs an artificial ideal that is unattainable by most women, especially in light of the changing social scene described earlier. For *Reader's Digest*, though, "double binds" and social contradictions for women are nonexistent, as there are virtually no references to problems for women outside of the realm of private domestic life. The narratives in the *Digest* produce norms and values that serve as ideals, no matter how greatly they contradict the lived experience of women during the 1980s and early 1990s.

It is important to note that women also participate in their own subjugation, as they recognize in *Digest* narratives a set of behaviors that are celebrated and rewarded. Shotter and Logan (1988) explain this tendency as a form of self-domination, in which "mastering" the rules of the system brings rewards, making individuals choose to conform to the system as it stands rather than challenge it and risk punishment.

CONCLUSION

Where feminist theorists encourage questioning, *Reader's Digest* seeks compliance. Most feminists would not argue for a complete reversal of traditional roles, but would instead agree with Hazou (1990), who argues:

> The ultimate goal of feminists is the social redefinition of women as neither evil temptresses nor angelic goddesses on a pedestal but simply as human creatures with the same needs and personality traits (good or bad, leader or follower) as any other persons, regardless of sex. (p. 101)

Thus, Hazou and other feminist theorists argue in favor of constructions that open up possibilities for women, rather than maintaining the standard descriptions and prescriptions promoted by society through tradition.

Through examination of the consistent images of women presented within the *Reader's Digest*'s narratives, I have identified recurring themes that seem to share a significantly limited—and limiting—view of the personal, social, and political potential of women.

These images are not unique creations of the editorial staff of the *Reader's Digest*. Still, their potential impact as recurring messages within this globally circulated publication is immense. In short, the magazine with the largest circulation in the world is promoting ideas that are limiting and subordinating women, that bear little resemblance to the available sociological data about contemporary U.S. society, and that, ultimately, provide women with little or no chance to ever become more than merely "the Second Sex."

REFERENCES

David, M., & Levitas, R. (1988). Antifeminism in the British and American new rights. In G. Seidel (Ed.), *The nature of the right* (pp. 141-152). Philadelphia: John Benjamins Publishing.

De Beauvoir, S. (1952). *The second sex*. New York: Vintage.

Hazou, W. (1990). *The social and legal status of women: A global perspective*. New York: Praeger.

Luke, T. (1989). *Screens of power: Ideology, domination, and resistance in informational society*. Urbana: University of Illinois Press.

Offen, K. (1988). Defining feminism: A comparative historical approach. *Signs, 14*, 119-157.

Opie, A. (1992). Qualitative research, appropriation of the "other" and empowerment. *Feminist Review, 40*, 52-69.

Quinn, S. (1992, June). The feminist betrayal. *Reader's Digest, 140*, 84-86.

Schreiner, S. A. (1974). *The condensed world of the Reader's Digest*. New York: Stein and Day.

Shotter, J., & Logan, J. (1988). The pervasiveness of patriarchy: On finding a different voice. In M.M. Gergen (Ed.), *Feminist thought and the structure of knowledge* (pp. 69-86). New York: New York University Press.

Ulrich's International Periodicals Directory: 1991-92. (1991). (30th ed.). New Providence, NJ: Reed Publishing.

4

The Pornography of
Everyday Life
Jane Caputi

Almost every woman knows something about what it is like to travel down a street and be met with the standard gamut of interrelated put-downs/come-ons: *girlie, honey, whore, sweet thing, baby, bitch, fatso, pussy, cunt, old bag*, as well as specifically sexually racist epithets: *squaw, brown sugar, hot tamale*; homophobic ones: *dyke, lezzie* and more of all types, increasingly hurtful and hateful. However removed from the realm of academic theory this everyday experience seems, it serves as a micro-cosm of the process that cultural studies scholars describe as working to form subjectivity. *Subjectivity* comprises our sense of ourselves, and our relations to other people, to other creatures, to society, to the cosmos. Both psychoanalytic and social theory stress the role played by dis-course in the ongoing construction of our very *political* subjectivities, however "natural" they seem. Subjectivities are based in power relations and are *hegemonic*, reflecting and serving the interests of dominant groups (Fiske, 1987/1992).

Everyday language and popular culture address us, hail us, or, in the terminology of critical theory, *interpellate* us. They call out to us with certain social names to which we are expected to identify and respond. If we do, usually habitually and unconsciously, we position ourselves within a hegemonic frame of reference; if we do not, we adopt a stance of resistance. For some the interpellation is meant to be flattering: the hailing of Americans as free citizens of the greatest country in the world; of humans as a superior, godlike species; of the rich as suave, beautiful, and sophisticated; of those of European descent as superior, winners of the "master race." Yet, for subjected peoples, the address most frequently takes the form of an epithet and must be understood as a form of abuse.

Tuchman, Daniels, and Benet (1978) use the term *symbolic annihilation* to describe the systemic treatment of female images in the mass media. Such annihilation is expressed in two ways: *absence*—women are simply disappeared from roles that convey social power, significance, and validity; or negative *stereotyping*—women are projected in images that are condemnatory, belittling, and/or victimized. Here, I look specifically at some of the ways that women as a gender class (with variations according to such factors as race, economic class, and age) are socially addressed as inferior in the mass media, whereas men as a gender class (again, with those same variations) are socially addressed as superior.

I am loosely using the term *pornography of everyday life* to refer to these mainstream images of gender dominance and subordination, exploitation and abuse, that proliferate throughout everyday culture in order to highlight the function of pornography as a paradigm for the development of all manner of oppressive discourses. By *pornography*, I do not mean mere sexual depiction or nudity, no matter how explicit; I support nonexploitative erotica based on sexual equality and justice.[1] Rather, I draw on feminist theory that has analyzed pornography as a form of sexual abuse, its narratives and iconography developed around exploitation, objectification, and "denigration of women and a fear and hatred of the female body" (Kaplan, 1991, p. 322). In a proposed civil ordinance, MacKinnon and Dworkin (cited in Dworkin, 1989, pp. 253-275) define pornography as the "sexually explicit subordination of women" that constructs feminine and masculine subjectivities based in gender inequality, conditioning us to eroticize domination, subordination, violence, and objectification.

Any examination of popular culture reveals an enormous range of nonsexually explicit imagery and language that pornographically addresses its viewers. Popular culture messages are polysemic; they are constructed to carry multiple meanings. Many individual viewers embrace the hegemonic/pornographic message. Others negotiate their own interpretations, sometimes even resistant ones that go against the grain of entrenched power. Others deliberately avoid exposing themselves to images that offend or enrage. However, these latter practices offer only partial protection against those who are empowered by abusive imagery. I use the word *abusive* deliberately for, as I argue, these images not only represent violence but function as a form of psychological/emotional assault. Mass-mediated battery exists in all venues of popular culture, including fiction, music, film, folklore, and so on. Here, though, to make my scope manageable, I largely limit my discussion to advertising imagery.

GENDER PORN

Pornography depends for its vitality on the gender stereotypes that support the fundamental structures of our social order. (Kaplan, 1991, pp. 342-43)

The headline of the January 20, 1992, cover of Time Magazine reads: "Why are Men and Women Different? It isn't just upbringing. New studies show they are born that way." The cover image is of a probably Latino boy and a girl, about 8 years old. They are standing in front of a brick wall. The boy takes up most of the frame. Pulling up his sleeve, flexing his right bicep, and admiring his small, swollen muscle, he is turned away from the girl and focused entirely on his display. She gazes indulgently at him and places one hand under his elbow, offering support. Contained in this simple image are a number of charged messages. We learn, visually, that males and females are utterly different, with self-absorbed males defined primarily by superior strength. This strength, as well as his placement in the bulk of the space, connotes dominance, both physical and social. The girl is subordinated, yet supportive, and absorbed totally by the little boy. Finally, there is that brick wall they are up against. As this image has it, there is no way out; biology is destiny and that destiny is male dominance and female subordination, male self-centeredness and female self-denial. Of course, although the whole thing is about that supposed immutable core of gender hierarchy, this profoundly staged image participates in the ongoing construction and legitimation of unequal gender.

Some viewers might wonder why children are shown to illustrate a statement about "men and women," and why Latino children are chosen when in a racist system whiteness is generally taken as the norm, and Latinos are usually symbolically annihilated through absence from mass media depictions. Racist ideology has it that people of color, like children, are "closer to nature" and more subject to instinctual drives than white people. Hence, the biologically deterministic subtext here supports the equally determinist argument for male dominance.

A grown-up Euro/American version of this pornographic couple appears in a Calvin Klein underwear ad from 1992. The ad is spread out over two pages. On the first page, Markie Mark appears clad only in his

Calvins, with a threatening look on his face and grabbing his crotch. On the next page, Markie is relaxed and sitting on the floor. He faces front; turning to him and wrapping a supportive arm around his waist is the notoriously slender "waif" Kate Moss (also dressed only in her underpants).

These gender-porn images point to power, violence, and control of space as intrinsic and defining components of masculinity. In patriarchal consciousness, *power* is not usually understood as an ability, such as the power of speech, but rather as being able to compel obedience, to dominate. At the same time, as these images testify, power becomes highly sexualized and hierarchically gendered. Not only male musculature but the penis itself is graphically associated with power, as well as self-absorption and aggression. Femininity, on the other hand, is represented as contained, side-lined, insubstantial, intrinsically supportive, controlled, and fundamentally powerless. Moreover, as this one-way power dynamic implies, one day the feminine counterpart will find herself at the other end of hardened muscle or hostile penis.

In the pornographic paradigm, male and female are defined as inevitably attracted to each other and, at the same time, inherently unequal. Domination is identified with masculinity and submission with femininity. The male partner is supposed to be taller, stronger, richer, and older—in short, more powerful. The female partner is supposed to be shorter, weaker, poorer, and younger—in short, powerless. Under this paradigm, such forms of domination as enslavement (of allegedly "primitive," "childish" peoples), imperialist conquest (of a "virgin land"), scientific "mastery" of the elements, and even technological exploitation of and violences against the body of (Mother) Earth acquire an undeniably sexual component. Such power dynamics are enacted and symbolically represented as a masculine gazing at, unveiling, taking, and even raping the (passive, inferior, weaker, backward) feminine. The language of heterosexual intercourse—*fucking, screwing, balling, banging, having, taking, possessing, scoring, nailing*—reveals a sexualization of domination and submission, even to the point of injury and death.

Henry Kissinger once remarked that power is the ultimate aphrodisiac. A political cartoon in *The Nation* (February 25, 1984) visualizes Kissinger's power by showing him taking/raping the Earth (a woman's body with the Earth as her head). We have no trouble getting the joke. Rena Swentzell (1993), a Native American scholar from Santa Clara Pueblo in New Mexico, scoffs at the normative/pornographic belief in "power as an integral part of sexuality" (p. 167). Yet, she demands that we recognize the historical implications of that belief: "That is what the whole conquest of the Southwest was about—power and control by males" (p. 167).

When men rape, it is an act of sexualized violence in which they conceptualize and use their penises as weapons. A 1987 porn feature, *Mr. MX*, features a white man with a monstrously long penis: "Take a long look at the real weapon of the '80s. . . . See his 16-1/2-inch missile." How different is this overtly pornographic notion of male sexuality from every-day notions? Support for such a cultural construction of the penis is lit-tered throughout popular culture where lethal implements (from knives to bomber aircraft) are continually associated with the penis and bran-dished as the paradigmatic icons of heroic masculinity (e.g., *Top Gun, Dirty Harry, Lethal Weapon, Rambo, True Lies*). Consider the July 1992 cover of *Vanity Fair* featuring sex symbol Luke Perry. He is shirtless, wearing only blue jeans and boots, and sprawled with one leg outstretched and one knee up. Nestled in his crotch, he holds a gun. Together, he and the gun are the symbol of a pornographic sexuality built on male dominance and female subordination until death do them part.

RHAPSODY IN BLACK AND BLUE

> Every breath you take, every step you make, I'll be watching you. Oh can't you see, you belong to me. (Sting, "Every Breath You Take")

Female models used in the advertising of all types of products are rou-tinely presented in tableaux suggesting bondage, rape, and battery. Such motifs were introduced into mainstream fashion imagery in the 1970s by such internationally known photographers as Helmut Newton and Guy Bourdin. These themes have now become commonplace. One of Newton's earliest spreads appeared in *Vogue* in 1975. Called "The Story of Ohh" (referring to the 1954 sado-masochistic classic by Pauline Réage, *The Story of O*), it showed a white man pushing and shoving a white woman before slapping her across the face. Is this an ad for perfume, as alleged, or one for woman beating? More recent versions include a 1994 May Company ad in which, with one hand, a dark man grabs a blonde woman with such force that her head is thrown back. With the other hand, he shakes an admonishing finger in her face. In a 1990 ad for Bonjour apparel, a glaring, close-mouthed man stands behind a woman, whose body is positioned with head thrust back, mouth open, and neck and chest exposed. Her shirt is strangely tied in front of her, suggesting bondage. Her torso juts forward awkwardly and it appears that her dis-torted posture is caused by the man holding her arms behind her back. The woman's eyes are half shut and her mouth open in an expression of pain and vulnerability. The clothes in this ad take a clear back seat to its more obvious message: the eroticization of manhandling.

Battery is a long-term process of torture and intimidation meant to break the will of the victim. This is accomplished not only by physical assault but through repeated humiliations and attacks on the victim's sense of self (Jones, 1994). One of the most audacious visual targetings of female self-esteem can be found in a 1994 ad for boots that appeared in *Details*, a men's magazine. In it, a white woman is positioned on hands and knees with her buttocks high in the air. She is licking the floor. The copy reads: "An acquired taste." The pornographic message here is that if an abuser humiliates his partner long enough, she will learn to love it; she will learn to eroticize her own submission.

Batterers generally claim to love their victims—a love defined by possession and obsession in which ownership and control of the partner is intrinsically tied to the batterer's sense of self. A 1994 ad for Calvin Klein's perfume, "Obsession," depicts a naked man striding off with his captive, a naked, unresisting, and perhaps unconscious, woman slung over his shoulder. As with Sting's "love" song, this image is a stalker's rhapsody—in black and blue.

THE JOY OF RAPE

A 1996 ad in Seventeen for Bonnie Bell "no shine" cosmetic products reads: *"No means NO."* It tells teenage girls that when they were little "no" meant things like "no cookie before dinner." Now, they proclaim, "NO takes on a whole new meaning." That meaning according to Bonnie Bell is: "No more greasy makeup." One 1992 study found that girls younger than 18 accounted for 62% of rape victims (Johnston, 1992). The well-known feminist retort "no means no" counters the pornographic insistence that a woman's no to sexual contact actually means yes. In this ad, anti-rape activism is grossly trivialized for the age group most susceptible to rape.

The word *no* also features prominently in a 1993 ad for Old Spice deodorant that appeared in *Sports Illustrated*. At the very top of the page is the huge bold-faced word **No** (at the bottom, in much smaller print, we find the word *sweat*). Underneath that caption, we see a white woman, her back against a brick wall. A white man towers over her, his arms outstretched; her hands press up against his chest. The two are both smiling, yet, despite the smiles, this ad's narrative can be read as a rape scenario. He has backed her up against the wall and is physically blockading her; she ineffectively tries to push him back. The unmistakable transmission is that of a woman being overwhelmed by a man, easily—*no sweat*. Perhaps the meaning her smile conveys to many readers is the quintessential pornographic dictum—that even when women say "NO" they mean "yes."

In September 1991, the "Tailhook" convention of Navy pilots in Las Vegas provided an occasion for the mass sexual abuse of women. Dozens of women, including officers and civilians, were accosted by dozens of naval officers. During the three-day event, Navy and Marine Corps pilots formed gauntlets in the hallways of the Hilton, shoving terrified women down the line, grabbing at their breasts, buttocks, and genitals, and ripping at their clothes. In April 1992, Harper's Bazaar made an extraordinary fashion statement about this event in "Maritime Dash," a photo spread featuring women's clothing with a military flair. The pictures were shot aboard a Navy ship, not at the Las Vegas Hilton, but the connection to the Tailhook convention was unmistakable. Nearly all of the photos feature a single woman, flanked by rows of uniformed men. The first shows the woman striding through a gauntlet of eight saluting sailors. The tongue-in-cheek copy reads: "Today's nautical report: the navy is coming." A subsequent photo shows the female model lifted adoringly in the arms of six uniformed men, one of whom is fondling her breast. The last photo shows her looking arch and utterly in control while six sailors flank her, rubbing broom handles in frustration. This photo essay recalls the sexist abuse but with a significant twist: the woman is smiling; the gauntlet is friendly. She wants it, these pictures say; she is in control. Such a skewed reconstruction after the fact is reminiscent of the 1992 Simi Valley verdict acquitting four Los Angeles policemen in the beating of Rodney King. That jury, after watching the videotaped beating more than 30 times, concluded that King was "in control," a perception indubitably aided by years of conditioning to the pornographic mindset that eroticizes power, domination, and violence; sexually fetishizes the uniformed man of violence; and insists on the willing, pleasurable, and, indeed, causal participation of victims.

Alcohol was deemed by all observers to expedite the Tailhook abuses and, as many analysts of rape concur, alcohol consumption by both victim and perpetrator frequently plays a role in facilitating rape, particularly gang rape (Sanday, 1990). Many liquor ads subtly teach perpetrators about the efficacy of alcohol. For example, a 1995 ad for Bacardi rum that appeared on the back cover of Vibe showed three white men and one woman (perhaps African American). One of the men is lifting her up in the air; her legs are spread and a huge bottle of Bacardi rum is aimed into her crotch. All parties are smiling. Advertised here are the joys of (gang) rape and the uses to which alcohol can be put in facilitating it.

BITCH

> Where white women are depicted in pornography as "objects,"
> black women are depicted as animals. Where white women are
> depicted as human bodies if not beings, black women are depicted
> as shit. (Walker, 1980, p. 103)

A horrific ad for "Bitch Skateboards" appeared in 1994 in the magazine *Big Brother* (and later was sent in to the "No Comment" page of *Ms.*). It depicts the universal stick figures for a man and a woman. The man holds his right arm outstretched, pointing a gun execution style at the head of a woman. *Bitch* functions as a universal term of contempt for women; here it doubles as a death sentence.

Bitch names femaleness as being animal-like, "sub" human. Yet at one point in human history, bitch was as honorific as the terms *queen* and *goddess*; indeed, they were in some ways synonymous. Barbara Walker (1983) reveals that *Bitch* was "one of the most sacred titles of the Goddess Artemis-Diana" (p. 109). Indeed, around the world, "in India to the Mediterranean, in Asia Minor, Crete, Greece, Syria, Mesopotamia, Egypt, Africa, and westward to Malta, Sicily, and Southern Spain," as Neumann (1963, p. 268) notes, the Great Mother or Lady of the Beasts assumed the form of an animal or appeared surrounded by animals. This ancient, powerful, and divine Bitch is the sacred archetype behind the contemporary profanity, reflecting fear of the sexually sovereign, creative, awesome elemental figure for whom there is no place save caricaturization or outright demonization in the patriarchal pantheon.

Sexist/racist logic, although resting on that universal contempt for femaleness, when necessary makes expedient distinctions among women, scapegoating some as particularly animalistic—women of color and/or prostitutes, poor women—and others as "pure"—upper class white woman who are installed as the closely guarded symbol of "white purity, white culture, of whiteness itself" (Doane, 1991, p. 41). This ideology is enacted in two disparate magazine ads from 1994. One, appearing in *Cosmopolitan*, is for Neutragena soap and pictures a standing women. She is young, blonde, smiling, and wearing faded blue jeans and a white blouse against a white background. The boldfaced word—*PURE*—comprises the principal text and obviously is meant to refer equally to the woman and the soap. Whereas the young, blonde white woman, as racist symbolization insists, is the emblem of purity—racial, moral, spiritual—conversely the dark-skinned woman is not only deemed a member of an inferior animalistic race, but also to be contamination personified, to be *shit*.

This message is proclaimed in a 1994 ad for Diesel jeans appearing in *Details*. An unsmiling brown-skinned woman lies on a bed covered

with zebra-striped sheets. She wears a black bra, unbuttoned jeans, and a crucifix (symbolizing colonization as well as religious systems based in theological notions of female sexual filth/evil). Obviously, this woman is available for invasion and conquest. The headline reads: "HOW TO CONTROL WILD ANIMALS." In smaller print, this advice is given:

> We all want a safer world. So, come on, let's build more zoos. 1000s of them! Right now, there are far too many dangerous animals running around, wasting space, wasting time, using the planet as a toilet! Take our advice. Don't be fooled by "natural" beauty, stick em in practical, easy-to-clean metal cages.

Here the imperialist culture, which, as Morrison scathingly points out, is characteristically wasteful and waste-obsessed (1981, pp. 184-175), absolves itself and targets the colonized woman of color as animal, as lethal danger, and as infinite waste/corruption/evil. Just as pornography is necessarily rooted in sexist notions of hierarchical gender, sexual objectification, and sexual "dirtiness," so, too, is it dependent on racist notions of hierarchy and objectification, purity and filth.

(SWEET) THING

Sexuality is socially organized to require sex inequality for excitement and satisfaction. The least extreme expression of gender inequality, and the prerequisite for all of it, is dehumanization and objectification. The most extreme is violence. Because sexual objectification and sexual violence are almost uniquely done to women, they have been systematically treated as the sex difference, when they represent the socially situated subjection of women to men. (MacKinnon, 1989, p. 243)

When feminists began to decry the projection of women as sex objects, the pop culture pimps objected: Objectification, they declared, is a necessary component of female sexual agency. The cover photo of the December 19, 1979 issue of *Esquire* displayed a young, blonde model in lingerie. The headline read: "The Year of the Lusty Woman: It's All Right to Be a Sex Object Again." According to this logic, it is feminism that is out to destroy female sexual agency—not those who traffic women as sex objects. Sexual objectification and its logical accompaniment, ownership or enslavement, is a key component of pornography. Objectification does not simply mean that someone is the object or aim of your sexual desire. Rather, it is a systemic process whereby a sentient being is dehumanized, reduced to a thing, a being without social significance or stature, someone turned into something that can be exchanged, bartered, owned, shown off, kept, used, abused, and disposed of. Dehumanization of an enemy is an essential tactic to enslavement and to prepare forces to commit violence against an enemy.

Women learn their status as objects through not only the harassment and surveillance they encounter regularly on the streets (euphemistically called "girl watching"), but through all the mass forms and rites that confirm the status of woman as spectacle and object of possession—pornography, fashion, cheesecake, beauty contests, tourist advertising, and so on. Drawing on the history of European art, particularly "the nude" which is always female, Berger (1972) notes that in a sexist system "men act and women appear" (pp. 46–47). Moreover, the one who does the looking is in a position of power over those who are positioned as spectacle. Indeed, those who are positioned as spectacle are reduced to slave, animal, and/or commodity status.

Collins (1990) argues persuasively that African American women are not included in pornography as an afterthought, but that the history of racist enslavement and sexual exploitation of African American women forms a "key pillar on which contemporary pornography rests" (p. 168). Because of slavery, black women's bodies were continual objects of display on the auction block, reduced to commodities for purchase and used for prostitution and forced reproduction. Collins (1990) writes: "The process illustrated by the pornographic treatment of the bodies of enslaved African women . . . has developed into a full-scale industry encompassing all women objectified differently by racial/ethnic pornography" (p. 169).

Bondage, objectification, submission: the sexualized iconography of slavery pervades mainstream imagery. A 1994 ad for Jaïpur perfume is shot in black and white. A shadowy, naked, partial (torso to knee) female body is shown from the rear. Her hands are held behind her buttocks, glamorously cuffed into bondage by a jeweled bracelet. The November 1996 issue of *Vibe* contains an article deploring Muslim Arab enslavement of black African people in Sudan and Mauritania. This righteous denouncement clashes loudly with "Vibe Fashion," a layout that follows a few pages later. The fashions are for men because the men (of various races) are the only ones wearing clothes. The white woman who is tossed among them is either wholly naked or clad only in a black lacy bra. One image that especially suggests slavery has her kneeling naked at the feet of a seated man. In another image, she is pressed between the bodies of two identical twins, very dark-skinned black men. Their sweaters are raised to reveal their nipples. It appears that they, too, are on the auction block.

Contemporary slavery encompasses much of what is understood as prostitution (Barry, 1979). Due to First World military occupation, whole countries in Asia and Africa have been turned into sex tourist colonies for men from Japan, Australia, and the West. The sexual use of local women, dehumanized as *different* or *other* both racially and sexually, is a core practice of colonization. Possession of women by conquering men serves as both a symbolic equivalent to and actual facilitator of political, ideological, and military conquest (Alloula, 1986). Consistently, in popular narratives, both fiction and nonfiction, the masculine is represented as mobile boundary violator; the feminine constitutes the primitive; undeveloped (virgin) space that is to be exploited, consumed, violated, re-mapped (de Lauretis, 1987; Lotman, 1979). Hence, in sexually racist colonial fantasies, Third World women are either fetishized—as passive, accessible, welcoming or seductive "virgins," veiled mysteries to be penetrated, exotic fruit to be tasted—or phobically feared as contaminating *femmes fatales*, voracious cannibals who must be annihilated.

The pornographic/colonial fantasy that images the woman of color as consummate comestible is epitomized in a layout featuring Naomi Campbell, a dark-skinned woman of African, Chinese, and European ancestry (*Harper's Bazaar*, April 1994). The layout uses fashion images, set off by quotes from French painter Paul Gaugin ("I had been seduced . . . by this land and by its simple and primitive people"). The first image is of an offered, cut-open tropical fruit, glistening with moisture. The second is of Campbell also offered and open—naked and face down on a bed. In another, she wears a white dress and holds a fruit at womb level; she too is presented as "good enough to eat." The bodice of the dress is absurdly low and her "primitive" breasts (no doubt pushed up by a Wonderbra) spill out.

Here, the body of a woman of color is identified with that which can be consumed and possessed, in hooks' (1992, p. 23) words—"an alternative playground where members of dominant races, genders, sexual practices, affirm their power over in intimate relations with the Other" (p. 23). Because *Harper's Bazaar* is pitched primarily to white women, one must wonder how these images are read. Do white women desire Campbell as objectified Other, want to be her, hate her as a rival with whom they cannot compete, and/or rage against the sexual racism in which they are supposed to be complicit? Do women of color identify with, desire, and/or disdain Campbell, and recognize that, however exotic the setting, the scene transmits the stereotypic indignities that mar everyday existence? As hooks and others detail, women of color in utterly mundane settings are conspicuously hit with attitudes of consumption. Baines (1994) writes:

> It is not a compliment . . . .
> When each day I push through the sea of white eyes staring at
> me on the bus as if I were some strange fruit
> as if my vulva was hanging outside of my skirt whispering exotic
> welcomes. (p. 150)

What Baines experiences as pornographic abuse, *Harper's Bazaar* pretties up and proffers.

VIRTUAL NECROPHILIA

The end result of objectification is death. In the early 1980s, Helmut Newton bragged that he deliberately mixed in plastic mannequins with actual models and dared viewers to be able to detect the difference (Behr, 1978, unpaged). In the same vein, female models are frequently represented as corpses, suffocated under plastic bags, partially buried under cement, and dismembered and presented as "parts" (legs, eyes, heads); they are killed into machinery and rendered indistinguishable from projections on television screens. In all such depictions, the attack is on what we culturally understand as the soul, that which makes us significant, self-aware, unique, precious beings. Some critics might read these images as reflecting what postmodernist critics speak of as *depthlessness*, or a flattening out of affect in an age dominated by mechanical reproductions, visual simulations, and apocalyptic technologies. Although this is certainly partially true, any analysis that ignores the *misogyny* in these conventional depictions—and the connection of that misogyny to the totality of sexualized domination informing such apocalyptic and pornographic technologies as nuclear weaponry (Caputi, 1993)—would be radically incomplete.

Symbolic dismemberments have long been the norm in fashion photography (decapitated heads to sell us perfume, amputated legs to push pantyhose, even crowds of disembodied eyes to sell us eye shadow). These dismemberments usually are not recognized as such, so habituated are we to them. We might notice them if they were being done to male bodies, but they are not in any comparable way.

The lethal misogyny underlying such depictions is clear in a 1993 Kenneth Cole two-page spread that appeared in *Vanity Fair*. On one page, a handbag is featured. It hangs on the shoulder of a one-armed, headless, pale plastic torso; its legs are cut off at the knees. The next page features shoes on a pair of mannequin feet cut off just above the ankle. A quote from Mr. Cole is included: "We considered using models, but they ended up being an arm and a leg." This "joke" implies that the models were murdered and mutilated, ending up dismembered to showcase his products.

An extreme form of violent pornography is the snuff film or photograph, images of someone (usually a woman) actually being murdered: her killing is understood as the climactic part of the sex. A "virtual snuff" sensibility informs countless fashionable images that have appeared in fashion and feminine product advertising since the 1970s. Glamorous models (including Linda Evangelista and Madonna) are showcased in positions that suggest they are dead: suffocated under plastic bags, laid out in gift-box coffins, sprawled brokenly on stairs and boutique floors.

After the flesh-and-blood women have been thus cut down to size, misogynists can bring in the artificial substitutes. A full-bodied, if wholly uncanny, sex object is used in a 1985 promo from the Canned Food Information Council. To illustrate their message that "In the year 3000, food will come in . . . cans," the Council depicts a reclining, leg-spread pornographic *fembot*, a simulated or artificial woman (Daly with Caputi, 1987), in this case replete with stiletto heels and sculpted, uplifted breasts. If the woman here is the can that can be opened, in another pictorial she is a motorcycle to be ridden, a cyber-woman made for rape.[2] A 1985 ad for Carrera motorcycle equipment depicts a woman's body fused to a motorcycle; her skin appears to be polished black metal, her arms become handlebars, her rump the seat.

Marshall McLuhan (1951) pointed to what he found to be "one of the most peculiar features of our world—the interfusion of sex and technology . . . a widely occurring cluster image of sex, technology, and death" (p. 101). This cluster coheres in widespread representations of the eroticized (and dehumanized) mechanical simulated woman and a counterpart—the sexualized, humanized, and ensoulled machine. McLuhan (1951) saw the ubiquity of this image as bespeaking an underlying cultural necrophilia, a jaded and numbed sensibility that could only experience sensation through sadism, "plucking] the heart out of the mystery" (p. 101). Such imagery, then, not only bespeaks the soullessness of the consumer/technological culture, but also points to the core connection between that culture and a pornographic animosity to both female flesh and what that flesh historically has represented— nature, matter. That pornographic animosity against nature, as documented by Merchant (1980), Keller (1985), and others, is riddled with scientific language and metaphor that regularly refers to "mastery" over nature, "penetrating" the mysteries of the universe, and so on.

An extraordinary representation of this normative sadism linked not only to sexual violence (represented by these fragmented and dehumanized women) but to a porno-technological power over nature can be found in a 1993 ad for Eclipse Fax machines. The headline reads: "Eclipse FAX: If It Were Any Faster, You'd Have To Send and Receive Your Faxes Internally." The image is the severed head of a white woman, whose hair fans out around her head. Two electrodes are attached to her forehead. Jammed into her eyes, ears, and mouth are cruel-looking metal pipes with wires going in multiple directions. Every visible opening is penetrated. The last line of the ad informs us that "to fax any faster, you'd have to break a few laws. Of physics." The reference to law-breaking alludes not only to the crime of rape, but to an overall eroticization of taboo violation. This sexualization of law-breaking is one of the structuring principles of both overt pornography as well as the pornography of everyday life.

BREAKING THE LAWS OF NATURE

[Our] mission: To boldly go where no man has gone before. (From the introduction to Star Trek)

Stick it where the hell you like. (Line from an ad for the Nissan Patrol GR, Esquire (British), June 1995)

A 1989 ad for Forbidden perfume foregrounds a woman in a red dress hiked up to her buttocks. She is seated with one knee bent. A man passionately kisses her knee; she seems to be in ecstasy. Why, we might wonder, is this clearly consensual and enjoyable passion "forbidden." The ad reminds us: "CAUTION: You could be banished from Paradise for using it."

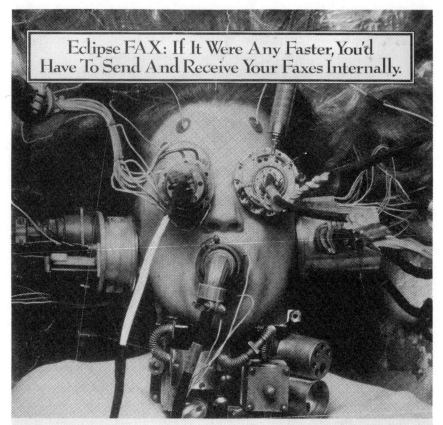

Eclipse FAX: If It Were Any Faster, You'd Have To Send And Receive Your Faxes Internally.

Here's the inside story on Eclipse FAX - the fastest, easiest Windows fax software available today. With Eclipse FAX, you save time since all your faxing is done from your own personal computer. You can fax to or receive from any fax machine and easily track, file, mark-up and store your faxes.

With a click, you can send or receive a fax - even if you're in a word processor or other Windows application - without being interrupted. And Eclipse FAX also includes OCR, which converts your faxes into editable text.

Of course, the nature of fax software has other unbeatable benefits. Like the ability to annotate and type comments on faxes with your PC; the ability to print out plain paper faxes from your PC; and the privacy and convenience of faxing from your own personal computer.

If you already own a fax software program, we'll let you trade up to Eclipse FAX for just $59*. So pick up Eclipse FAX, because to fax any faster, you'd have to break a few laws. Of physics.

Phoenix

1-800-452-0120

Phoenix Technologies Ltd. 846 University Avenue, Norwood, MA 02062

©1993 Phoenix Technologies Ltd. Available now at Egghead, Comp USA, Computer City and other dealers.   *Competitive upgrade offer.

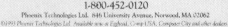

Most everyone learns the story of Adam and Eve at a very early age and usually in a didactic context. Continual references to the story pervade popular imagery, ensuring that we never forget that elementary lesson. One of these lessons is that women were created by an all-male God—a reversal of the reality whereby women birth men into being (Daly with Caputi, 1987). Such a sacred narrative endorses the view that women are afterthoughts to creation, made for men.

On November 19, 1994, unknown vandals defaced and hid over 100 bound volumes of women, gay, and gender studies journals at the library of the University of New Mexico. Some journals had "bitch propaganda" scrawled on them. Others, such as one issue of *Lesbian Ethics*, had more extensive markings. The cover had a large swastika drawn across its surface. The title was crossed out and replaced with "God's Ethics"; underneath that, the listing of contents was effaced by the pronouncement: "God made women for men." Ironically, this scrawl reveals the profound connection between male supremacist religion and male supremacist pornography. In both systems, women are made for men. In both overt pornography and the pornography of everyday life, women are projections of male fantasy, whether as fetish dominatrix or fetish submissive, all-forgiving mother or seductive daughter, naked girl next door or scapegoated "whore." Whatever role she occupies, she is accessible, open, her secrets revealed, the heart of her mystery plucked.[3]

Another all-important lesson that we learn from the story of Adam and Eve is that sex is sinful, with special venom reserved for assertive female sexuality (Daly, 1973). It is in this morality that locates sex as the basis for original sin that pornography is ineluctably rooted. As Sjöö and Mor (1987) write, "wherever you find a puritanical God, you also find a pornographic God" (p. 234). However opposite these belief systems seem, they are profoundly linked. Pornography owes its existence to and utterly depends on its alleged opposite—a misogynist and antisexual morality. That is, it depends on religiously legitimated disgust and hatred for the body and sexuality, particularly female sexuality, which is identified with dirt, filth, "whoredom," and evil. Under this system, sex and sexual depiction become taboo and, concomitantly, sexuality becomes infused with the aura of the forbidden. Taboo-breaking inevitably becomes sexualized—transgression is bold and erotic, and the forbidden is increasingly seductive.

As MacKinnon (1989) has noted, the "frontier of the taboo keeps vanishing as one crosses it" (p. 200). Hence, ever greater violations are required in order to generate the same charge of eroticism. A billboard displayed throughout Albuquerque in 1995 was dominated by an image of a baby's buttocks. "The only thing softer than our water," averred the advertiser. When I object to this image, the standard response is that babies are innocent, so there is nothing dangerous in this. Because of this rhetoric of "innocence," the nudity of children (especially from the rear) in mass imagery is not considered pornographic or even sexually explicit. Yet, expediently constructed childhood "innocence" is actually far sexier than we might like to think.

A 1975 ad for Love's Baby Soft Fragrance works very hard to sexualize girlish "innocence." The image is of a white child, about five or six years old. Her hair (or a wig) is arranged in an adult style. She is obviously made up and wears some sort of ruffled white top. A hand which is far too large to be hers—perhaps representing the molester who is the inevitable presence in this tableaux—holds a white Teddy Bear in front of her. The headline reads: "Love's Baby Soft. Because innocence is sexier then you think."

In the pornographic paradigm, the bottom line is that domination and violation are sexual. Thus, for some, sex becomes most exciting when the scenario allows the dominator to rule most completely and to despoil the most pure, to violate the most sacred taboo. The construction of childhood "innocence" serves by no means to protect children. Rather, it sets them up as the most delicious targets in the culture where breaking the rules and indulging in the forbidden are fundamentally sexualized. Kaplan (1991) argues that when women demand and express intellectual, sexual, and emotional freedom, patriarchy responds with both overtly woman-hating pornography and the increased sexualization of children. In regular as well as everyday pornography, children can be used as a repository of the idealized feminine: helpless, weak, passive, pliable, and "innocent"—pure and asexual until awakened, sometimes forcibly, into the "forbidden" by the superior and experienced man. Child pornography, a "cottage industry, pretty much run by child molesters" (Kaplan, 1991, p. 348) who take photographs of children either posing naked or engaging in sexual activities with adults and/or other children, is mirrored in the widespread sexual objectification of children (primarily girls but also boys) as well as the normative use of childhood nakedness in all sorts of advertising imagery. In a 1996 pitch for funds for The Breast Cancer Research Foundation, a little, white moppet with fly-away tousled curls is pictured naked from the waist up. She is standing with her hands folded beneath her exposed nipples. In pornography as well popular culture, a woman's open mouth signifies her accessibility, her openness to penetration. This little girl's full-lipped (and probably lipsticked) mouth is open, much in the manner of the rubber mouth of a sex doll. The copy, written across her undeveloped breasts, reads: "Mommy, when I grow up will I get breast cancer?" This overt message could have been as effectively conveyed by a fully dressed little girl shown conversing with her mother. This image is pitched to the pedophilic gaze by setting up the child as a fully available and vulnerable sex object.

Another common motif is the conflation of little girls with adult sex objects. A 1987 ad for Bonnie Doon hosiery features a blonde girl about five years of age. She wears a white frilly dress and white, adult-sized, high-heeled shoes. Her dress blows up around her, revealing her underwear. Such a ploy deliberately recalls Marilyn Monroe's star turn in *The Seven Year Itch*, deftly paralleling the child with the consummate white American sex goddess.

Calvin Klein demands our attention again with a 1994 image from his Obsession line. In the four-page spread, the pictures of the perfume bottle are in color; the sexual image is in black and white. It depicts a naked, and apparently short-haired, Kate Moss spread out face down and with legs opened on a couch in some decaying edifice. The floor is obviously cracked and crumbling. Here Moss's "waif" characteristics—those that make her resemble an adolescent boy—are exploited to evoke titillatingly decadent adult "obsessions" for young boys.

Sometimes the images promote not only pedophilia but incest. In 1979, *Playboy* featured a nude layout of a 21-year-old woman photographed by her father. It was coyly entitled "Father Knows Best." Underneath that headline is a full nude portrait of the daughter when she was three. Her backside is in view as she turns to look at her father. The accompanying copy reveals that the father would shoot nude models at home and that the little girl would take her clothes off, mimic the model's poses, and beg her daddy to photograph her too. He just had to comply for, "She had the cutest little tush." He continued to photograph her nude throughout her childhood. This arguably incestuous abuse, as well as the production of child pornography, is applauded by *Playboy*.

The always tenuous borders between actual pornography and the pornography of everyday life threaten to collapse when we juxtapose the *Playboy* image with a nearly identical picture of a naked child that appears in a 1995 issue of *Newsweek*. The photo is in black and white. A small naked girl looks back over her shoulder as she hurries away from the spectator. The room is utterly empty. The headline reads: "Make Your Father's Day." Then in smaller print are these words: "Show him you love him. Father's Day." This bizarre image was sponsored by an advertising agency to plug itself as an effective mass communicator. Perhaps some readers see an image that reminds them of a time in their life when they were utterly dependent on their father and that causes an upswelling of love. Others, including but not limited to the many who have been the victims or perpetrators of incest, might view this in a different way. There is no color or warmth but, rather, coldness, isolation, and intimidation. "Make your father's day" is a phrase with both sexual and threatening undertones.

Radical theorists frequently speak of the value of transgression. Certainly, the deliberate flouting of sexist rules is a key strategy of feminism. Yet we must refrain from overgeneralizing the value of transgression, for certain acts of transgression are structured into the patriarchal system and serve to support it. Select rules literally are made to be broken—rules against rape, lynching, incest, battery, and *gynocide* (Daly with Caputi, 1987) to name a few. However nominally forbidden, these acts of terrorism are tacitly encouraged because they serve to produce and maintain the power structure.

IMAGE BATTERY

In her rich and complex reading of Julie Dash's 1991 film, *Daughters of the Dust*, Bambara (1993) describes hegemonic popular culture as one that "masks history and addicts us to voyeurism, fetishism, mystified notions of social relations, and freakish notions of intimate relations" (pp. 132-133). The experience of viewing such fare, for African American women, she avows, is a "mugging." bell hooks (1992) also understands such representation as a form of violence: "Our present entertainment is the spectacle of contemporary colonization, dehumanization, and disempowerment where the image serves as a murder weapon" (p. 7). Similarly, in his study of postcards of Algerian women manufactured by French colonizers, Alloula (1986) locates the "practice of a right of (oversight) that the colonizer arrogates to himself and that is the bearer of multiform violence. The postcard fully participates in such violence; it extends its effects; it is its accomplished expression, no less efficient for being symbolic" (p. 5).

Mugging, murder, violence "no less efficient for being symbolic." Pornography's defenders frequently admonish its critics by averring that pornography is simply a form of fantasy, with endless negotiable meanings, no fixed reading, and great subversive power (Kipnis, 1996). Yet, Cade, hooks, Alloula, and others take a very different view, declaring that the misogynist, objectifying, and racist imagery of everyday life not only endorses and normalizes violence but is itself a form of violence. We know that in intimate violence such as wife abuse the battery need not take the form of physical blows. Abuse takes an emotional and psychological form as well, one which some researchers conclude may well be the "most hidden, most insidious, least researched, and perhaps in the long run most damaging form of intimate victimization" (Gelles & Straus, 1988, p. 67). Emotional/psychological abuse encompasses verbal assaults, belittlement, cultivation of anxiety and despair, mockery, blaming, accusation, humiliation, degradation, disrespect, and reality control—a control that includes denying the harm of the abuse, creating an atmosphere of threat, and blocking awareness of alternative ways of living and being. Moreover, just as such abuse is meant to destroy the self-esteem of the victim, it is meant to enhance that of the abuser.

The formulaic, ritually repeated, and negatively stereotyped symbolic representation of a subjected group is a public, mass-mediated analog of intimate psychological/emotional violence. It, too, serves as a form of reality construction and control. It, too, serves as a form of torture and psychological destruction meant to squelch resistance and destroy self-esteem. It, too, feeds the sense of omnipotence of the dominators.

Pornography, overt and everyday, is crucial to the maintenance of women's oppression—cutting across lines of race, class, sexual orientation, and age. It promotes disabling images of gender and relations between women. It batters female psyches, calling us names that are meant to injure and disable us. And it pushes the master-slave perception that sentient beings can be possessed as objects. Feminist philosopher Mary Daly (1984) contends that "total arrogance in the promulgation of deception" (p. 55) characterizes pornographic degradations of women throughout all spheres. Contra *Esquire*'s self-serving lie, it is never "All Right To Be A Sex Object."

ENDNOTES

1. In contemporary feminist theory, the sexually political implications of pornography are hotly debated and usually dichotomized. Some, calling themselves "pro-sex," point to the danger of feminists being associated with right-wing, repressive, puritanical, antipornography agendas, and stress the importance of women claiming desire and sexual identities resistant to patriarchal notions of normalcy (i.e., heterosexual, passive, romantic, monogamous, and so on). They tend to locate pornography in an historical tradition of opposition to the status quo, protection of free speech rights, and the resistant culture of sexual minorities (Califia, 1994; Gibson, 1993; Kipnis, 1996). Certainly, the cultural denial of women's sexual agency, the repression of lesbianism, and the inculcation of feminine bodily shame has been core to women's oppression. The countering and rejections of patriarchal sexualities, including the creation of nonsexist erotica, are key modes of feminist resistance. Yet this by no means implies that women's claim to sexual agency is synonymous with responding to the hateful names which which pornography hails them—quite the opposite.
2. The rape script written into this pictorial was played out literally in July 1997 in Firozpur Namak, India. A 15-year-old girl, Baskar, was married that month to a stranger selected for her by her Muslim family. In accordance with tradition, her family sent a dowry to the

bridegroom. It consisted of household goods but lacked one item he had requested—a motorcycle. On her wedding night, Baskar reported, her inebriated husband and three of his friends beat her and took turns raping her, taunting her that they had made her into a motorcycle. Although her family reported the rape, the traditional all-male council declined to reach a verdict in the case (*San Francisco Chronicle*, July 21, 1997).

3. I thank Cara MariAnna for her tremendous insights into the ways that the pornographic paradigm demands that women be constantly open and how, mythically, this corresponds to the destruction of sacred female mysteries.

REFERENCES

Alloula, M. (1986). *The colonial harem* (M. Godzich & W. Godzich, trans.). Minneapolis: University of Minnesota Press.

Baines, M. (1994). Bus fucking. In C. Camper (Ed.), *Miscegenation blues: Voices of mixed race women* (p. 150). Toronto: Sister Vision, Black Women and Women of Color Press.

Bambara, T. C. (1993). Reading the signs, empowering the eye: Daughters of the dust and the black independent cinema movement. In M. Diawara (Ed.), *Black American cinema* (pp. 118-144). New York: Routledge.

Barry, K. (1979). *Female sexual slavery*. Englewood Cliffs, NJ: Prentice-Hall.

Behr, E. (1978). *Introduction to sleepless nights*. New York: Congreve.

Berger, J. (1972). *Ways of seeing*. London: The BBC and Penguin Books.

Califia, P. (1994). *Public sex: The culture of radical sex*. Pittsburgh: Cleis Press.

Caputi, J. (1993). *Gossips, gorgons, and crones: The fates of the earth*. Santa Fe: Bear and Company.

Collins, P. (1990). *Black feminist thought: Knowledge, consciousness, and the politics of empowerment*. New York: Routledge.

Daly, M. (1973). *Beyond god the father: Toward a philosophy of women's liberation*. Boston: Beacon Press

Daly, M. (1984). *Pure lust: Elemental feminist philosophy*. Boston. Beacon Press.

Daly, M., with Caputi, J. (1987). *Websters' first new intergalactic wickedary of the English language*. Boston: Beacon Press.

de Lauretis, T. (1987). *Technologies of gender: Essays on theory, film, and fiction*. Bloomington: University of Indiana Press.

Doane, M. (1991). *Femmes fatales: Feminism, film theory, psychoanalysis*. New York: Routledge.

Dworkin, A. (1989). *Letters from a war zone*. New York: E. P. Dutton.

Fiske, J. (1992). British cultural studies and television. In R. C. Allen (Ed.), *Channels of discourse, reassembled: Television and contemporary criticism* (2nd ed., pp. 284-326). Chapel Hill: University of North Carolina Press.

Gelles, R. J., & Straus, M. A. (1988). *Intimate violence*. New York: Simon and Schuster.

Gibson, P. C. (Ed.). (1993). Dirty looks: Women, pornography, power. London: British Film Institute.

hooks, b. (1992). *Black looks: Race and representation*. Boston: South End Press.

Johnston, D. (1992, April 24). Survey shows number of rapes far higher than official figures. *New York Times* (national edition), p. A9.

Jones, A. (1994). *Next time, she'll be dead: Battering and how to stop it*. Boston: Beacon Press.

Kaplan, L. J. (1991). *Female perversions: The temptations of Emma Bovary*. New York: Doubleday.

Keller, E. F. (1985). *Reflections on gender and science*. New Haven: Yale University Press.

Kipnis, L. (1996). *Bound and gagged: Pornography and the politics of fantasy in America*. New York: Grove Press.

Lotman, J. (1979). The origin of plot in the light of typology (J. Graffy, trans.). *Poetics Today*, 1(1-2), 161-184.

MacKinnon, C. (1989). *Toward a feminist theory of the state*. Cambridge: Harvard University Press.

McLuhan, M. (1951). *The mechanical bride: Folklore of industrial man*. Boston: Beacon Press.

Merchant, C. (1980). *The death of nature: Women, ecology, and the scientific revolution*. San Francisco: Harper and Row.

Morrison, T. (1981). *Tar baby*. New York: New American Library, Signet Books.

Neumann, E. (1963). *The great mother: An analysis of the archetype*. Princeton: Princeton University Press.

Réage, P. (1954, 1965). *The Story of O* (S. d'Esträe, trans). New York: Grove Press.

Sanday, P. R. (1990). *Fraternity gang rape: Sex, brotherhood, and privilege on campus*. New York: New York University Press.

Sjöö, M., & Mor, B. (1987). *The great cosmic mother: Rediscovering the religion of the earth*. San Francisco: HarperSanFrancisco.

Swentzell, R. (1993). Commentaries on *When Jesus came the Corn Mothers went away: Marriage, sex, and power in New Mexico, 1500-1846*, by Ramùn GutiÄrrez (compiled by Native American Studies Center, University of New Mexico). *American Indian Culture and Research Journal*, 17(3), 141-177.

Tuchman, G., Daniels, A., & Benet, J. (Eds.). (1978). *Hearth and home: Images of women in the mass media*. New York: Oxford.

Walker, A. (1980). Coming apart. In L. Lederer (Ed.), *Take back the night: Women on pornography* (pp. 95-104). New York: Bantam Books.

Walker, B. (1983). *The woman's encyclopedia of myths and secrets*. San Francisco: HarperSanFrancisco.

5

Mammy Goes to Las Vegas: *Showgirls* and the Constancy of African-American Female Stereotypes

Carmen R. Gillespie

Perhaps one of the most famous lines from the film *Gone With the Wind* (1939) is Mammy's reprimand of Scarlett O'Hara when Scarlett insists that she will go to Atlanta to meet Ashley as he visits his wife Melanie on furlough from *the* War. Mammy, played by Hattie McDaniel, angrily tells Scarlett that she will "be sitting there jes lak a *spider*." Despite Mammy's advice and to the horror of Atlanta confederate society, Scarlett journeys to Atlanta to be by Ashley's side. What this icono-graphic moment in film history reveals are the classic representations of the mammy stereotype. According to Christian (1980), the traditional mammy:

> is strong, for she certainly has enough girth, but this strength is used in the service of her white master and as a way of keeping her male

counterparts in check; she is kind and loyal, for she is a mother, she
is sexless, for she is ugly; and she is *religious and superstitious, because
she is black.* (p. 12; emphasis added)

As the aforementioned scene from *Gone With the Wind* illustrates, the
stereotypical religiosity and/or morality of traditional mammies corresponds with the role cinematic mammies often play as the moral
guardians of their white female charges.

THE CINEMATIC MAMMY TRADITION

In many Hollywood films, the mammy character frequently functions as
a moral arbiter and barometer for the white woman protagonist. For
example, one of Mammy's most frequently repeated reprimands of
Scarlett in *Gone With the Wind* is "'taint fittin'. It just ain't fittin.'"
Throughout the film, Mammy chastises Scarlett with this refrain when
Scarlett's behavior transgresses the boundaries of Mammy's superior
moral code.

> Like earlier film slaves, Hattie McDaniel's character is motivated
> almost solely out of concern for the master family, but her Mammy
> also feels confident to express anger toward her masters. She berates
> and hounds anyone who goes against *her* conception of right and
> wrong. . . . Not once does she bite her tongue. (Bogle, 1994, p. 88)

McDaniel's powerful performance in *Gone With the Wind* affixed moral
caretaking as one of Mammy's primary characteristics.
      Like the several cosmetic changes Proctor and Gamble has made
in the appearance of its trademark pancake symbol, Aunt Jemima, the
mammy stereotype has undergone a similar and equally superficial evolution. These surface alterations to the mammy type are present in the
1959 version of the film *Imitation of Life*. Reprising and revamping Hattie
McDaniel's Mammy, Juanita Moore's Annie is physically smaller than
the traditional Mammy and lacks her antagonistic spirit. Yet the essential qualities of Mammy remain intact as Annie insists that she enjoys
her servile position because she "likes taking care of pretty things," in
this case, her mistress, Miss Laura. Annie's self-effacement and extreme
humility act as a foil for Miss Laura's worldliness and self-absorption.
Annie functions as Miss Laura's conscience, and it is only with Annie's
dramatic death and martyrdom that Miss Laura is able to fulfill her own
obligations as mother and wife.

SHOWGIRL'S MOLLY ABRAMS AS MAMMY-FIGURE

By excavating the roots of the mammy stereotype, the source and the dimension of many contemporary depictions of African American women become evident. One such descendent of both Mammy and Annie is Molly Abrams of the 1995 film *Showgirls*. The controversial film *Showgirls* is a soft porn quest narrative notable for its bad acting and gratuitous exploitation of female sexuality. However, examination of this film is informative inasmuch as it reiterates the consistent patterns in the relationships between white female characters and their cinematic mammy-figures.

The film's protagonist is Nomi Malone, a young woman in search of success and self-esteem. Borrowing an old Hollywood formula, the film begins as Nomi, portrayed by Elizabeth Berkeley, travels to Las Vegas from Los Angeles with aspirations of becoming a dancer. Nomi hitchhikes and accepts a ride from an Elvis look-alike who offers her a job in a casino. The Elvis imitator is a scam artist who steals Nomi's suitcase and abandons her, leaving Nomi alone in her new city with no belongings and no money. This early moment in the film illuminates the multifaceted significances of the name Nomi Malone. Nomi Malone is easily translated into "No me. I'm alone," and thus outlines the twin conundrums of the protagonist: her lack of a solid and stable identity and her emotional isolation. Molly as mammy-figure is central to Nomi's resolution of both of these problems.

Later in the film, the audience learns that the protagonist created the name Nomi Malone and that her actual name is Polly Anne Cassell. Through personal sacrifice for and service to Nomi, Molly, played by Gina Ravera, aids Nomi's quest to reclaim her rightful identity as Polly Anne, along with all the correspondent connotations of innocence and purity inherent in the name Pollyanna.

The relationship between Molly and Nomi begins with Nomi's precarious arrival in Las Vegas. In her fury at the loss of her belongings, Nomi begins kicking and pounding on Molly's parked car. Molly appears and yells at her to stop, and Nomi inexplicably vomits and then runs out into the street into the path of an oncoming vehicle. Nomi's vomiting implies her lack of physical and moral health. Apparently moved by Nomi's illness and predicament, Molly, without hesitating or considering her own well-being, runs into the street to pull Nomi back to safety. This act is foundational to the entirety of Molly and Nomi's relationship. In the short-term, Molly saves Nomi from certain vehicular slaughter and in the long run from the moral onslaught of the Las Vegas world of professional sexploitation.

MOLLY AS SAVIOR

Molly's role reinscribes the traditional and historical juxtaposition between mammy and her white counterpart. At the center of this opposition is the hegemonic cultural tension generated by the fear of interracial rape.

> Since the planters accepted miscegenation between white men and black women as inevitable, they charged the white woman with the responsibility of being "the repository of white civilization." By giving birth to the white man's legitimate heirs, she became actually and symbolically his greatest treasure. Thus the fear of rape of the white woman by the black man reached mammoth proportions. . . . For any sexual activity between these two actors would constitute, from the white man's perspective, the rape of his birthright and legacy. (Christian, 1980, p. 7)

Throughout *Showgirls*, Nomi's true Pollyannic character is in danger of being debased, figuratively and literally raped by a variety of unsavory characters, including a black male. Molly's role is to deliver Nomi from the threat of sexual violation and objectification and restore her "rightful" iconographic place in the American hierarchy.

Following Molly's rescue of Nomi, Molly and Nomi stand in the parking lot and embrace in a maternal and familial gesture.[1] From that moment, Molly, despite her physical attractiveness, inculcates herself in the formulaic legacy of her mammy predecessors.

Central to the exchanges between Molly and Nomi is Molly's expression of overwhelming concern about Nomi's eating behavior. Characteristically, mammies exhibit their nurturing behavior in the guise of concern over the gastronomy of their charges. Like the memorable opening sequence in *Gone With the Wind*, when Mammy dupes Scarlett into eating, Molly is similarly concerned with feeding Nomi. Following the scene in the parking lot, Molly purchases dinner for Nomi. After asking Nomi about possible family and friends, Molly tells Nomi that she can share her trailer. There are three additional moments in the film when Molly feeds Nomi. Typical of these instances is an occasion when the two are shopping. After Nomi purchases her first designer dress, Molly offers to buy her "a burrito. I'll even buy you a fajita to celebrate." The caretaking impulse is consistently directed from Molly to Nomi.

Molly not only tries to persuade Nomi to eat well, she also provides the conduit for Nomi to access the dance world to which she aspires. Molly is employed as a seamstress at the dance show entitled, significantly, *Goddess*. Largely as a result of Molly's persuasive influence,

Nomi auditions and becomes a member of the *Goddess* pantheon. This new position enables Nomi to leave her job as a stripper in a club called the *Cheetah*.

After Nomi leaves the *Cheetah*, Molly is more effectively able to protect her from the dangers of Las Vegas. While Nomi advances her status, Molly remains *Goddess*'s seamstress, and functions as servant to the women who perform in the show. In every backstage scene, Molly clearly is at the base of the hierarchy. Molly's positionality is visually represented as she stands at the bottom of the stairs leading to the stage each night as Nomi and the others ascend to the glamorous artificial world of *Goddess*.

MOLLY'S SUBSERVIENCE AND HER SECRET DESIRES

Molly's subservience pervades her demeanor. When she first introduces Nomi to Crystal Connors, the lead dancer in *Goddess*, she cannot stop referring to her as Miss Crystal.

> "Molly, Crystal needs you." [Stagehand]
> "Yes, Miss Connors." [Molly]
> "Call me Crystal. What's your name?" [Crystal]
> "Molly Abrams. You were really great tonight Miss. . ." [Molly]
> "Crystal" [Crystal]

Obviously Molly does not feel equal to the star of *Goddess*. Indeed, she seems to delight in altering and repairing Crystal's appearance. Molly's employment as the show's seamstress enables her to fulfill the same role as that of traditional maids without actually being labeled as a servant. During this scene, Molly, dressed in nondescript overalls, introduces Nomi to Crystal. Nomi wears a short red dress that Molly has made and encouraged her to wear. The contrast is characteristic of Molly's habitual self-effacement.

Like Molly's mammy predecessors, the audience learns little of her personal life. Other than her interactions and obsessive involvement with Nomi, the only information provided about Molly Abrams as autonomous individual is her employment as a seamstress and cursory references to her pursuit of a college degree. When Molly tells Nomi "only four more courses and they'll have to give me that degree," she locates the impetus for her education externally and characterizes the impending degree as a gift rather than the earned result of hard work. The virtual silence about Molly's personal life further connects her to the mammy stereotype because traditional film mammies generally are without context. When mammies are portrayed with their families, their preference for their white charges is blatantly obvious. Nothing else about Molly's background or current situation, save her insatiable desire for the singer Andrew Carver, is ever revealed.

An explanation for Molly's singular attraction to Carver is located in the historical mythologies about the sexual interests of African American women. William Wells Brown's text *Clotel* (1861) evidences this mythology as the narrator maintains:

> Many a planter's wife has dragged out a miserable existence, with an aching heart, at seeing her place in the husband's affections usurped by the unadorned beauty and the captivating smiles of her waiting maid. Indeed, the greater portion of the colored women, in the days of slavery, had no greater aspiration than that of becoming the finely-dressed mistress of some white man. (Brown in Christian, 1980, p. 14)

This historically inaccurate mythology is at the heart of Molly's desire for Carver. As mammy, she is totally asexual, consistently dressed in baggy overalls and oversized jeans; however, with regard to Carver, the movie's white male icon, Molly embodies the myth of African American women's secret desire.

In a film that is heavily laden with images of nude and semi-nude women, objectification of the female form becomes normative; however, the objectification of the Molly character is particularized and unique. The venues in *Showgirls* in which nudity is pervasive are all public spaces. The film is rife with scenes of women and men dancing and striping in various clubs, in dressing rooms, and in rehearsals, but Molly is the only character, quite curiously including Nomi herself, who is ever seen nude or semi-nude in her own personal space. When Molly is initially seen in her domicile, she stands clad only in a black bra and underwear while she dresses for work in front of Nomi. Her room is filled with images of Andrew Carver, including a picture and a poster. Along with these visual images is a background voice-over from the radio announcing that the song playing is the latest hit by Carver. Later in the film, after Nomi gets an audition for *Goddess*, she runs into the trailer to tell Molly, who apparently is just coming out of the shower dressed in nothing but a towel. The reference to Molly as a sexual object in the domestic sphere reinforces the notion of the nurturing black woman as covertly sexual but incapable of attaining the dubious status associated with public objectification which the film's genre promotes as the ultimate female goal.

Although portrayed by a physically attractive actress, Gina Ravera, the character Molly Abrams does not attract any physical attention until the end of the film, when she is brutally assaulted. She tells

Nomi that she "hasn't been laid in six months" and confesses to auto-erotic behavior. Molly's lack of consensual adult sexuality aligns her with the Mammy stereotype and reinforces historical mythologies about the secret desires of African American women for white men.

ANNIE AS LOOSE WOMAN AND FOIL FOR MOLLY

On the other end of the spectrum of misconceptions about black women is the stereotype of the loose black woman.[2] The only African American dancer in *Goddess* fulfills this stereotype and serves as a foil to Molly's humility and nurturance. This dancer, known only to the audience as Annie, is crude and cruel. Her significance in the film is as exemplar of popular constructions of African American female sexuality as animalistic and exhibitionistic. Annie embodies the stereotype of the loose black woman as this type is "known to have an 'evil' disposition, a characteristic that constitutes rather than distracts from her sexiness . . . her animal nature rather than her human qualities are foremost in makeup" (Christian, 1980, p. 15). In her every appearance in the film, Annie displays the classic representations of this type. For example, as the dancers prepare for a show, Annie screams abuses at everyone in sight, particularly Molly.

> "Annie!" [Stagehand]
> "What?" [Annie]
> "You're naked." [Stagehand]
> "Fuck you! Molly, they're gonna see a smiling snatch if you don't fix this." [Annie]

Inappropriately angry, Annie screams expletives at everyone in sight and demeans Molly by treating her like a servant. Immediately following this exchange, one of the dancers inquires of another, "What is that smell?", and the dancer replies, "The goddamned monkey act." Although the reference is to an actual monkey act, the juxtaposition implies a connection between Annie's nakedness and sexuality and the animals. In Annie's other appearance in *Showgirls*, she is equally offensive and, not surprisingly, the monkeys are also present. Annie's presence in *Showgirls* and its contrast with the characterization of Molly reveals the common cinematic polarity of portrayals of black women.

Annie's demeanor contrasts sharply with Molly's and affirms Molly's self-sacrificing role as surrogate mother to Nomi. Despite Molly's attempts to guide Nomi's behavior through warnings and admonitions about the volatile dance world, Nomi is overcome by her ambition to become a star. As previously established, one of Molly's primary roles is as protector of Nomi's moral and physical health. Nomi's adventures in Las Vegas, including a near sexual encounter with a black man and a lesbian, and a sexual relationship with her employer, Zack, threaten her "actual" iconographic identity as Polly Anne.

MOLLY AS MARTYR

Molly consistently attempts to protect Nomi and guide her actions but falls short of these goals when Nomi pushes Crystal down the stage stairs in order to become the star of *Goddess* herself. Molly suspects her of this act and confronts Nomi on the night she replaces Crystal as the star of the show. Molly as mammy reprimands Nomi as if she were a child: "You pushed her, didn't you?" Although Nomi denies this, Molly refuses to accompany her to the opening cast party.

> "Have fun at your party." [Molly]
> "You've gotta come. Andrew's gonna be there. It ain't a party
>   without you." [Nomi]
> "Bye, Nomi." [Molly]

Although she clearly disapproves of Nomi's actions, Molly, forever loyal to her charge, compromises her values and attends Nomi's opening night party. There she encounters the man of her dreams, Andrew Carver.

This party solidifies the subtextual messages about sexuality and race that permeate *Showgirls*. When Nomi meets Andrew Carver and introduces him to Molly, he provides her with a warning about his actual character. Carver tells Nomi:

> "You were sensational tonight." [Carver]
> "I like your songs." [Nomi]
> "I like your ass." [Carver]

Despite Nomi's forewarning about Carver's character, she introduces Molly to him and to Molly's demise. While Nomi enjoys the feast and dances with Zack, who whispers in her ear, "I could fall in love with you," Molly goes upstairs with Carver. As soon as they enter the bedroom, Carver's two sidekicks enter the room and the three of them proceed to brutally gang rape Molly while exclaiming "slut pussy." Eventually, Molly tumbles down the stairs and lands partially clad sprawled in the middle of the dance floor. As a direct result of Nomi's inaction, Molly becomes a victim of Carver.

Simultaneous with Nomi's arrival at Molly's hospital bed, Zack appears bearing the results of an employment background report on Nomi. In addition to disclosing Nomi's identity as Polly Anne Cassell, the report reveals that prior to her arrival in Las Vegas, Polly, orphaned by her father's murder of her mother and his subsequent suicide, worked as a prostitute. Revelation of this fact silences Nomi and persuades her not to call the police to report Molly's rape. This silence about the cinematic rape of a black woman mirrors the silence and inaction with which reports of the rapes of actual black women are commonly received.

During his confrontation with Nomi about her past, Zack tells her that she, like Carver, is "part of the team" and that she cannot violate this bond by reporting Carver's actions to the police. Zack's allegiance to Carver is an economic one. Like Nomi, Carver is a Las Vegas commodity who belongs to the team of club owners and managers who control this underworld.

Following her discussion with Zack, Nomi makes two critical decisions. First, she attempts to avenge Molly's rape by beating up Carver herself. In the process of supposedly defending Molly, she symbolically extracts herself from the *Goddess* "team" and reasserts herself as an autonomous individual by demonstrating her ability to care for another person, Molly. Second, Nomi decides to leave Las Vegas and literally to return in the direction from which she has come, metaphorically reconnecting with her abandoned identity as Polly Anne Cassell. The consolidation between Polly Anne and Nomi represents self-affirmation. It is, however, Molly's rape and subsequently bruised and battered body that provide a bridge for Nomi to cross over into selfhood.

Molly's role as mammy is complete, and she becomes an expendable commodity when Nomi abandons her and Las Vegas. As she hitchhikes out of town, the Elvis look-alike picks her up. Her reclamation of her belongings mirrors her emergent identity. The dialogue between Nomi and the Elvis look-alike confirms Nomi's moral victory.

"Did you gamble?" [Elvis look-alike]
"Yes." [Nomi]
"Did you win?" [Elvis look-alike]
"Yes." [Nomi]
"What did you win?" [Elvis look-alike]
"Me." [Nomi]

Much like Miss Laura's conversion in *Imitation of Life* following the death of Annie, Molly's strength and nurturance is subsumed by Nomi, and this metaphorical merger explains the similarity between the names Molly and Polly. Nomi is able literally and symbolically to regain what was taken from her, her hierarchical legacy as a white woman. This reacquisition of status is confirmed by the final shot of the film as Nomi drives past a large billboard that reads "Nomi Malone is *Goddess*."

CONCLUSION

Showgirls functions as a significant encoder of racial stereotypes of black women and reinforces traditional racial and gender-based hierarchies. The film is part of a historical and contemporary pseudo-narrative that depicts black women as faithful companions to white women and, less frequently, men. Such African American female characters appear as regulars in the 1998-99 television season on the shows *Touched By an Angel* and *Early Edition*. These stereotypical black women serve only as guardians of their respective charges and, with little or no concern for themselves and their own well-being, sacrifice everything to protect and parole the moral and physical health of their surrogate children. As literary critics and historians such as Christian (1980) and Bogle (1994) have noted, these images persist and prevail because they reinforce hegemonic definitions of blackness. More insidiously, because these stereotypes establish black female subservience as desirable and normative, they validate the continued economic subjugation of real African American women who, like the fictitious Molly Abrams, are often forced to find jobs performing servile tasks.

ENDNOTES

1. Although I believe that Molly's sexual energy is exclusively aimed at the icongraphic Andrew Carver character, it is possible to view the relationship between Molly and Nomi as fraught with homoerotic tensions, particularly in light of the film's exploitation of lesbianism.
2. According to Christian (1980), the loose black woman stereotype validates the myth of the black woman as sexual animal: "Rooted in this particular image is the sense of sex as base, even violent, and an act of domination rather than sharing" (p. 29).

REFERENCES

Bogle, D. (1994). *Toms, coons, mulattos, mammies, & bucks: An interpretive history of blacks in American films*. New York: Continuum.
Christian, B. (1980). *Black women novelists: The development of a tradition, 1892-1976*. Westport, CT: Greenwood.

6

Tales of Difference: Representations of American Indian Women in Popular Film and Television

S. Elizabeth Bird

In the summer of 1995, the toy stores of the United States were flooded with dolls, books, play sets, dress-up costumes, and games, all carrying the name of Pocahontas, the Indian Princess. The Walt Disney marketing juggernaut was selling images of American Indians as never before, this time with the face and body of an Indian woman.[1]

The animated feature, *Pocahontas*, was the first mainstream movie in history to have an Indian woman as its leading character. It seems ironically appropriate that this role was a cartoon—the ultimate in unreality. For although women from other ethnic groups have had varied but definite success in transforming stereotypical media representations, American Indian women have continued to appear in a limited, narrow range of roles. Although *Pocahontas* capitalized on the boom in popular culture's Indian imagery that resulted from the unexpected success of *Dances with Wolves* in 1990, Indian women have generally not shared in any advances made.

With the rise in "Indian" movies and even a few TV shows, Indian women have been conspicuous by their absence, appearing usually in small, supporting roles, as loyal wives or pretty "maidens," whereas the plot lines belong to the men. To understand why this has happened, it is essential to understand one basic point: mass images of American Indians are created by white culture, for white culture, and the representation of Indian women carries the double burden of stereotyping by both ethnicity and gender. American Indians have only recently begun to influence the production of images of themselves, and the range of available imagery of Indians is remarkably small.

This has been demonstrated eloquently in the classic work by Berkhofer (1979), who points out that

> the essence of the White image of the Indian has been the definition of Native Americans in fact and fancy as a separate and single Other. Whether evaluated as noble or ignoble, whether seen as exotic or downgraded, the Indian as an image was always alien to the White. (p. xv)

As Berkhofer notes, interest in American Indians has ebbed and flowed over time. Depending on the era, the Indian male has usually been seen as either the "noble savage" or his alter ego, the "ignoble savage." As cultural images of whites change, so does the image of the Indian change—now becoming everything whites fear, in the person of the marauding, hellish savage, then becoming everything they envy, in the person of the peaceful, mystical, spiritual guardian of the land who is in vogue in the 1990s. However they are pictured, Indians are the quintessential Other, whose role in mass culture is to be the object of the white, colonialist gaze.

A central element in that gaze has been a construction of the Indian as locked in the past. Nineteenth century tourists paid for trips to pacified Indian country to see traditional clothing and quiet nobility; today, white audiences turn to movies, television, and romance novels for the same pleasure. These mass cultural productions are almost invariably set in the past, offering few opportunities for the portrayal of contemporary Indian life.

WOMAN AS PRINCESS OR SQUAW

Although this limited view of Indians has affected the representation of both men and women, it has curtailed the presentation of women far more. Again, to understand that, we need to go back in time to see how the current imagery developed. Just as male imagery alternates between nobility and savagery, so female Indian imagery is bifurcated. From early times, a dominant image was the Indian Princess, represented most thoroughly by Pocahontas, the 17th century sachem's daughter who, according to legend, threw herself in front of her tribe's executioners to save the life of colonist Captain John Smith. Even before this, the Indian Queen image had been used widely to represent the exoticism of America, evolving into the dusky princess who "continued to stand for the New World and for rude native nobility" (Green, 1975, p. 703).

As Tilton (1994) describes it, the Pocahontas/Princess myth became a crucial part in the creation of a national identity: "On a national level . . . it had become clear by the second decade of the nineteenth century that Pocahontas had rescued Smith, and by implication all Anglo-Americans, so that they might carry on the destined work of becoming a great nation" (p. 55). The Indian Princess became an important, nonthreatening symbol of white Americans' right to be here because she was always willing to sacrifice her happiness, cultural identity, and even her life for the good of the new nation. Endless plays, novels, and poems were written about Pocahontas, extolling her beauty and nobility, such as an 1861 poem written by John Esten Cooke, author of a famous 1885 novel, *My Lady Pokahontas*. In the middle stanzas of the poem, Cooke describes her:

> She comes!—like a fawn in the forest,
> With a bearing mild and meek,
> The blood of a line of chieftains
> Rich in her golden cheek.
>
> With the tender, fluttering bosom,
> And the rounded shoulders, bare—
> The folds of her mantle waving
> In the breath of the idle air.
>
> With a crown of nodding feathers
> Set round with glimmering pearls;
> And the light of the dreamy sunshine
> Asleep in her raven curls!
>
> Our own dear Pocahontas!
> The Virgin Queen of the West—
> With the heart of Christian hero
> In a timid maiden's breast! (quoted in Tilton, 1994, p. 167)

These verses sum up the prevailing view of the Princess—gentle, noble, nonthreateningly erotic, virtually a white Christian, and yet different because she is tied to the native soils of America. As Tilton (1994) explains, the Princess Pocahontas story enabled the white United States, but especially the South, to justify its dominance, providing a kind of origin myth that explained how and why Indians had welcomed the destiny brought to them by whites. The "Indian Princess" as a stereotype thrived in the 19th century. Francis (1992), in his study of the "Imaginary Indian" in Canadian culture, describes the late 19th century success of author and poet Pauline Johnson, the daughter of a Mohawk chief. Dressed in a "polyglot" costume of ermine tails, knives, and beads, the "Mohawk Princess" declaimed melodramatic tales of doomed love between Indian women and white men. Audiences "saw in her the personification of Pocahontas. . . . The original Miss America, Pocahontas came to represent the beautiful, exotic New World itself. Her story provided a model for the ideal merger of Native and newcomer" (pp. 120-121).

But just as popular imagery defined white women as either good or bad, virgin or whore, so it forced images of Indian women into a similar bipolar split. According to Green (1975), the Indian "princess" is defined as one who helps or saves a white man. But if she actually has a sexual relationship with a white or Indian man, she becomes a "squaw," who is lower even than a "bad" white woman. The squaw is the other side of the Indian woman—a drudge who is at the beck and call of her savage Indian husband, who produces baby after baby, and who has sex endlessly and indiscriminately with whites and Indians alike. Green documents the sad history of this image in popular songs and tales of the 19th century. The perception of Indian women as sexual conveniences is demonstrated with graphic horror in the eyewitness accounts of the 1865 Sand Creek massacre of Cheyenne, after which soldiers were seen to move the bodies of Indian women into obscene poses and to cut off their genitals for display on their saddle horns (Jones, 1994).

The inescapable fact about this dual imagery of Indian woman is that the imagery is entirely defined by whites. From early contact, white observers brought their own categories and preconceptions to indigenous American cultures, and "authoritative" sources defined the role of the Indian woman in ways that bore little relationship to reality. Thus, James Hall and Thomas McKenney (who was the chief U.S. administrator of Indian affairs from 1816-1830) wrote in 1844: "The life of the Indian woman, under the most favourable circumstances, is one of continual labour and unmitigated hardship. Trained to servitude from infancy and condemned to the performance of the most menial offices, they are the servants rather than the companions of man" (McKenney & Hall, 1844/1933, p. 199). No actual Indian culture saw women in these limited terms; in fact, the range of Indian cultures offered a variety of

roles for women, many of them holding a great deal of honor and prestige.[2] The complexity of these roles has simply been elided from both
mainstream history and popular culture because they were not compre-
hensible to white culture. Thus, as Green (1975) argues, stereotypes of
male and female American Indians "are both tied to definition by relationships with white men, but she (woman) is especially burdened by
the narrowness of that definition" (p. 713).

THE WESTERN AS DEFINING GENRE

As popular media evolved, the definitions of Indian woman remained
oppressively narrow. As I have noted, representations of Indians have
stayed locked in the past, and the popular genre that has ensured that is
the Western (Leuthold, 1995). Western film and television simply took
over where dime novels and wild west shows left off, endlessly reliving
the myth of the late 19th century frontier. The Western genre was hard
on American Indians, imprisoning them in their roles as marauding savages, and later as noble, doomed braves. Although we think of Westerns
as "cowboys and Indians," during the great era of Western film from the
1930s through the 1950s, actual Indian characters were surprisingly rare.
Rather they appear as yelling hordes, scenery, or in occasional bit parts.
And, as Tompkins (1992) points out, the Western is overwhelmingly
male, dealing with male quests and challenges. Women may be there as
an incentive or a reward, but they are not subjective participants in the
story. Indian women, above all, disappear. If they surface occasionally,
they are minor plot devices, like the character from the famous 1956
western *The Searchers*: "Her name was 'Look.' This woman is treated so
abominably by the characters—ridiculed, humiliated, and then killed off
casually by the plot—that I couldn't believe my eyes. The movie treated
her as a joke, not as a person" (p. 8).

Thus, in the "golden age" of the cinema Western, the "squaw"
was the most common image of Indian women. At the same time, the
sacrificing princess stereotype was still salient. Marsden and Nachbar
(1988) describe the princess image in such early films as the 1903 *Kit
Carson*, in which an Indian woman helps Kit escape and is killed by her
own chief. "For the next 10 years this romantic figure, young, beautiful,
and self-sacrificing, would come to the aid of Whites almost as often as
the savage Reactionary would murder or capture them" (pp. 609-610).
Although Pocahontas is portrayed in many movies, the theme is
replayed in other guises—*The Squaw's Sacrifice* (1909), *The Heart of the
Sioux* (1910), *The Indian Maid's Sacrifice* (1911), and *The Heart of an Indian*
(1913).

From the 1920s to 1940s, the portrayal of the Princess declined. She returned with the "sensitive" Westerns of the 1950s and beyond, led especially by director Delmer Daves's *Broken Arrow*, released in 1950. It told the story of a white man (James Stewart) who, in the course of setting up a peace accord with Apache chief Cochise (Jeff Chandler), falls in love with and marries Sonseeahray, or "Morning Star" (Debra Paget), an Apache woman who is, naturally, a princess. Sonseeahray dies after being shot by a white man who is breaking the peace, but, as always, her death is not in vain. As the Stewart character speaks over the final scenes in the film, "The death of Sonseeahray put a seal on the peace." The Princess figure again went into decline in the 1960s, seeming outdated and of less importance to white culture. Although the graphically obscene dimension of the "squaw" did not translate into the movie era, the remnants of it remained in the few, tiny roles for Indian women in Westerns from the 1950s onward. Without the princess stereotype, white culture had only the squaw, and she was, by definition, unimportant and uninteresting.[3] Like her princess predecessor, the newer squaw was devoted to a white man, but she had even less importance to the plot and was easily sacrificed if necessary. As Marsden and Nachbar (1988) point out, none of the famous "Indian" movies of the early 1970s had substantial roles for women: "*A Man Called Horse* (1970); *Little Big Man* (1971); *Jeremiah Johnson* (1972); and *The Man who Loved Cat Dancing* (1973)—all have Indian women married to whites who die either during the film or in the background of the film's story" (p. 614).

Thus, the most obvious and overwhelming aspect of portrayals of American Indians (male and female) is that these portrayals reflect a white gaze. Ironically, this has become even more pronounced in recent years, even as portrayals of Indians have become more "authentic" in terms of accurate detail, language, and, above all, the use of Indian actors. When non-Indian Hollywood stars played Indians, there were occasional films that saw events from the point of view of an Indian character. Thus, in Robert Aldrich's 1954 *Apache*, Burt Lancaster is cast as Massai, an Apache warrior who first defies white authority, but eventually learns to farm, and sets the stage for peace. His wife, a classic Indian princess, is also played by a white actress, Jean Peters, a woman who sacrifices everything and almost dies for love of Massai. ("If I lost you, I would be nothing," she mourns at one point in the film.) Like the casting of Debra Paget and Jeff Chandler in *Broken Arrow*, these many ludicrous casting choices are insulting, consigning actual Indian actors to minor roles. However, contemporary filmmakers, aware that it is no longer acceptable to cast whites as Indians, seem to have simply abandoned central roles for Indian characters. Clearly, this is an economic as well as a cultural decision—no Indian actor apparently has the drawing power of Burt Lancaster or Jeff Chandler. Inevitably, the lead roles go to white characters playing white roles. Even the television movie, *The Legend of Walks Far Woman* (1982), would probably not have been made without a star like Raquel Welch in the (Indian) title role. Thus, ironically, even though Hollywood now realizes that Indian roles must be played by Indian actors, those actors often find themselves playing only side-kick roles. The films look more "authentic" now, but as Leuthold (1995) writes, issues of representation go far beyond accurate detail into "questions of whether (Indian) women are depicted with a full sense of humanity" (p. 178). One device producers have used is to create a central role for a white actor to play a mixed blood Indian—Tom Berenger in *At Play in the Fields of the Lord* or Val Kilmer (who does have Indian heritage) in *Thunderheart* (1992). But once again, there have been none of these roles for women; the female role in *Thunderheart*, played with conviction by Sheila Tousey, is small and, predictably, ends in death.

CONTEMPORARY MEDIA REPRESENTATIONS OF INDIAN GENDER

Meanwhile, Indian men have fared somewhat better in media depictions. They, too, have been consigned to the past, defined by the western genre. But Westerns are about men, and Indian men since the 1950s have had roles as side-kicks to the hero. Most significant, however, Indian men have been the focus of the wave of fascination with things Indian that first crested in the 1960s and 1970s when the counter-culture embraced Indians (Brand, 1988). Although mainstream media interest subsided somewhat in the 1980s, the Indian "wannabee" phenomenon gained momentum in New Age-tinged popular culture (Green, 1988b) and rose again in the 1990s, this time in a more mainstream, ecologically minded form. The Indian elder who is wise beyond white understanding first began to appear in films like *Little Big Man* and *One Flew Over the Cuckoo's Nest* (1975), and returned in force after *Dances with Wolves*. In the 1990s, as never before, Indians are chic—mystical, wise, earth-loving and tragic. New Age culture appropriated Indian religious practices, clothing, music, and myths, and Indian-inspired art and design became all the rage.[4] In this trend, Indian culture is yet again commodified and made the object of white consumption, as it has been for centuries:

> This emphasis on the spiritual exoticism of Native Americans brings the screen Indian full circle. Just as Edison's one-minute movies in the 1890s were sold to audiences eager to view the strange otherness of Native peoples, so too do audiences in the 1980s go to the movies

for the pleasure of seeing Indians whose mystical lore makes them fascinatingly different. (Marsden & Nachbar, 1988, pp. 615-616)

This fascination is consistently associated in popular imagery with Indian men—artists, warriors, shamans. Indeed, in a recent study of male Indian imagery in film, romance novels, and other popular media, Van Lent (1996) convincingly shows that the image of the Indian male has become an important cultural icon in the 1990s. Perhaps in response to cultural uncertainties about "correct" male roles, the Indian man, usually placed in a "dead" historical context, has bifurcated in a slightly new way. Young men are handsome and virile, with the potential for decisive action when pressed, yet tender, loving, and vulnerable. Thus, Indian or mixed-blood men prove incredible lovers for white women in romance novels, whereas Indian women are invisible. Handsome young Indian men fight alongside white heroes in 1990s movies like *Dances with Wolves, Last of the Mohicans,* and *Squanto.* Meanwhile, older men act as wise sages in the same period pieces, and they provide a similar spiritual dimension in more contemporary films like *Free Willy, Legends of the Fall,* and even *Natural Born Killers.* They are stereotypical roles, usually subordinate to white storylines, and serve white cultural needs—but at least they are there.

In contrast, roles for Indian women in mainstream film and television have been meager at best. It is instructive to look, for example, at the one Indian woman who has become most familiar on both the large and small screen over the last 10 years. Tantoo Cardinal, a Metis (mixed blood) woman from Canada, has had roles in several recent movies, including *Black Robe, Dances with Wolves,* and *Legends of the Fall.* She also played a recurring role in the television series *Dr. Quinn, Medicine Woman,* until her character was killed at the end of the 1994-95 series. I will return to *Dr. Quinn;* first, I consider Cardinal's movie roles.

In *Dances with Wolves,* Cardinal plays Black Shawl, the wife of Kicking Bird, the medicine man who befriends Lt. John Dunbar, the lead character played by director Kevin Costner. Black Shawl is a definite advance on the sacrificial princesses of the past—she admonishes her husband when he is too curt with his ward, Stands with a Fist, and nudges him into authorizing her marriage to Dunbar. Kicking Bird and Black Shawl are permitted an enjoyable sex life, and their marriage is seen as warm and loving. Nevertheless, it is clearly a minor, supporting role. The lead female role is Stands with a Fist, a white woman who has been adopted into the tribe. This fact does make it plausible that she can speak English and thus can interpret for Dunbar and Kicking Bird. However, one wonders why some other device did not occur to Michael Blake, the author of the book and screenplay, opening up the possibility of a romance between Dunbar and an actual Lakota woman.

In *Black Robe* (1992), Cardinal again plays the wife of a more prominent character, although with less humor and light relief. Her character is killed midway through the film. The one other role for an Indian woman in the film is that of a chief's daughter with whom a young subsidiary character falls in love—an unrewarding role played by Sandrine Holt. *Legends of the Fall* (1994) is a classic example of Indian identity being appropriated to add mystery and resonance to white characters' life problems. The film is narrated by Gordon Tootoosis as a Cree elder who frames the life of hero Tristan Ludlow (Brad Pitt) in terms of an epic, spiritual identification with the Bear. Cardinal plays Pet, an Indian woman married to a hired hand on the Ludlow ranch. She is clearly loved and respected, but speaks hardly at all. Eventually her daughter (Katrina Lombard) marries Tristan, but is killed in a random act of violence, setting in motion a new twist in the main, white characters' lives.

Cardinal has spoken about her supporting roles and the frustrations that go with them: "If you've got those small roles, you're there on the (production) set but you're barely ever used" (Greer, 1994b, p. 152). She describes building the characters in her mind, giving them histories, and trying to make the experience more fulfilling: "You have to give yourself a reason for being there, a whole history where you live, what the whole place looks like, what your everyday life is like" (p. 152). One can only think how frustrating it must be for other Indian women, having to do their best with tiny, underwritten, and stereotypical roles. For example, Kimberley Norris, an Indian woman who had a small role in the TV miniseries *Son of the Morning Star* in the 1980s, reports how she was told to redo a scene in which she wept for the slain leader Crazy Horse. Instead of her tears, she was told, "Let's do it again and just take it with that dignified stoicism of the Indians" (Greer, 1994a, p. 144). As Norris commented, "That was a real quick lesson in their perception of how we don't have those natural human emotions" (p. 144).

THE DUAL BURDEN OF GENDER AND RACE:
DR. QUINN, MEDICINE WOMAN

American Indians are still virtually absent from popular television, largely because the Western is no longer a major TV genre (Taylor, 1996). They do appear occasionally, frequently as stereotypical "mystical wise men," in action adventures such as CBS's *Walker, Texas Ranger*, in which the supposedly part-Native hero (Chuck Norris) is advised and inspired by his Indian uncle and mentor on a semi-regular basis. *Northern Exposure*, which ran on CBS from 1990 to 1995, did succeed in challenging some stereotypes, and I return to that show later.

Aside from the no-longer-running *Northern Exposure*, the only other recent show to include Indians as regular characters is CBS's *Dr. Quinn, Medicine Woman*, a frontier drama set in the late 1860s. Generally despised by critics for its formulaic and sentimental predictability, *Dr. Quinn* has nevertheless proved very successful. The show features a crusading woman doctor, Michaela Quinn, played by Jane Seymour, who fights the bigotry and sexism of the people of Colorado Springs on a weekly basis. The show is especially popular with women, and one reason for this is its essentially feminist point of view (Dow, 1996). Created and produced by a woman, Beth Sullivan, the show was originally populated by a cast of strong women, surrounded by weak and bigoted men, although gradually the gender balance has shifted, and the men have become more likeable. As Dow (1996) suggests, the show takes many of the standard Western formulas, such as the hero battling for justice, and transforms the hero into a woman. And unlike traditional TV Westerns, American Indians are included in the form of a Cheyenne village. However, these Cheyenne are largely anonymous, functioning as plot devices to showcase the central white characters. Indeed, *Dr. Quinn* illustrates perfectly the point that the Indian of popular culture is a white creation (Bird, 1996).

Perhaps most striking of all, the show has not one strong female Cheyenne character. In fact, *Dr. Quinn* throws into sharp focus the double burden of race and gender stereotyping that has erased Indian women from popular imagery. The show demonstrates that in popular media, the traditional, restricted images of white women have often been challenged and transformed. Most of the strong characters are women, and, as in many other popular shows, white men often behave as ignorant buffoons (with the exception of the glamorous Indian "Wannabee," Sully, who is Michaela's love interest and eventual husband). Yet even within this context, there is no space for a significant Indian woman. The Cheyenne, although presented "authentically" and generally favorably, are not well-drawn characters and are never given stories that focus on them as individuals. Rather they are beautiful, serene, and spiritual, reflecting the current fascination with New Age-tinged mysticism.

The one Cheyenne who has a significant presence is medicine man Cloud Dancing, who is the epitome of the stoic, strong, noble male Indian, who suffers horrendous personal losses with dignity and forgiveness. In other words, he fits right into one of the prevailing permitted roles for Indian men—the noble wise man. There is no such role allowed for his wife, Snowbird, played until the character's death by the long-suffering Tantoo Cardinal. Her main role was to look wise and wifely, offering smiling advice to Cloud Dancing, just as she did as

Kicking Bird's wife in Dances with Wolves. Mostly, though, she appears briefly to allow Dr. Quinn to make a point—she suffers a miscarriage so that Michaela can become indignant about the Indians' lack of food; she looks on as Michaela vaccinates Indian children, uttering lines like, "You bring us strong medicine."

Cardinal must have had shows like *Dr. Quinn* in mind when she commented, "Native people are not brought into the foreground, or even accepted as an everyday part of life, not anywhere in the American media. It is rare, rare, rare that you see anything about Native people as human beings" (Greer, 1994b, p. 153). Other Cheyenne women drift around the village, smiling and carrying babies. In one memorable episode, the show displaced Indian women completely, while trying to use their cultural experience to make a 1990s moral point. It focused on a woman who is the sole survivor of an Army raid on her Cheyenne village. She is brought to town, where she faces the ignorance and racism of the local people, and meanwhile proves to be a temporary rival for Sully's affections. This story offered a chance to develop a Cheyenne female character more fully, and yet this is avoided—the woman is white and was merely raised Cheyenne. She fits perfectly into the pattern of white female Indian adoptees that we have seen in movies from *Soldier Blue* to *Dances with Wolves*. In this context, the white woman essentially stands in for the Indian woman, apparently making the character more interesting for white viewers, who can vicariously enjoy "going Indian" without having to see a real Indian woman as an engaging individual. Since the 1994-95 season, it appears that the producers of *Dr. Quinn* have found the strain of incorporating Indian characters too much—toward the end of that season, the real, historical massacre of Cheyenne at the 1868 "battle" of Washita was depicted. Snowbird and most of the villagers died. Snowbird's dying words to Michaela are typically designed to assuage white guilt: "One day, perhaps many seasons from now, my people and your people will come to understand each other and no longer be afraid." Since this episode, we have seen Indian land being sold off, and the Cheyenne have largely disappeared, with the exception of Cloud Dancing. The notion that viewers might have been interested in following the fate of the survivors apparently did not occur to the producers.

RETURN TO POCAHONTAS

So it seems that in the mid-1990s, living, breathing Indian women have become so invisible and irrelevant that the only way mainstream white culture could insert an Indian woman back into the cultural picture was to return to Pocahontas—and make her a cartoon. And in spite of being touted as a feminist rendering of the tale, with Pocahontas as a free-spirited, courageous, and strong-willed young woman, the story clearly echoes the old imagery. Pocahontas persuades her father to make peace, even though it is not clear why it is in her best interests to do so. Even though she loses her lover, she learns to recognize the inevitability of "progress," a crucial and guilt-reducing element in the white image of Indians. In the cartoon, Disney tells us also that Pocahontas taught John Smith respect for nature, implying that she had a profound impact on how the nation developed—a sentimentalizing of the way things actually happened, and a kind of collective fantasy that is strikingly close to the sentimental image of Pocahontas embraced in the 19th century. Disney's version harks back to Victorian imagery in other ways—the cartoon character is notably voluptuous and scantily clad, as were the earlier images. As Green (1988a) points out, "the society permitted portrayals to include sexual references (bare and prominent bosoms) for females even when tribal dress and ethnography denied the reality of the reference" (p. 593). Combining "superwoman" imagery of women as both strong-willed and eminently desirable to men, alongside the current image of Indians as guardians of the Earth, "Disney has created a marketable New Age Pocahontas to embody our millennial dreams for wholeness and harmony," as Strong observes (1996, p. 416).

"Our dreams," of course, refers to white dreams, for *Pocahontas* is still a white fantasy. Indeed, as Tilton (1994) writes, "We might argue that if one were to formulate the narrative from an Indian perspective, Pocahontas would have to be presented as an extremely problematic character" (p. 90). Yet Disney's *Pocahontas* has breathed new life into an Indian Princess stereotype that never really disappeared. We still see it, on Pocahontas-inspired merchandise, "collector plates," and so on. For instance, a recent advertisement for a "collectable" Indian doll named "Buffalo Child" described the figure: "She will be a princess among her people [who those people might be is not disclosed]. Her mother leads the Buffalo Clan, as her grandmother did before her. Now she will receive their wisdom and lore."[5] The image lives on in local legends about Indian maidens/princesses who leaped to their deaths for love of a handsome brave or a white man (DeCaro, 1986). But it has nothing whatever to do with the lived experience of American Indian women in the late 20th century—nor has it anything to do with the lived experiences of American Indian women of the past. As Green (1975) argues, "Delightful and interesting as Pocahontas' story may be, she offers an intolerable metaphor for the Indian-White experience. She and the Squaw offer unendurable metaphors for the lives of Indian women" (p. 714).

BREAKING THE STEREOTYPES

Although mainstream popular culture offers little subjectivity to the Indian, male or female, the impetus for change is mounting. Independent Indian film makers are producing their own movies that speak about who they are (Weatherford, 1992), and more Indian people are in production roles in Hollywood, although by 1995 no major feature film had been directed by an American Indian (Leuthold, 1995).[6] As always, resources for large mainstream productions go where money can be made, and as long as Indians are not considered marketable in their own right, change is slow. At present, with the popular infatuation with things Indian, there are probably more roles than ever for Indian actors. But these roles are inevitably subordinate and either rooted in the past or in a conception of Indians as "traditional." Female stars generally are less bankable than male stars; if conventional wisdom is that no male Indian star can carry a major film, what chance is there for a woman?

When the conventional wisdom is challenged, it is usually by nonmainstream producers. In documentary film-making, American Indians have made great strides in gaining control over their own representation (Prins, 1989). The National Film Board of Canada has produced many feature films, including a series of four one-hour television movies in 1986 called "Daughters of the Country." These features told four different stories of Indian or Metis women, from the 18th century to the present. They were unusual in that they used a mostly Native cast, but they were extraordinary in that they told their stories from the point of view of the women who were their central figures. Suddenly, instead of a movie that gazes at Indians through the eyes of white settlers, soldiers, or trappers, we see those whites as interlopers, whose ways are strange and alien. So accustomed are we to the standard way of seeing things, that it takes a while to adjust. I found myself expecting to have the story of *Ikwe*, the title role in the first film, produced and directed by Norma Bailey, told through the eyes of the white man she is forced to marry. Instead, he remains peripheral to the central story, and is ultimately dispensable. Life in the Ojibwa village is simple and mundane, concentrating more on survival and everyday tasks than on mystical ceremonies.[7] The women who play the lead roles, such as Hazel King as Ikwe, or Mireille Deyglun as *Mistress Madeleine*, are neither voluptuous princesses nor dumpy squaws, but ordinary women who face human dilemmas that are not defined by their ethnicity.

For as Tantoo Cardinal puts it, "So often when we have a story that they call a Native American story, the characters become cardboard, because the focus is on the issue, not about the human beings groping through that experience" (Greer, 1994b, p. 153). She was delighted, then, to participate in another unusual project—the 1993 film *Where the Rivers Flow North*. Jay Craven, the non-Indian director, co-producer and co-writer, adapted it from a novella by Vermont author Howard Frank Mosher and raised funding through many local efforts in Vermont. It is a film that, although not being "about Indians" at all, finally provides a major, co-starring role for an Indian woman—Tantoo Cardinal. This film tells the story of a couple, an aging white logger (Rip Torn) and his Indian housekeeper/common law wife Bangor (Cardinal), as they fight against the acquisition of their land in the 1920s. *Where the Rivers Flow North* is about people groping through a personal crisis. Bangor is written as an Indian woman, and there are moments in the film where that is clear, such as when the developers' strong-man refers to her as a squaw. But her ethnicity is not the issue—her complicated, bickering relationship with Torn's character is. In a reversal of the usual pattern, the male character dies in his quest for independence, leaving Bangor alone, not victorious but at least surviving. The film, by its nature and subject matter, could never be a "big" movie, but at least it may point to the possibility of roles for Indian women that acknowledge their ethnicity, while being "about" larger human issues.

Network television went some way in expanding the imagery of Indian women in the now-cancelled CBS series *Northern Exposure*, which ran from 1990 to 1995. As Taylor (1996) writes, *Northern Exposure*, which was set in contemporary Alaska, "casts its native population as alive, well, and flourishing, part of the dominant white society and modernity, yet still practicing traditional ways" (p. 229). As part of an ensemble cast, the show included two native Alaskan characters, Ed Chigliak (Darren E. Burrows) and Marilyn Whirlwind (Elaine Miles). Like all the characters on the show, neither was simple and one-dimensional, but rather displayed idiosyncratic, quirky characteristics. Ed was a film buff and would-be shaman, whereas Marilyn was a physician's receptionist who in many ways was wiser than the physician, Joel Fleischman. She was large and yet was allowed to be sexual, without being portrayed as "loose" or "squawlike." At the same time, Taylor points out that the program was vague and inconsistent when identifying Marilyn's cultural heritage; she seemed to move among the distinctly different Haida, Tlingit, and Athabascan cultures, whereas white characters were consistently rooted in specific ethnicities. "Television would never consider giving cajuns Russian accents, (or) putting Islamic women in bikinis," (p. 241), yet *Northern Exposure*'s producers moved Marilyn and Ed's tribal affiliation with abandon.

In the long term, it will be interesting to see if *Northern Exposure* has any impact on mainstream portrayals of Indians. The show was so distinctive, dreamlike, and "unrealistic" that it may be remembered as a unique and nonrepresentative moment in television. Yet when I asked Indian viewers to contrast *Northern Exposure* and *Dr. Quinn*, which is ostensibly presented as more "realistic," they all agreed that *Northern Exposure* was more "real," reflecting a sense of identification with the Native Alaskans as human beings, rather than cardboard characters (Bird, 1996). In that respect, *Northern Exposure* was in a different class from any television show, before or since.

Finally, we saw a hopeful sign in the 1994 Turner Broadcasting series on *The Native Americans*, which attempted to dramatize historic moments in Indian history in a series of feature-length television films. Although *Geronimo* and *The Broken Chain* were dismissed by at least one Indian critic as "feeble" (Merritt, 1994), the same writer had more encouraging words for *Lakota Woman: Siege at Wounded Knee*, a dramatization of the autobiography of Mary Crow Dog, who took part in the 1973 American Indian Movement seige at Wounded Knee. The movie was made with a 90% Indian cast, and 40% of the crew were Indians, offering unprecedented opportunities for Indian people to gain experience in film-making techniques. Executive producer Lois Bonfiglio described the filming as "an extraordinary spiritual and emotional experience" for everyone involved (Merritt, 1994, p. 90). Indeed, the movie proved exceptional in that, like the smaller budget Canadian films, it told the story from the point of view of Mary Crow Dog, played with skill and sincerity by Irene Bedard (the voice of Disney's *Pocahontas*). The film does not glamorize Indian women—Mary is seen to sink into a life of alcoholism and promiscuity before being transformed by the message of AIM. Neither does it stereotype her as a degraded squaw; she is simply a human being, dealing with a set of problems and issues, many of which confront her because of her ethnic heritage. Although some may be cynical that Ted Turner and Jane Fonda were merely jumping on the Indian bandwagon (Merritt, 1994), *Lakota Woman* does offer an encouraging step in the right direction.

Meanwhile, American Indian women novelists and poets have worked hard to cast off the old imagery. Leslie Silko, Paula Gunn Allen, Joy Harjo, and others "have established a 'voice' and an 'identity' for the Indian woman which are grounded in the realities of the present, rather than the stereotypes of the past" (Tsosie, 1988, p. 3). Eventually, just as white and African American women now have at least some voice in creating mass imagery, American Indian women will break into the consciousness of the mass culture industry. As Tantoo Cardinal says, "We have to get to a place where our Native women have a sexuality, a sensuality, an intelligence" (Greer, 1994b, p. 153). But the stereotypes of Indians, male and female, will be hard to shatter—their role as the exotic, fascinating "other" is so entrenched and so naturalized.

DOES IT MATTER?

As more women take part in the production of media, as scriptwriters, directors, producers, and actors, there is an opportunity to celebrate some of the huge advances that have been gained in the representation of women. As Cook (1993) writes, these female media makers "speak for themselves and not necessarily for all women: but they insist on their right to speak differently, and for that difference to be recognised" (p. xxiii). Yet overwhelmingly, these gains have been made by white women. American Indian women are still almost invisible in mass culture, and even when white women gain some power in media production, as *Dr. Quinn's* Beth Sullivan has done, their Indian counterparts remain invisible.

But does the limited picture of Indian women actually matter? After all, most people are surrounded by real men and women; they know that media imagery is not everything, and their understandings of gender are formed not only by media but by day-to-day interactions. In many parts of the country, however, non-Indians never see or encounter real Indians. Media representations take on an added power in this situation, filling a knowledge vacuum with outmoded and limited stereotypes. In my study of *Dr. Quinn* (Bird, 1996), for example, white viewers found the portrayal of the Cheyenne "authentic" and believable, especially when the Cheyenne behaved in ways that are indeed stereotypical—stoic, silent, and spiritual. It was these very aspects of behavior that Indian viewers found most problematic.

In a study by Shiveley (1992), in which whites saw Westerns as historically authentic whereas Indians did not, I found the same difference. Whites were impressed by the care with costumes and so on, whereas Indians saw the cultural details as phony. The point is that Westerns, even family ones on television like *Dr. Quinn,* feel "authentic" to white audiences—a myth that is "an affirmation of their own social experience" (Shiveley, 1992, p. 733). Without real-life experience to counter-act that myth, mainstream culture has only the media to constantly reinforce it.

Williams (1993) introduces an anthology that in many ways is a celebration of the transformations women have brought about in popular film-making. She presents the collection as the beginning of an answer to her own question: "So what happens when marginalised or repressed stories come to the fore? What happens when fantasies of power or tales of difference . . . become the conscious, overt, marketable stuff of mainstream cinema?" (p. xxv). When it comes to representations of American Indian women, the answer to this question is sadly clear. We do not know what happens, and we are nowhere near knowing. Only when mainstream white culture accepts the reality of Indian men and women as everyday Americans, and finds room for their tales of difference, will our mediated realities be able to break the lock of a mythic past.

ENDNOTES

1. Although some prefer to use the term "Native Americans," I have generally chosen to use "American Indians" because this is the more commonly used self-description in Minnesota, where I resided at the time of writing.
2. Tsosie (1988) discusses the range of traditional roles for women in several indigenous cultures. For a discussion of accepted alternative female roles in specific cultures, see Lewis (1941) and Medicine (1983). Many Native American cultures also offered alternative social roles for men: see Callender and Kodrens (1983). Foster (1995) describes how strong female roles have been erased from the historical literature on the Iroquois.
3. Indian actress Lois Red Elk commented in 1980 that of the many small roles she had played in her career, almost none of her characters was given a name (Leuthold, 1995).
4. For a discussion of the recent appropriations of Native culture, see Whitt (1995). Green (1991) takes issue especially with white feminists who appropriate Indian spirituality.
5. Advertisement for the "Buffalo Child" doll, produced by the Georgetown Collection of Portland, ME, appearing in an advertising supplement to *Parade* magazine, January 1996.
6. In 1998, however, "Smoke Signals," directed by Chris Eyre from a story by Sherman Alexie, was released to critical acclaim.
7. Appleford (1995) draws attention to the many "deceptively quieter Canadian films that are able to explore subjects such as female empowerment and community values, which often fall outside the purview of the epic feature film" (p. 115).

REFERENCES

Appleford, R. (1995). Coming out from behind the rocks: Construction of the Indian in recent U.S. and Canadian cinema. *American Indian Culture and Research Journal, 19*(1), 97-118.

Berkhofer, R.F. (1979). *The white man's Indian*. New York: Vintage Books.

Bird, S.E. (1996). Not my fantasy: The persistence of Indian imagery in *Dr. Quinn, Medicine Woman*. In S.E. Bird (Ed.), *Dressing in feathers: The construction of the Indian in American popular culture* (pp. 245-262). Boulder: Westview Press.

Brand, S. (1988). Indians and the counterculture, 1960s-1970s. In W.E. Washburn (Ed.), *The handbook of North American Indians, IV* (pp. 570-572). Washington, DC: Smithsonian Institution Press.

Callender, C., & Kodrens, L.M. (1983). The North American Berdache. *Current Anthropology, 24,* 443-490.

Cook, P. (1993). Border crossings: Women and film in context. In P. Cook & P. Dodd (Eds.), *Women and film: A sight and sound reader* (pp. ix-xxiii). Philadelphia: Temple University Press.

DeCaro, F. (1986). Vanishing the red man: Cultural guilt and legend formation. *International Folklore Review, 4,* 74-80.

Dow, B. (1996). *Prime time feminism: Television, media culture, and the women's movement since 1970.* Philadelphia: University of Pennsylvania Press.

Foster, M.H. (1995). Lost women of the matriarchy: Iroquois women in the historical literature. *American Indian Culture and Research Journal, 19*(3), 121-140.

Francis, D. (1992). *The imaginary Indian: The image of the Indian in Canadian culture.* Vancouver: Arsenal Pulp Press.

Green, A. (1991). For all those who were Indian in a former life. *Ms., 2*(3), 44-45.

Green, R. (1975). The Pocahontas perplex: The image of the Indian woman in American culture. *Massachusetts Review, 16*(4), 698-714.

Green, R. (1988a). The Indian in popular American culture. In W.E. Washburn (Ed.), *The handbook of North American Indians, IV* (pp. 587-606). Washington, DC: Smithsonian Institution Press.

Green, R. (1988b). The tribe called Wannabee: Playing Indian in America and Europe. *Folklore, 99*(1), 30-55.

Greer, S. (1994a). Imagining Indians: Native people voice their concerns, beliefs, and action plans at Arizona Film Festival. *Winds of Change, 9*(4), 142-144.

Greer, S. (1994b). Tantoo Cardinal: A part of all nations. *Winds of Change, 9*(4), 150-153.

Jones, M.E. (Ed.). (1994). The military savagely destroys Indians: Testimony from U.S. Congressional investigations. In *The American frontier: Opposing viewpoints.* San Diego: Greenhaven Press.

Leuthold, S.M. (1995). Native American responses to the western. *American Indian Culture and Research Journal, 19*(1), 153-189.

Lewis, O. (1941). Manly hearted women among the South Peigan. *American Anthropologist, 43,* 173-187.

Marsden, M.T., & Nachbar, J. (1988). The Indian in the movies. In W.E. Washburn (Ed.), *The handbook of North American Indians, IV* (pp. 607-616). Washington, DC: Smithsonian Institution Press.

McKenney, T.L, & Hall. J. (1933). *The Indian tribes of North America.* Edinburgh: John Grant. (Original work published 1884)

Medicine, B. (1983). Warrior women: Sex role alternatives for Plains Indian women. In P. Albers & B. Medicine (Eds.), *Hidden half: Studies of Plains Indian women* (pp. 267-280). Lanham, MD: University Press of America.

Merritt, J. (1994). Lakota woman: Authentic culture on film or exploitation? *Winds of Change, 8*(2), 90-93.

Prins, H.E.L. (1989). American Indians and the ethnocinematic complex: From native participation to production control. In *Eyes Across the Water: Amsterdam Conference on Visual Anthropology and Sociology, Proceedings* (pp. 80-90). Amsterdam: Het Spinhuis.

Shiveley, J. (1992). Cowboys and Indians: Perceptions of western films among American Indians and Anglos. *American Sociological Review, 57*, 725-734.

Strong, P.T (1996). Animated Indians: Critique and contradiction in commodified children's culture. *Cultural Anthropology, 11*(3), 405-424.

Taylor, A. (1996). Cultural heritage in Northern Exposure. In S.E. Bird (Ed.), *Dressing in feathers: The construction of the Indian in American popular culture* (pp. 229-244). Boulder: Westview Press.

Tilton, R. (1994). *Pocahontas: The evolution of an American narrative.* Cambridge: Cambridge University Press.

Tompkins, J. (1992). *West of everything.* New York: Oxford University Press.

Tsosie, R. (1988). Changing women: The cross currents of American Indian feminine identity. *American Indian Culture and Research Journal, 12*(1), 1-38.

Van Lent, P. (1986). Her beautiful savage: The current sexual image of the Native American male. In S.E. Bird (Ed.), *Dressing in feathers: The construction of the Indian in American popular culture* (pp. 211-228). Boulder: Westview Press.

Weatherford, E. (1992). Starting fire with gunpowder. *Film Comment, 28*, 64-67.

Whitt, L.A. (1995). Cultural imperialism and the marketing of Native America. *American Indian Culture and Research Journal, 19*(3), 1-32.

Williams, L.R. (1993). Everything in question: Women and film in prospect. In P. Cook & P. Dodd (Eds.), *Women and film: A sight and sound reader* (pp. xxiv-xxix). Philadelphia: Temple University Press.

7

Who is the Puerto Rican Woman and How is She?: Shall Hollywood Respond?

Jocelyn A. Géliga Vargas

"Mami, that lady is Puerto Rican, right?," the transplanted four-year old asked as she found her way to a window seat on the bus that daily rocked her from one inner city to the unrelenting remnants of another one. Her very Puerto Rican mom shook in a mixture of fear, shame and surprise at the question and the occasion that aroused it. *That lady* was "kicking and screaming," I mean, in a frenzy, raving and venting out all sorts of insults and epithets at the very-much-non-Puerto Rican bus driver who refused to let her on the bus because she was ten cents short for the ride. The mother hesitated to respond, if only for a few very long seconds, as she wondered "where could my *nena* have absorbed that *this* is what Puerto Rican women are like?" Her still intact sense of pride for *los nuestros* led her to affirm that yes, indeed, "*that lady* is Puertorriqueña."

... Later in the journey, and after the familiar bumps and rings of the bus ride had reshuffled her emotions back in place, the mother asked, "how did you know that *she* was Puerto Rican?" The "incriminating" answer brought Mami to a deeper sigh of relief: "Because she speaks Spanish, just like us!"[1]

111

So, how do we know that *she* is a Puerto Rican woman (Puertorriqueña)? Who is the Puerto Rican woman and how is she?[2] This question, which has perpetually entertained and tormented those of us who fervently adopt this cultural identifier, is of increasing importance for understanding cultural diversity and cultural politics in the United States in light of a confluence of sociohistorical events associated with multinational capitalist expansionism.

The marketing rhetoric of commodity capitalism has, since the mid-1980s, fronted peoples of Latin American descent as a fertile and unexplored ground awaiting the civilizing mission of assimilation through consumption. As Bureau of the Census reports began hailing Latinos as the fastest growing "minority" in the United States—and here is where State planning and corporate interests meet—millions of advertising agency dollars were spent researching the particularities of this newly discovered market. "Rising" from a mass of dispersed people to an organized catalogue of identifiable consumers is a way of "making it" in capitalist societies such as the United States. But attaining consumer status is not equivalent to achieving full membership in society. The confluence and contradictions of the relationship between the economic, the political, and the cultural can be heard loud and clear throughout the 1990s, in the speeches in favor of California's proposition 187 and similar initiatives attempting to deny Latino (and other) immigrants everything from the opportunity to work "legally" in this country to the right to speak their native tongue. Today's anti-affirmative action climate and legislation dismantling the public assistance system so carefully erected during decades of liberal democratic agendas affect Latinos in acute ways. Lest we sweepingly and carelessly understand these changes in public policy as a general conservative trend of the 1990s, we must turn back to the historical backdrop of the 1980s to comprehend how this backlash is directed specifically at Latinos and to assess the extent to which the cultural industries are a protagonist in this crusade.

The 1980s were often hailed as the "Decade of Hispanics." In 1988, a special issue of *Time* celebrated that "¡Magnífico!, Hispanic culture breaks out of the Barrio" (*Time*, 1988, p. 1). What was there to carouse, however, was not the long-deserved recognition that people of Hispanic American descent have been part of the processes of economic production and cultural creation in this country from its inception, but the sudden, and ethnocentric, realization that "Hispanics" have now a bright and spicy cornucopia to offer to the demanding palate of mainstream audiences. The enthusiastic clamor of "A Surging New Spirit: In film, music, theater, art, design—the Hispanic influence exploding into the American mainstream" (*Time*, 1988, pp. 46-49) powerfully served to legitimate Latino/a cultural productions and their appropriations by the dominant media as the newly captured prey for the never subsiding appetite of the cultural industries for the experiences and images of those exotic "Others":

America, the great receiver. From every culture to arrive within its borders, it embraces some new ingredient. Puritan wrath. Black cool. Irish poetics. Jewish irony. One after another, America draws them down the channels of its awareness and puts them into play in new settings. They collide and cross-pollinate and mix it up, nowhere more so than in the arts and popular culture. . . . Nowadays the mainstream is receiving a rich new current. More and more American film, theater, music, design, dance and art are taking on a Hispanic color and spirit. Look around. . . . Then there are the developments that are harder to pin down, the Latin flavors and inflections conveyed through all the intricate paths of daily life, in the offerings at a table or the bolero curve of a woman's jacket. You can't walk down the street without running into them. On the corner where the disco used to be, a Latin-beat club; kids hip hop on the floors that withstood the bump. For lunch, a burrito. What's that in the salad? It's jicama. (say *hee*-ca-ma.) Things that once seemed foreign now seem as American as . . . a burrito. With each fresh connection tastes are being rebuilt, new understandings concluded. The American mind is adding a new wing. (Lacayo, 1988, p. 46)

The diverse and often conflicting histories, cultural codes, and tastes of the peoples of Latin American and Caribbean origin are lumped together in the category Hispanic, stripped of their historicity and materiality and blanketed with the restricting bandage that would make them safe and palatable to mainstream audiences. As has been pointed out in reference to Latino (Vázquez, 1990-91) and African American (Jhally & Lewis, 1992) media representations, the resulting selective appropriation of minority subjects and themes in the mainstream media has often promoted an enlightened version of racism that justifies the hands-off approach currently in vogue at the State level with regard to discrimination and exacerbated social inequality. The distorted inclusion of Latinos in the media lends credibility to both the argument for increased police control of private and community life (consider that most of the films treating Latino subjects throughout the 1980s and 1990s belong to the gang genre) and the arguments against affirmative action, multicultural and bilingual education, and public assistance for the poor. For if, according to media representations, Latinos have now been able to secure a piece of the pie, there is no longer a need for white "America"[3] to extend its "philanthropic" hand.

Because, as Shohat and Stam (1994) argue, at the present historical juncture all political struggles necessarily pass through the filter of mass culture, the contemporary media are absolutely central to any discussion of cultural identity, and by extension to the exploration of how notions of cultural identity are utilized to shape and popularize public discourse.

> The contemporary media shape identity; indeed many argue that they now exist close to the very core of identity production. In a transnational world typified by the global circulation of images and sounds, goods and peoples, media spectatorship impacts complexly on national identity and communal belonging. By facilitating an engagement with distant peoples, the media "deterritorialize" the process of imagining communities. (Shohat & Stam, 1994, pp. 6-7)

The media also play a central role in creating a sense of psychosocial distance among people insofar as they establish distinctions about who is "us" and who is "them." The recent stream of news reports "investigating" the impact of Welfare and Medicare costs on taxpayers is a vivid example of how the media hail middle-class "America" with the inclusive "us," whereas the poor and the indigent are (dis)regarded as a peripheral and disassociated "them." This is how ideologies, "those images, concepts and premises which provide the frameworks through which we represent, interpret, understand and make sense of some aspect of social existence" (Hall, 1980a, p. 37), are crafted. And circulating ideologies is a major role of the media. Hence, the pertinence of turning to critical analyses of media representations as one pathway to a more connected and grounded understanding of multiculturalism and race relations in the United States.

WHAT DOES THIS HAVE TO DO, *SPECIFICALLY*, WITH THE PUERTO RICAN WOMAN?

In this chapter, I use the Puertorriqueña as a case study to explore the role of the cultural industries in constructing notions of ethnic identity that are not only digestible for the "American" stomach (to follow *Time*'s food-court metaphor) but are instrumental in endorsing the hegemony[4] of the white-supremacist, patriarchal, and imperialist ideologies of the State. The representations of Puerto Rican women in popular culture provide an ample map over which to trace the intricate configuration and sedimentation of dominant ideologies with regard to the politics of gender, race, and colonialism (or its more fashionable transmutations in capitalist expansionism and transnational corporatism).

In looking at the symbolic construction of Puerto Rican womanhood, I turn specifically to Hollywood because of its undisputed rank as an ideological state apparatus, as a hegemonic producer of multiple dis-courses that intervene in, affirm, and/or contest the socioideological struggles that are being fought in the culture (Althusser, 1971), and also because Hollywood cinema has played a historical role in the process of cultural identity formation of "self" and "others" in the symbolic realm. The beginnings of the U.S. film industry, as Shohat (1991) reminds us, coincided with the height of imperialism, and so dominant cinema has not only inherited and disseminated colonial discourse, but has "thus operated as an epistemological mediator between two spaces—that of the Western ["mainstream"] spectator and that of the ["ethnic"] culture represented on the screen" (p. 42). The suggestion that the implied Hollywood cinema spectator is preconceived as the "American" main-stream is grounded on historical facts because by 1918 the U.S. film industry was already producing about 98% of the films shown in the country (and 85% of those shown across the globe). During World War II, Hollywood became a catalytic agent in mediating public relations between Latin America and the United States (Géliga Vargas, 1996). President Franklin Delano Roosevelt's efforts to procure the support of the southern hemisphere in the war and to maintain necessary economic relations prompted him to resurrect the "Good Neighbor Policy" with Latin America. The Motion Picture Section of the Office of Inter-American Affairs received special attention and was commanded to hire "experts" in Latin America (all Anglo-Saxon males) to avoid representa-tional mistakes in film "that could offend the neighbors to the south" (Woll, 1980, p. 54).

Although stereotypes and flawed accounts persisted, there was a boom in what the United States thought were "positive" movie images about Latinos/as. The main celebrities that emerged in that period were all females: Dolores del Río (Mexican), Lupe Vélez (Mexican), and Carmen Miranda (Brazilian). Gender-specific ideologies prospered, and Hollywood's "positive" attitude toward Latin America and its peoples was transformed into mystification and objectification. These actresses became fetishes, goddesses to be admired, desired, and, hence, dehu-manized (López, 1991).[5]

But while the celebration of Latin Americanism inundated Hollywood and the ideology of Inter-Americanism punctuated domi-nant political discourse, where were the Puerto Ricans? Well, thousands of them were fighting the war. As U.S. citizens, Puerto Ricans were already politically and economically coerced into supporting the United States in WWII.[6] The first commercial film to feature (however distorted-ly) Puerto Ricans did not appear until 1959.[7] Despite the late arrival and the still scattered resurgence of media images of Puerto Rican people, and of Puerto Rican women in particular, Hollywood is the only dominant media form that has somewhat consistently embarked on the enterprise of constructing a Puertorriqueña identity.

It is not my intention to isolate the experience of Puerto Rican women in popular culture as unique. The Puertorriqueña is not the only cultural aggregate that has historically faced, in this country and back home, the three-tier system of oppression encompassed by racism, sexism, and colonialism. But she is certainly one that has been summarily condemned to oblivion in critical analyses of popular culture to this day.

At a more general level, then, this chapter responds to a pressing need to fill the gap in documentation and critical analysis of the Puerto Rican experience vis-à-vis U.S. cultural industries. The legal status of Puerto Ricans as U.S. citizens has generally excluded us from consideration in scholarship addressing the problematic of peoples of Latin American and Caribbean descent in the United States or in relation to the United States. Concurrently, our marginal social position as clearly non-"American" (if not earnestly un-American!) subsumes Puerto Ricans into silence and invisibility in a cultural context in which racial discourse is still by and large construed in the simple binary opposition of black/white. This project is thus fueled by the imperative to pursue radical multicultural revisions that attend to the complex multivocity of the contemporary cultural milieu. By exploring and critiquing dominant representations of Puertorriqueñas, this chapter engages in an exercise of multicultural expression that is corrective insofar as it seeks to expose the limiting and frequently oppressive character of Anglo-centric, patriarchal depictions of nondiminant constituencies. And it is also a prospective venture, for it sows the seeds for the continued manifestation and reconfiguration of cultural identity as a fluid, permeable construct. Radical multiculturalism, then, rests on the understanding that cultural accounts are always partial and dynamic, produced collectively through ongoing processes of social interaction. Hence, my intention is neither to develop a taxonomy of Puertorriqueña stereotypes broached by Hollywood, nor to affirm a definite, congealed Puertorriqueña essence. The goal is rather, as Shohat and Stam (1994) would agree, to decolonize representation, not only in terms of cultural artifacts, but in terms of power relations between communities.

Any attempt to study the conditions of Puerto Ricans in the United States must bear reference to the framework of colonialism. Given the widespread omission of the Puerto Rican experience in official accounts of U.S. history and politics, this merits some explanation. Since 1898, when U.S. troops invaded Puerto Rico during the elusively named Spanish American War, Puerto Rico has been a territory under the occupation of the United States. Despite continued institutional refusals to acknowledge this status, Puerto Rico is to this day a colony of the United

States because its economic infrastructure, militia, judicial system, political status, and cultural industries are controlled almost exclusively by "American" bureaucracies and "American" dollars. This historical and political legacy, as Flores (1993) persuasively argues, must inform and route any analysis and interpretation of the cultural experiences and exchanges of the Puerto Rican people in the United States.

In what follows I explore the representation of Puertorriqueña identity in recent Hollywood films with two parallel goals in mind: to expose the workings of racial, gender, and colonial ideologies in popular culture; and to speculate about the weight that these representations may bear in public discourse on the one hand, and in the processes of cultural identity formation of actual Puerto Rican women and girls on the other. A set of theoretic-political tenets sustain me through this journey. The first has to do with the rites of passage of ideologies in lived experience. According to Hall (1980a), in daily social practice ideologies tend to disappear from view into the taken-for-granted "naturalized" world of common sense. This is how racist, sexist, classist, and other problematic assumptions register into our consciousness as the way things ought to be. This process of cementing of ideologies is vital for the Puerto Rican woman as an ethnic and gender "Other": insofar as both gender and race appear to be given by Nature, racism and sexism are profoundly naturalized ideologies.[8]

The second theoretic-political motivation underpinning this critique derives from Deane's (1990) assertion that in the attempted discovery of its true identity, a community often begins with the demolition of the false stereotypes within which it has been entrapped. In looking at these texts, I am not a disengaged critic, but a black Puerto Rican woman in continuous search of fresh strategies to approach my own and my sisters' histories. To quote Hall (1980a) again, "how we *see* ourselves and our social relations *matters* because it enters into and informs our actions and practices" (p. 35; emphasis in original). In order for us, Puertorriqueñas, to displace the established hierarchies that oppress us and eventually replace them, we need to begin by understanding the processes whereby our oppression is constructed. In the context of film, I explore the politics of appropriation, for Hollywood's "naming and renaming of a race, a region, a person, is, like all acts of primordial nomination, an act of possession" (Deane, 1990, p.18). It is in the best interest of our liberation, then, that we shall face and subsequently confront the ways in which our names, bodies, and identities are seized, packaged, and marketed by the industries of culture.

IN SEARCH OF THE PUERTO RICAN WOMAN

In my attempt to discuss contemporary popular constructions of Puerto Rican womanhood I turn to three Hollywood productions that incorporate significant Puertorriqueña characters and that enjoyed relatively wide appeal by U.S. audiences.[9] Given the limited scope of this analysis, I focus on films from 1989 onward, beginning chronologically with *Do the Right Thing* (1989) and following with *White Men Can't Jump* (1992) and *It Could Happen to You* (1994). (For a more comprehensive study of Puertorriqueña representations from the 1960s to the 1990s, see Géliga Vargas, 1996).

It is impossible to loiter around the block allotted to Puerto Rican women in recent films without first paying a visit to actress Rosie Pérez. Brooklyn-born Pérez has become Hollywood's epitome of the Nuyorican (a gentile crafted, and proudly boasted of, by the generations of Puerto Ricans who have called New York their home) female: a talk fast, take none, fussin' and hustlin,' cunning woman who no matter where she goes moves at the pulse of her *barrio* ("turf"). Different from her predecessors on the screen, Pérez is not cast to ventriloquize the charicaturesque "Spanish-accented" Puerto Rican immigrants who were portrayed by Natalie Wood (*West Side Story*, 1961), Rita Moreno[10] (*West Side Story*; Popi, 1969), María Richwine (*The Buddy Holly Story*, 1978), and others. Rather she gives voice to the "take no shit," "give me mine" icon of the inner city Latina. I resort to the all-encompassing "Latina" label purposefully because one dominant trend in Hollywood's treatment of Latina/os is their ahistorical and often schizophrenic collusion in one unitary category.[11]

Pérez also represents an unusual hybrid for Hollywood, for she is the first black Puerto Rican woman to pave her way into and "make it" in the industry. Irene Cara (*Fame*, 1980) is possibly the only precedent to what I think is a progressive move in Hollywood, but her cinema days were short-lived. Because Pérez *is* a black woman, and because she has come to embody the urban poetics of "cool" on screen, sometimes it is hard to locate her characters in the continuum of cultural identities.[12]

In *Do the Right Thing* (DTRT), as in most contemporary films, the Puertorriqueña appears as a side theme-subject. That is, in contrast to earlier films like *West Side Story*, *Salsa* (1988), or *Popi*, which built on the story of a Puerto Rican family or community, here Tina (Rosie Pérez) is an isolated Puerto Rican individual in a plot about African American urban male youth confronting poverty, violence, racism, and police repression.

On the surface, Tina appears as an assertive, wayward woman who would not "take shit" from anyone. She has parented a child with

Mookie (Spike Lee), the film's protagonist, and she appears at first glance entitled and empowered to confront Mookie and make demands on his time and money. Yet, beneath the illusion of empowerment, lies her absolute powerlessness. She is objectified and victimized by Mookie and, in her most substantial scene in the film, ends up turning into his complaisant sex object. The gist of their relationship is that Tina wishes to continue her relationship with Mookie, but he refuses to commit. When the movie begins she appears tough, "but when it ends she is trapped into that old movie frame where the woman is seduced and abandoned, gaslighted again and again" (hooks, 1990, p. 183) or, in the colonial metaphor, occupied, conquered, and (s)exploited.

Although no one overtly opposes their miscegenation (which is different from the case of earlier films like *West Side Story* or *The Buddy Holly Story*), one is left with the feeling that it does not quite work. Tina is exclusively positioned in the domestic space—a dark, gloomy, and crammed apartment where she constantly quarrels with her mother in Span-glish. In the very private space of her bedroom, then, she can become involved (however subserviently and unsuccessfully) with a member of another ethnic group. In the public terrain, however, I agree with hooks (1990) in that the film's final moral is that everybody is safer and better off in their own neighborhood; that it works best if we remain with people like ourselves.

Tina is conspicuously framed as a sex object. Her objectification in the film makes it impossible for Tina to emerge as a subject. Tina's actions appear secondary to her uses, which are solely sexual and are formulated for the audience by Mookie. At its release, DTRT was praised for its counter-hegemonic discourse. However slightly, it challenges racial oppression and exposes some of the consequences capitalist accumulation and racial stratification effect on the metropolis. Nonetheless, gender oppression is not challenged but ratified, and it is the Puertorriqueña character who becomes the main target of such oppression. Her sexual involvement with Mookie turns Tina into his only secure property in an underclass urban setting where he and his black (male) community suffer the consequences of systematic dispossession. Sexual relations develop as a metaphor for domination: a pervasive ideology in the patriarchal colonialist imaginary. In a colonial situation the confinement of women to the domestic realm and the manipulation of their sexuality (and reproduction) serves both the interests of the colonized male and those of the colonizer. For the colonized man it serves as a way of safeguarding his dominance, honor, and pride in a context that constantly reminds him of his insufficiencies and impotence to achieve major changes. On the other hand, as long as the colonized male has someone to oppress and wield his power over, he channels in that direction the aggressive forces that could otherwise be directed against the empire (Ostolaza Bey, 1989).

The film splits off Tina's complex identity as a poor, black Puertorriqueña. Her woman-ness is emphasized at the expense of her Puerto Rican-ness and her condition as a member of the urban underclass. She is isolated and her only significant contact is with Mookie. Tina is not part of the Puerto Rican community which is presented a few times in the film, first fighting for their turf against Radio Raheem—one of the black youth—and later joining Mookie and other black males in rioting at the local white-owned business. The rebellious coalition of Puerto Ricans is a community of men only. Tina is not only absent from the political arena, but seems uninterested and remains ignorant of the motivations and repercussions of the violent incidents. By the end of the film she appears somewhat content with the tragic denouement of events, for now Mookie will not have a job to go to and may then stay in bed with her. As a Puertorriqueña, in contrast to some of the African American female characters, Tina appears withdrawn and apathetic to actions toward political/social change. She is clearly not a political being, but a sexual one.

This hypersexualization of Tina and her erasure from political life is lamentable, especially in the context of a story that lends itself to the possibility of imagining interethnic and cross-gender alliances. hooks (1990) has argued that *DTRT* subscribes to that strand of black nationalism promoting the exclusion of women and their role in liberation struggle. Filmmaker Spike Lee's depiction of his screen partner as a sexual artifact rather than a comrade in struggle ultimately serves to consolidate dominant ideologies about poor single women of color in urban centers. The stereotype of the hypersexual, parasitic, "Welfare" single-mom that has for so long justified massive sterilization campaigns,[13] racist litigation, and cutbacks in services for the poor, rallies support in this representation. On a contiguous and relevant front, as McClintock (1995) observes, denying colonized women any direct relation to the definition of national identity and the exercise of national agency perpetuates a gendered hierarchy that refuses women equal access to the rights and resources that may become available to their male counterparts through emancipatory struggles.

Spike Lee's (non)development of the character of Tina in *DTRT* invites us to recall how Rosie Pérez was cast for this, her very first film role. As she recounted it in an interview on the *Arsenio Show* some years ago, she was "discovered" by Lee in a Los Angeles club where she was on stage competing in a "butt contest." Lee liked what he saw and offered her the part immediately. Not to disregard the acting talents and merits that have won Pérez many other opportunities since, what the anecdote makes evident is what the director *really* had in mind when he envisioned the character of Tina.

In *White Men Can't Jump* (WMCJ), Gloria (also starring Rosie Pérez) is a more multidimensional portrayal of the "talk-tough," "let's-fuck" sex symbol embodied by Tina. Again, she appears as a deterritorialized subject in a plot about an interracial friendship between an African American man, Sidney (Wesley Snipes), and an Anglo Saxon man, Billy (Woody Harrelson). The men are basketball "hustlers" who play two-on-two games on (black) neighborhood courts for money. The action takes place in Sidney's "hood," and he is given a sense of community belonging insofar as his family and friends are involved in his movements and space. Billy is less rooted because he has recently relocated West, with girlfriend Gloria, from New York. But he soon finds his anchorage in the manly world of the basketball court. Gloria, however, remains uprooted and isolated and spends most of her time secluded in a motel room. In a scene in which she is determined to venture out into the black neighborhood (L.A's Crenshaw District), she is warned by Billy: "No, we can't go there. I'm telling you they do not let white people in the Crenshaw District; I don't know about Puerto Ricans . . . it's a reverse discrimination thing."

I have already discussed what patriarchal ideology accomplishes by circumscribing women to the domestic space in terms of disallowing their participation in the sociopolitical struggles that are being fought in the public sphere. But I think it pertinent also to consider the concomitant colonialist ideology at play when over and over again Puerto Rican women are symbolically uprooted from their communities and territory. To elaborate this point, allow me to go back to the "Good Neighbor Policy" years. During that period, most film presentations of Latin Americans located them in their homeland (even if artificially recreated in Hollywood studios). However, when films about Puerto Ricans hit the screen, they summarily ignored the native land. With few exceptions (the only one I know is *A Show of Force*, 1990), Puerto Ricans have always been situated in the United States and to this day have not been symbolically rooted via the connecting sagas that ground other Latino groups in films like Anna Thomas's and Gregory Nava's *El Norte* and *My Family*. This functions as an imperialist/universalist abstraction that denies the "real" existence of a colony. The Puerto Rican subject is isolated, removed from the land, which often functions as a metaphor for nationality. In film, the colonized Puerto Rican experiences and registers the transformations of First World life that accompany the imperial relationship. But the Puerto Rican is removed from the colonial experience, thereby hampering the emergence of nationalist discourses. This dislocation has acute political repercussions: Puerto Ricans become a people without a nation. As Jameson (1990) explains, when the "otherness" of the colonized, non-Western people is represented, this act becomes another fundamental imperialist structure of colonial appropriation: "its effects are representational effects which is to say a systematic block on any adequate consciousness of the structure of the imperial system" (p. 50).

What is interesting and potentially affirming in *WMCJ* about Gloria's escape from the domestic space is that, after episodes of distrust and indifference, she ends up "connecting" with the African American woman in the film (Sidney's wife Rhonda). They act together to set their men in place, after a dispute over money between them has made it apparent that "black and white don't mix." In an illusory act of empowerment, the women command Billy and Sidney to get together again and play in an upcoming tournament. The men appear submissive, which obscures the fact that it is precisely because they have both hitherto made all the time and money decisions and been free to move at the expense of their partners that the women are experiencing the material and emotional deprivation that made them "connect" with each other in the first place.

In the end, however, what the film really documents is the distresses and tribulations faced by Billy while trying to compete at a game and in a setting that allegedly excludes him for being white. As the title implies, *WMCJ* seeks to draw sympathy toward the white hero who, championing the cause of the "American Dream," is presented as working "honestly" and strenuously to overcome "reverse discrimination" in basketball. Billy becomes the object of mockery and ridicule by the black men on the courts, and yet he remains stoically perseverant and generally victorious. In *WMCJ*, the isolated white male appears as the triumphant victim of the story.

Gloria's character in this plot mostly works to provide comic relief and sexual gratification for both Billy and the audience. She is a former disco queen from Brooklyn whose new "trade" in L.A. is reading trivia books and waiting both for Billy to come back from the courts and for a call from "Jeopardy." They are in debt to a pair of gangsters named the Spookie Brothers, who have threatened to kill them if they do not pay back their debt. Billy is expected by Gloria to be making money on the courts so that they can get by until *Jeopardy* calls because: "It is [her] destiny to get a call from *Jeopardy*."

WMCJ echoes the depoliticization of the Puertorriqueña experience advanced by *DTRT*. Gloria's sexual identity (like Tina's) preempts her ethnic/racial one. Although the interracial friendship bond between the two males is flooded with references to ethnic conflict and racial awareness, none of these seems to affect Gloria. Unlike *West Side Story* and *Salsa*, her miscegenation with an Anglo man does not lift any eyebrows. Similarly, although Billy's interactions with African Americans are embedded in race-related arguments, Gloria's exchanges with Sidney and Rhonda do not present any such conflicts. I do not want to imply, however, that Gloria appears assimilated; she is clearly not in the mainstream of "American culture." Yet, her experiences of race and ethnicity are not as politicized as those of the males in the film. As in *West Side Story*, *Salsa*, and *Do the Right Thing*, the politics of race relations continue to be the domain of males.[14]

Nevertheless, in some respects Gloria is many steps ahead of Tina and her predecessors on the big screen. At times she appears as a subject capable of changing the course of action. Indeed, by the end of the film she has not only triumphed on *Jeopardy*, but has left Billy because he insisted on "hustling" instead of getting a job. Nevertheless, I would argue that what Gloria's departure ultimately accomplishes is the foregrounding of male bonding as the most precious alliance in the narrative. What is potentially liberating in this Puertorriqueña image, however, is that, unlike her counterparts in *West Side Story*, *Popi*, *Salsa*, and *Do the Right Thing*, Gloria is not abandoned by the man. She leaves him. She may have not controlled the conditions that led her to this, but she assumed the (qualified) power to take off. Indeed, one of the underlying subthemes in the film is that money is power, and at the end Gloria is actually the character who has made the most cash.

This presents an interesting shift in Hollywood presentations of Puertorriqueñas. In contrast to the Puerto Rican women characters in *Popi*, *Salsa*, and *Do the Right Thing*, Gloria appears more interested in securing money than in securing "her" man. Indeed, in her very first line in the film she asks Billy, "How much money did you make today?" Only later in the exchange does she ask him, "How much do you love me?" But there is not much to celebrate in this representational shift for the Puertorriqueña, for it basically endorses the very dominant patriarchal ideology that money buys sexual favors. All of the sexual encounters in the film, which are always initiated by the women and mostly by Gloria, follow scenes in which the men have brought money home.

Film and television are historically established disseminators of class expectations and notions of upward mobility. Meritocracy, or the notion that if you work hard you get a piece of the pie, is a deeply rooted ideology in popular culture. What is provoking about the cases of Gloria and Muriel (as is discussed in the analysis of the suggestively titled film *It Could Happen to You*) is that their way of "making it" is not by subscribing to the legitimized, honorable ethos of "hard work" but through more fortuitous and less dignified means, like top-scoring in *Jeopardy* or winning the lottery. This plot recourse works to keep Puerto

Rican women "in place" as members of the underclass, for their economic gains bring them money but not "class." An anecdote about the casting of Pérez for the role of Gloria in *WMCJ* provides a lucid example of
how expectations of class position and mobility are mediated in popular
culture and public discourse through ideologies of race and gender.
Gloria had been initially written as a WASP Ivy League student who
rebelled against her class and ran off with a college basketball player. In
an interview with the *New York Times*, director Ron Shelton recounts that
in the audition, Pérez's reading of the screenplay was so surprising and
truthful that he signed her immediately and changed Gloria. What
Shelton does not explain is why a Puerto Rican woman could not have
played an upper class, Ivy League college girl, and why, upon deciding
that Gloria would be a Puertorriqueña, the character had to be demoted
to the less socially laudable role of a former disco queen.

The theme of class mobility or, rather, "immobility," is an adequate segue to expand on the character of Muriel (Rosie Pérez) in the
film *It Could Happen to You*. Nicholas Cage plays Charlie, an honest, sim-
ple-minded Queens cop who is rather satisfied with his life. His wife,
Muriel, is a hairdresser who detests Queens and her husband's contentment and is filled with dreams and ambitions of living the high life. The
couple play and win New York City's $64 million lottery. But when
Muriel is about to claim the cash, she finds out that her husband has
abdicated half of their fortune. Charlie had promised a waitress
(Yvonne, played by Bridget Fonda) to whom he owed a tip that if he
won, he would split the prize with her in payment. The ensuing drama
is rather predictable. Muriel becomes greedy, pretentious, and ever
more disregarding of Charlie's "decent man" sensibilities. He seeks
refuge in the arms of Yvonne, who is herself economically and emotionally bankrupt thanks to her ex-husband's scams. Although by the end of
the story Charlie and Yvonne are broke again, New York City saves
them and their "earnest" love by sending in thousands of dollars in contributions to the "good Samaritan" couple.

Muriel is presented as nothing more than a self-absorbed, oppor-
tunistic caricature, and her on-screen pathology becomes a justification for
the "naturalized" and comfortable union of the two soft-hearted, well-
intentioned, hard-working "Americans" in the film. Ideologically loaded
notions of work ethics and ambition permeate the constant counterpoising
of Muriel and Charlie in the film. Charlie is a committed, zealous, and
heroic policeman who is totally immersed in the duties of his job, to the
point of putting his life on the line to save his "favorite Korean" from
ruthless, though imbecilic, muggers. Charlie's virtuous act refills the popular imaginary with the all too familiar image of the police as benevolent
guardian angels—symbolism that is particularly at odds with the lived

experiences of many urban communities of color (as *Do the Right Thing* attempts to expose). Muriel, on the other hand, is an ambitious hairdresser who yearns for the vanity and frivolity of high-class standards. Her actions, in contrast to Charlie's, are depicted as rather wicked, if not downright pathological, and Muriel appears as nothing more than a "fussing, greedy bitch." The opening sequence of the film, structured as a fairy tale, sets the tone for how Muriel will be read throughout::

10-year-old boy:	You are not gonna see your wife?
Charlie:	No, she doesn't like me to surprise her at work.
Narrator:	Charlie was married to Muriel. She hated Queens!
Muriel:	If he was a detective or another kind of cop, at least he'd have some decent clothes. But that's not for him. He's gotta wear that uniform.
Customer:	I feel for you honey, 'cuz you got driving ambition.
Muriel:	I never pushed him enough. If he was on the take, at least I'd say, "OK, he has initiative." But no!
Customer:	My sister was married to a cop for 10 years, and it's a no-win situation. Either they are honest and you're broke, or they are crooks and they never come home.
Muriel:	So, your sister, what did she do?
Customer:	She left the cop and married an electrician. That's your real money.
Muriel:	I'm running out of patience. I tell you, I'm a person who needs money.

And as the story evolves, we witness that she will do anything to get it. But her zealousness is not rewarded.

There are two film codes through which Muriel's "pathology" is exacerbated. The first one is speech as her fast-paced, agitated talk in heavy New York-accented English with some splashes of Spanish contrasts with the soft-spoken, caring demeanor of both Charlie and Yvonne. Thus, in the ensuing exchanges, Muriel appears "out there" and "beyond control," which elicits negative responses from nearly all the characters in the film. Muriel's speech invites curtailment, which is accomplished in the "I-told-you-so" tone with which the final words about her failure are pronounced in the film. The second code is costume, and Muriel once again stands out as an "Other." Her taste and choices in clothing and decor appear tacky to the eyes and in the context of those around her. These codes function, much more concertedly and vividly than in *WMCJ*, to ridicule the notion of upward mobility for Puertorriqueñas, for money buys neither "class" nor entry into the Anglo framework of aesthetic sensibilities.

By the end of the film, the ideology has been reinstated that God rewards those who are good, honest, and content with what they have.[15] And to further consolidate the film's alignment with the racist, sexist, and classist status quo, Muriel's ambitions and eccentricities are condemned. The moral of the story is built around Muriel's punishment, as could be distilled from the narrator's marshaling remarks:

> It took Charlie and Yvonne three days to open up all that mail, and when they were done, New York had given them a $600,000 tip. Charlie happily went back to the force. Yvonne got her coffee shop back . . . and Muriel!: She married Jack Gross who cleaned out that checking account and fled the country. Muriel lives in the Bronx with her mother now . . . and works in a nail salon.

And so Muriel returns to where she began. Is this metaphor for social "immobility" a presage of what awaits the Puerto Rican woman struggling today to survive in urban centers under decaying social and economic conditions? Or is it a admonition regarding the permitted range of movement for nondominant constituencies in the empire? Either way, and similar to the preceding examples, the Puertorriqueña is bound to remain in symbolic marginality.

SO WHAT? THEY ARE JUST MOVIES!

Yes, they are. But they also have intent and meaning and are part of the popular imaginary to which we subconsciously turn when we need to find a piece to the puzzle.

Given the inveterate history of racial segregation in the United States and its contemporary permutations in the increasing gentrification of the nation's cities, these Hollywood images are the only contact that millions of "Americans" and other groups have with Puertorriqueñas. Even if they eventually interact in "real life" with Puerto Rican people, these representations are frequently the sediment through which any subsequent contact percolates. Or else, why is it that to this day, upon entering the Anglo-dominated spaces of the workplace or school, so many of us are still greeted with the humiliating, though admittedly catchy, tune of *West Side Story*'s "I like to live in America"?[16] And these are only the subtle consequences. Some of the more profound and life-threatening ones can be heard daily in the rhetoric of anti-immigration, Welfare reform, English-only, and enforced sterilization sponsors. But this is not just about extremists on the Right. Many of our fairly well-intentioned teachers and public service providers operate from the same mindframe, as the autobiographical novel by Esmeralda Santiago, *When I was a Puerto Rican* (1994), so forcefully and poetically recounts.

As decades of research in cultural studies have taught us, the intended meaning of a cultural product need not remain intact when its consumers make it their own. As audience members, we actively engage with media texts and negotiate their meaning, reinterpreting their codes in correspondence to our own personal and social baggage of knowledge and experiences. My interpretations of these characters and films, although privileged inasmuch as it is grounded on detailed analysis and engaged in a broader project of social critique, is by no means exclusive. Other plausible interpretations may emerge. But those are going to need to rely on some other frames of reference, in ways that may reflect the popular imaginary so tightly encircled within racist, patriarchal, and capitalist ways of seeing. This popular imagery has been instrumental in maintaining the racist status quo, a dynamic that Hall (1992) explains most eloquently:

> One aspect of racism is that it occupies a world of machinean opposites: them and us, primitive and civilized, black and white. . . . The great divisions of racism are a way of masking how deeply our histories intertwine and interpenetrate: how necessary the "Other" is to our sense of identity; how even the colonizing power only knows who and what it is and can only experience the pleasure of its own power of domination in and through the construction of "Other." And the Other is not out there but in here. (pp. 16-17)

How much different would public policy be if "America" ceased splitting itself, claiming the "good" (like in the characters of Charlie and Yvonne) and transferring its negative parts onto us? How different would Puertorriqueña processes of cultural identity formation and affirmation be if the media presented a world in which the Puerto Rican woman is not isolated, is not uprooted, is not (s)exploited, in which she is the focus of attention, her concerns and experiences not on the margins but at the fore?

The images offered by Hollywood have acute repercussions for the identity construction of Puerto Rican women and girls. We have our lived experiences to turn to for a context and to reflect on, but we, like everybody else, have a need to *see* ourselves reflected. For many women whose stories I have listened to, it has been a cold-blooded stab when their children return from school, the mall, or the movies and say, "I want to be white." This speaks of a dire need to escape the isolation that comes from not seeing ourselves as part of the world around us, from speaking a language that does not speak us. This is why Tina, Gloria, and Muriel matter: because they fill a void and become "representative." And they do so authoritatively, given that Hollywood's monopoly over Puerto Rico's film industry has obliterated the possibility of the emergence of a sizable national cinema. The few films that are produced locally cannot compete with Hollywood's mega-productions and thus end up circulating in narrow, cinema-art circles. The constraints in funding for distribution also ensure that the progressive work of U.S.-based Puertorriqueña filmmakers like Ana M. García and Frances Negrón Muntaner rarely reach beyond academic and film festival contexts.

But Tina, Gloria, and Muriel also, and importantly, matter because they open a space and incite reflection on who is the Puertorriqueña. They do for audiences pretty much what the angry *lady* wanting to get on the bus did for the proud Puerto Rican *nena*. They add a dimension, a reference for the ever-evolving reconfiguration of Puertorriqueña cultural identity.

ENDNOTES

1. My heartfelt *gracias* to Juana for blessing me with the wisdom of her revealing and ever-captivating stories. My apologies to her and the reader for a translation that could never replicate the liveliness of her original words.
2. This framing of the question of Puertorriqueña identity is not entirely original. Three decades after the military invasion of Puerto Rico by the United States, which brought an end to four centuries of Spanish colonial control over the territory, the debate over national identity for Puerto Ricans could not be postponed. The editors of the journal *Índice* orchestrated a forum in 1929 to address the question *¿qué somos y cómo somos?* ("what are we and how are we?"). Today, after nearly a century of U.S. domination over Puerto Rico and with generations of Puerto Ricans now settled permanently in the United States, this discussion continues to be as pressing for Puerto Rican intellectuals. (For a comprehensive review of the contemporary debate, see Flores, 1993). However, with very few exceptions (notably, Acosta-Belén, 1980), gender/sexual identity has not figured in the ever-extending equations of what constitutes Puerto Rican national/cultural identity.
3. In my writing I use the word "America" and its gentile "American" in quotations in order to make explicit my discomfort with the imperialist construction of this term. The notion of "America" as one country (the United States) as opposed to two

continents is a prime example of the ethnocentric, universalist abstractions informing U.S. imperialism. America extends all the way from Argentina to Alaska, and Americans are all the peoples and cultures that occupy and transform this multiethnic landscape.

4. *Hegemony*, a concept developed by Antonio Gramsci (1971), is a way of understanding the distribution of power in the contemporary social order. It designates the cultural leadership of the dominant classes in the production of generalized meanings, of "common sense," and of consent to the prevailing arrangement of social relations which in turn stabilizes the enduring leadership of the dominant class. Hall (1980b) notes that the dominant class is not a unitary, fixated, and unproblematic "ruling class," but rather an alliance of class strata that is subject to changes and regeneration. The wielding of power under hegemony is thus never absolute, as it perpetually needs to reinvigorate itself by a combination of coercion and consent of the dominated classes.

5. For a well-researched and compelling account of how the sexual fantasies created and marketed by Hollywood impacted social life, see the documentary *Carmen Miranda: Bananas is my Business* (directed by Helena Solberg and David Meyer, 1994).

6. U.S. citizenship was forced onto the Puerto Rican people in 1917.

7. The permutations of the racist common sense that inform popular representations of Puerto Ricans in the United States can be traced back to the pioneer enterprise of *Cry Tough* (1959). The film presents Sarita, a dance hall hostess who will be deported to Puerto Rico unless she marries a U.S. citizen. Miguel agrees to marry her although he cannot fulfill her ambition for wealth. Eventually, she leaves him because she can no longer stand poverty (Oshana, 1985). In addition to its sexist and racist (albeit still typical) characterization of women of color as opportunists who find their way to upward mobility through the granting of sexual favors, the film reflects the reigning state of ignorance about the Puerto Rican people. The producers overlooked the fact that all Puerto Ricans are United States citizens. Although the film industry invested in documenting their presentations of Latin America during the war years, a decade later they did not even bother to corroborate the most basic information about the country's own "possession."

8. Here I am paraphrasing Hall (1980a) and expanding on his elaboration of the workings of ideology, which he caters primarily to questions of race.

9. A recent and important film, *I Like it Like That* (1994), has a Puertorriqueña as its protagonist. However, because it was a low-budget production, its circulation and audiences were rather limited. It would be interesting, although certainly the task of a separate investigation, to compare notions of Puertorriqueña identity aired by this low-budget and female-produced film to those of mainstream Hollywood.

10. In the insightful documentary *Carmen Miranda: Bananas is My Business* (1994), Rita Moreno reflects on the absurdities of characterization for most of the roles she played during her Hollywood acting career, which totaled more than a dozen films. She talks about how she was coached to talk in an exaggerated, charicaturesque, high-pitch Spanish accent that bore no resemblance to anybody's, and certainly not her own "Spanish" accent. This reaffirms the degree to which Hollywood films interpellate an Anglo, mainstream imaginary for whom the farce allegedly provokes comic relief while neatly maintaining the *cordon sanitaire* between what is "normal"—us—and what is "strange"—them.

11. One place where this is painfully palpable is in the character of Chi Chi Rodríguez in the 1996 film *Too Wong Foo, Thanks for Everything!* Played by Colombian actor John Leguizamo, Chi Chi is a "Latina" drag queen from New York who, given the location and setting of the story and her peculiar Span-glish accentuation, may be seen by most as Puerto Rican. Yet, when she is first approached by the queens who will eventually become her "aunties" and mentors, she is addressed by Vida (Patrick Swayze) and Noxeema (Wesley Snipes) as "little Latin boy." During the course of their journey through middle "America," Chi Chi will be called everything from "piñata," to "Sandinista," "Spanish soul," "border-crosser," "spic," "puta Spanish fly," and "swayed back Third World thing." Following the all too familiar melting pot recipe, here Mexico, Nicaragua, Spain, Puerto Rico, possibly all of Central America, and nearly half of the world come together in one single character! This convolution of Latino experiences and icons (and certainly stereotypes) is also present in some of the characters played by Pérez, such as her role as Carla in *Fearless* (1993).

12. In the New York stop of Jim Jarmusch's road movie about cabbies and their passengers (*Night on Earth*, 1991), Pérez plays Angela, and it is very plausible to assume, as most of my students have over the years, that she is an African American woman. What these ambiguities call for is a detailed exploration of spectators' engagement with cinema language and codes so as to unveil the mechanisms whereby audiences are able to "tell" (regardless of whether their impressions are "accurate") the ethnic identity of the characters displayed on the screen. Because this is the task of a much more encompassing project, I adhere here to films in which it is made explicit that the character in question is a Puertorriqueña.

13. Curtailment of reproductive freedom has been possibly the most pervasive form of US. control over the Puerto Rican woman. After World War II, the U.S. government devised two ways to counter the alleged overpopulation of the Puerto Rican archipelago. One was to "facilitate" migration of Puerto Ricans to the United States; the other was to coerce women into sterilization. The results are appalling: nearly 50% of the Puerto Rican women of childbearing

age had been sterilized by the mid-1980s. (For more on the capitalist rationale underpinning migration and sterilization policies in Puerto Rico, see Ostolaza Bey, 1989).

14. A more recent film featuring the same interracial duet of Wesley Snipes and Woody Harrelson (*Money Train*, 1995) once again turns to a Puerto Rican woman (played by Jennifer López) as the deracialized object of desire for both the characters and the implied audience. John (Snipes) and Charlie (Harrelson) are work partners, life-long best friends and foster brothers, and yet their exchanges are flooded with expressions of racial consciousness and conflicts. However, their interactions with their female Puerto Rican co-worker (who they both want to claim as a sexual conquest) bear no references to her ethnic/racial identity or to her experiencing any such conflicts.

15. As the denouement of the story makes evident, it is indeed God who intervenes! The film ends as Charlie and Yvonne are lifted into the sky in a hot air balloon that billboards "Cop weds waitress," and the oracular voice of the narrator captions: "Charlie, Muriel and Yvonne all lived in a city where people prayed for miracles everyday . . . and sometimes they happened."

16. For a compelling account of how this was the case even in encounters with European people, see Vázquez, 1990-91.

REFERENCES

Acosta-Belén, E. (1980). *La mujer en la sociedad puertorriqueña* [Women in Puerto Rican society]. Río Piedras: Huracán.

Althusser, L. (1971). *Lenin and philosophy and other essays*. London: New Left Books.

Deane, S. (1990). Introduction. In T. Eagleton, F. Jameson, & E. W. Said (Eds.), *Nationalism, colonialism and literature* (pp. 3-18). Minneapolis: University of Minnesota Press.

Flores, J. (1993). *Divided borders: Essays on Puerto Rican identity*. Houston: Arte Público Press.

Géliga Vargas, J. (1996). Expanding the popular culture debate: A case study of Hollywood's constructed Puertorriqueaña identity. *Studies in Latin American Popular Culture, 15*, 2-19.

Gramsci, A. (1971). *Selections from the prison notebooks*. London: Lawrence and Wishart.

Hall, S. (1980a). The whites of their eyes. In G. Bridges & R. Blunt (Eds.), *Silver linings: Some strategies for the eighties* (pp. 33-42). London: Lawrence and Wishart.

Hall, S. (1980b). Cultural studies at the Centre. In S. Hall et al. (Eds.), *Culture, media, language* (pp. 117-121). London: Hutchinson.

Hall, S. (1992). Race, culture, and communications: Looking backward and forward at cultural studies. *Rethinking Marxism, 1*, 10-18.

hooks, b. (1990). *Yearning: Race, gender and cultural politics*. Boston: South End Press.

Jameson, F. (1990). Modernism and imperialism. In In T. Eagleton, F. Jameson, & E. W. Said (Eds.), *Nationalism, colonialism and literature* (pp. 43-66). Minneapolis: University of Minnesota Press.

Jhally, S., & Lewis, J. (1992). *Enlightened racism: Audiences, the Cosby Show, and the myth of the American dream*. Boulder, CO: Westview Press.

Lacayo, R. (1988, July 11). A surging new spirit. *Time*, pp. 46-49.

López, A. (1991). Are all Latins from Manhattan? Hollywood, ethnography and cultural colonialism. In L. Friedman (Ed.), *Unspeakable images* (pp. 404-423). Urbana & Chicago: University of Illinois Press.

McClintock, A. (1995). *Imperial leather: Race, gender and sexuality in the colonial contest*. New York: Routledge.

Oshana, M. (1985). *Women of color: A filmography of minority and third world women*. New York & London: Garland Publishing.

Ostolaza Bey, M. (1989). *Política sexual en Puerto Rico* [Sexual politics in Puerto Rico]. Río Piedras: Ediciones Huracán.

Santiago, E. (1994). *When I was a Puerto Rican*. New York: Vintage Books.

Shohat, E. (1991). Imaging terra incognita: The disciplinary gaze of empire. *Public Culture, 3*, 41-70.

Shohat, E., & Stam, R. (1994). *Unthinking Euro-centrism: Multiculturalism and the media*. London & New York: Routledge.

Time. (1988, July 11). Vol. 132, no. 2.

Vázquez, B. (1990-91, Winter). Puerto Ricans and the media: A personal statement. *Centro, 3*(1), 4-15.

Woll, A. (1980). *The Latin image in American film*. Los Angeles: UCLA Latin American Center Publications.

8

From Rags to Riches: The Story of Class Advancement in Women's Figure Skating Coverage

Bettina Fabos

Three weeks before the 1994 Olympics in Lillehammer, Norway, figure skater Nancy Kerrigan was brutally clubbed on the knee after a routine practice during the National Championships in Detroit. Her fragile, sobbing image quickly dominated the nation's news media (television cameras had been present at her practice), and investigations soon implicated associates of rival American figure skater Tonya Harding. Reports suggested that Harding herself had masterminded the attack. Harding, an athletic skater with a muscular physique and—like Kerrigan—a working-class background, was quickly cast as a wicked, jealous "witch" who had just handed Snow White a poisoned apple (Gibbons, 1994).

The media's adoration of Kerrigan and dislike for Harding had been evident as early as the 1992 coverage of the Winter Olympics at Albertville, France. Kerrigan was described as elegant and gorgeous by sideline commentators. She had classic Northern European features and thus epitomized the western ideal of what a princess was supposed to look like. She had a humble blue-collar background, doting parents, and a mother who was legally blind (and, as the story went, could never see how *beautiful* her daughter was). She also was a contender for the gold medal (or "crown jewel"). In essence, Kerrigan fit perfectly into the familiar narrative of a rags-to-riches fairy tale, in which a poor girl acquires fame and fortune because of her beauty and comportment.

Harding was one of two skaters in the world capable of mastering fantastically difficult jumps and beating Kerrigan, but the media had cast her as reckless, shattered, thoughtless, overweight, and sexually tainted. By 1994, and in the spotlight of an incredible media blitz, Kerrigan had become an icon representing the proper image, behaviors, and values that would triumphantly bring her access to middle-class status and beyond. Harding, who lacked Kerrigan's beauty capital, represented an evil opposite and was framed as hopelessly, unforgivingly, and permanently working class.

This analysis shows how the mass media negotiates, interprets, and reinforces an American value system that is based on: (a) largely uncontested constructs of gender roles in our society, and (b) rigid behavioral expectations. Rather than broaching the uncomfortable topic of culturally constructed beauty capital as a root of female class difference, the media identified the individual attributes of personality and behavior as the underlying causes of inequality between Kerrigan and Harding. These individual inequalities made for dramatic stories—stories in which Kerrigan was cast as an icon representing (and reinforcing) female class mobility.

THE SKATING WORLD AS A PLACE FOR CLASS ADVANCEMENT

Although it has a history of upper class attachments (coaches on the sidelines often wear furs, commentators sport tuxes, and "serious training can easily cost $40,000 a year in coaching fees, costumes, skates, and living expenses" [Duffy, 1994a, p. 55]), figure skating has recently been transformed from a sport for the privileged leisure class into a money-making enterprise for all classes. Training money from the U.S. Figure Skating Association is now allocated to skaters who show promise, and lucrative corporate endorsements are handed to young, amateur skaters who not only skate well but are considered marketable. As skating events became more popularized during the 1990s, stories began to routinely acknowledge the substantial monetary possibilities in a successful skating career. "There's more to having relatives in the Olympics than medals and national pride," NBC's Pete Wilson reported. "Champion skaters can earn up to $10 million in product endorsements" (Wilson,

1994). With such big money, the skating world has become an attractive site for the media to explore stories about upward mobility.

CLASS AND GENDER

Kerrigan's story, like most fairy tales, explained class access for women in terms of beauty capital. Beauty capital, in American culture, is a legitimate and necessary qualification for a woman's rise in wealth, power, and class status. According to Wolf (1992),

> Since men have used women's "beauty" as a form of currency in circulation among men, ideas about "beauty" have evolved since the Industrial Revolution side by side with ideas about money, so that the two are virtual parallels in our consumer economy. A woman looks like a million dollars, she's a first-class beauty, her face is her fortune. In the bourgeois marriage markets of the last century, women learned to understand their own beauty as part of this economy. (p. 20)

Popular stories and folk tales, like *Cinderella, My Fair Lady*, and *Pretty Woman*, link class access for women with beauty capital. Even real-life fairy tales, like the rise of Grace Kelly from middle-class Philadelphia native to princess of Monaco, reinforce the cultural myth that all women need is beauty to achieve stability and wealth. Whereas Horatio Alger-type rags-to-riches stories (repopularized during the Reagan era) dwell on men's uncommon savvy and determination to explain their class transcendence (e.g., Lee Iacocca, Steven Spielberg, Bill Clinton), women's rags-to-riches stories rely on culturally approved and endorsed images of beauty to explain their class advancement.

Competitive figure skating makes it easy for the media to celebrate women's beauty as a means for success. Skating judges traditionally favor artistic skaters (thin, long-limbed—code "feminine" and "beautiful"), and looks are as paramount for the mass media. "What appeals to the sports audience," said sports commentator Frank Deford, is "whatsoever is most beautiful, whatsoever is most lovely, whatsoever is most sexy" (Deford, 1992, p. 50). Whereas male skaters are described in terms of their technical merit, intelligence, steely resolve, and an extraordinary determination to master their routine, their female counterparts have pluck and luck and can only dream of, instead of impel, their success. Consequently, media narratives for women's skating competitions are spun around the sport's "prettiest" skater. Without her culturally approved and endorsed image of beauty, Kerrigan's media stardom and subsequent corporate sponsorships would have been far less likely.

Although Kerrigan was almost universally characterized as a working-class Cinderella with upwardly mobile looks, she was also understood as a "girl next door" with upwardly mobile behaviors and desires. Whenever Kerrigan exhibited an upwardly mobile middle-class mannerism, the media applauded it to firmly position her in that world. In effect, Kerrigan was cast to join the other middle-class characters that dominate American media. According to Butsch (1995), characters with middle-class occupations drastically outnumber characters from all other classes in mainstream media (p. 403). These middle-class characters, Ehrenreich (1990) writes, are "taken as a social norm—a bland and neutral mainstream, from which every other group or class is ultimately a kind of deviation" (p. 3). Whereas working-class characters are generally described in terms of sloth, imprudence, or self-indulgence (e.g., Harding), upper class characters are often depicted as spoiled, arrogant, or goofy. Characters from these "deviant" classes are embraced only when they exhibit "normal" middle-class behaviors and desires (e.g., Kerrigan) (see Thomas & Callahan, 1982; Thomas & LeShay, 1992).

By saturating their pages and programs with "normal" middle-class stories, the mass media appear legitimate and relatively autonomous from upper class interests and influence. However, stories about middle-class upward mobility ultimately reinforce upper class dominance by maximizing audience revenues (they address the largest public segment) and by depicting characters who aspire to—and thus validate—upper class lifestyles. According to Hall (1977), "the media serve, in societies like ours, ceaselessly to perform the critical ideological work of 'classifying out the world' within the discourse of the dominant ideologies" (p. 346). Kerrigan, for instance, was "classified" to represent and celebrate middle-class upward mobility. Whereas her beauty capital promised her a middle-class identity and with it the possibility of further advancement, Kerrigan was further cast as the embodiment of all middle-class values. These values—of not failing, not indulging, remaining pure, secure and focussed on reaching "higher goals"—are handily represented in the skating world. Thus, Kerrigan was positively positioned in terms of authenticity, hard work, and strong "family values," proper mannerisms to which she was expected to adhere.

KERRIGAN IS AUTHENTIC AND NONCOMPETITIVE

That Kerrigan was described as "authentic" socially identified her as upwardly mobile. "The middle class uses consumption to establish its [educated] status, especially relative to the working class. Typically, this has meant an emphasis on things 'authentic,' 'natural,' and 'frequently imported'" (Ehrenreich, 1990, p. 14). Kerrigan's natural hair color and hairstyle were seen as uncomplicated, honest, and pure. Reports that Kerrigan's skating costumes were original designs from prestigious designers (e.g., Vera Wang, the celebrated designer of wedding dresses for the East Coast's elite) increased her luster of authenticity. In contrast to Harding, who was lambasted for her cheap, homemade, immodest costumes and "common" styles of dress, Kerrigan shone as the desirable alternative. Confirmed Margaret Carlson of *Time*: "The millions of people who have followed this drama want an international duel in which good sportsmanship, staying within type and fair play are triumphant; where intact families, modest costumes, chemical-free hair and good teeth are rewarded" (1994, p. 58).

Kerrigan was similarly applauded for upholding the glamour and prestige of her sport. Her graceful body lines, routines with classical ballet movements, and orchestral musical selections won her gushing comparisons to Grace Kelly, Jacqueline Kennedy Onassis, and Katherine Hepburn for her "disciplined poise." In addition to princess status, the media gave Kerrigan a virginal, wholesome, girl-next-door representation that cornered on her modest appearance and "tasteful," upwardly mobile behavior. During her press conferences after the knee-bashing, Kerrigan was described as silent and serene, with reports marveling at her tact, lack of pretension, and seeming lack of outward competitiveness and desire for revenge. "Kerrigan's only comment," explained ABC's Bob Jamieson, "was that the attack could have been worse" (Jamieson, 1994).

Kerrigan's representation as "noncompetitive" was an important distinction. The Olympic Figure Skating event is, obviously, a competition. But figure skating, unlike football, basketball, or hockey, has long been positioned in terms of the more prestigious realm of artistic spectacle (such as a ballet or opera), and thus it upholds signifiers of "high culture" enjoyed primarily by the upper and upper middle classes (Gans, 1974). In Bourdieu's (1993) discussion of class habitus in the realm of sport, he relates the more privileged class sports, such as equestrian sports or figure skating, with body development, expertise, rational noncompetitiveness, and deferred satisfactions (scores), while associating working-class sports with elements of risk, strength, body contact, and competitiveness. That Kerrigan was described as noncompetitive in a sport idealized as "noncompetitive" reaffirmed her upwardly mobile social standing.

During the past decade, skating has become more outwardly competitive, however. When freestyle figure skating was made the most important element in skating competition[1] the event evolved into a drama in which artistic skaters, typically favored by judges and the media, were "challenged" by athletic skaters who threw in risky and physically demanding jumps. Although the artistic versus athletic tension was good for ratings, the media echoed skating industry worries that athletic jumping threatened to defeminize the sport and represented an intrusion of working-class culture. For instance, of the two women able to successfully complete a triple axle in competition in 1994, one of them was Tonya Harding.

Comments from skating coach Sonya Dunfield illustrate the fear of skating's new athletic "jumpers":

> The fact that we don't do any school figures, it's just jump jump jump jump jump now, we've forgotten part of our sport. The grace of figure skating is not really there anymore. Just because we don't go over a finish line we should still try to do a rounded sport and not just barrel and think you're going to do one jump and you're going to make it. So that I think — that it is changing, and I came from Brooklyn, too, so I have a background from where I was brought up and I don't think that should have anything to do with my thoughts. (cited in Tillotson, 1994)

As Dunfield implies, even working-class skaters, like herself and Nancy Kerrigan, can embrace upper class aesthetics if they try hard enough, eschew risky jumps, and have the right body type and image. The ultimate message, we are reassured, is that if artistic skaters continue to be rewarded as they have been in the past, then the skating world is safe as a bastion for the upper classes and as an arena for middle-class aspiration.

Figure skating's stylistic struggle between rationalized artistry and competitive athleticism was strained even further with the physical assault on Kerrigan. Suddenly the glamour sport, according to the media, was transformed from an abstract competition into a "contact" sport. Commentators feared that the pristine image of figure skating was forever smeared, again, by a working-class affront. Although other examples of mean-spirited rivalry among skaters—including physical harm, tripping, torn costumes, and other forms of skate sabotage—later crept into the narrative (Gibbons, 1994; Raphael, 1994), Tonya Harding was continually used as the primary example of invasion and corruption.

KERRIGAN SACRIFICES AND WORKS HARD

The idea of sacrifice so commonly associated with the arduous world of ice skating competition meshes nicely with the American model of upward mobility that honors strict regimen, physical, emotional and financial sacrifice; and the gradual amassing of cultural capital for future gain. One must avoid indulgence because, the rhetoric intones, the goal is to rise up, not slip back. Accordingly, Kerrigan's knack for personal sacrifice was celebrated well before she was bashed on the knee. In the months before the Olympics, the media told audiences that Kerrigan had been "training harder than ever. Brimming with more confidence than ever. . . . She's never worked this hard before . . . she's never done the run-throughs she's doing now. Double run-throughs. Going for perfect run-throughs" (Swift, 1994, p. 17).

Kerrigan's ultimate testament to striving and sacrificing was her tenacity after the vicious attempt by a rival faction to destroy her career, her "life work" (Starr, p. 41). Now, she had to face physical pain and emotional stress to attain the 1994 gold medal. The story played as a perfect example of overcoming extenuating circumstances through perseverance and a positive attitude. "Nancy's not a victim," fellow skater and Harvard graduate Paul Wylie wrote in a *Newsweek* column. "She's a survivor" (Wylie, 1994, p. 21). Kerrigan's apparent ability for sacrifice was systematically enhanced during CBS's coverage of the U.S. National Championships, where the injured skater was videotaped through the tinted glass of a luxury box, sitting out the rest of the event. The coverage returned to the shot as a point of juxtaposition after every skater finished her routine and each time the program cut to a commercial break. We were guided to feel Kerrigan's sorrow and yearning, so that her point of view came to dominate the event's media narrative.

Reports of Kerrigan's prevailing determination were accompanied by reports of Kerrigan's emotional and physical hardships during childhood. She was commanded to "suffer in silence" when her skates were too small (Plummer & Reed, 1994, p. 59). She would rise at 4 a.m., skate before school, do her homework, and crash at 7 p.m. Kerrigan also had "earned a two-year associate degree in business at nearby Emmanuel College" (p. 61), reinforcing her image of sharing the middle-class drive for education. Because her life was so full of regimen, we learned that she had few friends: sexual flirtations or any other deviations or vices were out of the question. This profile of abstinence and sacrifice was further reinforced when CBS and all but the rarest of media coverage avoided the fact that Kerrigan had at one point been engaged (see Sherman, 1993, p. 203).

Beyond Kerrigan's personal sacrifices, her family also was described in terms of their stoic ability to scrimp and save. Precariously remortgaging their family home and taking out loans to finance their daughter's "life work," Kerrigan's family was applauded for their continued sacrifices, which made them likable and "normal." "'Since Nancy started skating,' her father Dan was quoted as saying, 'the family hasn't been on a real vacation. We go to skating events'" (Plummer & Reed, p. 59).

The ultimate sacrifice, in many ways, seemed to come from Kerrigan's father. Viewers were continuously reminded he was a welder, a job that firmly positioned him as a blue-collar patriarch. Besides Dan Kerrigan's other working-class jobs, which had included opening the ice rink in the early mornings where his daughter had trained, we also learned that he did the shopping, cooking, and laundry because his wife, Brenda, was legally blind. Dan was thus presented as sacrificing his "proper" role within the family while working long hours in the public sphere—a double sacrifice.

KERRIGAN HAS AN INTACT FAMILY

The representation of the Kerrigan family mirrored the post-World War II sentiment—repopularized during the 1980s—that the nuclear family was the favored model of family bliss and upward mobility (Coontz, 1992; Spigel, 1992). If there ever was an intact family that turned toward home and worked together for family betterment, it was, we were told, the Kerrigan family. We first got to know the Kerrigans two years prior to the 1994 Winter Games during CBS's 1992 Winter Olympic coverage, through constant images of Kerrigan's parents, Dan and Brenda, cheering their daughter and waiting anxiously for her marks. These parents, we were told early on, were not too busy to help their children with their homework. The 1994 coverage of the assault on Kerrigan exploded with defining shots of and references to Kerrigan's family: Her father gently scooping her up—child-like—after her attack; her family by Kerrigan's side; extensive press commentary on how Kerrigan's "close family has always been her mainstay, the lump of gold Harding never had" (Duffy, 1994b, p. 53); and sympathetic interviews with the Kerrigan family in their home, including shots with roses carefully arranged in the background, and scenes in which the Kerrigans ate cake with Connie Chung (Chung, 1994). The Kerrigans were shown to embody everything that seemed to be right with the intact American family.

The media's tendency to position this intact family as a middle-class phenomenon was evident in the shifting descriptions of Kerrigan's hometown, from "blue-collar Stoneham, Mass," (Adler, 1994a, p. 70) to a "middle-class Boston suburb" (Starr, 1994, p. 44). The Kerrigan household was described as a "sanctuary" (Plummer & Reed, 1994, p. 56) to which Kerrigan came home to mend, where it was warm and comfortable, and where, we were led to assume, everybody got along—again, a testament to the success of nuclear family values. The Kerrigans even watched television together in their living room and marveled—along with so many other Americans—at the unfolding stories of the seedy, working-class world of Tonya Harding. "Even the Kerrigan family, holed up in their home in suburban Stoneham, Mass., was finding the tale of low-rent—and, fortunately incompetent—lowlifes mesmerizing"(Adler, 1994a, p. 70). Reports highlighted the skater's dependency on her family network by noting that despite all of her endorsements, Nancy still needed the help of her family. "Even now, when the money from Campbell's Soup and Reebok is starting to flow, the Kerrigans still pitch in, ironing their daughter's fancy dresses: Brenda, barely able to see, wields the iron, Dan guides her on where to place it" (Duffy, 1994b, p. 56). The Kerrigans were shown to embrace class advancement and would not, we were assured, lose or forget their middle-class ideals.

PERSONALIZING CLASS DIFFERENCE

In the onslaught of media coverage that tried to make sense of Harding's "hardness" and Kerrigan's "perfection," the media chose to compare the two skaters in terms of their individual characters and personal tastes, rather than investigate a broader underlying context for their culturally determined social placements. The ultimate conclusion of the media was that Kerrigan, having the proper looks and embracing middle-class values, was to be adored. Harding, who had no intention of changing her ways, was to be admonished. Media comparisons between Kerrigan and Harding became the basis for most figure skating narratives of 1994:

> Kerrigan's smile was dazzling even in her press conference the day after the beating, while Harding's expression is a wolfish grin. Kerrigan has taken up the hobby appropriate to her new station in life—golf—while Harding has pursued interests including auto repair, hunting and pool. Kerrigan's first scheduled public performance after the attack was at a benefit for her favorite charity, the Lion's Club SightFirst campaign (her mother is legally blind). Harding, afforded an opportunity to say something inspirational on her return home from Portland, Ore., after the Nationals, ringingly declared that "what I'm really thinking about are dollar signs". . . . In Detroit, Kerrigan dressed in a demure white outfit; Harding posed in an eye-catching, lavishly spangled purple costume. Kerrigan swoops across the ice with the effortless grace of a young sapling in the breeze, while Harding hurls herself into her jumps like a steeple chaser. At 5 foot 1, three inches shorter than Kerrigan,

she cuts a powerful but not especially elegant figure on the ice.—
Jerry Adler, *Newsweek* (1994b, p. 20)

Nancy Kerrigan has already cashed in as the girl next door. But
Tonya Harding, who can fix a pickup truck, has struggled with an
image of toughness, not quite the one advertisers would bring back
home.—Brian Rooney, *ABC* (1994)

Kerrigan, talking to the press last week, showed the natural elegance
and smile that could be worth millions.—Photo caption, *Time*
(January 24, 1994, p. 54)

Harding is neither politic nor polished, sociable nor sophisticated.
Instead, she is the bead of raw sweat in a field of dainty perspirers;
the asthmatic who heaves uncontrollably while others pant prettily;
the pool-playing, drag-racing, trash-talking bad girl of a sport that
thrives on illusion and politesse.—Jill Smolowe, *Time* (1994, p. 51)

Without Harding in the gritty shadows—as symbolically illustrated by the *Time* cover featuring Kerrigan in the foreground, dressed in
white, leaping lightly over a darkened, grainy enlargement of Harding's
face (1994, Feb. 21)—Kerrigan would not have seemed so resolute, so
perfect, such an ideal embodiment of everything that is right and good
with America. According to Fiske (1987), "social and political issues are
only reported if they can be embodied in the individual, and thus social
conflict of interest is personalized in the conflict between individuals"
(p. 284). By personalizing conflict, difference, and inequality, and by letting these stories represent the broader realm, the media can consequently make sense of the conflict while vigorously maintaining and
defining what is considered to be normal.

The class lines between Kerrigan, as upwardly mobile working
class, and Harding, as immobile working class, were not only clearly
defined, they were defined viciously, openly, and with the moralistic
implication that these contrasts—exalted for Kerrigan, punitive for
Harding—made perfect common sense. Ehrenreich (1990) observes the
ease with which the media disparages working-class Americans:

Enlightened people who might flinch at a racial slur, have no trouble
listing the character defects of an ill-defined "underclass," defects
which routinely include promiscuity, and sloth. There is, if anything,
even less inhibition about caricaturing the white or "ethnic" working class: Its tastes are "tacky"; its habits unhealthful; and its views
are hopelessly bigoted and parochial. (p. 7)

Even though Kerrigan's and Harding's pursuits were the
same—skate well enough to win a gold medal and hope for payoffs in

the form of publicity and endorsements—the media mocked rather than rewarded Harding's desire to work hard and succeed in the skating world. Instead of striving and sacrificing, words consistently used to describe Kerrigan, Harding was described as struggling and barely surviving. "A different person," wrote Adler of *Newsweek*, "handed this autobiography could have fashioned an inspiring story of transcending poverty, but somehow Tonya's personality keeps getting in the way" (Adler, 1994b, p. 23).

Harding's sacrifices, we learned, of gathering bottles on the side of the road to afford expensive skating fees, skating in homemade costumes, working at a Mr. Spuds potato stand in the mall, and self-reliantly scraping funds together to make the smallest ends meet, paled next to the monolithic sacrifices of the entire, bonded, striving, Kerrigan family. We heard more about Harding's penchant for pool, hunting, and auto repair—extracurricular vices—than we heard of her constant training and "suffering in silence." Constant media references to Harding's cigarette smoking—despite her asthma!—not only reinforced her lack of discipline but exposed what was seen as her knack for compulsion, spending her money on irrelevant, nasty habits. Other "facts" we learned about Harding included: she met her future husband at 15, suggesting a rampant, uncontrolled sexuality; she could not decide if she was married or divorced, constantly returning to and leaving an abusive marriage; she threatened a woman with a baseball bat during a traffic dispute; and she parked in illegal parking places.

Even though it was granted that Harding, too, had to "work hard" to meet her expenses ("she has worked so hard, tried for so long, wanted so bad" [Duffy, 1994a, p. 52]), her inability to get beyond her "personality," her "behavior," or her "turbulent background" was seen as an individual liability. Harding's problem character was irrevocably linked to her recalcitrant mother, LaVona. A woman who had been married and divorced six times and worked as a night waitress, we learned how she provided instability as well as hostility. Harding's father, Al, served a more naturalizing function: he taught Harding how to hunt, play pool, and build up her muscles. In another sense, he was held accountable for the unfortunate masculinization of his daughter. The typical one-dimensional portrayal of LaVona Harding as "evil mother" was momentarily cracked in a *60 Minutes* package (the interview used had been conducted years earlier for a Yale student's video project). LaVona Harding's comments about Tonya briefly brought broader class issues back into the skating narrative: "She can't come up to their standards no matter how hard she tries. That gets to me. No matter how hard we try, we're always wrong. That's perfectly *normal*" (Croft, 1994; emphasis added).

That Harding was described as being destined to become the heroine of the shopping mall, a place for mass consumerism and teenage sexual display, illustrated the limitations assigned her endorsement image and her skating career. Harding had no beauty capital, no cultural capital, and was not willing to embrace the proper value system; she would never be allowed to climb the class ladder. The social and cultural reasons for these barriers, and the media's implicit storytelling devices that marked Harding's overall image, style, behavior, family instability, and poverty as an aberration from middle-class norms, were absent from all mainstream coverage. Her implied involvement with the assault aside, Harding's entire working-class self was positioned as a hopeless deviation from what should be embraced: Kerrigan. As Ehrenreich (1990) notes,

> there are no models, in the mainstream media, suggesting that any-thing less than middle-class affluence might be an honorable and dignified condition, nor is there any reason why corporate advertis-ers should promote such a subversive possibility . . . the more the poor are cut off or abandoned, the less they are capable of inspiring sympathy or even simple human interest. (p. 250)

A question must be asked: how different would the working-class media status of Tonya Harding be if Harding fulfilled standard notions of beauty and, therefore, had a place reserved for her in the mid-dle and upper class? If Harding had high cheekbones, a longer line, less bulky muscles, and the will to change her "rough" sides—like Liza Doolittle in *My Fair Lady*—how would the story work differently, and what kind of class access would Harding have had early on in her skat-ing career?

KERRIGAN BACKLASH

Nancy Kerrigan, after being built up to middle-class icon status, was poised to fall from grace. "Caught on tape" is the way Doug Bruckner of *Hard Copy* described it. "Could it be that American's sweetheart isn't so sweet, or is she finally buckling under pressure?" (Bruckner, 1994). With so much publicity about her $2 million deal with Disney, her continuous cascade of endorsements and appearances, and her upcoming hosting of *Saturday Night Live*, Kerrigan's humble Stoneham beginnings were already paling next to her (and her family's) new and comfortable status as a millionaire. Kerrigan had arrived at celebrity, wealth, and security, and the American public and American media felt responsible for putting her there. They had "bought" the carefully constructed rags-to-riches story of Kerrigan, they had supported her from victim to silver medalist, and they had participated in the verbal bashing of her rival.

Kerrigan's responsibility in this unspoken contract with her fans was to continually serve as an icon for class mobility. Thus, when she did not skate well enough to win the crown jewel (her level of beauty, in a sense, was not high enough), and when cameras snagged images and sounds of Kerrigan complaining, acting spiteful, and looking sour at the 1994 Olympic medal ceremonies (she was awarded a silver medal to Oksana Baiul's gold), her inability to sustain perfection triggered the news media's moralistic middle-class ire. *Hard Copy's* Doug Bruckner had the scoop: "The medal ceremony was delayed by 10 minutes. . . . Nancy Kerrigan and skater Chen Lu thought they were waiting for Oksana Baiul to be made up. [CUT TO KERRIGAN ON TAPE] Kerrigan: Oh come on . . . so she's going to go ahead and cry again . . . what's the difference?" (Bruckner, 1994). Kerrigan was scrutinized for other acts of intemperance and indulgence. Leaving the Olympics before the closing ceremonies to wave in a Disney parade was interpreted as a selfish snub to the "team spirit" of the Olympic Games. Sitting next to Mickey Mouse on a float and commenting within the range of microphones and television cameras that "this is the corniest thing I've ever done, it's so dumb, I hate it," was evaluated as a spoiled, tactless, and ungrateful jab at her new corporate sponsor. A new class lesson was in the making. "When you wish upon a star, maybe you should act like one," scolded Ann Oldenburg in *USA Today* (1994, p. 1A). Syndicated news magazine show *Hard Copy* documented calls on a radio talk show. "Everyone is sick of it," one caller said. "Well, I think that she's a spoiled little itch with a B in front of it," another caller added, with the radio talk show host representing the voice of middle-class common sense: "People who make billions have to be gracious, and if you're not gracious, people won't like you" (Bruckner, 1994).

With concrete examples of Kerrigan slipping and "not working hard," she was chastised for her sudden lack of discipline, striving, and sense of sacrifice. When she commented that her Olympic performance "was flawless" (Fortin, 1994), her sense of modesty evaporated, drawing parallels to Harding's overconfident and loudly repudiated remark about seeing dollar signs when she skates. In essence, Kerrigan no longer had the villain, Harding, to offer a comforting contrast. Without Harding's working-class glare and with Kerrigan's miscalculated behavior, the silver medalist's human imperfections were now exposed: she was never worthy of the gold medal, the media suggested, and was consequently undeserving of her newfound wealth. As Stacey D'Erasmo wrote in the *Village Voice*, "Did Kerrigan's jaw get bigger overnight, or were we just noticing it for the first time? What big teeth you have, Snow White. No one ever got anywhere without them, my dear" (1994, p. 140). In a *USA Today*/CNN/Gallup nationwide telephone poll of 1,016 adults conducted in December 1994, 53% had a favorable impression of Kerrigan, down from 61% in March. "Solomon says Kerrigan's relationship with the media 'needs' to be rebuilt," *USA Today* reported, quoting Kerrigan's agent, Jerry Solomon. "They jumped on the bandwagon to build her up before the Olympics and jumped even harder to tear her down after the Olympics" (Becker, 1995, p. 2C).

Kerrigan's image was further smudged when it became public knowledge that she had become her agent's partner. Solomon had divorced his wife, the media reported, and Kerrigan was cast as a homewrecker. She had abandoned the safe environment of her stable family and disrupted family stability elsewhere. She was no longer virginal and dependent, but sexually indulgent and independent (Terry, 1995).

Meanwhile, Baiul was quickly being framed as an even better fairy tale. As her story would be told and retold, Baiul had been orphaned by her mother's tragic death when she was 13, and she had skated on inferior rinks in the harsh environment of the Ukraine. With indisputable grace, a "sweet face," and princess charm, she won the gold "crown jewel" at the 1994 Olympics, edging out Kerrigan on artistic (feminine) merit while Kerrigan's skating was reinterpreted as "cold." Like Kerrigan, Baiul was skating on an injured leg,[2] but only had one day of recovery time compared to Kerrigan's three weeks: "bruised and battered Oksana Baiul, with pain in her back and stitches in her leg, turned in one of the gutsiest performances in Olympic history" (Reilly, 1994). Her musical choices, including Tchaikovsky's *Swan Lake*, embraced high musical culture—her routine was even reminiscent of ballet. Fitting the mold of a rags-to-riches princess far more precisely than Kerrigan, Baiul also was cast as a carefree, young, uncorrupted fawn next to a rude and jealous Kerrigan; in effect, she was Bambi and Cinderella combined.

Baiul, coming from a newly capitalistic former Soviet bloc country, also came to represent success the "American" way. She was shown to embrace American shopping culture, having been deprived for so long. Even without an intact family, Baiul came to represent nuclear family values. When asked why she was crying after she won her gold, Baiul said her tears were kisses from heaven, where her mother was looking down on her—a quote that was widely circulated and warmly applauded by the media. Had her mother been alive, it was suggested, she surely would have watched Baiul skate, cheered her on, held her hand, and guided her. On the second to last day of 1994, the *USA Today* sports section published a list of who was "IN" and "OUT" that confirmed the sentiment about Nancy Kerrigan ("one last time," 1994, p. 1C): Kerrigan was OUT, Baiul was IN. The media had found another middle-class champion, and the skating world had found another star.

CONCLUSION

Gender plays a fundamental role in the character configurations of women in mass media's coverage of women's figure skating. Along with a constant search for media icons to represent a feminine ideal, there also is a search to identify an upwardly mobile ideal. In most cases, what is "feminine" and what signifies class advancement is quite the same. Skaters believed to have a "feminine" skating style and body image are coded in terms of their "artistic" approach and couched in terms of class mobility, which is further justified by their adherence to the values of authenticity, hard work, and nuclear family stability. Skaters culturally defined as "unfeminine" are labeled "athletic" skaters who can then be understood as undesirably working class.

How much did Kerrigan's white, Northern European features and long, model-like legs have to do with her class mobility? Five-time gold medalist speed skater Bonnie Blair, who was sturdy, muscular, and 30 years old at the time of her many victories at the same 1994 Winter Olympics, was represented by CBS Olympic commentators as "the kid sister" and was not slated for class advancement, although her hard work, discipline, and family cohesiveness were, as with Kerrigan, celebrated in the media narrative surrounding her performances.

How would the story change if Harding—denigrated for her athletic feats, muscular body type, and hard-nosed sense of ambition—had been given class access and endorsements from the onset? Perhaps such an act of desperation, the clubbing of a rival, would not have been considered by those surrounding Harding, or Harding herself. Would Kerrigan's star have faded slowly and gracefully if she had not had a behavioral lapse? If Kerrigan had won the gold medal and assumed her position as the sport's most beautiful skater, would her skating ever be described as "cold as ice"?

That there is a constant search for upwardly mobile feminine icons—as we first saw with Kerrigan, then with Baiul—means that these women athletes are expected to adhere to and exemplify almost impossible standards of appearance and behavior as they compete on and off the ice. Kerrigan's star faded and Baiul's star rose. Within three years, Baiul was arrested on drunken driving charges and accused by the media of being an indulgent party girl. In a subsequent promo for a show on *Oprah* in which Baiul was to appear, Oprah Winfrey confirmed

Baiul's big slide: "The last time Oksana was on our show, she was a golden girl—the perfect role model. I want to find out what happened" ("Skater," p. D1). Ultimately, Kerrigan, Baiul, and all the skaters to follow are just characters in the continuous narrative that defines an ideal for women.

ENDNOTES

1. Skating figure-8 patterns was abolished in the 1980s.
2. Baiul's leg had been injured by an accidental on-ice collision during warm up.

REFERENCES

Adler, J. (1994a, January 24). On thin ice. *Newsweek*, 69-72.

Adler, J. (1994b, Winter). Tonya trouble. *Newsweek* (Special edition), 18-23.

Becker, D. (1995, January 5). After the hoopla, Kerrigan needs a break. *USA Today*, p. 2C.

Bourdieu, P. (1993). How can one be a sports fan? In S. During (Ed.), *The cultural studies reader* (pp. 339-356). London: Routledge.

Bruckner, D. (Anchor/Correspondent). (1994, March 3). *Hard Copy*. Detroit: WJBK.

Butsch, R. (1995). Ralph, Fred, Archie and Homer: Why television keeps recreating the white male working-class buffoon. In S. Dines & J. M. Humez (Eds.), *Gender, race and class in media* (pp. 403-412). Thousand Oaks, CA: Sage.

Carlson, M. (1994, February. 21). Now for the skate-off. *Time, 143*(8), 58.

Coontz, S. (1992). The way we never were. New York: Basic Books.

Chung, C. (Anchor/Correspondent). (1994, January 20). On edge. *Eye to Eye with Connie Chung*. New York: CBS.

Croft, S. (Correspondent). (1994, January 16). My name is Tonya Harding. *60 Minutes*. New York: CBS.

Deford, F. (1992, February 10). The jewel of the games. *Newsweek*, 46-53.

D'Erasmo, S. (1994, March 8). An American tragedy. *The Village Voice*, p. 140.

Duffy, M. (1994a, January 24). No holiday on ice. *Time, 143*(4), 55-57.

Duffy, M. (1994b, February 21). With blades drawn. *Time, 143*(8), 53-58.

Ehrenreich, B. (1990). *Fear of falling*. New York: HarperPerennial.

Fiske, J. (1987). *Understanding television culture*. London: Methuen.

Fortin, J. (Anchor). (1994, March 3). *CNN Headline News*. Atlanta: CNN.

Gans, H. J. (1974). *Popular culture and high culture*. New York: Basic Books.

Gibbons, L. (Anchor). (1994, February 20.). *Shattered glory: The Tonya Harding, Nancy Kerrigan story*. New York: NBC.

Hall, S. (1977). Culture, the media, and the "ideological effect." In J. Curran, M. Gurevitch, and J. Woollacott (Eds.), *Mass communication and society* (pp. 315-348). London: The Open University Press.

Jamieson, B. (Correspondent). (1994, January 17). *ABC World News Tonight*. New York: ABC.

Oldenburg, A. (1994, March 3). Kerrigan draws fire for Disney performance. *USA Today*, p. 1A.

One last time: The "ins" and "outs" of sports (1994, December 30). *USA Today*, p. 1C.

Plummer, W., & Reed, S. (1994, January 24). Poisoned ice. *People, 41*(3), 56-62.

Raphael, S.J. (Executive Producer). (1994, January 20). *Sally*. Detroit: WDIV.

Reilly, B. (Anchor). (1994, March 3). *Inside Edition*. Detroit: WXYZ.

Rooney, B. (Correspondent). (1994, January 13). *ABC World News Tonight*. New York: ABC.

Sherman, W. (1993, December). The sexy, scandalous world of women sports stars. *Cosmopolitan*, 202-203.

Skater facing drunken driving charges to appear on Oprah (1997, February 6). *The Waterloo Courier*, p. DI.

Smolowe, J. (1994, January 24). Tarnished victory. *Time, 143*(4), 50-54.

Spigel, L. (1992). *Make room for TV: Television and the family ideal in post-war America*. Chicago: University of Chicago Press.

Starr, M. (1994, January 17). I'm so scared. *Newsweek*, 41-43.

Swift, E.M. (1994, January 17). Violence. *Sports Illustrated, 80*(2), 16-21.

Terry, L. (Anchor/Correspondent). (1995, March 27). *American Journal*. Detroit: WXYZ.

Thomas S., & Callahan, B.P. (1982). Allocating happiness: TV families and social class. *Journal of Communication, 32*, 184-190.

Thomas, S., & LeShay, S. (1992). Bad business? A reexamination of television's portrayal of business persons. *Journal of Communication, 42*, 95-105.

Tillotson, M. (Anchor/Correspondent). (1994, January 20). *CNN & Company*. Atlanta: CNN.

Wilson, P. (Correspondent). (1994, January 13). *NBC Nightly News*. New York: NBC.

Wolf, N. (1992). *The beauty myth*. New York: Doubleday.

Wylie, P. (1994, January 24). Tougher than she looks. *Newsweek*, 73.

III

LIMIT/ED/ING CHALLENGES

9

"More Power!":
Negotiating Masculinity
and Femininity in
Home Improvement

Charlene Dellinger-Pate
Roger C. Aden

In a 1992 episode of *Home Improvement*, the sitcom's main character, Tim
Taylor, who is host of the home repair television show, *Tool Time*, faces
the camera and says, "Women, I don't think you're stupid just because
you don't know anything . . . you just haven't been taught." Following
this tirade, Tim's *Tool Time* co-host, Al, warns Tim to check the trigger
switch on the saw before plugging it in. "Any idiot knows that Al," Tim
smugly replies. But as soon as he plugs in the saw, it runs away from
him, cutting the board completely in half, nearly falling to the floor and
causing a great calamity.

Because of stunts like these, *Home Improvement* is described in
the popular press as different and a welcomed change to the prime-time
sitcom. Moreover, the popular press suggests that *Home Improvement*
succeeds because it offers messages that appeal to both women and
men. *TV Guide*, for example, regards Tim and Jill Taylor as "America's

favorite TV couple" (Hall, 1993, p. 10). Nielsen ratings support this account as *Home Improvement* consistently remained in the top seven prime-time television shows from February 22 through April 5, 1993 ("Ratings," 1993a, 1993b, 1993c). Prime-time demographics for the first week of February 1993 placed *Home Improvement* as the number one show for both men and women ages 18-49 ("Ratings," 1993a). As of February 1995, *Home Improvement* remained within the top five most watched television programs by both males and females ("Nielsen prime-time ratings," 1995a, 1995b). In 1996, *Home Improvement* not only maintained its prime-time status but was also in syndication.

Although the humorous "macho" antics may satisfy male audiences, by themselves they do not earn the show's continuously high ratings among both male and female audiences. In order to understand the sitcom's appeal to both sexes, we turn our attention to the character Jill Taylor and her representation within the text. Jill's strong character, which is widely commented on in popular media texts, provides audiences with a sense of balance and equality between masculinity and femininity. Tim's attempts to assert his masculinity are typically rebuffed by Jill, described by one reviewer as "more than just the show's token female" (Frolick, 1993, p. 14). Generally, writers characterize Jill Taylor as a feisty female who can counter Tim's machoism while serving as a role model for women in the 1990s.

Home Improvement implies that masculinity (represented by Tim) consents to femininity's (represented by Jill) calls for equality through three strategies: (a) Jill's strong character, (b) Tim's failed efforts at home improvement, and (c) Tim's apologies for his insensitive masculine behavior. These three strategies thrive on Jill's representation within the text, for she appears to be an equal counterpart to Tim. Jill remains unblemished during Tim's foolish antics, and she inevitably accepts Tim's attempted apologies. However, as our textual analysis indicates, these strategies do more to maintain masculine hegemony than they do to create equality between masculinity and femininity.

Following a brief discussion of the hegemonic process within media texts, we identify how *Home Improvement*'s three compensatory strategies are enacted by referring to excerpts from programs aired during May 1992.[1] Then, we explain how what is left unsaid in these episodes allows hegemonic masculinity to circumvent these strategies.

HEGEMONIC MASCULINITY

Italian scholar Antonio Gramsci (1987) argues that the most popular beliefs, values, and ideas in a culture constitute an ever-changing system of hegemony, or cultural domination. This domination occurs not through coercion, however, but through consent. In other words, the process of developing cultural consensus disguises hegemonic strategies that help more powerful groups maintain their influence. Subordinated groups participate in the on-going negotiations and compromises that produce consensus, but the result reflects the more powerful parties' ability to incorporate and redefine others' beliefs, values, and ideas.

Importantly, Gramsci (1987) says that hegemony works not so much through overt, collective discussion as through the simple every-day practices that mark a culture (e.g., going to the movies, watching television, reading the newspaper). When ideas or statements that challenge the status quo are absent from these simple practices, Gramsci claims hegemony is perpetuated. Thus, when Tim and Jill Taylor butt heads on *Home Improvement*, their conflict challenges the hegemony of masculinity. Tim's desire to charge ahead, to add power, and to control what others do represents the culturally valued "take charge" attitude associated with masculinity; he shoots first and asks questions later. Jill's concern for the feelings of others, for maintaining harmony, and for seeing all individuals as possessing equal power represents the "nurturing" attitude associated with femininity; she asks questions first. Their process of conflict, negotiation, and resolution appears to favor Jill's belief, but the absence of certain statements and the lack of particular discussions—as we illustrate in the following pages—ensures the continued hegemony of masculinity in the Taylor household.

HOME IMPROVEMENT'S IMPRESSION OF GENDER EQUALITY

Home Improvement's appeal to both women and men may well lie in its structuring of an apparently balanced relationship between Jill and Tim. Men can appreciate Tim's macho musings and drive for more power, whereas women can appreciate both the follies that Tim's actions produce and Jill's reactions to those occurrences. We isolate three strategies that seem to construct an impression of equality in *Home Improvement*.

Strategy 1: Jill and Tim Taylor

Although the popular press recognizes *Home Improvement* as a "celebration of power tools, macho musings, and the battle of the sexes" (Hall, 1993, p. 8), and its *Tool Time* show-within-a-show as a "dream lair for any New Age caveman" (Frolick, 1993, p. 15), it is also cheered for its portrayal of a strong, genuine Jill Taylor, played by Patricia Richardson. Reviewers distinguish Richardson from the "cookie-cutter blonde or blow-dried airhead" (Hall, 1993, p. 9) of many situation comedies and regard her as a "refreshingly unaffected" (Shales, 1991, B1) actress who has the stage presence to usurp actor Tim Allen when necessary.

Not only is Jill's character acclaimed as the bonding fiber between the "ever-manly Tim" and her three sons, she is also equated with a "more opinionated wave of TV wives" (Hall, 1993, pp. 8-9), such as the character Roseanne in the situation comedy of the same name. Because Jill has a "dry, unaffected take on the often thankless wife-mother role" (Hall, 1993, p. 8), her character is viewed, according to Tim Allen, as the "type of woman other women would like to be around" (quoted in Hall, 1993, p. 8). Consequently, Richardson's Jill is regarded as someone who can "match wits—and then some—with Tim" (Frolick, 1992, p. 14) and counter the very macho views and antics of Tim Allen/Taylor. As Hall (1993) writes, "Allen may wield electric drills, grunt virile grunts, and yell his trademark, chest-thumping slogan, "More Power!" in the forum of his *Tool Time* show, but at home, he and Richardson are affectionate and feisty equals" (p. 9).

Various signifiers are employed throughout *Home Improvement* to instill the sense of equality or balance between Jill and Tim Taylor. Mostly, these signifiers are in the form of Jill's comebacks to Tim's sexist remarks and putdowns. Jill is not only unshaken by Tim's remarks, but simply reciprocates his jabs with smart remarks of her own. In fact, in most of the couple's verbal sparring, Jill is afforded the last laugh. For example, when Tim attempts to show Jill how to unclog a sink, Jill, refer-ring to the tool, asks, "Why do they call it a monkey wrench?" Tim uses the question to poke fun at Jill and answers, "Because even a monkey can use it." Jill, however, gains the upper hand when she replies, taking the wrench from his hands, "Thank you, Cheetah."

Jill also is quick to tease Tim for his foolish macho behavior on the set of *Tool Time*. In another episode, Tim returns home from work with a piece of table glued to his forehead. When Jill asks him if he went to the emergency room, Tim sarcastically replies, "I just came from there. They said I wasn't a priority." Jill laughs and retorts, "Why? Was there a guy with a whole table stuck to his head?"

In a more elaborate example, another episode begins as Tim coaxes Jill into keeping score during a "friendly" bowling competition by remarking, "You can't help it if you're a lousy bowler—you're a woman." This remark gets a huge laugh from the audience for its unabashedly sexist generalization. However, in her "unaffected" man-ner, Jill gets the last laugh when she says, "Nothing gets by you, huh, Tim?" The sparring continues in the bowling lanes when Tim, after throwing a gutter ball, becomes the brunt of Jill's jabs. Prior to his second ball, Tim says, "Jill, would you mind going down there and dressing up like a bowling pin?" to which Jill retorts, "Sure, that's the one place I wouldn't get hit by a bowling ball."

As a couple, then, Jill and Tim apparently possess a balanced relationship. Jill is perfectly capable of handling Tim's humor-driven attempts to exert power in the relationship, whether they are engaged in competition inside or outside of the home. In fact, by getting in the last word, Jill can be seen by viewers as frequently winning the battle of the sexes.

FEMININITY AND MASCULINITY AS UNEQUAL COUNTERPARTS

What is not said in the relationship between Jill and Tim reveals more of the process of hegemonic masculinity than what is said. A closer look reveals that masculinity and femininity are ordered within a traditional structure that valorizes masculinity while reframing femininity as its inferior.

In exploring Jill's feisty character and "unaffected" demeanor, one sees that Jill's last laugh is afforded only in response to Tim. Her comebacks, such as "Nothing gets by you, huh, Tim?", are exactly that—comebacks. As a balancing tool, Jill's humor reciprocates Tim's original putdowns. Her wit is rarely used to instigate a jab in the first place, which would illustrate a more equal depiction of humor within Jill and Tim's relationship. Moreover, Jill's humor is created to complement masculinity in that she is unaffected by Tim's sexist comments. Instead of confronting Tim's women-bashing generalizations, she actually adds laughs of her own to them or ignores them completely. Thus, this impression of equality created with Jill and Tim's verbal sparring disguises the construction of masculinity as aggressive and femininity as either reactive or cooperative.

A closer reading of Jill's victory on the bowling lanes reveals another instance of inequality between masculinity and femininity in that Jill's win is actually due to Tim's mistake. During Tim's last turn, he commits a foul which Jill does not fully recognize. Tim's fans, who are watching the match, call attention to the fact that Tim failed to beat his wife "fair and square," for without the foul, Tim would have won. Thus, the impression of equality disguises the fact that Jill wins not on her own terms but only because Tim loses. Moreover, as the next section illustrates, Jill and Tim's characters reveal how femininity is afforded an equal status only when masculinity "goofs."

Strategy 2: The Home Improvement Gags

Home Improvement's humor depends on Tim as the "one-gag wonder and klutzy tool- meister" (Frolick, 1992, p. 14) for its staying power as a top-rated, prime-time show. However, Tim's antics also work narratively to balance his sexist behavior. The viewer gets a he-had-it-coming-to-him sense when Tim's macho, grunting ways are ridiculed or countered. For example, during the bowling competition with Jill, Tim brags to some of his male fans of the *Tool Time* television show that he is a good bowler. However, after Jill completes four strikes in a row, Tim explains to one of the fans that he is going easy on Jill because her mother was just convicted of grand theft auto. This excuse, of course, is a macho response to a statement by one of his fans: "Boy Tim, you're really taking this well. If my wife were beating the pants off of me, I'd find somewhere to hide."

Throughout the rest of the bowling match, Tim and his fans take turns poking fun at Jill's "girlish" bowling technique. Tim, asserting his masculinity once again, assures Jill that he is going to make a comeback and declares that the winner "has to kiss the loser's bowling shoes." As the reader anticipates from Tim's extremely macho behavior, Jill wins the bowling match, Tim's fans declare that he has let them down, and Jill gloats ostentatiously. The sequence ends with Tim foolishly and shamefully nuzzling Jill's bowling shoes declaring, "You're the best, Jill. You're the best."

Other instances that signify a sense of balance in the text occur as slapstick fiascos involving Tim and powerful machinery. These antics, which usually leave Tim in ridiculous situations—such as hanging from the rooftop upside down or riding an out-of-control clothes dryer in the garage—narratively function as a counter to Tim's egotistical, sexist behavior. In fact, as Tim's sexist jabs reach an optimum point of women bashing, they cue the reader that something extraordinary is about to happen to make Tim look foolish. For example, on the set of *Tool Time*, Tim speaks to his all-male audience about how women never help with mens' chores around the house. In a false woman's voice, Tim pokes fun at a woman's response when she is asked to help with jobs such as unclogging the sink and says, "I could break a nail." He then says, "This is an excuse. Women, you don't know anything because you've never been taught." He continues by saying that he wants to alleviate this unfortunate situation by having women on the show next week and "teaching them home repair using a simple language even women can understand." His derogatory remarks peak when he says, "I mean, it's not a woman's fault—they grew up spending half their time playing with plastic ovens and dolls and don't know a thing about tools." Immediately following this monologue, Tim loses control of his saber saw and nearly destroys the entire *Tool Time* stage.

Another foolish incident follows Tim's exaggerated macho behavior when as host of Tool Time, he shares with his all-male audience feelings he has after an altercation at home with his wife's "feminist" friend, Karen. He laments: "I'm a little cheesed. Some say men are into tools because we're insecure. These same people say men are into power because we're destructive or aggressive. Let me explain something to you—we're neither destructive or aggressive. What we are is creative.

He continues by pointing out that famous structures, such as the Great Wall of China and the Leaning Tower of Pisa, were built by men and tools. Here, Al corrects Tim by saying that the tower was actually considered a mistake. However, Tim points out that, "This tower has been leaning for over 800 years and hasn't fallen over—kind of reminds me of my mother-in-law." As the macho talk continues, the viewer anticipates the calamity that is about to occur as Tim and Al instruct the audience on how to laminate a table. Following Al's warning to the public that the glue is strong and will "bond instantly to the skin," Tim reprimands him with "everyone knows not to play with glue" and begins calling him "Mr. Negativity." Tim then bends to pick something off of the floor, touches his forehead to the laminated table and is permanently stuck to the plywood.

The gags in *Home Improvement*, the result of Tim's fearlessly independent, masculine behavior, are all at Tim's expense. As an apparent symbol of masculinity gone awry, Tim demonstrates the failures that result from an unquestioning belief in the ability to use power—and that more power is always better.

MASCULINITY AS SPECTACULAR

The process of hegemonic masculinity often entails the reconstruction of masculinity in order for it to remain superior to femininity. Here, the consequences of Tim's sexist behavior are exaggerated, fictional calamities. However, these calamities are humorous because the audience knows they are unreal. In real life, even macho men, unlike Tim Taylor, do not put helicopter engines in their riding lawnmowers or turn washing machines into giant life support systems. These visual images are for humorous effect. A piece of plywood glued for two days to Tim's forehead, for example, is an absurd visual image that the viewer processes as pure fiction. Similarly, even when Tim forgets to check the safety switch on his saber saw and it flies to the end of the table, the reader knows Tim is really not going to cut off his legs.

Contrary to Tim's spectacular goofs, some observers commend *Home Improvement* for its strong sense of "realness" at home (Shales,

1991, p. B1). As Richardson herself notes, "People tell me, `Boy, the fights between you and Tim are just what happens in our house'" (Hall, 1993, p. 8). Similarly, the executive producer, David McFadzean, says *Home Improvement* "is more about building a modern relationship than a deck or a door" (Hall, 1993, p. 8).

Yet, the narrative structure contains a significant contradiction between Tim's stunts and the relational issues between Jill and Tim Taylor. Whereas Tim's antics are imaginative and sometimes surreal, the relational issues—such as sharing housework, making romantic dinner plans, and engaging in competitive sports—are grounded in the mundane lives of relational partners. These issues, pertaining to the domestic sphere of life and the "real life" of marital partners, are mostly represented in Jill's character, for the story often depends on her to present the domestic or relational "problem" or issue to the viewers. Tim's character is represented much more through exaggerated antics and buffoonery. Moreover, the home-improvement gags, all of which appear to be exaggerated and unreal, are used to balance Tim's sexist ideology or, as represented in *Home Improvement*'s dialogue and narrative, to provide a counterpoint to the real issues between men and women. Thus, buffoonery is proposed as equal to both male chauvinism and the trivialization of interpersonal issues. In this relationship, however, masculinity is privileged as spectacular, and femininity is constructed as its opposite—the mundane.

The impression of equality between masculinity and femininity is created with the juxtaposition of domesticity as represented by wife/mother Jill Taylor and the fictional, exaggerated, and cartoon-like escapades of Tim Taylor. A false dichotomy is created with femininity being balanced by its counterpart, the ridiculous.

Strategy 3: Tim's Apologetic Behavior

When an issue of importance arises between Tim and Jill, Tim goes to his neighbor, Wilson, for advice. Wilson offers Tim tidbits of information ranging from a feminist reading of the customs in patriarchal societies to the meaning of metamessages and the teachings of Plato. Following these trips to the fence, Tim attempts to make right his wrong. In one episode, the wrong involves Jill's broken dinner plans. Tim is seen in a poolhall, with his buddies, phoning Jill to tell her he will be home in 15 minutes. Jill, who is planning to surprise Tim with a romantic dinner at home without the kids, tells him seductively, "I'll be waiting." Two hours later, Tim returns home to a very angry wife. During their argument, Jill asks him why he did not understand from her comments over the phone that she was planning a romantic evening. The issue then focuses on the fact that Tim failed to pick up romantic signals from Jill. The next morning, Jill comes downstairs to find Tim preparing a nice breakfast for one which she mistakenly believes is for her. "About last night," she begins to apologize, then she realizes Tim did not prepare breakfast as an apology but had made it for himself. She storms out of the room.

After talking to Wilson, Tim realizes he was not "tuned into" Jill's needs. He makes amends by coming to the front door in the middle of the day dressed as a telephone worker. When Jill answers the door, she questions Tim's behavior, but Tim insists on role playing Fred, the telephone worker. He begins: "The name's Fred, and I had a report that there was some faulty wiring at this household." Tim walks to the kitchen phone and begins unscrewing the telephone receiver. "Here's your problem," he says. "The receiver is not picking up signals." Jill responds by saying, "Maybe it's my fault. Maybe—sometimes I don't speak clearly enough." Tim then says, "No, it's not your fault. Your signals are quite clear. There's your problem right there. Your wires are crossed." The two continue role playing as Fred and Jill kiss and pretend to have an affair while her husband is away.

In a similar example, Tim attempts to make up with Jill for yelling at her while teaching her how to unclog a drain. A visit with Wilson makes Tim realize that men often use complicated and technical language in order to remain in power. Tim attempts to make amends by having women on *Tool Time* to teach them basic home repair. When asking for volunteers, Tim deliberately chooses a reluctant Jill to participate in the show. Again, the viewer watches Tim role play his apology, as Jill introduces herself as "Rita." Tim asks Rita: "How would you like to help me unclog this sink?" Rita replies, "No, I don't think that's a good idea. My husband always yells at me a lot when he tries to teach me something." Tim continues talking as host of *Tool Time* and explains, "That's probably because he's using metamessages—making things seem more complicated than they are—using technical jargon to make women feel inferior. And I'm sure he didn't know he was doing that, and I'm sure he's real sorry he did that." The apology works, for the next scene shows Jill and Tim at home with their children with Jill saying, "Tim, you were a pretty good teacher today."

Tim's apologies in *Home Improvement* emphasize the need for masculinity to recognize its errors. If equality between masculinity and femininity is considered the desired state of affairs—and Jill and Tim's relationship seems to suggest that it is—Tim must apologize to restore the balance. His macho actions and quest for more power in all situations lead to a disruption of his relationship with Jill. His elaborate apologies reaffirm the notion of equality as natural, as well as the need for masculinity to make the changes necessary to restore balance. Tim's extravagant performances, such as going to the trouble of dressing up like a telephone repairman, seem to indicate his commitment to restoring equality.

FEMININITY, NOT MASCULINITY, IS APOLOGETIC

Tim's apologies seem to exonerate him in all situations. However, a closer look at Tim's actions finds them not only unapologetic, but failing to address issues for which he should be apologizing. In the episode in which he attempts to make up for missing a romantic dinner with Jill, Tim finds the "faulty wiring." The underlying question that Tim and Jill never discuss, however, concerns the fact that he did not come home "in 15 minutes" when he said he would. In other words, the issue focuses on miscommunication rather than Tim failing to keep his word. Moreover, Tim never directly says, "I made a mistake," but conveys his message metaphorically through Fred, a fictional character. In contrast, Jill is quick to admit the problem might have been her fault and that "maybe I wasn't speaking clearly enough." Consequently, Tim's inability to keep his word is transformed into Jill's inability to be straightforward. In accepting Tim's indirect apology, Jill allows him to avoid the issues for which he should be apologizing. Masculinity thus remains unapologetic, whereas femininity is presented as accepting and nondemanding.

In another episode, Tim again apologizes indirectly by enacting a role-playing scenario. As host of *Tool Time*, Tim apologizes to his wife, "Rita," for using what he terms "metamessages" or complicated language when trying to show her how to do repairs around the house. Jill readily accepts this apology and later praises Tim for his teaching ability. However, again, Tim has circumvented the very issue for which he is apologizing. Tim and Jill's altercation, in which Tim made unkind remarks to Jill while teaching her how to unclog a sink, is disguised as man's "natural" tendency to use technical language. Consequently, Tim's character flaw, or his inability to control his temper, is reframed as Tim's natural and intellectual superiority over Jill. In contrast, Jill's acceptance of Tim's apology with no reference to the original altercation signifies her acceptance of an inferior position within the relationship.

Like Tim's absurd antics, his apologetic acts distract the viewer from recognizing masculinity's refusal to acknowledge femininity as an equal. More importantly, however, the text provides the impression of equality because of Jill's representation within the text. Here, Jill accepts the conflict between Jill and Tim only as Tim defines it, making femininity accepting and complacent. Masculinity is the victor due to its ability to avoid relational issues, usually regarded as "feminine," and reframe them to its advantage.

CONCLUSION

In analyzing Jill and Tim's representation, *Home Improvement* becomes a collection of texts in which femininity is constructed as inferior to masculinity. By placing Tim and Jill in conflict—a traditional narrative device, to be sure—a pattern of competition between masculinity and femininity emerges. Tim and Jill's "battles" occur within the masculine realm of competition rather than the feminine realm of cooperation. The confrontations between Jill and Tim are played by Tim's rules; the competitions are established at Tim's goading. Thus, even when Jill ostensibly wins a confrontation, as she does at the bowling alley, she has had to "act like a man" by becoming overtly competitive to win, thus reaffirming the hegemony of masculinity.

In addition, as the bowling match demonstrates, femininity only wins in *Home Improvement* when masculinity blunders. Femininity is therefore recognized not as a worthy equal to masculinity, but as an inferior construction privileged only when masculinity is flawed. Masculinity's flaws, however, are glossed over in the metanarrative of *Home Improvement* because the competition and mode of conflict resolution occur on masculine terms.

In this respect, femininity gives its consent to masculinity's leadership. Playing by Tim's rules means that Jill *must* accept Tim's initiation of banter, his control of the spectacular, and his indirect apologies. When Jill directly raises the issue of equality, Tim can beat a strategic retreat through indirect apologies and/or initiate a flanking action through humor. His repositioning of himself, and thus masculinity, offers the appearance of a new, egalitarian dimension to the relationship, especially because Jill consents to this apparently new definition. Yet Tim's control of the ground on which this battle of the sexes is played out ensures that Jill will never have the last word.

ENDNOTES

1. The excerpts of *Home Improvement* are culled from four episodes that aired during the sweeps period in May 1992 (May 5, 12, 19, 26). Although sweeps shows are generally considered to be more sensational to draw a larger audience, the episodes aired during this period remain representative of the series and the relationship between Jill and Tim Taylor.

REFERENCES

Frolick, B. (1992, April 18). How to build a hit show. *TV Guide*, pp. 12-15.

Gramsci, A. (1987). *Selections from the prison notebooks* (Q. Hoare & G. N. Smith, trans. & eds.). New York: International Publishers.

Hall, C. (1993, April 24). More Power. *TV Guide*, pp. 8-14.

Nielsen prime-time ratings. (1995a, February 8). *Philadelphia Inquirer*, p. ABBE.

Nielsen prime-time ratings. (1995b, February 15). *Philadelphia Inquirer*, p. D.

Ratings week: Broadcast. (1993a, March 8). *Broadcasting & Cable*, p. 31.

Ratings week: Broadcast. (1993b, March 15). *Broadcasting & Cable*, p. 36.

Ratings week: Broadcast. (1993c, April 5). *Broadcasting & Cable*, p. 29.

Shales, T. (1991, September 17). Handyman special. *Washington Post*, pp. B1, B.

10

"We Are Your Neighbors": *Serving in Silence* and the Simulated Lesbian

Amy Villarejo

The theme of the 1995 Gay Pride march in Pittsburgh—"we are your neighbors"—echoed the closing speech that Margarethe ("Grethe") Cammermeyer (Glenn Close) gave at a similar event in Seattle in 1994 in the made-for-TV-movie *Serving in Silence* (which aired in February 1995):

> People ask, who are we? We are their daughters, their sisters, their sons, their nurses, their athletes, their police. We're your doctors, your fathers, your politicians, your soldiers, your mothers, your friends. We live with you, care for you, help you, protect you, teach you, love you, and need you. All we ask is that you let us.

The film, based on the "real-life" experiences of the highest ranking military officer discharged on the basis of sexual preference, is an exemplary case through which to explore the central question of gay and lesbian representation in popular culture: what does gay or lesbian emerge as in the discourse of rights-based politics and pleas for acceptance? What are the limits of this picture, whom does it exclude, and what does it efface? Whereas the Pittsburgh event emphasized "neighbor," community, and

165

property ownership, Cammermeyer touched on the constellations of family, law, professionalism, the nation, and the associated values of nurturance, care, and support.

These values partake of the national right-wing rhetoric the film both espouses and complicates. Beginning with an implicit address to a gay and lesbian audience at a gay pride event, Cammermeyer's question assumes that *straight* people do not know who "we" are. But the address quickly shifts to a straight *audience* (we are "your" doctors, fathers, etc.), revealing a tension between self-definition of a community and definition for the perceived mainstream television audience. Some have dismissed prime-time television's few "watered-down" versions of homosexuality for their narrowly drawn portraits of gay lives. Others have celebrated the "positive images" paradigm, insisting that any expansion of the repertoire of gay and lesbian images signals wider social acceptance (even if those "positive images" are limited to the white, middle-class, hard-working and sensitive homosexual). What is interesting, however, about *Serving in Silence* is less the representation of the white, upper middle-class, property-owning, maternal lesbian soldier than the film's use of melodrama to score an uneasy counterpoint between the so-called public concerns the film ostensibly takes up (gay and lesbian military service) and the so-called private domain that structures Cammermeyer's internal motivations, goals, community, love-relationships, and family.

This chapter argues that *Serving in Silence* mobilizes a number of well-delineated oppositions to mirror the tension between heterosexuality and lesbianism: among them a dichotomy between North and South, between rigidity and creativity, between "real" community and "false" hierarchy, and, most important, between identity and role/position. All of these make visible the ideological crises surrounding lesbian representation during this period of intense retrenchment and contestation over sexual politics.

THE POLITICS OF MELODRAMA

As Landy (1991) has suggested, melodrama is characterized generally by the presence of these bold dichotomies, as well as "its emphasis on sexuality and sentiment, its inflation of personal conflicts, and its internalization of external social conflicts" (pp. 15-16). That is, melodrama works on the terrain of clear oppositions—good versus evil, masculinity versus femininity, home versus work—to condense a complicated social order into baldly drawn personal conflicts. Political readings of melodrama such as this one counterbalance the overwhelming tendency among cultural critics to dismiss melodrama as trash, ahistorical, or a distraction from more "fundamental" expressions of social conflict or political resistance. These readings eschew distinctions between "melodrama" and "real politics," a dichotomy that often takes as self-evident the distinction between the public and private, and rather insist on the connections between the political and the personal, or the translation of the social sphere into personal conflict through what Brooks (1976) has called the "melodramatic imagination." Brooks' term underscores a sense of movement rather than stagnant oppositions between "exterior" social conflict and "interior" personal motivations (heightened pain and suffering, jealousy and envy, love and its attendant anguish). What is therefore essential to the study of melodrama is to probe its political and ideological strategies, refusing to see it, on the one hand, always as a mystification of social class resulting in political powerlessness or, on the other hand, always as "subversive" or "resistant" in its excesses which reveal self-reflexive possibilities. As with any other genre or mode of expression, melodrama is dynamic, adapting continuously to changes in sociopolitical exigencies, technological innovations, and televisual and cinematic styles.

Even in the popular media, these tensions between political commentary and internalized narrative expression are operative. Carswell (1995) interviewed the "real" Grethe Cammermeyer's lover, Diane (last name withheld for reasons I discuss later), regarding the making of *Serving in Silence*:

> Grethe is more interested in the political nature of her story being made into a movie. She's more interested in what it can accomplish and what it says about the issues and family first, rather than to deal with it as a love story. I choose to view it as a love story first. The love story is an accessible way for the audience to care about the people. Once they care about the characters they can accept anything. (p. 60)

These comments square with certain recent strategies in lesbian filmmaking (such as Rose Troche's *Go Fish*[1]) to "humanize" or naturalize lesbian characters, reducing the threat of their difference by appealing to the "universal" nature of their stories: love, dating, family conflicts, and so on. The movement in these texts is, to borrow a term from Gilroy's (1993) characterization of Afrocentrism, "implosive," concentrated on an ever-decreasing repertoire of images of "lesbianism" in order to render the category acceptable and "accessible" to a mainstream audience perceived as increasingly hostile to the radical potential of certain "homosexual" positions.[2] Simply put, the potential alliances gay-and-lesbian interests might form with struggles around the family's relation to the state or other marginalized groups are squashed—by limiting the sense of "lesbian" to registers more congenial to dominant interests. This is not to dismiss media translations as "simply" retrogressive; rather, the translations effected by the "melodramatic imagination" are precisely what need to be investigated for their ideological ramifications.

TELEVISION GENRES: THE "TRAUMA DRAMA"

Television domestic melodramas and the "trauma dramas" of the 1980s provide the frame into which these implosive registers of "lesbianism" become inserted in the case of *Serving in Silence*. Made-for-TV-melodramas have a history and a set of formal conventions which, although not static, tend to accommodate only slight variation because television networks require a known and "acceptable" product to sell to advertisers. To understand how *Serving in Silence* is structured, it is helpful to look at the moment, the end of the 1970s, in which "trauma dramas" were born. That moment confirmed a crisis in progressive politics with Ronald Reagan's election. An increasing concentration of power in the hands of wealthy individuals and corporations characterized the 1980s, as well. Popular culture was the terrain on which battles over the meaning of "politics" and "America" were fought. Made-for-TV-movies, for example, turned their focus to individual, rather than collective, efforts to effect change. Feuer's (1995) discussion of the trauma drama highlights the contradictory nature of Reagan-era populism, wherein frustration with the state (in particular, the law and unyielding bureaucracy) tends to emphasize the efforts of a charismatic individual as opposed to the collective struggle that characterized earlier strains of American populism. As detailed by Feuer, these telefilms developed recognizable narrative strategies and ideological underpinnings, all of which appear in *Serving in Silence*: the family represents the ideal and norm of happy American life; a trauma occurs; the victim(s) seek help through established institutions; the institutions are unable to help them and are shown to be inadequate; the victim(s) take matters into their own hands; they join a self-help group or form a grass-roots organization; the new organization is better able to cope with the trauma; normality is restored (however inadequately).

Because the majority of these films are docudramas, the resolutions (often indicated through intertitles at the end of the film) are meant to spur the now-sympathetic viewer into action. It is not unusual for local television newscasts to offer follow-up segments providing local contacts, organizations, and telephone numbers, as was the case with *Serving in Silence*. In addition, the "real" Grethe Cammermeyer granted interviews, to promote both her victory and her book, which were fed to local television stations.

Both the narrative structure of *Serving in Silence* and the "extra-textual" (literally, outside of the film itself) events, such as Cammermeyer's celebrity, follow the trauma drama's focus on the exemplary individual. That focus may seem "natural" in the 1990s, but it is in, fact, a product of many years of repetition of a now-familiar format. The importance of the film's structure, then, lies in the fact that even though *Serving in Silence* may address a "new" theme for television in the 1990s (homosexuality), it does so by following a conception of politics born years earlier. This conception, however, is introduced into the context of contemporary debates, and that insertion proved uneasy for *Serving in Silence*. As with any narrativizing of history, the "facts" on which docudramas are based are filtered through the available structures of expression.

GAYS IN THE MILITARY

Serving in Silence was developed and exhibited within the context of heated debates on "gays in the military," including contestation around issues of nationalism and citizenship in a country that flatly ignored the immediate needs of gay men and lesbians and denied us basic membership in legal foundations of American humanity, as well as whether the military issue was displacing attention from AIDS-related struggles. In addition, more radical challenges to the assumptions of those debates circulated, assumptions involving the contours of the state and its power, the interdependence of global capital and global arsenals, and the constraining tentacles of gender and sexual definition in the disciplining of citizens and citizen-service. Feminism, especially lesbian feminism, had long been committed to peace politics, to an understanding of the global effects of war and the expansion of capitalism into the "Third World." Feminist resistance to the "inclusion" of gays and lesbians in the military emphasized: (a) gays and lesbians were already *in* the military; and (b) building a war machine with gay and lesbian bodies threatens the life of the planet and its citizens. These debates were located within contestation over the nature of activism itself, the leadership and platforms of gay and lesbian political organizations, and the overwhelming priority granted to the military issue during 1993 and 1994.

Melodrama is not external to these questions and conflicts. To the contrary, melodrama has for more than a decade served as the cen-

mode of expression of AIDS and gay-and-lesbian concerns in the popular media.[3] And gay and lesbian intellectuals are challenged to investigate the politics of desire and emotion associated with melodrama in their work on popular culture. *Serving in Silence* simply capitalizes on the forms available for articulating discontent with inflexible structures that deny "rights" to gays and lesbians, in this case the military bureaucracy. The question is: what is the structure of this discontent? How is it mapped in *Serving in Silence*, what are its limits, and how is this expressed within the televisual representation of Grethe Cammermeyer?

READING *SERVING IN SILENCE*:
THE SIMULATED FAMILY

Serving in Silence begins with a simulation in three parts, in the first three sequences of the film. In the first, Grethe Cammermeyer is the commanding officer in a National Guard enactment of a bombing on a medical facility. The film opens with Cammermeyer and her soldiers in camouflage; she is shown as a capable, butch commander of a unit under fire, and her troops respond bravely and triumphantly to an enemy attack. As Carswell (1995) comments, and the film bears out, Glenn Close as Cammermeyer is shot in low angle both to approximate more closely Cammermeyer's height and to inflect her image with authority. Close commented, "I wish I had grown a foot and a half for this part" (p. 58). Also, the film's attention from the outset to Close's rigid gestures, down to the clenched jaw, and her carriage detract from her star image as she emulates a controlled officer. After her troops' successful simulation, Cammermeyer comments, "I hope this is as close as you'll get to the real thing." Cued by this opening moment, the film will be concerned with delineating the simulation from the real, appearance from the truth, costume from identity. If the opening segment poses an enigma, it is geared toward distinguishing the "real thing" from its simulation, which functions as a metaphor for the question, "What is a real lesbian?" These concerns are played out on a narrative level but also through the film's form. To see this, we must attend to the film's deliberate cinematography (placing and moving the camera), *mise-en-scene* (setting, lighting, costuming, make-up, and figure behavior), and editing (joining together of individual shots).

    The opening segment gestures toward two components of Cammermeyer's story which become intimately woven together: her achievements in the military and her strong-willed, determined, motivated personality. We see at the outset melodrama's tendency to produce internal or psychological explanations, rather than social ones, to account for the power of the charismatic individual protagonist. We see here, too, the emphasis the trauma drama places on local, isolated crises. Cammermeyer's military accomplishments, which include the Bronze Star for service in Vietnam and increasing positions of authority within the Army and National Guard, combined with academic achievement (she pursues and is awarded the Ph.D. in nursing during the course of the film) are invoked in the representation of the capable and revered officer in the opening moments of the film. The film presents a number of explanations for her success: Nordic lineage, a strength of character formed in opposition to a cold and repressed father, and a commitment to the hierarchy of the military based on patriotism and "family values." Indeed, the film bangs the spectator over the head with references to her Norwegian upbringing, from sweaters to folk songs to diminutive Norwegian appellations for "mother" and "father."

The film wastes no time in charting these paths. From the opening segment, it cuts to Grethe's reunion with her sons upon her return to Seattle to serve in the National Guard. Within a sequence of a few minutes' duration, we see Cammermeyer's Jeep Wagoneer (a timely signifier of the upper middle-class's turn to larger, "rugged" vehicles), loaded with her teenage sons, arrive at a suburban house, the opulence of which is tempered by its outdated layout. Grethe means to simulate a family after her service in San Francisco, but the sons' tension with their father is soon disclosed, as is the impending marriage of the oldest son (Matt), about which Grethe knew nothing. With the brevity of realist narrative economy, the film establishes the idealization of the suburban family as well as something askew within that unit: a divorced mother whose career has distracted her from a significant benchmark of heterosexual life. Grethe is nonetheless hip enough to take her sons out for burgers, and that sense of connection to her sons is reinforced in the following sequence at a beach-house picnic, thrown by lesbian friends.

The third and final establishing sequence sets an idealized lesbian community against the idealized but faltering family unit. Grethe's Birkenstock-wearing lesbian friend and her companion invite Grethe and her children to a beach weekend and, unbeknownst to Grethe, invite an artist friend, Diane, along to meet her. Diane (played by the spectacular Judy Davis) is Grethe's antithesis: dressed in black and leather as opposed to Grethe's suburban garb, lithe as opposed to Grethe's tight trimness. Diane will become the counterpart to the film's project of defining "lesbian" through both Diane and Grethe. Their expected attraction is secured in a shot/countershot in the rear-view mirror as Grethe "picks up" Diane at the train station, an editing motif that will be repeated at key moments of identity-definition and literal mirroring of tension and conflict in the film. After beach football, where

Diane acquires the nickname that the sons will repeat throughout the film, "Dud," the ever-helpful sons accompany the two hostesses back to the house. Grethe and Diane remain at the side of a romantic bonfire, with Grethe strumming a folk song on the guitar. Their ensuing conversation approaches a clichéd recitation of candidacy for a lesbian relationship, in which Grethe reveals her significant traits of character ("persistent," convinced that "you can usually get around the rules if you know how") and family situation. She adds that her former husband, Louis, is now a Mormon, as are her children. Diane exhibits her artistic talent in a sketch (simulation/representation) of Grethe by the fire. The final shot of the sequence brings us inside the house, at another romantic fireside, where Grethe strengthens her self-portrait of truth with the declaration that "I don't pretend well," and Diane invites Grethe to her opening show in Los Angeles. A romance is born.

THE FAMILY OF THE LEGITIMATE SOLDIER

The film thus establishes the three central concerns of the film: Grethe's military career, her family, and her new relationship with Diane. To follow the melodramatic strands of the familial crises and to domesticate Grethe's impending crisis over her allegiance to the military and its fixed bureaucracy, the film is required to dispense with any political challenges to the legitimacy of the military. For the viewer to secure a position of empathy with Cammermeyer, there cannot linger any significant challenges to the institutions which she holds dear and which will present the obstacle to a rights-based vision of American citizenship. Diane, predictably, raises these challenges in the first moment of translation of political conflict over military allegiance to a conflict over sexuality. In the sequence that follows the beach house episode, Grethe travels to Los Angeles to attend Diane's art gallery opening; they flee the art gallery crowd for a romantic dinner, during which a conversation over protests to the Vietnam war ensues. Diane describes parades on the streets of Los Angeles ("Hey, hey, LBJ, how many kids did you kill today?"), though she comments that she was too busy attending art school to participate in the marches (a lesser version of Grethe's careerism).

> Grethe: We were *dying* in Vietnam.
> Diane: That was the whole point.
> Grethe: It was demoralizing.
> Diane: The dying or the marching? . . . . Are we going to
>   have an argument on our first date?
> Grethe: Is that what this is, a date?

The conflict over Vietnam is neatly displaced onto a conflict about the status of the relationship between the two protagonists. At this moment, even *before* Grethe's career is threatened by the revelation of her lesbianism, the trajectory of the film twists away from any antagonism over the role of gays and lesbians in the military and the legitimacy of that issue within a broader liberal "rights" agenda or within a more radical challenge to the military per se. It is by speaking the existence of anti-war politics that they are whisked away by the film, and the military is legitimized by ignoring all of its registers except its firm rejection of its lesbian and gay personnel.

This conversation also invokes a problematic involving history: how do past challenges to American intervention and to the role of the military as a colonial force become neutralized? In a later discussion, in which Grethe asserts that "the Army is a reasonable organization" that "judges a situation as to its merits," Diane responds, "Not according to history." Grethe's comeback, "Were you there?", suggests that a knowledge of history relies on presence, first-hand experience, and an involvement only granted to "soldiers" who were "in" the war and not to those who contested its necessity. In *Serving in Silence*, that conflict is further rendered internal by displacing questions of inclusion or acceptance onto a familial register, introduced in the person of Grethe's father, who is seen as the origin and locus of her motivations, (lack of) sense of accomplishment, and "personality."

Before the film introduces the "trauma"—Grethe's revelation to the military investigator that she is a lesbian—the film sets its agenda for resolving familial strife (as represented by the father) through the alibi of a timely political issue. Grethe's father exemplifies Oedipal turmoil for Grethe (who wishes only to please him) but also continuity in her heritage: it is he who carries the ideological weight of Northern rigidity, lack of warmth, misogyny, and principled (if nostalgic) resistance to injustice. Through the course of the film, he must be humanized, warmed by Grethe's trauma, and he must be convinced that he can "accept" her both for what she "is" and for what she comes to "represent." His stories of her mother smuggling weapons for resistance fighters in Grethe's baby carriage seem to indicate that he has the potential for sympathy, and his revelation that he refused to hug his sons because he feared that they would become homosexual narratively questions both the origins of homosexuality and the "proper" role of the family in nurturing and supporting its gay and lesbian members. The father, a "fool for genealogy," must learn that homosexuality is not inherited (as Diane explains to Grethe's younger son, David, toward the end of the film) and that the idealization of the family does not suffer any damage through its gay and lesbian members. Diane's task is to stoke fires of affection underneath his cold Norwegian heart. This absolves Grethe from affective or familial labor in the film. Instead, she is freed to pursue her career and her struggle with the military. Yet, it remains Grethe's task to earn her father's pride, his paternal seal of approval.

DEFINING THE TRAUMA

Grethe's sons, her father, and Diane are thus established as the ground which will shake after the "trauma" occurs, a "trauma" that is framed in dual registers: of revelation and of definition. Grethe announces her ambition to become head nurse of the National Guard to Diane following a recitation of her father's cold neglect toward her achievements. That step up the hierarchical ladder requires a higher security clearance, and a Department of Defense investigator is sent to interview Grethe—a routine procedure, he tells her: "I ask, you answer. Very basic." Framing the inquiry as routine serves two functions: it heightens the shock of the unusual, the surprise, disclosed during the inquiry, and it masks the connections between the inquiry and the central, undisclosed concerns of the film, concerns that have to do with knowledge and power. The inquiry is meant, after all, to determine who can have knowledge of secrets, who is "fit" to know, who will gain power *by* knowing. The "trauma," too, is a crisis of knowledge, of revealing a secret. It is a question of who can handle that knowledge, and what disturbances in power and hierarchy that knowledge will cause. But as soon as the question is framed as revelation, it becomes a question of definition, first of morality: the interviewer asks whether Grethe has engaged in immoral conduct. She quickly responds in the negative, pauses to reconsider, asks after the definition of "immoral," learns that it includes homosexuality, and declares "I am a lesbian." This is the trauma—but why, and for whom?

Unlike the standard "trauma drama," in which the trauma is clearly accepted as such and consensually understood as criminal and sufficient to provoke crisis (rape, incest, battery), Grethe's traumatic declaration initiates a crisis of definition that must be played out along several axes to secure her status as victim. First, the Army, represented by the agent, cannot "hear" this avowal. The utterance is prohibited by the institution which requires it to speak itself, and, indeed, the agent demands more definition, clarification, description—in short, a taxonomy of lesbian identity for mass consumption. The interview proceeds from Grethe's declaration to parse out the components of that which goes under the name "lesbian":

Grethe: I'm a lesbian.
Agent: You're an active lesbian?
Grethe: I have an emotional. . . . I connect emotionally with women.
Agent: Sexually?
Grethe: It doesn't have anything to do with sexual activity.
Agent: Then, what makes you a lesbian?
Grethe: My feelings.
Agent: About women?
Grethe: More about myself. It's who I am.

As she ties "lesbian" to the mystical interior, severing emotion from sexuality, the camera moves to a close-up. Then, Grethe's voice-over description of acts prohibited by the Uniform Code of Military Justice accompanies a new shot of the two at a long table, the agent pacing in his frustration, a cinematographic distance metaphorically anticipating their discord:

Agent: So, how many women have you had sex with?
Grethe: I never said I did.
Agent: But you have had relationships. I'm trying to understand. Help me out?
Grethe: This is who I am. How many ways can I explain it to you?
Agent: So, if you didn't engage in conduct, how do you know you're a lesbian? Maybe you're celibate.
Grethe: You're not listening.
Agent: I am.
Grethe: Being a lesbian is part of someone's identity. No more, no less. I have patients. . . . I've got to go back to work.

If the interview opens the question, "What is a lesbian?", it closes routes of explanation or contestation over the intersecting but distinct matrices of desire, companionship, sexuality, and intimacy by anchoring identity in amorphous conviction rather than in social relations: one "simply" is a lesbian, "no more, no less." The very tentacles of gender and sexual definition and behavior that "gay and lesbian" challenges in the social arena, in which "gay" or "lesbian" can be seen to function as varied social markers and practices, become displaced onto something that is and, more important, that Grethe Cammermeyer *is*. The uncomprehending agent cannot, however, separate "lesbian" from sexuality. And out of a vague desire to "save" Grethe's career, he wants her not to have uttered the traumatic phrase, a declaration less significant for its substance than for its motivation and effects. The agent is joined in his disbelief by Diane, who wonders to Grethe in the next sequence why she felt compelled to "come out" to the Army. It comes as no surprise that Grethe's reply is that she has never been asked before, that she "belongs" to the Army, and that a good soldier tells the truth when asked.

Consonant with the protocols of melodrama, motivation becomes located in personal traits rather, at least initially, than in a desire to change an injust or inflexible institution. And the effects are similarly routed into personal conflict: the "trauma" is not a trauma for the Army, which will dispense with her statement by demonstrating in a subsequent interview and final hearing that it is simply inconsistent with regulation number AR135-175 (although we learn as well that over 15,000 gay and lesbian soldiers have been discharged from the military). It is instead a trauma for her family, for her father, for Diane. What has been personal—Grethe's identity—will now become a public problem, and it is the entry of the domain previously marked as internal into the so-called public sphere that provides the meat of the domestic melodrama which the film becomes.

The film effectively becomes divided after the trauma occurs, a narrative division that belies the tension between the external political issues the film addresses and the internalization or domestication of those conflicts. On the one hand, Grethe must do battle with the immovable though individually sympathetic Army bureaucrats, who hold to the regulation without regard for the stellar nature of Grethe's accomplishments within the military. On the other, Grethe must reconcile the public disclosure of her lesbian identity with her other social roles and positions. The former path follows the trajectory outlined by Feuer (1995), in which the Army represents an inflexible institution that victimizes gay and lesbian personnel and justifies its discriminatory policy through unyielding regulations. Grethe turns to more accommodating structures, the Lambda Legal Defense team, to fight the Army. This alternative institution supports Cammermeyer, even though she claims that she is not like *those* lesbians, and she forges a temporary solution. As a title tells us at the end of the film, Cammermeyer was reinstated in the military on June 1, 1994, after the United States District Court ruled that the government had violated her constitutional rights to due process and equal protection. And, as the closing sequence of the film demonstrates, she becomes an active spokeswoman in gay and lesbian politics, reconciling her lesbian identity with her career in the military. The speech at the Seattle event continues in voice-over as we see Cammermeyer's Jeep pull into the National Guard facility as she returns to work after her court verdict.

CONCLUSION: DEFINING "LESBIAN"

This political battle with the Army, however, is possible for Grethe only after she resolves the traumatic tremors reverberating throughout her "personal" life. The film deals neatly with Grethe's father, who expresses his pride in Grethe at her final hearing, and who has revealed the sources of his misogyny and coldness, sources which rest in common misconceptions about the causes of homosexuality. His awakening serves as a model to spectators who might harbor similar misconceptions or condemnations based on fear, which the film shows to be misguided. Grethe also resolves the tensions with her children, expressing to Matt and Linette, his fiancée, her resistance to their pastor's view of her lifestyle. When they tell her that he is not in favor of her lifestyle, she responds, "Which part? The part where I pay my taxes, the part where I hold a job, where I make a home for my father and kids, where I defend my country?" Anticipating her final speech, these remarks align lesbianism with "family values" neatly and without concern for lesbian practices, such as peace politics, which challenge their centrality. Her other sons, who had at moments in the film expressed varying levels of support and disdain, return to the bosom of the family she has created with Diane, understanding that they are not in danger of "becoming" gay as a result of her parenting. All of these reconciliations facilitate Grethe's resistance to the Army's policy. By restoring the family, Grethe is able to contest an injustice carved out of the social relations in which it is located without contradictions remaining on the narrative level.

Although the film abandons those contradictions, it must address the relationship between Grethe and Diane. They represent the two co-constituted and interdependent axes of "lesbian" in *Serving in Silence*. As indicated earlier, Diane is the counterpoint to Grethe's character (fluid, creative, compassionate, easy-going, caring), and those differences are highlighted by reference to Grethe's heroic, Viking, Northern traits. The relationship between Grethe and Diane is generally depicted as asexual, peppered with caresses, hair-fondling, heads on shoulders, and affection (including the exchange of rings). Although the film insists narratively that Grethe and Diane simply *are* lesbians, it bows to the demand to link this version of lesbianism to sexuality, in the sequence in which Grethe and Diane (finally) kiss. What is significant about the kiss beyond its scarcity on prime-time television is that it reveals the instability of lesbian-as-identity through an odd attention to costuming, which becomes significant in the kiss sequence. Without tracing the motif of *mise- en-scene* in great detail, one can point to several moments in the film which would seem to indicate that lesbianism, as well as femininity, maternity, and other social positions, is worn rather than being an intrinsic component of identity. These moments include the attention to Cammermeyer in camouflage (a butch image which Diane offhandedly acknowledges and denies), the sequence in which Linette helps Grethe on with her officer's uniform, the sequence in which Diane begins to remove it, the sequence outside the Mormon church where Matt and Linette are married, and, finally, the sequence involving the kiss between Grethe and Diane. What each of these moments shares is an attention to costume, to drag, in the creation of social position and the role of appearance in undermining a stable sense of how and what "lesbian" *means* to others. Grethe moves from soldier, an historically alluring image in the lesbian community, to officer, and in that move Linette's assistance with her uniform helps them to bond as future relations and as women. In that sequence, Grethe struggles to fit into an old uniform that has become too small, and Linette and Grethe engage in a little girl talk over weight gain. The film's desire to secure some naked "truth" of lesbian is frustrated at this moment, because Grethe is shown to simply "put on" her costume, and she will put on another, that of mother of the groom. Grethe and Diane's exclusion from the wedding ceremony (not "because they *are* lesbians" but because they are *not* Mormons) similarly indicates that social positionality is relational and not intrinsic, not identity-driven unless there exists another term of comparison. The removal of her uniform functions not only as a heavy-handed metaphor of her victimage but also strips Grethe to her essence-as-lesbian: a woman with another woman, without camouflage or authority. But this sequence is quickly followed by several short sequences involving other roles: as nurse with a patient who confirms that Grethe can still be a good soldier, and as mother with her son, just beaten up in a fight at school over her lesbianism, whom she tells: "I'm supposed to be the soldier, not you."

The costuming component of *mise-en-scene*, as with many films, thus sets an agenda which works in tension with the film's narrative. That tension culminates in the kiss sequence, which begins with the family watching a report on television news about Cammermeyer's hearing that catches a glimpse of Diane's face on screen. Diane, in the kitchen making popcorn, tells those gathered that she will watch it on tape. Diane thus provides the cue that this sequence, too, will be concerned with simulation. As Diane sees herself on the small screen, she receives a telephone call from her sister; she hesitates to take the call that will confirm that she has been "outed" on television. Diane emerges from the bedroom to join Grethe on the porch and tells her that her sister had called simply to tell her that she hated Diane's hat. This little moment of levity sparks intimacy. Diane has seemingly overcome her fear of the public disclosure of her lesbianism, and the lifting of that weight allows Grethe and Diane to embrace and kiss (nicely and with genuine affection, as Carswell [1995] sees it). From the kiss in tight close-up, the film dissolves to Grethe's Bronze Star award, and cuts to her on television about to make the speech which closes the film. From this editing, it would seem that the kiss authorizes the reconciliation of Grethe's "identity as lesbian" and her identity as soldier. But, curiously, the motivation for the kiss is in fact Diane's own resolution of the private/public conflict into which she has been thrown as Grethe's lover. As I suggested at the beginning of this chapter, however, the "real" Diane remains reluctant to make her last name public, and she retains the sense that the priority of the film rests with "the love story," with acceptance rather than with political challenges to the military as an oppressive, hierarchical, exploitative institution.

The "conclusion" that the film represents, then, does not curtail the melodramatizing of conflict, the internalization of external strife, the offering of personal/internal explanations for social oppression, or the impulse to curtail the contradictions emerging from hierarchies of knowledge and power. Although *Serving in Silence* makes one lesbian's story available to millions of American television spectators, its version of resistance and 1980s populism (in the body of the charismatic individual) is thwarted by its own strategies and makes visible the ideological stakes in processing lesbianism through the techtronics of the melodramatic imagination. If speaking lesbianism is preferable to silence, we must persistently evaluate the terms of that speech and the stories that remain silenced in the name of the popular.

ENDNOTES

1. The press packet for *Go Fish* proclaims it as "a groundbreaking new film about life and love, offering a candid slice of urban lesbian life in the '90s. This romantic comedy follows a closely knit group of friends as they go on dates, endure fashion crises, oversleep, wish for and encounter love." (Press packet courtesy of the Samuel Goldwyn Company).

2. I borrow Gilroy's description of Afrocentrism, which shares with contemporary engagements with sexuality an increasing abandonment of the public sphere and a focus on what has traditionally been understood as individualized, private symbolic registers. This is not to say that the public/private distinction should be easily maintained theoretically or that sexuality, the register of human experience most often assigned to the "private," cannot be understood as a social phenomenon; to the contrary, the public/private distinction is what is at stake as a social operation in consigning matters sexual to the bedroom, "where they properly belong."

3. These include AIDS storylines on soaps to the movie *Philadelphia* to domestic melodramas on lesbian custody, and so on.

REFERENCES

Brooks, P. (1976). *The melodramatic imagination: Balzac, Henry James, melodrama, and the modes of excess.* New Haven, CT: Yale University Press.

Carswell, S. (1995, February). An officer and a gentleman. *Out,* p. 60.

Feuer, J. (1995). *Seeing through the eighties: Television and Reaganism.* Durham, NC: Duke University Press.

Gilroy, P. (1993). *Small acts: Thoughts on the politics of black culture.* London: Serpent's Tail.

Landy, M. (1991). Introduction. In M. Landy (Ed.) *Imitations of life: A reader on film and television melodrama* (pp. 15-16). Detroit: Wayne State University.

11

Only a Joke?: The Standup Comedy of Women of Color

Cristina Bodinger-deUriarte

In the 1980s, stand-up comedy enjoyed a popularity boom, and women comics enjoyed increased visibility:

> Women stand-up comics are fashionable these days. It was not always thus. Indeed, according to erudite and popular opinion, women comics were an incongruous, indeed rare, lot . . . philosophers like Bergson and Schopenhauer had declared that women had no sense of humor; ergo they could not perform humor. (Sochen, 1991, p. 141)

By the 1990s, this boom had been captured by television. Numerous stand-up comedy shows were broadcast on cable, independent, and local and national network television stations. However, very little contemporary scholarship has been devoted to stand-up comedy and the content of stand-up routines. An even smaller body of work addresses female comics. Fraiberg (1994) believes this is because few academic disciplines comfortably include the subject: "Mainstream women's stand-up is too performance or drama oriented for the social sciences; it's not dramatic enough for drama studies; it's too popular and nonfictional for literary studies; and it's evidently too mainstream for feminist studies" (p. 318).

In addition, with the exception of a few articles discussing Moms Mabley (Williams, 1991) and Whoopi Goldberg (Dresner, 1991), virtually no research focuses on comedy performed by women of color. Most studies of women's stand-up comedy discuss a few comics in-depth (Dresner, 1991, 1994; Fraiberg, 1994; Pershing, 1991; Sheppard, 1991; Sochen, 1991; Walker, 1991) to provide case studies that test established theory or to generate new theories about why female comics may address particular issues in their humor. However, without a broader collection of data, these studies cannot with any certainty tell you what most women of color (or women in general) actually do in their stand-up routines. This chapter looks at the televised stand-up comedy routines of black women and Latinas[1] in order to discover what they do and do not joke about in a public forum, how this relates to established theories and feminist studies on humor, and what this communicates about the social position and self-representation of women of color.

Most work on humor addresses literary humor, humor in the workplace, humor as folklore, or joke books. Although little scholarship specifically addresses stand-up comedy, scholars in communications, literary criticism, psychology, and sociology have long addressed the social roles humor plays. Generally, humor has been seen either to reinforce aspects of society (Burma, 1946; Chapman, 1983; Coser, 1960; McWhirter, 1994; Wilt, 1980) or to challenge them, (Blakely, 1980; Fraiberg, 1994; Sheppard, 1991; Walker, 1988, 1991). Humor also has been looked at as an expression of group experiences and viewpoints, presenting positive group images or exposing perceived conflicts or hardships (Coser, 1960; Martineau, 1972). Much has been written about the racial and ethnic humor of whites (Apte, 1987; Barron, 1950; Ehrlich, 1979; Gadfield,1979). A few articles also look at self-stereotyping or self-denigrating humor by minority comics (Saper, 1991). Empirical work examining joke content that challenges stereotypes and comments on the social concerns of particular racial or ethnic groups is strangely absent.

Because humor is seen as a safe avenue for communicating and confronting social frustrations or inequities (Barreca, 1991; Duncan, 1962; Eastman, 1943; Martineau, 1972; Walker, 1991) most theories treat humor as potentially expressing the possibility of social change:

> It is risky to admit to one's self that a situation might be funny or absurd, because to do that means taking into account the idea of change. When you see humor in a situation, it implies that you can also then imagine how the situation could be altered. Once you can

imagine altering a situation that is not to your liking, you confront your own desire for change (Barreca, 1991, pp. 19-20)

Feminist studies of female humorists have focused particularly on the confrontational aspect of humor in "recovering and defining women's distinctive comedic traditions" (McWhirter, 1994, p. 189).

> The humor of American women has in fact functioned as a means of establishing and representing a community of shared concerns about oppression. Despite the daunting effects of female socialization to be passive and dependent on male approbation . . . women have nonetheless used humor to connect with one another and to announce their superiority to cultural myths about their nature and behavior. (Walker, 1991, p. 60)

As Walker (1988) points out, women's humor challenges the basic assumptions about women's roles:

> Instead of passive, emotional beings, women in their humorous writing show themselves to be assertive and insightful, alert to the absurdities that affect not only their lives, but the values of American culture in a larger sense. The tradition of women's humor is a record of women's conscious denial of inferiority and subordination and a testament to their spirit of survival in a sexist culture. (Walker, 1988, p. 183)

The resulting picture is one of women empowering women through humor that frequently challenges patriarchal values.

> Such comedy is risky. It is confrontational and boundary breaking, since you walk away feeling angry even as you laugh. This sort of comedy does not do away with women's feelings of powerlessness—instead it underscores the political nature of a woman's role. It should make us even more determined to change those aspects of our situation that confines us. It is comedy that inspires as well as entertains. (Barreca, 1991, pp. 14-15)

These observations grow out of studies focusing on literary humor, television situation comedy, or a few white female comedians. As will be shown, stand-up routines performed by black women and Latinas paint a different picture.

METHODS

All stand-up comedy programs broadcast on basic cable, independent, regional, and national network television over a 16-month period (April 1993 through July 1994) were taped[2] to obtain the comic routines of black women and Latinas for analysis.[3] Included were three "specialty venues" that target a particular audience by casting only a specific type of comic: *Comedy Compadres* (Latinos), *Comic View* (blacks), and *Girl's Night Out* (women). The five "mainstream (nonspecialty) venues" are: *A&E's An Evening at the Improv, The A-List, Caroline's Comedy Hour, Comedy on the Road,* and *Comic Strip Live.* This yielded 405 comic routines, of which only 33 (8%) were performed by black women and Latinas.

Stand-up routines were analyzed for themes and intergroup relations.[4] Themes are the specific subject matter on which the punchline depends. Only the punchline-dependent theme in a given joke was coded. For example, the following two jokes by black female comics have an imbedded sports theme, but were coded for their substance abuse theme because that is the "hook" for the punchline—the focal point of the humor, the behavior being "sent up":

> I just love professional athletes, don't you? Yeah, you know they're always so involved in community service and all—of course that's because they're all *addicted to drugs.*

> You know that one guy who was suspended for using cocaine but the Yankees took him right back? I don't think he should have been given back his position as *snort-stop* and *free-base.*

The analysis of intergroup relations includes the characterization of male-female, black-white, or Latino-Anglo relations. Content concerning intergroup relations may be attached to punchlines or imbedded in the lead-in material. Themes and intergroup relations were considered in terms of the presence or absence of humor that challenged stereotypes or oppressive intergroup relations. Finally, the routines were considered in terms of their cumulative value in constructing a representation of these women and their communities.

WHO'S JOKING?

Three-quarters of the comics featured on televised stand-up programs are men, and most are white men. White women also are represented, but to a much smaller degree. Minority female stand-up comics are the smallest demographic subgroup.

Table 11.1. Breakdown of Comics by Gender and Ethnicity/Race Across All Venues.

	White Men	Men of Color	White Women	Women of Color
Sample Total (n = 405)	53% (216)	21% (84)	18% (72)	8% (33)
Male vs. Female Total	74% (n=300) Males		26% (n=105) Females	
White vs. Nonwhite Total	71% (n=288) Whites		29% (n=117) Nonwhites	

Female, racial, and ethnic visibility is largely provided by specialty venues that target particular demographic groups. Consequently, women of color rely on specialty programming for about two-thirds of their air time.

Table 11.2. Breakdowns of Comics by Gender and Ethnicity/Race by Specialty Venues.

Specialty Venue (n = 111)	Men of Color (n = 51)	White Women (n = 39)	Women of Color (n = 21)
Comedy Compadres (Latino)	69%	NA	31%
Comic View (Black)	86%	NA	14%
Across Both Ethnic Venues	71%	NA	29%
Girl's Night Out	NA	93%	7%

An investigation of mainstream venues, those venues meant to appeal to a broad audience, reveals that they are, actually, predominately white, male venues. As shown in Table 11.3, 74% of comics performing on mainstream venue programs are white men; an additional 11% are men of color. Thus, on mainstream programs, only 15% of the comics are women, less than one-third of whom are women of color. This means that only a tiny proportion (4%) of the humor on nonspecialty shows is generated by women of color.

Table 11.3. Mainstream Venues: Breakdown of Comics by Gender and Ethnicity/Race.

Mixed Venue (n = 294)	White Men (%)	Men of Color (%)	White Women (%)	Women of Color (%)
A&E at the Improv	73	14	7	6
A-List	90		10	
Caroline's Comedy Hour	76	5	19	
Comedy on the Road	70	10	10	10
Comic Strip Live	62	23	15	
Totals Across all Venues (%)	74 (n = 216)	11 (n = 33)	11 (n = 33)	4 (n = 12)
Male vs. Female Totals			85% (n = 249) Males	15% (n = 45) Females
White vs. Nonwhite Totals			85% (n = 249) Whites	15% (n = 45) Nonwhites

Although no data are available on just how many women choose this career and what proportion of them are women of color, stand-up programs specializing in female and minority comics show this to be a casting issue. For example, when *Girl's Night Out* was aired, female comics were plentiful enough to provide a nonredundant cast for a weekly, hour-long program. However, booking agents for the programs apparently follow a formula, booking one or, rarely, two women or persons of color for each five to six performers on a show.[5] Perhaps the observations Collier and Beckett (1980) made over a decade ago still provide the best explanation: "Comedy is a business that has traditionally been the domain of males, and their influence still dominates—in numbers, in attitudes, and in determining the way things are done and who does them" (pp. xi-xii).

Women of color receive the least airtime among professional comics. With the exception of the irregularly aired *Comedy Compadres* and *Comic View*, the sampled comedy programs present themselves as culturally mixed, mainstream venues—that is, as shows that do not feature a specific demographic group. However, these shows are primarily white. *Girl's Night Out* is presented as a culturally mixed female venue; but it also is primarily white.

The three specialty shows specifically featuring females, Latinos, or blacks increase the overall visibility of women of color among televised stand-up comics from 4% to a mere 8%. This underrepresentation is more serious than might initially be apparent because women of color are the *only* group fitting the casting criteria for every program. Yet, they are the smallest proportion of performers.

Again this seems to be the result of casting decisions as 20% of the black comics on the nonsampled *Def Comedy Jam* were females "missing" from the sampled programs. Further, almost one-third of the Latino venue performers were female. Proportionate representation should be more than 4% within mainstream venues and certainly, among female comics in a female venue, more than 7%.

White males enjoy the greatest visibility and the greatest access to audiences. As a result, they maintain the majority voice across comedy despite their absence from the specialty venues. Four of the five mixed venue programs appear on basic cable, whereas the fifth is a network show. By contrast, two of the three speciality shows are aired only regionally, whereas the third, which appears on basic cable, is aired irregularly. In other words, unless you lived in the targeted neighborhoods, you could not view the specialty programs. Thus, the voices of black and Latino comics are further marginalized.

Pershing's (1991) observations on conditions faced by Kate Clinton, a lesbian comic, also summarize the context of stand-up for all types of minority female comics:

> Her access to the public role of stand-up comedian is restricted and negotiated by cultural norms. Hence, within this traditionally male-dominated domain, she has to work very hard to find a forum for validation and public recognition. This affects her performance by putting additional pressure on her, as a woman performer, to measure up to conventionally male-identified standards, while simultaneously attempting to call them into question. (p. 203)

Kate Clinton, Joan Rivers, and Abby Stein have all referred to this difficulty in interviews. White women are less visible than white men, yet still enjoy more than twice the airtime and have greater access to broad audiences than do women of color. They may, therefore, have achieved a type of "critical mass" that occupationally empowers them and allows them to better resist dominant norms.

WHAT DO WOMEN OF COLOR JOKE ABOUT?

> The topics of women's humor reflect their lives as women, their
> interests as women, their positions as women in male-dominated
> cultures, and, consequently, their world as women—a world always
> a little apart from that of men. (Dresner, 1991, p. 180)

Just what themes are included in contemporary stand-up comedy performed by women of color? Do they, as Dresner (1991) says of Whoopi
Goldberg, use humor to communicate the absurdity and flawed logic of a
"system that discriminates against minorities," and does their humor focus
on their status as women "in male dominated cultures" (pp. 183-184)?

For most minority women comics in this study, humor specifically addressing experiences unique to women is infrequent. These
infrequent experiences, as two black comics demonstrate, include jokes
about breast feeding and mammograms:

> My sister has a new baby boy which she breastfeeds in public. We're
> at a Raiders game and she whips it out. I'm trying to cover her with
> my coat and she says, "This is perfectly natural," and I say, "Well, is
> it natural to have your breast up there on the big screen? Wow, it's
> huge!"

> My sister-in-law was really upset because she went to a gynecologist
> and got a mammogram. They put her breast between two cold
> plates and tried to smash it flat like a waffle. . . . They should make it
> special—Yeah, a singing mammogram where a guy in a clown suit
> sings . . . [has a little song ending with] "and if we pull a little too
> hard, well, here's some balloons and a nice little card."

These jokes have a subtext, an implied message, about the objectification of women's bodies. In the first example, there is an interplay
between the breast in its natural function and the sexual objectification
of the female anatomy. In the second example, the cold and impersonal
objectification of a women's body in medical procedures is noted. The
humorous alternative is not a true suggestion but still functions to imply
that there might be a means of humanizing the experience.

The level of confrontation in these examples is minor. Women of
color in the study rarely made jokes that were more directly challenging
or critical of society. Further, little of their humor addressed the unique
experiences of women in the manner that these examples do. And
although the more traditional roles of women sometimes set the scene in
the jokes, white female comics are more likely to make use of domesticity for humor. For example, with white female comics like Rosanne, "the

emphasis in housewife humor is on the liberation of the individual from the constraints of the nuclear family" (Dresner, 1994, p. 229). This is not the case for minority female comics. Instead, they set the scene with references to cooking or shopping or cleaning, but domesticity is not the subject of their jokes. This reinforces traditional views of the woman's place. McWhirter (1994) commented on this in refuting claims that women's humor is generally subversive and antitraditional: "Women's laughter may be subversive, but comedy as a genre, it would seem, is almost fatally overdetermined in its reinscription of fixed, traditional gender roles and hierarchies of power" (p. 190).

In fact, any of the themes most popular with minority female comics could be used as avenues for critique, but they are not (see Table 11.4).

For all groups of comedians, sex and dating are two of the most popular themes. What distinguishes the dating and sexual humor of women of color, however, is its nonconfrontational nature. Sexual humor takes place primarily outside a relationship context and generally does not involve any criticism of a sexual partner. Rather, the humor centers more on fantasy and on enjoying the appearance of sexy men:

> Latina comic: I do love the Dallas Cowboys—All right!! But I hate commentators like Pat and John. They make every play the most important play of the game. Pat-John-John-Pat-John. "Well, John, will you explain to us what happened." "Sure Pat." And he talks very fast about nothing. No, really, I could care less. I just want to know if Troy is wearing any underwear. Sssi! Wouldn't it be great if we could have our own female sports announcers like Joan Rivers? Oh, can we talk? Will you look at Troy's pants? Look at his pants!

> Black comic: My man got mad 'cause I took my girlfriend to Tigers—for all you White folks, that's a Black version of Chippendales. He said, "I don't think you should be lookin' at all those naked men." "Well, I made love to you when I came home." "But all those names you screamed, not one of them was mine."

Appearance jokes are made by more than half of these minority women, frequently about their own weight or about the weight of a female relative or friend.

> Latina comic: I went to an aerobics class a few weeks ago with a friend of mine who knows the instructor and afterwards she introduced us. And my friend says, "This is Jackie, and she's recently lost over 100 pounds." And the aerobics instructor looks at me and with a straight face she says, "Oh my God, you must have been *so* fat!!"

Table 11.4. Most Popular Humor Themes for Women of Color (Percent Reflects the Proportion of Comics Mentioning the Theme).

Sexuality & Dating	70%
Appearance & Weight	55%
Family & Kids	48%
Celebrities	48%
Stupidity	42%

> Black comic: My mom is big, y'all. Soon as she gets in the car, the seat sinks down, the hubcaps pop off, the car's saying "Tilt, tilt, tilt!" The seat belt won't fit around her, so we just tie her in with a rope.

Although one might argue that this reinforces stereotypes about minority women as "fat mamas," jokes about personal appearance, particularly "fat jokes," are too common and too long-standing a tradition among comics of all ilks to be seen in this light. Interestingly, women do not target men with appearance humor. The fact that women tell personal appearance jokes only about themselves and other women reinforces that part of the social order that evaluates women by their appearances rather than by their accomplishments.

Family and children tie with celebrities for third place as topics of humor and are used as material by almost half of these comics. For Latinas, family jokes most often involve insecurity about parenting:

> I don't care if you're brown, black, white, pink, whatever. It's very hard being a parent because you never know if you're making the right mistakes.

> Kids are dropping out of school like flies because their parents are helping them with their homework.

For the black female comics, family jokes most often revolve around discipline and materialism:

> Children have really gotten out of hand these days, don't you think? Right now, beat your kids—just go on home and beat them.

My child gave me a dozen roses. They were dead—I'm talkin' Elvis dead. I said, "Baby, how come you give your mama dead roses?" He said, "Don't think of them as dead. Think of them as potpourri on a stick." They all want something for nothing.

He says, "Mama, take me down to the mall for some sneakers." So I take him down to the mall 'cause that's my boy. I said, "Hey, that's my boy, give him some of them shoes over there." And the man told me, "That's $169.95." Now, I'm diggin' all through the box and I can't find no NBA contract, so I ask, "Now why would a child, 4'9", D minus average, need some $169 shoes?" And he gonna tell me that for $169 he can get those shoes and pump, pump, pump, pump, pump. I tell my child, "You know what? You can get those $20 shoes and I'll buy you a $5 bicycle pump, and you can pump your butt off for $25."

Such humor either refers to male children or leaves the gender unspecified. This reinforces a patriarchal value system by supporting the relative cultural importance of men. Further, family humor does not include spouses or ex-spouses. The humor remains fairly well within traditional roles and is not confrontational.

Celebrity humor tied for third most popular theme. This humor can be either derisive or complementary. In both cases, however, the humor remains "safe":

Black comic: My dad is a Pentecostal minister. He preaches about everything. Sometimes he's preaching, and I don't even know what he's talking about. One time he was preaching, he says, "God is not straight or gay; God is not woman or man; God is not Black or White." I say, "Dad, is God Michael Jackson?"

Black comic: [Dances in] That's Cris Cross "Jump, Jump." Well, that's all you *can* do if you put your pants on backwards!

Latina comic: If you haven't seen *American Me* yet, I'll give you three good reasons to see it: Edward James Olmos. He actually created a brand new technique of acting: The triple M: Monotone, Mexican, Macho.

Blacks joked about black celebrities, and Latinas joked about Latino celebrities, investing the humor with an element of racial/ethnic group identity. However, neither group referred to female celebrities. The only fame acknowledged in their humor belonged to men. Again, this can be seen as reinforcing traditional gender roles.

Finally, stupidity was the only other topic to be humorously treated by more than 40% of the women of color. For all types of comics, stupidity is a traditional topic:

Latina comic: My brother is kind of stupid. He doesn't steal VCRs. No, no—that would be too easy. He actually tried to make a bootleg VCR headcleaner for a friend.

Latina comic: The aerobics instructor says [strong valley-girl accent], "You know what? I work on my body four hours every day, and you can too. But you have to start off slow, like at one hour, and then it's one and a half and then two and then two and a half and then three and then three and a half and then you're up to four!" All I could think of was, "How about giving your brain five minutes. You know what? You could start off slow, like with a coloring book, and then a magazine, and then books!"

Black comic: Have you ever dated someone so dumb they didn't qualify as a second person for the car pool lane? Nothing like sitting in traffic with an idiot.

One might use this topic to focus on the stupidity of particular socially significant behaviors, like racism or sexism, or to address particular political issues. The earlier examples show that, once again, women of color avoid humor critical of the status quo.

The striking thing about their humor is the ability to be noncontroversial—making innocuous jokes about sex and dating; exaggerating a critique of one's own appearance or that of another; sharing anecdotes about one's grandparents, parents, and children; poking fun at a celebrity; and ridiculing stupid people.

One more theme bears mention as the most popular theme among Latina comics—the misuse of the English language by Spanish speakers. Punchlines are dependent on or underscored by this misuse:

My kids asked me about euthanasia. "Well, mi hijo [my son], there's a lot of them. They're good at math, but, hey, they're just like everybody else in the world."

Ironically, aside from jokes about celebrities, humor about the misuse of English provides the only example of content that addresses group identity and may serve to reaffirm the values of bilingualism. By joking about language misuse and recognizing it as a widespread "problem," Latina comics also may help to desensitize a touchy subject by providing reassurance that these embarrassing errors are common experiences. However, one also might argue that such jokes merely reinforce derisive majority attitudes about more recent immigrants. This view gains credence given the dearth of counter-balancing humor depicting other (noncelebrity) persons of color as literate and accomplished. Further, whereas male Latino comics often use Spanish words in their jokes to build a sense of community among Latino audiences, only one Latina comic did this.

> Eddie Olmos is so sexy, man—*Feo pero* [ugly but] sexy. I love his big Mexican *bigote*—That's Spanish for "mustache," for all you perverts!

As can be seen, confrontational humor does not really figure into the topics most popular among women of color. Further, their jokes do not use role reversal, irony, or any other technique to address a "system that discriminates against minorities." One might suggest, however, that confrontational humor could well be found in the less popular topics. For this reason, the topics deemed to have the highest social comment potential also were examined.

POTENTIAL TOPICS OF SOCIAL COMMENTARY AND CONFRONTATIONAL HUMOR

Analysis of comedy routines across racial, ethnic, and gender groups reveals that quite a few stand-up comics use their performances as a means of addressing their social positions and other socio-political realities. Sometimes this involves making nonhumorous, direct statements about social concerns. As Blakely (1980) states: "The natives are restless. We use our humor to deliver our complaints about the status quo. We tend to be a bit edgy at times because we know from experience just how many potential toes we are stepping on" (p. 10).

By and large, however, female black and Latina comics do not use their humor to complain about the status quo. Only 11% of the female black and Latina comics include serious commentary. Further, physical abuse was the only topic presented in such commentary.

> Black comic: I learned a long time ago, I learned from Tina Turner: If you're being abused, you gotta run, right? I mean don't stick around and get abused by anybody.

Comedy produced by women of color might reasonably be expected to contain themes concerned with their social condition, such as being female or of color, having a lower status position than other groups, and being underrepresented in the occupation of their choice. However, as is shown later, women of color perform stand-up routines that avoid jokes dealing with occupational status, gender, race or ethnicity, and social, economic, and political conditions.

Despite well-established demographic information that indicates that women of color are underrepresented in many higher status occupations, their comedic representatives do not address this issue. The black female or Latina stand-up does not even address occupational inequities within her own occupation of professional comic. No black comics and only one Latina joked about job experiences:

> Hey, it's really tough being a Chicana actress in Hollywood—you know it. But it's finally changing 'cause when I first came here, all I played was—Maria, the gang-member's sister; Maria, the gang-member's girlfriend. But not anymore. Just the other day I got to play Lupe (strikes a proud pose), the gang-member's *mother*. Or maybe I'm just getting old.

One might argue that occupational humor is the least important of the potential arenas of confrontational humor for Latina and black female comics—that women of color may have bigger issues to confront. Indeed, numerous studies have documented the continuing use of sexist themes in humor (Bergmann 1986; Bill & Naus 1992; Moore, Griffiths, Payne 1987). Thus, one might expect there to be potential for redress or revenge in the humor of both majority and minority women. Women of color, however, do not use gender humor to "address shared concerns about oppression" (Walker, 1991, p. 60).

Lauding successful women also is virtually ignored, as is the conspiratorial style used by many white female stand-up comics. Comments such as "We girls know . . . " or "Now, we ladies are . . . " are almost completely absent from the humor of the minority female comic. The exceptions are jokes about being overweight—hardly a positive or progressive contribution to building group identity—as these jokes by two black comics show:

> I don't know what happens when you turn over 30. And ladies, you all know this is true. We fall asleep in 5/7 and wake up in Lane Bryant.

> I found a product called "I Can't Believe It's Not Butter." Why don't they say what they really mean? "Your big ass don't need no more butter." 'Cause women are very sensitive about their weight. We're very sensitive because we want to look good.

Black women and Latinas do not make jokes about women as a group; they do not make jokes about men as a group; they do not make jokes about boyfriends or husbands; and they barely touch on male-female relationships or sexism.[6] There are rare exceptions. One black female joked about controlling her relationships with her purse strings:

> My man is always on my back trying to get me to lose weight. "Annie, either me or the fat has got to go." "The fat one's paying the bills—you know who'll be leaving, doncha?"

The deadbeat boyfriend theme might be seen as contributing to negative majority stereotypes about minorities. However, this was the only joke of its kind so no representational pattern emerged. It was, in fact, the sole example of minority female humor with a male-female relationship theme. Boyfriend and husband jokes have not disappeared; they are still alive and well and being told by white women. White women are also the ones telling stereotypic "men" jokes involving slovenly habits, cheapness, remote control possessiveness, and so forth.

Black women do not address sexism in their humor. And although some Latinas (19%) addressed sexism, it received superficial treatment. Latina jokes about sexism primarily focus on men who make rude remarks:

> There's always some 4 foot 11 inch guy on the street corner with no shirt in February with a name like Juan Jose Puneta Tu Madre—and he's got a boom box, you know. And I don't know what happens, but when a butt goes by and the boom box is on, he's like (grabs crotch and gyrates) "Boom-boom mommy-mommy-mommy, boom-boom!" (pauses) And what am I supposed to do? (wide-eyed expression) "Boom-boom poppy- poppy-poppy, boom-boom"?

> I'm walking along and I get to a stop light and this guy catches up to me and he smiles, so I smile back. And to a guy, you know, this is like *license to start a family*. And he looks at me and he goes, "Ooo-eee-damn-mmm-mm-mmM!—For a skinny girl you got yourself a nice little onion. (Makes exaggerated confused looks).

> I was recently in the Deep South—Yeah, I know *that's* scary, *me* in the Deep South. Anyway, I said to one of these girls down there "You are so lucky that guys don't say things to you in the street." And this perky little blonde goes (southern accent) "Oh, yes, they do!" And I'm thinking—Oh, great, you mean there's no difference between 8th Avenue in Manhattan and Maple Drive in Alabama? She says, "Oh, they look at me and they go, 'Uh-huh, mm-hmm'." I'm thinking—Uh-huh, mm-hmm? You're buggin' on uh-huh, mm-hmm when every day of my life I get (makes obscene sounds) "I want to sniff your panties"—and *that's* just from my *doorman*.

Sex and dating are the only gender-linked themes Latinas and black women joke about with any frequency. For black females, this ranks first in popularity; every black female comic joked about sex or dating in her routine, as did 42% of the Latina comics. However, their treatment of the topic is devoid of comment on the nature of male-female relationships. Sex and dating appear unconnected to the unequal status between men and women. Rather, the treatment of dating and sexuality is circumstantial or topic-specific, as in the routines of two black comics:

> I was reading the personals and I got confused. It said: Single Black male seeks Nubian queen, must be Afrocentric, culturally aware, and celebrate Kwanza (pause) *race unimportant*—so, I'm wondering?

> You know, women reach their sexual peak at 35 and men do at 18. I'm surprised there aren't more 35-year-old women cruising the high schools. "Come on, I got Nintendo and I'm old enough to buy beer!"

Latinas and black women do not joke about their personal dating experiences, their difficulties with being single, the sexual ineptness of their partners, inequities and dysfunction in relationships, or sexual double standards. This generic and decontextualized treatment of sexuality and dating divests the humor of any potential power to confront gender inequality.

Only 2 of the 33 minority female comedy routines included instances of racial or ethnic humor that challenged stereotypes. Both comics were Latina:

> They ask me such stupid questions, like, "How long have you been working on that accent?" What accent? This is original dialect, *Que no*? Then they ask me "Are you *really* Mexican?" No, I'm just pretending to be one because I thought I'd enjoy being an oppressed minority.

> My professor told me if I would answer some questions for my fellow students on Mexican culture and Mexican history, then I could get extra credit. Lucky for them (heavy sarcasm in voice and face) I *am* the spokesman for *all* Mexican people. Anyway, one of the students says to me, "Well, you claim to be Mexican and that's all right and everything, but if you are a Mexican, why don't you look like a Mexican?" I said, "Oh, I'm sorry, I left my leaf-blower in the dorm."

The relative dearth of such humor among women of color is puzzling, particularly in that these jokes are very well received. Not only is their humor devoid of socially significant racial and ethnic commentary, but race or ethnicity is seldom mentioned once the comics have been introduced.

The social and economic oppression of minority groups makes it reasonable to anticipate some treatment of these topics in the routines of minority comics. In fact, their routines are virtually apolitical. Poverty is the only social issue that is treated with any frequency by Latina (38%) and black women (25%) but, as seen next in the routines of two Latinas, in a decontextualized and merely personal way. Again this diverts the humor from its potential as social commentary:

Someone broke into our house, but we weren't mad—we knew *it was a mistake*. My father grabs the thief and says (heavy Mexican accent), "Hey, if you find anything worth to steal, I'll split it with you 50-50!"

We decided to go for a drive and about 40 of us pile into my dad's Plymouth. And I noticed we must have left the neighborhood 'cause we were driving on pavement.

VEXATION WITHOUT REPRESENTATION

This chapter clearly indicates that most of the comics performing these routines do not engage in reflective commentary on what it means to be a woman of color. Nonetheless, the images imbedded in these routines tell us much about the representation of these comics as black women and as Latinas. The patterns of representation often are not established through punchlines, as they are not the target of play, negotiation, or satire. Rather, the performers present images of everyday life that set the stage for the comic content and, thus, provide a backdrop of normalcy. It is here, then, that these women construct the "taken-for-granted" aspect of self-representation.

These routines overwhelmingly represent everyday life for women of color as a nonconflicted filling of traditional roles within patriarchy. As the preceding analysis demonstrates, women of color are presented as fairly passive heterosexuals who do not criticize their spouses or boyfriends. Single women may look at and appreciate sexy men but do not initiate action (as in the jokes about football players in tight pants and male strippers). In addition, they do not critique their domestic roles or a gender-typed division of labor. Not only are jokes about work absent, but jokes never even take place in a work setting. Even celebrities are only included in humor when they are male. Thus, the humor reinforces older patriarchal views of a woman's place by predominantly setting jokes in the home or at the mall. Representations embody homemaking, caretaking, and mothering sons (daughters are not mentioned).

Leisure time is represented as revolving around shopping and concerns about appearance. Although white female comics often critique the objectification of women's bodies, minority female comics often reinforce that objectification with jokes deriding the physical attributes of other women and through humor concerning their own attempts to measure up to this criterion:

> Latina comic: This guy was following me and he was really fine, so what did I do? I was suckin' in my stomach—you know when we are being looked at we suck in stuff we didn't know was even out!

> Black comic: My grandma was right about one thing. She said, "Some day, you gonna gain a li'l weight." We're out there buying those little panties and everything and I realized I couldn't wear those bikini ones anymore. I was in a department store and I thought I was looking at a *fun house mirror*—my butt was just *all around* back there.

Diet and exercise humor is also prevalent. As previously mentioned, the appearance of men is not targeted. Thus, comics who are women of color represent themselves as accepting a value system that judges them according to their appearance.

These comics do not challenge racial or ethnic stereotypes or deal with the social realities of being minority females. A few female comics even reinforce negative stereotypes of minority women as inadequate mothers. For these few, jokes included representations of abusive child-rearing practices and children born out-of-wedlock:

> Black comic: I whipped my child before I left home. He hadn't done nothin', but I was gonna be gone a couple hours so I figured he was gonna do *something* when I was gone. I might get home late and be too tired, so I just whipped him before I left.

> Latina comic: I have two teenage sons—Hey, *that's* probably why I'm still single.

Jokes about illiteracy also reinforce negative stereotypes:

> Black comic: Curfew really blew my mind—everybody in my house looked like spooks—and we ain't no good at Scrabble.

> Latina comic: The other night I was burning dinner when my 13-year-old asked me, "Mom, what about calculus?" . . . . I said "Isn't that what grows on your teeth? Get a toothbrush and take care of it."

English-misuse humor reinforces representations of the Latino community as primarily immigrants or marginal participants in U.S. culture. Similarly, comic routines that included typifications of minorities as criminals—blacks as "crack heads" and looters; Latinos as thieves—reinforce negative stereotypes of the African American community.

Low-income backgrounds were frequently the setting of comic scenarios. This reinforces majority conceptions that all minorities are members of the lowest income status groups. Naturally, this representation gains further power through the dearth of work-related scenarios. Unfortunately, comics do not simply set the scene in low-income areas with low-income participants, but represent upward mobility as a humorous anomaly.

> Black comic: My grandmother worked for a wealthy Mexican family—well, let's pretend for a moment that such a thing exists.

Two Latinas presented themselves as middle/upper class. However, in both cases, they reinforce the misperception of Latinos as impoverished by referring to themselves as exceptions:[7]

> My family are important historical figures in San Antonio. We're actually the first Hispanics on our block to actually own a house instead of clean it.

> I am originally from Mexico but now I live in L.A. California—oh, it gets better—I live in the *valley* (a moderately affluent area). . . . I went to Yale. I was in the Chicano Studies Program—I was the program.

In the Yale alumna's joke, achievement and academic excellence are again seen as the sole province of the majority. However, 20 years before this comic made her joke, I enrolled at Yale University along with 99 other Latinos, many of whom are now in leadership and professional positions. Rather than reflecting reality, humor emphasizing the supposed uniqueness of upward mobility and achievement for minority females denies their intelligence and competence while supporting a conservative political agenda that views affirmative action as foisting the unqualified minority employee on the hapless majority employer.

In sum, then, black women and Latinas are represented as lower class, passive, traditional heterosexuals whose place is in the home and whose concerns are appearance, shopping, and family. They are represented as women who fulfill traditional roles in a patriarchal system without reflection and without conflict.

CONCLUSION

Latinas and black women virtually ignore work, relationships, and gender as themes for humor. This is even true for women of color performing on *Girl's Night Out,* where the venue implies an "us-and-them" or "our turn" comic tone. Minority female comics tell jokes about sex and dating that are devoid of social comment. This might be due to racial or ethnic solidarity—that is, avoiding even humorous public critique of other blacks and Latinos. However, they do not otherwise use their humor to promote positive group identity. The cumulative impression is one in which minority women represent themselves as nonproblematically inhabiting traditional roles in a patriarchal system.

One might expect the least occupationally secure group, women of color, to avoid routines that use racial and ethnic solidarity building or confrontational humor in a mainstream venue. However, such jokes are anticipated in venues where other performers employ this humor and in specialty venues where racial and ethnic group identity is celebrated. Regardless of venue, women of color do not address their racial and ethnic identities and experiences through humor.[8]

Latina and black females also generally avoid jokes with a socioeconomic or political context. Instead, they share humorous personal experiences with poverty devoid of social critique. Even when the group is represented, poverty is presented as "taken-for-granted" rather than addressed as a consequence of economic oppression and long-standing discrimination. This anecdotal treatment, in combination with the absence of work-related humor, acts across routines to represent blacks and Latinos as inhabiting only the lowest social status positions. Such representations reinforce negative majority stereotypes of minorities as underachieving and economically dependent.

Overall, women of color choose noncontroversial, nonconfrontational material. This may be because they are aware of their relatively weak occupational position as well as their undervalued status in U.S. society. Chapman (1983) says that "for the individual, instances of humor can serve a number of functions simultaneously, and these depend on the social context" (p. 135). The apolitical nature of minority female humor generally remains unexplained by established humor theories but may well reflect the comics' social context. For televised stand-up comics, this means who has the greatest audience access and who receives the most airtime. One of the most pertinent aspects, then, is the fact that televised stand-up comedy is overwhelmingly dominated by white males.[9]

Not only are women of color less visible than white women, they also are females in a male-dominated realm. These combined factors may make the minority female performer feel particularly vulnerable to the social context in which she performs. It may well increase the difficulty with which she obtains "validation and public recognition" and multiply her perceptions that her own "access to the public role of stand-up comedian is negotiated by cultural norms" that are too risky to violate in confrontational humor (Pershing, 1991).

Media are often looked at as a reflection of the values of their audiences. Because Latinas and black women are nonconfrontational in their routines, one might think their concerns differed not at all from those of white males or that they had no real concerns. Studies of media content, thus, should be augmented by an awareness of how media are produced and who has access to the production.

ENDNOTES

1. Comics are referred to as blacks and Latinas or Latinos rather than African Americans and Hispanics in order to remain consistent with the terms overwhelmingly used by the comics in reference to their own group identities.
2. Only programs that consisted of complete, multiple stand-up routines as the only form of entertainment were taped, transcribed, and analyzed. Two coders worked together to guard against possible biases in interpretation. Intercoder reliability was 92% for the 10% of data coded in common. Shows on premium cable channels requiring additional pay from viewers were not included. Duplicated routines and rerun programs were dropped.
3. Asian comics were omitted because too few appeared during the sampling period.
4. All comedy routine excerpts are quotes taken from female comics unless specified otherwise.
5. A recent Oprah Winfrey show featured minority comics discussing this very issue. The black male comic, Sinbad, said that performing on mainstream programs was difficult because agents would cast only one black per show. One of the females agreed this was also true for female comics saying that she had been told by a booking agent that two women could not be on the same show because they would talk about all the same things. Presumably, agents do not notice that the five to six male comics per show perform overlapping material.
6. Although *Def Comedy Jam* fell outside the sampling criteria, black female comics performing on *Def Comedy Jam* followed a different pattern. Some of them specifically discussed dysfunctional relationships. They also joked about women. It is, therefore, puzzling that women in the other black venue, *Comic View*, did not address

women as a group, men as a group, male-female relationships, or sexism.

7. The misperception that important positions and leadership roles are devoid of minority membership created embarrassment at the Texas Capital recently when an extensive photo exhibit depicting the history of Texas was unveiled in the newly remodeled Capital building. Press reaction caused the exhibit to be hastily revised because no persons of color had been included. The following important figures were among those Texas minority women overlooked: Mrs. Walter Burton, first black to refuse to vacate a white-only seat on a train (1882); Lucy Gonzales-Parsons, black leader, labor organizer, writer and orator; Lena Guererro and Irma Rangel, two of the first Latinas elected to the State House of Representatives; Barbara Jordan, first Southern black woman elected to Congress; and Ann Lundy, founder of the Scott Joplin Chamber Orchestra featuring works by black composers. At the time of this exhibit, Texas Latinos accounted for three seats in Congress, four state senateships, and 21 state representatives.

8. A small number of Latinas and black females in the sample gave performances in both venues—their material did not differ by venue.

9. The fact that most of the televised shows simply broadcast the performances staged at different successful comedy clubs indicates that the preferred live stage venues are also dominated by white male comics.

REFERENCES

Apte, M. L. (1987). Ethnic humor versus sense of humor: An American socio-cultural dilemma. *American Behavioral Scientist, 30*(1), 27-41.

Barreca, R. (1991). *They used to call me Snow White . . . but I drifted: Women's strategic use of humor.* New York: Viking Penguin.

Barron, M. L. (1950). A content analysis of intergroup humor. *American Sociological Review, 15,* 88-94.

Bergmann, M. (1986). How many feminists does it take to make a joke? Sexist humor and what's wrong with it. *Hypatia 1*(1), 63-82.

Bill, B., & Naus, P. (1992). The role of humor in the interpretation of sexist incidents. *Sex Roles, 27*(11/12), 645-663.

Blakely, M. K. (1980). Commentary. In G. Kaufman & M. K. Blakely (Eds.), *Pulling our own strings: Feminist humor and satire* (p. 10). Bloomington: Indiana University Press.

Burma, J. H. (1946). Humor as a technique in race conflict. *American Sociological Review, 11,* 710-711.

Chapman, A. J. (1983). Humor and laughter in social interaction and some implications for humor research. In P. E. McGhee & J.

Goldstein (Eds.), *Handbook of humor research, Volume 1* (pp. 132-145). New York: Springer-Verlag.

Collier, D., & Beckett, K. (1980). *Spare ribs: Women in the humor biz.* New York: St. Martin's Press.

Coser, R. L. (1960). Laughter among colleagues: A study of the social functions of humor among the staff of a mental hospital. *Psychiatry, 23,* 81-95.

Dresner, Z. Z. (1991). Whoopi Goldberg and Lily Tomlin: Black and white women's humor. In J. Sochen (Ed.), *Women's comic visions* (pp. 179-192). Detroit: Wayne State University Press.

Dresner, Z. Z. (1994). Alice Childress's *Like One of the Family*: Domestic and undomesticated domestic humor. In G. Finney (Ed.), *Look who's laughing: Gender and comedy* (pp. 221-229). Amsterdam: Gordon and Breach.

Duncan, H. D. (1962). *Communication and social order.* New York: Bedminster.

Eastman, M. (1943, April). What we laugh at and why. *Readers Digest, 42,* 66-68.

Ehrlich, H. J. (1979) Observations on ethnic and intergroup humor. *Ethnicity, 6,* 383-298.

Fraiberg, A. (1994). Between the laughter: Bridging feminist studies through women's stand-up comedy. In G. Finney (Ed.), *Look who's laughing: Gender and comedy* (pp. 315-330). Amsterdam: Gordon and Breach.

Gadfield, N. J. (1979). Dynamics of humor in ethnic group relations. *Ethnicity, 6,* 373-382.

Martineau, W. H. (1972). A model of the social functions of humor. In J. Goldstein & P. E. McGhee (Eds.), *The psychology of humor* (pp. 101-125). New York: Academic Press.

McWhirter, D. (1994). Feminism/gender/comedy: Meredith Woolf and the reconfiguration of comic distance. In G. Finney (Ed.), *Look who's laughing: Gender and comedy* (pp. 189-204). Amsterdam: Gordon and Breach.

Moore, T. E., Griffiths, K., & Payne, B. (1987). Gender, attitudes towards women, and the appreciation of sexist humor. *Sex Roles, 16*(9/10), 521-531.

Pershing, L. (1991). There's a joker in the menstrual hut. In J. Sochen (Ed.), *Women's comic visions* (pp. 193-236). Detroit: Wayne State University Press.

Saper, B. (1991). A cognitive behavioral formulation of the relation between the Jewish joke and anti-semitism. *Humor, 4*(1), 41-59.

Sheppard, A. (1991). Social cognition, gender roles, and women's humor. In J. Sochen (Ed.), *Women's comic visions* (pp. 33-56). Detroit: Wayne State University Press.

Sochen, J. (1991). Slapsticks, screwballs, and bawds: The long road to the performing talents of Lucy and Bette. In J. Sochen (Ed.), *Women's comic visions* (pp. 141-157). Detroit: Wayne State University Press.

Walker, N. (1988). *A very serious thing: Women's humor and American culture*. Minneapolis: University of Minnesota Press.

Walker, N. 91991). Toward solidarity: Women's humor and group identity. In J. Sochen (Ed.), *Women's comic visions* (pp. 57-81). Detroit: Wayne State University Press.

Williams, E. A. (1991). Moms Mabley and the Afro-American comic performance. In J. Sochen (Ed.), *Women's comic visions* (pp. 158-178). Detroit: Wayne State University Press.

Wilt, J. (1980). The laughter of maidens, the cackle of matriarchs: Notes on the collision between comedy and feminism. In J. Todd (Ed.), *Gender and literary voice* (pp. 173-196). New York: Holmes and Meier.

12

Madonna: Transgression and Reinscription

Carolyn Lea

Madonna has long been a site of contention among feminists, with one side seeing her as offering a progressive and transgressive challenge to phallic hegemony and the other seeing her as reactionary and the antithesis of feminism. Although most feminists would probably agree that Madonna deserves kudos for her marketing savvy and longevity in a field predisposed toward male rockers, disagreements would most certainly emerge when considering the image(s) which have secured Madonna's success.

The perspective that Madonna poses a radical challenge to existing gender and sexual scripts is most prevalent among those academics who align themselves with sex radicalism or sexual libertarianism,[1] queer theory, and postmodernism. Kaplan (1987), for example, sees Madonna as representing "the postmodern feminist heroine in that she combines unabashed seductiveness with a gutsy kind of independence. She is neither male nor female identified, and seems mainly to be out for herself" (p. 122). hooks (1993) has said that "early on I was enamored of her . . . [she was] feminist in that she was daring to transgress sexist boundaries . . . a symbol of unrepressed female creativity and power—sexy, seductive, serious, and strong" (pp. 66-67). Henderson (1993) claims that "Madonna distinguishes herself as queer icon against the ground of commercial pop culture" (p. 122), whereas Paglia (1992) sees her as "the true feminist . . . she shows girls how to be attractive, sensual, energetic, ambitious, aggressive, and funny. . . . Madonna loves real men . . . [and] has a far profounder vision of sex than do the feminists. . . . Madonna is the future of feminism" (pp. 4-5). Schwichtenberg (1993) is among the many postmodern theorists who see Madonna as "an envoy of postmodernism" (p. 130) who, "from her disengendering polysexual display in *Justify* to her drag dance in *Express Yourself* to her representation as space-age dominatrix in the Blond Ambition tour, Madonna will continue to simulate and deconstruct the 'truths' of sex and gender" (p. 141). And Morton (1993) argues that "Madonna's displays of sexuality can be understood as politically subversive" (p. 220).

Others, however, suggest we not be so easily seduced. hooks (1993), for example, now feels betrayed by Madonna's "role of high priestess of a cultural hedonism that seeks to substitute unlimited production and pursuit of sexual pleasure for a radical, liberating political practice" (pp. 68-69). Bordo (1993a) sees the claim of a liberating postmodern subjectivity in the form of Madonna to be "a new inscription of mind/body dualism. What the body does is immaterial, so long as the imagination is free . . . disembodied freedom . . . celebrates itself through the effacement of the material praxis of people's lives . . . the sadly continuing social relations of dominance and subordination" (pp. 288-289). Mandziuk (1993) sees Madonna as the "perfect example of a postmodern heroine, selling the virtues of political indeterminacy in her insistent play with sexual expression . . . in her transformation of politics into pleasure: Madonna sounds the same old cultural message that a woman's place is to be sensual, stylish and self-involved" (pp. 183-184). For Tetzlaff (1993), Madonna serves as an example of "Boy Toy feminism" resting on the cynicism of the premise that "sexual autonomy is a lost cause anyway and the female body is already a token for male exchange, so we might as well try to get control of the transaction and attempt to get some cultural and economic independence out of the deal" (p. 254).

Schulze, White, and Brown (1993) have pointed out that Madonna is a figure who most often evokes either love or hate, even speculating that for the female Madonna hater, "the rejection is manifestation of a barely displaced 'abjection of self,' a self-loathing resulting from the interiorization of the patriarchal feminine" (p. 31). This suggests that, as Paglia (1992) forthrightly proclaims, "feminists who still loathe Madonna have a sexual ideology problem" (p. 11).

I argue that although we can appreciate that Madonna does, as Schwichtenberg (1993) puts it, "push the envelope" (p. 140), thus posing the possibility of subversion, we also must recognize that the progressive elements in her work are consistently undercut and marginalized. Madonna does transgress cultural norms: she positions herself as center, as subject; and she displays an active, rather than passive, female sexuality. However, these transgressions are, at the same time, undermined; her decoding always re-encoded, leaving the structures she has challenged intact and negating the potential for subversion in her texts. To expand on this critique, I consider texts from Madonna's video release of The Immaculate Collection, a "greatest hits" collection released along with the album of the same name and representative of Madonna's work from 1984 to 1990.[2] In addition, I look at the *Justify My Love* video, as well as *Rain* (1992) and *Take A Bow* (1994).[3]

Madonna's work has often been divided into two periods: the first period covers the years 1983 through 1985, and the second period covers the years 1986 to the present.[4] The break is accorded different reasons. Bordo (1993a) sees the early years as Madonna's fleshy years, when she rejected dominant standards of female beauty, and the later years as when she shaped up and "self-normalized" (p. 283). Tetzlaff identifies the phases as Boy Toy phase, a period of "self-conscious trashiness and excess" (p. 243), and the Chameleon Madonna phase in which she presents herself in ever-changing roles and settings, sometimes with the trappings of trash and excess and sometimes without.

I see Madonna's work as being on a continuum, with the video productions becoming more artistic and sophisticated by 1986, and Madonna herself adopting a svelte, more sophisticated look. These changes parallel Madonna's move from the position of a relative lack of power within the music industry to a position of power. The themes and basic elements remain the same: Madonna presents herself as having sexual agency, which she equates with freedom and autonomy; sadomasochism is threaded throughout her work; and throughout Madonna's work there is an appropriation of subcultural iconography promoting an image of rebelliousness and outlawry, much appreciated by the academic avant-garde.

THE IMMACULATE COLLECTION (1984-1990)

Dating from Madonna's early "fleshy period," *Lucky Star* was released in 1984. The video opens with a black-and-white image of Madonna with sunglasses—which she lowers to look into the camera. Then we see Madonna on the floor with a completely white background. She is wearing a black net top over a black dance bra, with black skirt over black tights, which hit mid-calf. Her hair is tousled; she wears red lipstick and smoky eyeshadow. Raising herself from the floor, she dances, moving seductively and suggestively, touching her own body and pulling her hands through her hair. The camera moves back and forth, providing wide-angle shots, then moves in for close-ups on body parts, such as her exposed belly and navel. These shots are intermixed with close-ups of her face, in which Madonna looks into the camera seductively, her head raised with her eyes brought down to meet the camera or lowering her head as she looks up. She peeks over her shoulder, her eyes still looking into the camera, her face in a pout, and she licks her lip invitingly. The last close-up shot shows her biting her lip then slowly inserting her finger into her mouth. Throughout the video, mid-range shots and several close shots emphasize her mouth and the movement of her tongue. The video ends by cutting to Madonna, again in black-and-white, raising her sunglasses. There are two dancers in the video, a black woman and white male with dark hair, who appear in the wide angle shots, although their presence seems almost irrelevant as the camera remains centered on Madonna.

The opening and closing shots frame the dance scene as performance. We are invited to look, to be the voyeur, as Madonna places herself as the object of the gaze. She is aware of the gaze, aware of the objectification of her body, of her desirability, and she invites it. The close-up shots fragment the body into body parts to be fetishized. She winks at her naughtiness, she is our accomplice. She implies that in choosing the position of object and commodity she is in control of her sexuality. But the dynamic of dominance and subordination remain in place. She remains object, with the words to the song reinforcing this message with "what you *do to me*, baby." The lyrics also imply an escape from responsibility and of sex making everything all right. The lucky star, read "stud," will be her guide, place his body on hers, and she will be the "luckiest by far." As Tetzlaff (1993) comments, "we would have to say that interpretations of . . . *Lucky Star* as parodic critiques of voyeurism are simply not supported by the text" (p. 245).

Madonna uses her costuming and dancers to identify with street culture, with punk, the dance form itself resembling street dance. Paglia (1992) calls this Madonna "raffish, gamine, still full of the street urchin mischief" (p. 9), and it is the street punk subculture that Madonna most often aligned herself with in her early work, the symbol of her rebelliousness and "outlaw" status.

In *Open Your Heart*, from 1986, Madonna plays a porn star in a peep show. The video opens with the image of a sign of a nude woman with light bulbs for nipples. A young boy, who reads as not-white, approaches the box office and is forbidden access. He must satisfy his curiosity by looking at the photographs displayed outside, all of which have the breasts blackened out. He looks, covering one eye, then another, and uses his hands to block out sections of the bodies, learning how to fetishize the parts of women's bodies. The boy comes to a portrait of Madonna looking upward earnestly. We are invited inside to act again as voyeurs. Madonna is dressed in black satin, her breasts accentuated by gold metal points and tassels. She is sitting sideways on a chair, and moving her hands up her own body, removes a black wig to reveal her white-blond hair. The men inside are shown as rather slimy and drooling, peering at Madonna through glass windows. In one window, there is a black male; in another, two twins who are touching each other and appear gay. A black, androgynous woman sits in one booth. The greatest part of the time is spent with the camera moving over Madonna's body. She looks seductively through the back of the chair into the camera while singing, "I think that you're afraid to look in my eyes," then straddles the chair, the chair reading as phallus. She peels off long black satin gloves seductively. Ending her dance, she lies on the floor, arm outstretched toward one of the (white) peepers. The booths are panned and we see her audience responding with their satisfaction with the performance. The woman lights a cigarette. Then we see Madonna outside, dressed identically with the boy, reaching over to kiss him on the mouth before they skip away together.

The possibility of reading this as a serious critique of the male gaze is undercut by the clearly objectifying gaze the camera invites us to participate in. Bordo is critical of Susan McClary's argument that *Open* destabilizes "'[t]he usual power relationship between the voyeuristic male gaze and object'" and that the ending represents an "'escape into androgyny,' which 'refuses essentialist gender categories and turns sexual identity into a kind of play'" (cited in Bordo, 1993a, p. 287). Rather, Bordo argues, "the female body is offered to the viewer purely as spectacle, an object of sight, a visual commodity to be consumed . . . there is a dominant position in this video and it is that of the objectifying gaze. One is not *really* decentered and confused by this video, despite the 'ambiguities'" (pp. 287-288; emphasis in original). Bordo sees the postmodern elements as facilitating rather than hindering the reading of Madonna's body as object of display, "[f]or in the absence of a coherent critical position *on* the images, the images themselves become preeminent, hypnotic, fixating" (p. 288; emphasis in original). The video becomes "entirely about Madonna's body," showcasing "the physical achievement of the star," and "any parodic or de-stabilizing element appears as utterly, cynically, mechanically tacked on" (p. 288).

This reading is supported in the findings of Brown and Schultz (1990). Showing the *Open* video to undergraduate students at three universities, they found males felt "comfortably hailed as masculine subjects" (p. 98), and they aligned themselves with the male characters in the video. The male students identified themselves as being "turned on," "hot," and "pumped" and described in detail their pleasure in watching Madonna's body. The female students tended to try to build on the narrative in a way that relieved Madonna of responsibility for positioning herself as object, whereas some female students spoke of their own body as being fat.

The introduction of the gay male and, presumably, lesbian, into the peep show audience provides Madonna an opportunity to broaden her appeal to a gay and lesbian audience while, at the same time, "the incorporation of ethnic, gender, and sexual difference into Madonna's image enhances the mainstream appeal of her own sexuality as exotic or taboo" (Curry, 1990, p. 21), again positioning her as outlaw. Nor are these images positive. Despite the fact that Madonna portrays both the black and gay characters in a more positive light than the white males, a woman objectifying a woman is no less oppressive than a male doing so. As De Lauretis (1988) notes, "[T]his notion of lesbian desire as commodity of exchange is rather disturbing. For, unfortunately—or fortunately as the case may be—commodity exchange does have the same meaning 'between women' as between men, by definition" (p. 170). Patriarchal sexual dynamics again go unchallenged. There is no room for intersubjectivity, only subject/object.

Madonna repeats the idea of escape, this time from the material body, when she skips off with the boy, implying that "what the body does is immaterial, so long as the imagination is free" (Bordo, 1993a, p. 288). Unlike a real woman, she is unscathed by her environment; she simply dances out of it.

The video *Express Yourself* came out in 1989 and is a collage of images drawn from various sources. The video begins with images from the 1926 German film *Metropolis*, which are interspersed with images reminiscent of the film *Cat People*, as well as take-offs of Michael Jackson. The video begins with Madonna perched atop an eagle and calling out to "girls" to hear what she has to sing about love. Madonna, in the role of Teutonic dominatrix, stands over a scene of bare-chested workers with muscular builds, glistening bodies, and dark hair, working in an area which is dimly lit. She is dressed in a long gown, looking down. In almost all the scenes of Madonna, there seems to be white light, making her pale skin appear even whiter. A "boss" with light brown hair watches Madonna. There are images of Nazi icons, such as a loudspeaker,[5] interspersed. We see Madonna in black corset and stockings looking seductively into the camera. Then, she is behind a screen touching her body, dancing suggestively, and thrusting her pelvis. She is next dressed in a "man's" suit with the low-cut jacket revealing her bra. Dancing, she grabs her crotch several times, mimicking Michael Jackson.[6] A shot of a worker is intercut with these scenes; he is seen lying down, then raising his body to gaze up at Madonna. The boss is also shown watching her, but the door to her room closes when he appears to move toward her, thus denying him access. We see images of her as cat/sex kitten, dressed in black leather, slinking along the floor, hair disheveled, heading for a saucer of milk, which she pours sensuously over her shoulder. Next she appears on her bed, an iron collar with chain around her neck. She is approached by the worker as she lies nude on the bed. He appears to pull her up forcefully, then goes down on his knees beside her.

Despite the multiplicity of images, the dominant one remains Madonna as object of the gaze. As Curry (1990) notes, this video "is laced with conventional pornographic representations," including its use of sadomasochistic iconography (such as the collar and chain), corset and garter, and slinky sex kitten images, whereas the scenes of the workers employ the "conventions of gay male pornography," the "wetness," and the "the men's muscular nude bodies glistening in blue light as they flex and move" (p. 23). Madonna holds the position of power over the working-class male she beckons to be her lover. Sexuality and power are inextricably linked. In masculine attire, Madonna portrays herself as having access to male prerogatives, of being in control of her sexuality, and of inverting the heterosexual dynamic. Yet "the representation of female sexuality in *Express Yourself* is clearly that of the fetishized icon configured within phallocentric modes of representation, which the video seems simultaneously to parody and to exploit" (Curry, 1990, p. 24). In juxtaposition to the song lyrics, which eschew material concerns, the video images "assert that desirable bodies and superior sexual performance are the ultimate good" (Curry, 1990, p. 24).

Madonna's use of S/M iconography and identification with the "worker," rather than the "boss/overseer," are again employed in her attempt to maintain her identification with the "other." However, as Curry (1990) points out, the "stance on racial and ethnic 'otherness'" in this video is not consistent. Shots of an Asian businessman with the "boss" present a negative reference to Japanese business interests (p. 24), whereas the use of both Nazi and sadomasochistic iconography proves to be similarly problematic.

Although many Madonna videos have been controversial,[7] only *Justify My Love* was banned from MTV. It was subsequently shown on *Nightline* on December 3, 1990. Shot in black and white, the video opens with Madonna moving down the hallway of a hotel, passing a topless woman, a couple in leather with the man moving in a thrusting motion behind her, and another woman, this one alone and pulling a leather corset up around her breasts. Tony Ward, Madonna's then real-life lover, is seen moving toward her. She squats, her coat opening to expose thighs and garter belt, and she touches her thighs. She whispers to Ward, "You put this into me, now what are you going to do with it?" They move into a motel room. She removes her coat to reveal black lace bra and panties, garter belt, and stockings. He removes his shirt to reveal—crucifixes. As he moves on top of her she pushes him back, saying, "Not like that." An androgynous figure replaces Ward, lying on top of Madonna and kissing her. You see Madonna's tongue move into her (?) mouth. Ward is seen behind the figures, watching. Two drag queens are also watching. Ward replaces the woman (?) on top of Madonna and thrusts his pelvis, as if he is fucking her. A leather-capped, bare-breasted S/M woman enters the room. Ward is sitting in a chair wearing some type of S/M garb. The S/M woman lifts his face and kisses him. The camera pans the room, revealing a crucifix on the wall. At this moment Madonna says, "Poor is the man whose pleasure depends on the permission of another." Madonna is on top of Ward. The camera moves to a close-up of her derriere moving up and down. Then we see Ward, lips moving down the body of a woman in a black lace corset, and, moving down to her high heels, he begins to remove one. Then his mouth is moving up the body of Madonna. Two people face each other, one penciling a moustache on the other. Madonna giggles. Ward's mouth moves up her chest, she throws her head back, arching her neck, then falls backward. Ward is on a couch with drag queens, then alone. Madonna is moving back down the hallway giggling and pulling her coat closed at the neck. She looks back over her shoulder, bites her hand, and shakes it as if enjoying the pain. She continues down the hallway (toward the camera) until she blurs out of focus. The "scenes" are broken through intermittent appearances of a black male dancer moving gracefully in arching motions. "Poor is the man whose pleasure depends on the permission of another," appears written on the screen as the images fade.

This video reveals the paradoxes of Madonna's work. The ambiguous gender identities of the actors offer an opportunity to unsettle our ideas about gender. Without "masculine" and "feminine" signs, I found it impossible to determine the biological sexual identity of the performers. The essays of Henderson and Robinson indicate the confusion. In reading the video, Robinson (1993) identifies the figure on top of Madonna as a woman, whereas Henderson (1993) sees several figures, none definitely identifiable as women. Robinson identifies the mustache painters as two women, Henderson as two men. I thought there was one of each. Robinson sees all the performers, with the exception of the dancer who she identifies as "not-white," as white. Henderson sees black, Latino, and white.

The impact is marginalized, however, by the context. The characters are ensconced in what appears to be a whore house, thereby refuting a positive feminist reading, as they appear within a source of women's traditional subjugation. All of the sexual encounters are seen in the context of S/M, maintaining the women's dependence on eroticizing dominance and subordination. Madonna maintains her identity as explicitly heterosexual, despite her foray with "otherness." The "lesbian" sex scene served as foreplay for the "real" sex between Madonna and Ward. He is the voyeur, turned on by the spectacle.

Madonna also retains her very unambiguous version of femininity, made-up, costumed in lacy bra and panty, setting herself apart from the freakish appearance of the "other," just as Ward clings to his masculine cues. Madonna is in underwear, whereas Ward remains partly dressed. She has again positioned herself as object of the gaze and has placed us in the position of voyeur, looking into a private space. And again she relies on pornographic conventions to fetishize parts of the body—her mouth, her derriere, her breasts, the other woman's shoe. Frolicking gleefully through this sadomasochistic underground world, she retains her claim to outlawry, posing as rebel in the midst of avant-garde decadence.

However, Madonna's supposedly radical statement about a man not being dependent on societal sanction puts her, along with all sex radicals, in the camp of liberal humanism, rather than posing a serious threat to sexual norms. The very concept of privacy and individual right has protected men from being confronted in regard to issues of sexual abuse of women and children. The concept of privacy and individual right protects those with power and privilege, not marginalized groups. It is not an argument that should be advocated by heterosexual women, lesbians, and gays.

RECENT WORK: *RAIN* AND *TAKE A BOW*

Madonna's more recent work similarly fails to offer any serious challenge to the status quo. Like Madonna herself, however, her new videos are fashionably sophisticated productions. The *Rain* video, from the Erotica album, opens with Madonna, earphones on her ears, resting on a futuristic looking divan, her hair cropped short and dyed black. Ostensibly, she is on the set of the *Rain* taping and we are "watching" the video being produced.[8] Despite the pastiche of images, and her use again of the "other," the video seems to be primarily about the sensuousness of Madonna's body. Moving from the "set" to the "video" we see a close-up of Madonna's face behind a very phallic looking microphone head. And "head" seems to be exactly what Madonna is giving us as she caresses the mike with her fingertips, at times brushing her cheek with her hand, the camera zooming in on her open mouth and tongue, and at times positioning her head so that her mouth disappears behind the "head" of the mike. This image from the "video" is interspersed with images from the set; we see the Asian director giving instructions, an Asian woman fixing her hair. She kisses a Latino-looking man, as an Asian woman brushes her cheek sensuously with a make-up brush. We see her standing between prop walls with water cascading down them. On the "video," she runs her hands caressingly up and down her body, her black dress drenched and clinging, or caresses her bare, wet arms. There are cuts of her behind a shower glass with the Latino lover, water running down the glass. Back on the set we see the director, as well as several other Japanese men and one short-haired Asian woman, all wearing dark glasses, watching Madonna, and holding cameras. Other Asian women turn from their positions at video monitors to look at Madonna. There are repeated cuts to the close-up of Madonna's face with the mike, her fingers touching it ever so suggestively. The video closes with the Latino looking at Madonna. She returns his look. Then we see the shower head spraying water. Next, an overhead shot shows Madonna standing among open, black umbrellas. Then, we again see her standing on the "set" as the light fades.

The lyrics add to the suggestiveness of the video, with Madonna singing, "Till I feel your/ Rain/ I feel it/ Its coming/ Your love's coming down like/ Rain/ Feel it on my fingertips," and telling us that "rain" can wash away her sorrow and her pain. Madonna situates herself firmly within a traditional scenario. Not only is she the object of our gaze, she tells us she will wait for her lover to come and take away her pain, again implying that sex will make everything all right.[9] Moreover, despite the fact that Madonna is the only "white" member of the video's cast, she again is positioned as center. She is the dominator—the "other" is exoticised and colonized. The lighting always highlights the whiteness of her skin, always setting her apart. In the scene with the Asian "crew" in dark glasses, they are made to appear freakish, almost insect-like, and the Asian men are never shown looking at the Asian women—only at Madonna. Despite all the high-tech trappings and sophistication, the video seems once again to be about the selling of Madonna—particularly her body.

Take A Bow not only showcases Madonna's body, but her high-fashion sense as well. The song is about the loss of a lover, which in the video is portrayed by the always present "other," a Spanish matador. Despite the collage of images, the story line is clear, never confusing. The video opens with two boys hanging a poster for a bullfight, then cuts to Madonna, her hand caressing a television screen on which we see the matador. The video cuts to the matador, waking to dress for his "role," and images of him dressing are juxtaposed with images of Madonna dressing—we see him putting on his sash—then a close-up of Madonna's hand on her thigh as she pulls black stockings up to meet black, lacy panties, then her hands pulling together and fastening a black corset. The close-up of her torso displays her hourglass figure, her body in black, silhouetted against a white background. We move back to his hands on his jacket—then Madonna's hands buttoning her suit jacket. He pulls a lance from a container—she puts a pin on her jacket, pricking her thumb and sucking it. We see them both looking at themselves in mirrors as she sings "Watching you, watching me," and she positions a hat on her head, pulling its veil over her face. There is a shot of his calf resting against his horse, then Madonna's calf as she climbs into her limousine. She pulls the shade on the limo window. We see her at the stadium, looking down at her matador. Then the video cuts back to Madonna's room, where she frolics on her bed, the TV screen at its foot. She is dressed in bra, panties, and stockings, and she writhes seductively, arching her back and raising her breasts. Then the camera moves to a close-up of her parted knees, then moves in toward her crotch as she moves, legs spread-eagled as if to enclose the TV screen. She pulls a sheet over herself, singing "The show is over, say goodbye." The video then cuts back and forth between images of the bullfight, a cut of her alone in her room inserting her middle finger in her mouth, and her matador lover in the bedroom, kissing her. We see glass fall from a night stand and break. He smears her lipstick with his thumb, then he turns from her. We see his bare feet walking on the broken glass, then Madonna outside and running away, scraping her nails along rock walls as she runs. The video ends with us looking at a close-up of Madonna's face and hands, positioning the viewer as inside the TV monitor, then moving to a shot of Madonna standing beside the monitor.

Despite the multiple references to role playing and performance in both the video and lyrics, Madonna fails once again to challenge traditional gender codes or heterosexual dynamics. If anything, the video tends to imply that our "roles" are predetermined as she asks, "But how was I to know which way the story'd go." Echoing her earlier work, Madonna again defines herself within traditional parameters; in the video's "story" she plays the role of rejected lover, and she remains framed as the object of the viewer's desire, the looked at. She, not her lover, is scantily clad; he is positioned as matador. Despite the implication of her wealth, she is seen only in the position of sensuous lover, sucking her fingers as she fantasizes about her lost love. In 1994, Madonna's work seems, despite its slick presentation, to be far less subversive than her work in 1984. In this piece, she seems to have moved from inversion to passivity.

SUBVERSION AND/OR INVERSION?

The contention that Madonna poses a challenge to femininity and pas-sive female sexuality is problematic, ignoring that Madonna does not so much subvert the dynamics of heterosexuality as invert them. Madonna does transgress the boundaries of a passive female sexuality, but in so doing, she becomes the libertine, the willing victim/collaborator, who puts her chain around her own neck, "and she loves it, so she is free" (Dworkin, 1979, p. 94). The position of the libertine is not a new one and poses no serious threat to the heterosexual dynamic. As Kappeler (1986) explains:

> The slaves conditioned to see only one choice, to be master or slave, to cause suffering or to suffer, ensure the very continuation of the Master even in his coup d'etat. Locked into the mutual mirror-gaze of master and slave, the two will see-saw endlessly, changing places now and then, leaving the structure intact. The slave has accepted the master's law that there will be masters and slaves, he has agreed to play. (p. 149)

Madonna promotes herself as a free and independent sexual agent, whereas in fact she has simply seen sexual agency as merely having access to male privilege. In the role of libertine, she "re-creates herself in the image of the cruelest (most powerful) man she can find and in her alliance with him takes on some of his power over others" (Dworkin, 1979, p. 95). And, as Kappeler (1986) continues, "The sexual story may be written from the female-object's point of view, an enticing variant of the male writing on his own pleasure. She may write it because, as liber-tine, she will have acquired the point of view of the scenario, the per-spective of the master: she will write as a male cultural subject, as author, as artist" (p. 160). Madonna does not interrogate the text of het-erosexuality, the dynamic of dominance and submission she advocates, but instead proudly proclaims on *Nightline*, "I have chained myself. There wasn't a man that put that chain on me. I did it myself. I was chained to my desires. I crawled under my own table, you know? [This is in reference to her video *Express Yourself*.] There wasn't a man stand-ing there making me do it. I do everything of my own volition. I'm in charge" (cited in Anderson, 1991, p. 312). Madonna not only fails to question the construction of her sexuality, she evokes the same old song and dance of a woman being a slave to desire, a desire over which, despite her protestations, she has no control. Madonna never affords us an opportunity to imagine a sexuality not modeled on a patriarchal model.

Madonna has also transgressed the boundaries of traditional femininity by engaging in direct address within her videos. Throughout her work Madonna displays an acute awareness of the process of looking. If, as Mulvey (1989) has claimed, looking has been split by an active/male and passive/female position, Madonna challenges female passivity by looking back. Such decoding, however, is again undercut and recoded as Madonna positions herself in what Mulvey refers to as women's "traditional exhibitionist role," "displayed as sexual object" "of erotic spectacle" (p. 19). Despite Madonna's play with looking, her body continues to be, as Bordo (1993) noted, "offered to the viewer purely as spectacle" (p. 287), and the dominant position of the videos continues to be that of an objectifying gaze.

Similarly problematic, as Mandziuk (1993) has noted, is Madonna's insistence on equating personal freedom with sexuality and displacing a politics of liberation with a politics of personal gratification. Madonna purports that the "free" expression of sexuality is freedom, never examining or letting herself be touched by the struggles of those whose identities she appropriates to increase her market share. hooks (1993) says, "Madonna consistently appears in these images as if she is with them, but not of them. Posed in this way she can invite her status quo readers to imagine that they, too, can consume images of difference, participate in the sexual practices depicted, and yet remain untouched—unchanged" (p. 72). And Tetzlaff (1993) says of her, "She is the Teflon idol, nothing sticks to her. . . . Madonna only inhabits these positions as if she were modeling a collection of fashions . . . [the videos] end with Madonna seemingly unfazed by the cultures and struggles she has encountered, dancing off the screen" (p. 259). He sees her as a subcultural tourist, visiting on her way to upward mobility.

In Madonna's work, difference is fetishized, eroticized, and exoticized, and we are invited to touch it, use it for our personal pleasure and escape. Homosexuality, blackness, browness, are appropriated in our attempts to fill our own emptiness and sense of lack (Hawthorne, 1989; Moore, 1988). But, in tourism, we are always only visiting, we always return home. "You may 'be' another person while you are away. You may feel different but that is because your identity is firmly established elsewhere" (Moore, 1988, p. 167).

Despite the fact that Madonna's videos abound with images of the "other," the "other" remains marginalized in her work. Surrounded by the "other," Madonna remains centered, as her "others" adore her from the margins. Such a move can again be seen as transgressive, in that Madonna moves herself, woman, from the margins to the center, as both center and narrator of her texts. However, in so doing Madonna re-encodes the power of the phallus by "taking up the phallic position of dominator and controller of the Other" (O'Brien Hallstein, 1996, p. 130). Recoding a hierarchy of oppression, Madonna privileges her whiteness, her heterosexuality, and her wealth to position herself as subject, and, as such, she relies on the objectification of those lower on the hierarchal ladder. Madonna maintains an image of whiteness and blondness, the whitest skin, the blondest hair. Hair color is noted in the videos I looked at because it is never blond, except for Madonna's. Even Madonna's white dancers seem to be of a darker, more olive complexion. She sets herself apart and above the darker "other." Looking through her work, I found only one blond—a black male in her Blond Ambition tour tape. The lighting in the videos is also used to highlight the whiteness of Madonna's complexion, setting her apart even in videos in which Madonna's hair is dark, such as *Like A Prayer* and *Rain*. According to hooks (1992), Madonna is "[f]ascinated yet envious of black style, Madonna appropriates black culture in ways that mock and undermine, making her presentation one that upstages" (p. 161). For hooks this is most apparent in the *Like A Prayer* video, in which Madonna becomes the "saviour" of the black male while the black women play a "mammy" role, supporting Madonna (p. 161).[10] Similarly, despite the suggestions of homosexuality in her work, her own heterosexuality remains firmly anchored in the texts, and the homosexuality is represented as freakish, a technique which serves to distance these characters from Madonna herself.

The accolades accorded Madonna within academia may be due primarily to the fact that Madonna is seen as "playing with" and "deconstructing" gender. According to Kaplan (1993) "much of what Madonna does can be read, via [Judith] Butler,[11] as mobilizing for the purposes of subverting the constitutive categories of gender" (p. 156). "Drag," for example, has come to play an increasingly important role in Madonna's work. Schwichtenberg (1993) argues that Madonna wears female drag by displaying femininity in excess and that this foregrounds femininity as masquerade. I would argue, however, that her work, taken in the context of MTV, does not support this view. What is seen as "metafeminine" is normalized in the texts of MTV, in which male rock singers are the norm and images of women remain highly sexualized and fetishistic. And Madonna is not alone in the realm of female stars projecting this image, as women musicians bend their image to meet consumer demand. Even out lesbian Melissa Etheridge underwent a "make-over" on her road to success, as her rather "butch" image was transformed into a sexy, nonthreatening one.

It is also not evident how, if all gender is perceived as drag or masquerade, we can determine when a subversive strategy is being engaged in. As Jeffreys (1993) points out, "There is snobbery involved here . . . a distinction of value is being made between women's choice to wear precisely similar clothes according to whether they are ignorant . . . or . . . read Lacan and have made a deliberate and revolutionary choice to wear lacy low-cut bodices" (p. 87). Similarly, Tyler (1991) points out that:

> For the camp or mimic difference must be visible as such if it is to make a difference in the way gender or sexuality are lived or understood. But if all identities are alienated and fictional, then the distinction between parody, mimicry, or camp, and imitation, masquerade, or playing it straight is no longer self evident. What makes one credible and the other incredible when both are fictions? The answer, it seems, are the authors intentions . . . confusion of the two is eliminated by a focus on the theories of production rather than on reception or perception. (p. 54)

Furthermore, we might ask, if all gender is drag and naturalized through repetition, how will this drag of drag resist this very same naturalization? If Madonna is dragging femininity by "taking it over the top," doesn't her repetitive performance naturalize it as Madonna, as simply "the way she is?" And doesn't this beg the question that Tyler (1991) poses—"what passes for passing for or impersonating a gender when gender is always and already an impersonation" (p. 54)? If the parody is to be known through the use of exaggeration and excess, are we not, as Tyler (1990) suggests, assuming a correct femininity (or masculinity) against which the difference becomes obvious?

What if no one gets the joke? As Bordo (1993b) comments, subversion of cultural assumptions does not take place in the text but in the reading of the text. And, because the author has no control over the interpretation, both drag and role playing can just as easily reinscribe as subvert our concept of gender. Erickson (1990) points out that we should be leery of romanticizing the subversive potential of texts:

> Too often theorists . . . assume that the audience is simply a projection of themselves, and that, since they desire a certain theatrical strategy to work (usually to illustrate an already assumed theory), it does indeed work for everyone. It is assumed without qualification that a particular strategy "undermines" or "subverts" or "resists," whatever representational system it is engaged with, whereas for other audience members without such agendas, these effects might not be experienced at all. In fact, the more sophisticated these strate-

gies become in their use of irony, for instance, the more likely the
opposite meaning will be assumed and be reinforced, not undermined. (p. 235)

Neither does Madonna's appearance in a man's suit in any way
seem unsettling. In our culture, women wearing an article of masculine
clothing are seen as accentuating their femininity through contrast,
rather than detracting from it. In fact, the disjunction is seen as adding
an erotic charge. Madonna's sexual identity is never obfuscated by her
male attire; lacy bras reveal her breasts, and her make-up remains perfectly feminine. Ambiguity seems far more destabilizing than either the
wearing of feminine clothing as feminine clothing or the wearing of
male suits which reveal the female body underneath, as the ambiguous
figures in *Justify* demonstrate. As Bordo (1993b) points out, ambiguity
proves unsettling not because it reveals gender as artifice through parody, but because "the familiar dualities . . . had been forced to yield to an
unclear and uncharted continuum" (p. 293). Unfortunately, only the
"other" inhabits such an ambiguous position in Madonna's videos, in
which, even in *Justify*, both her gender and her heterosexuality remain
firmly grounded.

SUMMARY

Madonna's texts provide us with a landscape of contradictory messages.
She transgresses the boundaries of traditional femininity by assuming a
stance of active female sexuality, by positioning herself as center, and
through her "looking at." These decodings, however, are always re-
encoded as Madonna negotiates her sexuality through the phallic paradigm of dominance and submission, positions herself as dominator over
an exoticized "other," and positions herself as spectacle and sexualized
object of the gaze, albeit male or lesbian. The potential for subversion is
always undermined in her work. As O'Brien Hallstein (1996) notes,
Madonna "remains locked into the codes of Oedipus and the phallus
because Madonna takes up the phallic position of dominator" (p. 129).
She is the libertine, the sex object willing to participate in the master's
narrative. In some ways, too, Madonna is like the butch or dominatrix,
in that she asserts "masculine" phallic privilege in a way that does nothing to subvert, denaturalize, or challenge traditional gender constructs.
Her performance tends, in fact, to further naturalize those constructs by
suggesting that the only way any one can assert him- or herself is at the
expense of others—that is, by marginalizing and dominating that which
is "other." Erickson (1990) suggests that resistance only makes sense if

there is an alternative vision, one not "defined by what we are trans-gressing, resisting, or deconstructing" (p. 235). Madonna, whose texts operate only within a phallic economy, never ventures into such uncharted territory, never provides such a vision.

ENDNOTES

1. Thompson (1991) defines the sexual libertarian position as:

    [A]n insistence on freedom from constraint, a rejection of any form of restriction on sexual behaviour especially moral prohi-bition, the advocacy of a plurality of "sexualities," and a reluc-tance to relinquish the vision of "sexual liberation" . . . . Underlying this commitment is a belief that there exists some "true" kind of sexuality, an intrinsic property of the individual which is suppressed by "society," but will come into its full flowering once the social restrictions have been removed. The political strategy which follows from this commitment to the "repression hypothesis" involves the refusal to take a stand against any form of sexual desire or activity, and the pejora-tive labeling of any such stand as "moralistic." (p. 10)

2. The Immaculate Collection video includes the following: *Lucky Star, Borderline,* and *Like A Virgin* (1984), *Material Girl* (1985), *Papa Don't Preach, Open Your Heart,* and *La Isla Bonita* (1986), *Like A Prayer, Express Yourself, Cherish,* and *Oh Father* (1989), and two versions of *Vogue*—the 1990 video and the version performed for The 1990 MTV Awards Show. *Justify My Love* (1990) was included on The Immaculate Collection album, but the video was released as a "sin-gle," selling 250,000 copies at a cost of $9.95 each (Anderson, 1991).

3. *Rain* is from the album Erotica (1992), and *Take A Bow,* Madonna's 11th number one hit, is from the Bedtime Stories album (1994).

4. O'Brien Hallstein (1996) has divided Madonna's work into three periods: the first, the nomad phase, she associates with Madonna's very early work (1983); the second, a transitional phase, covers the years from 1984 to 1986; and the sophisticate phase from 1986 to the present. These phases reflect Madonna's move from what O'Brien Hallstein sees as Madonna's early identification with street culture and lack of power within the music industry, to her assumption of power within the industry and subsequent identifi-cation with power and wealth.

5. Morton (1993) explains: "[T]he loudspeaker is a densely coded sign. [The loudspeaker was a] propaganda tool and Nazi icon pur-portedly responsible for much of the successful mobilization of Adolf Hitler's popular support" (p. 231).

6. Both the jerky dance movements and the repeated grabbing of the crotch reference the performances of Michael Jackson (Curry, 1990; Patton, 1993).

7. The video *Like A Prayer* was viewed as sacrilegious and lost Madonna a contract with Pepsi, although they paid her $5 million, despite pulling the plug on their ad. Her *Papa Don't Preach* created controversy over what was seen as a pro-teenage pregnancy message. The *Erotica* video, from the album of the same name, had strong sadomasochistic undertones and was pulled from MTV after only three nights.

8. Such Brechtian distancing techniques are not new to Madonna's work and are evident in even her earliest videos; the cut from Madonna behind dark glasses to Madonna with dancers is an early example from *Lucky Star; Like A Prayer* ends with the entire cast taking a bow and curtains closing; and *Material Girl* also toyed with the idea of watching the video in production, although to a lesser degree than *Rain*.

9. A far more overt connection between love and pain is found in the title song from this album, *Erotica*, in which Madonna sings "There's a certain satisfaction / In a little bit of pain / I can see you understand / . . . Only the one that hurts you / Can make you feel better."

10. A different view is offered by Ronald Scott (1993), who sees *Prayer* as an "enlightened work that emphasizes positive aspects of the black community" and is "devoid of traditional stereotypes" (pp. 73-74).

11. Butler has argued that gender is a performance maintained through endless repetition. Drag serves as a "parodic repetition of gender," destabilizing and exposing gender as illusion. Drag, in its exaggeration, reveals the "phantasmatic" status of gender and exposes it as a copy for which there is no original (1990, pp. 146-147; 1991).

REFERENCES

Anderson, C. (1991). *Madonna unauthorized*. New York: Simon and Schuster.

Bordo, S. (1993a). Material girl: The effacements of postmodern culture. In C. Schwichtenberg (Ed.), *The Madonna connection* (pp. 265-290). Boulder: Westview Press.

Bordo, S. (1993b). *Unbearable weight: Feminism, Western culture and the body*. Berkeley: University of California Press.

Brown, J. D., & Schulze, L. (1990). The effects of race, gender, and fandom on audience interpretation of Madonna's music videos. *Journal of Communication, 40*, 88-102.

Butler, J. (1990). *Gender trouble*. New York: Routledge.

Butler, J. (1991) Imitation and gender insubordination. In D. Fuss (Ed.), *Inside/out: Lesbian theories, gay theories* (pp. 13-31). New York: Routledge.

Curry, R. (1990). Madonna from Marilyn to Marlene—Parody or pastiche? *Journal of Film and Video, 42*(2), 15-30.

De Lauretis, T. (1988). Sexual indifference and lesbian representation. *Theatre Journal, 40*, 155-177.

Dworkin, A. (1979). *Pornography: Men possessing women*. New York: Plume.

Erickson, J. (1990). Appropriation and transgression in contemporary American performance: The Wooster Group, Holly Hughes, and Karen Finley. *Theatre Journal, 42*(2), 225-236.

Hawthorne, S. (1989). The politics of the exotic: The paradox of cultural voyeurism. *NWSA Journal, 1*(4), 617-629.

Henderson, L. (1993). Justify our love: Madonna and the politics of queer sex. In C. Schwichtenberg (Ed.), *The Madonna connection* (pp. 107-128). Boulder: Westview Press.

hooks, b. (1992). *Black looks: Race and representation*. Boston: South End Press.

hooks, b. (1993). Power to the pussy: We don't wannabe dicks in drag. In L. Frank & P. Smith (Eds.), *Madonnarama: Essays on sex and popular culture* (pp. 65-80). San Francisco: Cleiss Press.

Jeffreys, S. (1993). *The lesbian heresy*. Melbourne: Spinifex.

Kaplan, E. A. (1993). Madonna politics: Perversion, repression or subversion? Or masks and master-y. In C. Schwichtenberg (Ed.), *The Madonna connection* (pp. 149-167). Boulder: Westview Press.

Kaplan, E. A. (1987). *Rocking around the clock: Music television, postmodernism and consumer culture*. New York: Methuen.

Kappeler, S. (1986). *The pornography of representation*. Minneapolis: University of Michigan Press.

Mandziuk, R. M. (1993). Feminist politics and postmodern seductions: Madonna and the struggle for political articulation. In C. Schwichtenberg (Ed.), *The Madonna connection* (pp. 167-188). Boulder: Westview Press.

Moore, S. (1988). Getting a bit of the other—The pimps of postmodernism. In R. Chapman & J. Rutherford (Eds.), *Male order: Unwrapping masculinity* (pp. 165-192). London: Lawrence and Wishart.

Morton, M. (1993). Don't go for second sex, baby! In C. Schwichtenberg (Ed.), *The Madonna connection* (pp. 213-235). Boulder: Westview Press.

Mulvey, L. (1989). Visual pleasure and narrative cinema. In *Visual and other pleasures* (pp. 14-26). Bloomington: Indiana University Press.

O'Brien Hallstein, D. L. (1996). Feminist assessment of emancipatory potential and Madonna's contradictory gender practices. *Quarterly Journal of Speech, 82*, 125-141.

Paglia, C. (1992). *Sex, art, and American culture*. New York: Vintage.

Patton, C. (1993). Embodying subaltern memory: Kinesthesia and the problematics of gender and race. In C. Schwichtenberg (Ed.), *The Madonna connection* (pp. 81-106). Boulder: Westview Press.

Robinson, A. (1993). Is she or isn't she? Madonna and the erotics of appropriation. In L. Hart & P. Phelan (Eds.), *Acting out: Feminist performances* (pp. 337-361). Ann Arbor: The University of Michigan Press.

Schwichtenberg, C. (1993). Madonna's postmodern feminism: Bringing the margins to the center. In C. Schwichtenberg (Ed.), *The Madonna connection* (pp. 129-148). Boulder: Westview Press.

Schulze, L., White, A. B., & Brown, J. D. (1993). A sacred monster in her prime: Audience construction of Madonna as low-other. In C. Schwichtenberg (Ed.), *The Madonna connection* (pp. 15-39). Boulder: Westview Press.

Scott, R. B. (1993) Images of race and religion in Madonna's video *Like A Prayer*: Prayer and praise. In C. Schwichtenberg (Ed.), *The Madonna connection* (pp. 57-77). Boulder: Westview Press.

Tetzlaff, D. (1993). Metatextual girl> patriarchy> postmodernism> power> money> Madonna. In C. Schwichtenberg (Ed.), *The Madonna connection* (pp. 239-264). Boulder: Westview Press.

Thompson, D. (1991). *Reading between the lines: A lesbian feminist critique of feminist accounts of sexuality*. Sydney: The Gorgon's Head Press.

Tyler, C.-A. (1991). Boys will be girls: The politics of gay drag. In D. Fuss (Ed.), *Inside/out: Lesbian theories, gay theories* (pp. 32-70). New York: Routledge.

Tyler, C.-A. (1990). The feminine look. In M. Kreiswirth & M.A. Cheetam (Eds.), *Theory between the disciplines: Authority/vision/politics* (pp. 191-212). Ann Arbor: University of Michigan Press.

13

New York Times Coverage of Anita Hill as a Female Cipher

Linda Steiner

In September 1991, acting on a tip, aides to Democratic senators asked a University of Oklahoma law professor to tell them about being sexually harassed years before by a conservative federal appeals court judge whom President George Bush had nominated to the Supreme Court. Weeks of negotiations ensued with Anita Hill, who had worked for Clarence Thomas at both the Education Department and the Equal Employment Opportunity Commission. Because Hill eventually made a statement, the FBI questioned both Hill and Thomas. The Judiciary Committee did nothing with the FBI report. Instead, the Committee forwarded the nomination to the Senate without recommending Thomas (N. Lewis, 1991a, pp. 1, 8). A couple of days after the Senate began its debate—and, by all accounts, Thomas seemed to be on his way to an easy confirmation—Hill's name and portions of the FBI report were leaked to *Newsday* and National Public Radio. They broke the story on October 6, 1991.

A firestorm of debate erupted once the public heard that Supreme Court nominee Clarence Thomas had been accused of sexual harassment. The vote was delayed one week so that the Judiciary

Committee could hold public hearings. The public's acute interest in these hearings was not surprising. The case involved several political and sexual elements that often make for high drama. Yet, even though some of the issues were articulated at a fairly prurient level, the stakes were significant. On the one hand was the reputation and career of an African American man nominated to the nation's highest court. On the other were the reputation of an African American woman struggling against racist and sexist images of black women, and the status of an important issue that corporations, the public, government, and mass media were just beginning to take more seriously. The controversy still reverberates, despite the October 16 confirmation of Thomas as Justice, by a 52-48 vote.

The U.S. news media devoted huge amounts of premium time and front-page space to the story. ABC, CBS, NBC, and C-SPAN all carried the hearings live. In October 1991, The *New York Times* carried more than 3,000 column inches of news articles and analyses. Yet, although both scholarly discussions (see, e.g., the special issue of *The Black Scholar*, published as Chrisman & Allen, 1992), and public perceptions were almost entirely based on print and television accounts, the news coverage itself has received little analysis.[1] For instance, in interpreting the hearings as an example of how "poststructural politics" generated contradictory tactical alliances, John Fiske (1993, 1994) uses "facts" from news accounts, without examining the stories themselves. Toni Morrison's (1992) collection of essays about Hill and Thomas includes one very insightful analysis of how news photographs visually distributed power and authority, ultimately asserting the power of the judge (Lubiano, 1992). Essays collected by Anita Hill and her legal adviser (Hill & Jordan, 1995) ignore news accounts, although several deal with the impact of the hearings.

The reportage about Anita Hill and her testimony illustrates journalism's discomfort in dealing with black women, race, sex, and sexual harassment—alone and in combination. Sexual harassment in U.S. government circles goes back at least to 1864, when a Treasury department supervisor forced women to use sexual favors to purchase their jobs, for which they were paid half of what men earned (Phelps & Winternitz, 1992). Yet, legal prohibition of sexual harassment is relatively recent,[2] perhaps because men in power are not victims of harassment, and partly because victims are loathe to expose themselves to the kind of scrutiny, even if to a lesser degree, that Hill endured.

Precisely because Hill's accusations received such intense attention, her case presents an opportunity to investigate not only how the press covered the issue of sexual harassment in this case, but how it dealt with successful professional black women, who otherwise had been rarely seen on the front pages, raising this unsettling issue. The chapter suggests that reporters' commitments to objectivity may have distorted their accounts. Anita Hill was particularly emptied of meaning. The *Times* called her "a symbol of one of the most sensitive and complex political issues of the day" (Suro, 1991a, p. 22). She indeed became a symbol, even a cipher.

This chapter describes how the *New York Times* constructed the Hill-Thomas story. It is based on textual analyses of all 80 articles and news analyses the *Times* published between October 8, 1991, when the media reported Hill's first news conference, and the end of the month, when the story was finally no longer a daily front-page story.[3] Not every U.S. newspaper operates the same way, but the *Times* has long been considered paradigmatic for the elite press. As research about other news events suggests, reporters across the United States tend to choose fairly similar frames for a given story. Both university-level journalism pedagogy and newsroom socialization tend to standardize news values and professional practices. Social and market vectors (van Zoonen, 1994) and the structures that enable journalists to move up the career ladder (often toward the *New York Times*, specifically) have analogous impact. Therefore, professional practices at the *Times* may represent the operative paradigm for elite metropolitan dailies.

After reviewing literature about press coverage of black women and in news sociology, this chapter describes how reporters discursively moved people into separate camps based on distinct identity factors. As Fiske (1994) put it, "[The hearings] stirred up all the murkiest currents of race, gender, class, and party politics into a maelstrom that involved a multiaxial complex of struggles in which . . . the only certainties were instability, fluidity, and contestation" (p. 75). The point here is that reporters treated each of these factors—one by one—as competing and independent, not interstructured. As the research shows, journalists construed several factors as tainting everyone's interpretations. First and above all, reporters represented the controversy as the struggle of angry females to be heard by the "old boys." Reporters subsequently calculated the impact of other bases of social identity, including race, age, party affiliation, ideology, and geography, as well as the experience of having been victimized or accused of sexual harassment. Meanwhile, reporters buried the context for their own judgments, responses, and values. The research finds that reporters defined themselves as uniquely able to see through everyone. Reporters implied that they sat in a flawlessly clear observation booth while other audiences watched the drama being staged for them through lenses dramatically tinted by their different identities, if not fractured by their experiences.

RACE AND JOURNALISM

Very little published research addresses how the press has dealt with
women of color. Indeed, women of color are only now being studied as
subjects, audiences, and producers of mass communication. Martindale
(1985, 1986, 1990) shows that the white press paid increasing attention to
African Americans in the 1970s and 1980s; she attributed this new-found
interest in black "everyday life" and community activities to the increased
employment of black journalists and the emergence of the black middle
class as both a source of news and target audience. Nonetheless,
Martindale (1990) also found stereotyping and "reduced attention to the
situations and forces still obstructing equality for African Americans" (pp.
110-111). The impetus for Martindale's research was the 1968 Kerner
Commission, whose criticisms of the news media's failure to cover the
black community ignored gender issues. Martindale did not address gender. Nor did post-Kerner analyses of print content by Stempel (1971),
Chaudhary (1980), and Sentman (1982). Wilson and Gutierrez's 1995
study of minority media ignored women, as do most studies of television
news coverage of blacks (see Entman, 1990 and 1992). One of the few projects attentive to black women is Fair's 1993 study of television coverage
of black violence in South Africa. Echoing Rakow and Kranich's (1991)
valuable point about women as signs rather than as active agents, Fair
found that South African black women were used to *represent* the ills of
apartheid, but they were not allowed to *speak* about apartheid.

Reporters seek strong narrative hooks for their stories—especially
when struggling with topics that are relatively new, complex, or abstract.
Because reporters are therefore likely to borrow fictional devices and
images, the scholarship now emerging about the representations of
women of color in popular culture is worth mentioning here. Mass mediated popular culture both circulates these images and relies on them—
especially when the media institutions employ a homogeneous workforce.
Black women's film roles have been confined to a small set of images such
as tragic mulattos, exotics, matriarchs, and whores. These images have
less to do with the realities of black women's lives and more to do with
racism (Mapp, 1982). Black men have been portrayed in overlapping and
equivalently restricted images (Bogle, 1991; Dates & Pease, 1994). One
black feminist scholar says analogously of television roles: "Black women
play two kinds of parts: tragic chippies and weeping mothers" (Wallace,
1992, p. 658). Other scholars find, however, that in recent years both soaps
and prime-time television have offered African American women more
complex and positive roles (Lindsey, 1995; Merritt, 1994).

As it turns out, several key players in the Hill-Thomas story
themselves relied on racial type casting. Thomas defended himself by

resorting to cardboard-cutout monsters. He even portrayed his own sister as a "welfare cheat"—an example of what Painter (1992) refers to as the "pernicious power of negative stereotype" (p. 202). More importantly, Thomas, his wife, and their supporters relied on old stereotypes of black women in order to cast Hill as a traitor to her race and/or desperate for sex (Painter, 1992). Fiske (1993, 1994) blames the agonizing controversy over Hill on racism generally and white discourse about the hypersexualized black female that is embedded in racism. Certainly this was a tactic of some conservatives. Senator Orrin Hatch, for example, a key member of the Judiciary Committee, challenged Hill's sexual practices. Lubiano (1992) persuasively argues that Thomas's supporters tried to exploit coded references to welfare cheats and the upright black "lady" to demonize both Hill and affirmative action.

As will become evident, while several aspects of the Hill and Thomas case dramatize racial and gender politics, the *Times* reporters avoided this crude racism. Reporters also tried to downplay or bury the discourse of both sexual looseness and primness. One of the factors that helped reporters in this respect was that, with their middle-class professional status, Hill and Thomas simply refused to fit the available roles. But this refusal cut both ways. As Painter (1992) says, "Hill chose not to make herself into a symbol Americans could recognize, and as a result she seemed to disappear, a fate reserved for black women who are well educated and are thus doubly hard to see" (p. 210).

These extreme images also have appeared in other news stories about individual black men—black political figures, entertainers, and athletes. Analyzing press coverage of the trial of the heavy weight boxer Mike Tyson, who was subsequently convicted of raping a Miss Black America pageant contestant, Lule (1995) says reporters degraded—or "raped"—Tyson by reproducing two highly racist stereotypes: Tyson was either a violent, monstrous savage or a victim of terrible social circumstance (Lule, 1995). Alternatively, the black press, especially, picked up on defense team tactics and treated Tyson as the victim of a promiscuous gold-digger operating at the behest of whites (Awkward, 1995, p. 105). Again, such insinuations reproduce all-too-common stereotypes of black women as oversexed Jezebels and Sapphires.

PROFESSIONAL ROUTINES AND SEXUAL HARASSMENT

If ideological interests and stock cultural images do not wholly explain how different social groups and processes are presented in the news, another route to understanding news content starts with professional routines. Sociologists of news have long noticed how reporters, constrained by inexorable institutional structures, organize their data-gathering and their data around narrative (Gans, 1979; Tuchman, 1972, 1978). Reporters structure their work around a "core conception of what constitutes the story" (Darnton, 1975). The question is which core conception reporters choose. The literature described earlier predicts that reporters will choose among the prevailing "types" already in circulation. Narratives also are constrained by the need to produce on deadline something that looks timely, complete, and that will attract readers. Given the requirement to appear balanced and to avoid alienating political interests, newspapers adhere to a neutral code of professionalism that standardizes and homogenizes all reporters beyond a certain fact and skill base.

　　　Most of the newly emerging literature about internal problems besetting news organizations examines hierarchal disputes, especially between reporters and management, although class, gender, race, and ethnicity can also fracture newsrooms (van Zoonen, 1994). Meanwhile, given journalists' fear about job stability and their superiors' fear of organizational instability, reporters and management tend to avoid and suppress internal conflict (Turow, 1994). No wonder that most histories of the *New York Times* and other press institutions by male insiders ignore both gender per se and sexual relationships. Gay Talese (1970) came close, in mentioning a sexual double standard at the *New York Times*: "Sex has been the traditional excess of so many of the paper's most prominent reporters, editors, executives, and shrine keepers" (p. 218).[4] Even female insiders have, at least until recently, tended to describe newsroom discrimination and sexism without specifically mentioning sexual harassment by journalists. Although women journalists (see Mills, 1988; Robertson, 1992) dispute men's exaggerated sense that women exploit their sexuality to obtain information, their accounts do not complain about "intimate" interactions with colleagues.

　　　Consistent with this view of reporters as tough and sexually unflappable was the case of Angela Wright, an assistant editor at the *Charlotte Observer*. Wright offered to corroborate Hill's description of Thomas as lecherous. But she made clear that she personally had not been upset by Thomas's sexual comments (Clymer, 1991a). Wright was not allowed to testify formally at the hearings, but she described how Judge Thomas had commented on her physique when she worked for him as chief spokeswoman for the Equal Employment Opportunity Commission. "It's not something that intimidated or frightened me. At the most, it was annoying and obnoxious," Wright insisted (cited in Tyler, 1991, p. 17).

　　　In any case, the Hill-Thomas hearings clearly provoked study of the newsroom, as well as other workplaces. In 1992, the Associated Press

Managing Editors found that 2% of men and 11% of women journalists said sexual harassment or fear of it had affected their work habits (Walsh-Childers, Chance, & Herzog, 1995). Responding to a 1993-95 survey, one-fourth of the women journalists said they had endured some amount of nonphysical sexual harassment from men in positions of authority; 29 percent received it from co-workers; and nearly a fourth were harassed by subordinates. News sources had sexually harassed (nonphysically) more than 70% of the respondents (Walsh-Childers, Chance & Herzog, 1995). Almost 5% had been physically harassed by other journalists. A survey of female Capitol reporters showed 80% calling sexual harassment a problem for women journalists; over 60% said they personally encountered it (McAdams & Beasley, 1994).

ANITA HILL AS A CIPHER

After Hill's allegations first became public, initial accounts in the *New York Times* said no more about Anita Hill than that she was a tenured law professor at the University of Oklahoma. Headlines and leads continued during the month to refer to Hill as "Law Professor" or, less often, as "former aide" to Thomas. In part, the *Times* reported, this silence about Hill resulted from the White House's immediate move to depict Thomas as "victim of a desperate final gambit" by political opponents. Republicans claimed this otherwise unknown 35-year-old professor was being manipulated by liberals. Furthermore, Hill was a reluctant public figure, albeit one who took on skeptics with "calm defiance" and "lawyerly prudence" (Suro, 1991a, p. 22).

Reporters themselves seemed not to know what to make of Hill. Two profiles (Suro, 1991a, 1991b) compared her to Thomas: "Like him, she overcame obstacles of discrimination and poverty by force of intellect and hard work in school" (1991a, p. 22). Both attended Yale Law School. Both sought the mentoring of powerful men (in her case, this was Thomas himself). The difference was—here reporter Roberto Suro's comment was prophetic of Thomas's later reference to being a victim of a high-tech lynching—that Thomas underscored his experience of discrimination, whereas Hill rarely mentioned it (1991b).

Suro's October 11 profile described "an intensely private person who now finds herself in the most public of roles, a sometimes enigmatic individual who must now explain herself to the nation" (1991b, p. 1). Of course, at some level, Hill was not obligated to explain herself. The problem was that reporters were not accustomed to being blocked from providing a clear, simple explanation. More than once in that profile, Suro described Hill as "complex" and "enigmatic." Suro employed these words, for example, when he noted that, after drafting her first public statement about the accusation, Hill went for a five-mile walk with her best friend. And Suro acknowledged, "But even knowing her personality and character does not answer the question of what, if anything, happened between Professor Hill and Judge Thomas" (1991b, p. 1).

Early stories briefly mentioned that Hill's and Thomas's families were religious. Suro said Hill's rigidly moral upbringing in rural Oklahoma "left her somewhat naive and more than a little idealistic" (1991b, p. 17). Subsequent discussions virtually ignored her intense Christianity. Having defined her as a female with a not-unique biographical history of virtuous hard work in school and law, reporters never asked whether religion might explain Hill's revulsion at discussions of human anatomy. Hill was serious enough about Christianity that she accepted a teaching position at Oral Roberts University, where, as required, she pledged fidelity to a social-religious code. Indeed, Christian values and beliefs might have undergirded Hill's embarrassment at Thomas's behavior, her sense of herself as the invaded victim, and her reluctance to file formal charges. Nonetheless, accustomed to predicting behavior from single causes and dealing primarily with religion when reporting on clergymen who abuse children or swindle listeners (or Mother Theresa), journalists did not take religion seriously as a formative standpoint.[5]

As the story progressed, reporters faced even greater difficulty writing about Hill, who they still found "enigmatic" and "cool" despite virulent attack. Meanwhile, reporter Maureen Dowd (1991c) claimed, "In an extraordinary political psychodrama, nasty charges are flying in Congress about character assassination, ruined lives, chicanery and sandbagging, a legislative process run amok, sex, lies and raunchy movies" (p. 1). (Dowd, whose analyses of the White House had already been running on the front page, wrote a front-page story about the Hill-Thomas controversy nearly every day.) Dowd quoted Sen. Alan Simpson, the Wyoming Republican, saying, "When you go for the jugular, the beast comes out." Indeed, Dowd chose fairly passionate verbs when quoting certain Congressmen: Sen. John Danforth (as Thomas's mentor, he was in charge of steering the nomination through the confirmation process) "railed," Rep. Newt Gingrich "blasted away," and Sen. Simpson first took "a backhanded approach" and then "screamed" (1991c, p. B15). Several articles more generally described President Bush's aides plotting a counterattack to present Thomas as a family man. But these articles said nothing about Hill except that she had raised an explosive issue. Indeed, taken collectively, the *Times* ran far more discussions about various Senators than about Hill.

Despite its attempt to avoid sensationalized details, the *Times* could not altogether ignore the language used to attack Hill. Published transcripts of the testimony showed what was being said against Hill: opponents called her "erotomaniac," "ruthless," "vindictive," "mad." Dowd's post-hearings analysis (1991f) also described the "worst nightmare" for women's groups: a credible woman emerged from telling her story "so bloodied as to be almost unrecognizable" (p. 1). Furthermore, when Dowd quoted Thomas's female supporters, she correctly noted that these women attacked Hill with the words that men have always used to suggest insidious motivations and character flaws in women: "stridently aggressive," "arrogant," "scorned," "opinionated," "tough" (1991f, p. 18). Ironically, the very next day, Dowd (1991g) said the Senators regarded Hill as having acted in a way that was not sufficiently feminine. Dowd said she borrowed from women's groups and feminists the speculation that Senators did not find Hill "convincing" as a female. Dowd herself said that Senators found Hill "too controlled and unemotional to really tug at the heartstrings of the heartland, especially when compared with Judge Thomas's hot and emotional television appearances in which he cast himself as a martyr to the process and to racial discrimination. Senators believed that even if her story was true, she seemed too calculating and career-centered" (1991g, p. 1).

FIRST ROUND: MEN DON'T GET IT

Whether or not Hill accommodated dominant conceptions of the female, she was not alone in being reduced to gender. The *Times* initially relied on gender to explain everyone's attitudes about sexual harassment. Maureen Dowd (1991a), the *New York Times's* White House correspondent, offered this lead on October 8: "The bitter 'he said, she said' case of Anita F. Hill and Clarence Thomas has offered a rare look into the mechanics of power and decision-making in Washington, a city where men have always made the rules and the Senate remains an overwhelmingly male club" (p. 1). Dowd's article, whose subhead referred to the "Mostly Male Club," suggested that "the boys here don't get it." On October 9, Dowd linked the delay in the confirmation vote to Washington's "highly charged sexual politics" and to women's increased clout: "Women's groups and female lawmakers swarmed through the [Congressional] halls, trying to make the male senators see the issue through their eyes, explaining why Professor Hill could very well be a victim whose words should carry weight" (1991b, p. 1). An accusatory tone marked the assertion that gender produced specific standpoints: "Women's groups, which had seemed to take Ms. Hill's side before she even testified, complained that Republican Senators were taking Mr. Thomas's side before all the testimony was completed" (Dowd, 1991e, p. 1). One of Dowd's male colleagues, R. W. Apple, agreed: "With only two women members, one from each party, and no minority members, the Senate still operates like a men's club, mostly taking the white male viewpoint as the universal norm, and it is therefore highly vulnerable to suggestions of insensitivity" (1991a, p. 1).

Already a *Times* star in the early 1960s, Apple did not mention age. Other reporters, however, wrapped gender, age, and race into a neat package. Referring to "white males over 50 years old," reporters rhetorically constituted white middle-aged men as a powerful, monolithic category with the authority to define and redefine reality for everyone else. Syndicated and in-house male columnists, it should be added, likewise treated maleness as a singular, global position—and likewise declined to identify themselves as male. Columnist Tom Wicker said, "Perhaps the male world will be made somewhat more aware that it has usually preferred to blame the victim rather than question itself" (1991, p. 27).[6] One of Wicker's colleagues said the initial F.B.I. report about Hill's allegations was ignored because "the 14 Judiciary Committee members, all men, were insensitive to women's experiences and feelings" (A. Lewis, 1991, p. 31).[7] Meanwhile, whether quoting well-known feminists, leaders of women's groups, or token individuals, the early reports implied that any woman could speak for all women. Just as all men failed to listen, women spoke as one.

For conservative critics, attacking Hill became a way to attack feminism, the intelligentsia, and liberal social programs. Thus, although Hill had not aligned herself with feminism, several op-ed writers undermined Hill by linking her—negatively—to feminism. In a highly controversial *Times* op-ed piece whose title referred to "Liberal Fallacies," Harvard sociologist Orlando Patterson (1991) mocked middle-class, neo-Puritanical feminists who, he said, stubbornly misconstrued what happened between Hill and Thomas. According to Patterson, most of the white working class and nearly all African Americans understood that Thomas was not unreasonably attracted to a woman apparently from a similar culture who admired him. Patterson ultimately justified Thomas's repudiation of Hill on the utilitarian grounds that "any admission would have immediately incurred a self-destructive and grossly unfair punishment" (p. E15).[8]

Other op-ed pieces melded feminist-bashing with media-bashing. Republican speech writer Peggy Noonan (1991) branded feminists and media professionals as elites waging "class division" on "real people." Noonan's *Times* op-ed piece applauded people like J.C. Alvarez, a woman who testified that she never had problems working for Thomas, whom she regarded as a victim of a lynch mob. Noonan contrasted "real people" like the "straight-shooting Maybellined J.C. Alvarez" to representatives of the "chattering classes" like National Public Radio's Nina Tottenberg. Another snobbish member of the chattering class was "the professional, movement-y and intellectualish Susan Hoerchner, with her unmakeupped face" (p. 25), referring here to the judge who testified on Hill's behalf that Hill had once tentatively confided that she was being harassed.

New York Times reporters located themselves outside or above the "battle of the sexes." Despite having posited a huge gender chasm, no reporter had trouble understanding anyone. Male reporters routinely spoke for/about women. Women reporters could read men's minds. Lena Williams (1991), for example, claimed Thomas's words "struck a chord . . . in the black male psyche" (p. 1).

The claim that reporters transcended gender bias may have been undermined in a story on so-called "women's" criticism of a Republican senator from Arizona for automatically believing Thomas over Hill. "Even some female journalists seemed to have a flash of gender-based anger," Dowd said (1991a, p. 22). Without conceding any gender-based anger of her own, Dowd quoted a sister reporter who accused Sen. Dennis DeConcini of misunderstanding how women empathize with rape victims whose character is challenged. A second incident hinting at intraprofessional criticism involved the Supreme Court reporter for the *Washington Times*. The daughter of a conservative fundraiser, Dawn Ceol had resigned after her managing editor changed her article about the testimony of John Doggett, who claimed that Hill appeared disappointed when he made clear that he was not romantically interested in her. The editor's rewrite highlighted accusations that Hill had "fantasized." An open defender of Thomas, Coel's editor had decried media harassment of Thomas as fueled by hysterical feminists, but he denied any ideological bases for his edits. Otherwise, however, reporters were reluctant to allege that their colleagues were not neutral, transparent, objective.

R. W. Apple (1991b) observed that, given this explosive, highly public, and televised situation, the Judiciary Committee had carefully moved female aides to prominent positions. Consistent with the press's notion that reporters are disembodied, however, the *Times* felt no particular compunction to make women reporters visible. Over the three weeks, 68 *Times* news reports and news analyses, for a total of 1,570 inches, carried male by-lines; 25, totalling 835 inches, carried female by-lines.[9] Despite the newspaper's explicit claim that harassment was a woman's issue, it was not in women's hands as a writing assignment.

THE BIAS OF PERSONAL EXPERIENCE

The *Times* noted that both Thomas's co-workers and Hill's boosters took their experiences as signalling truth. According to the *Times*, having been either a victim of sexual harassment or a victimizer determined how one saw Hill and Thomas.[10] This idea was at the heart of Jane Gross's (1991) description of "many women celebrating the sudden public discussion of a heretofore private subject and many men wondering about their own conduct, present, past and future" (p. 8). Gross commented: "Certain viewers had special agendas as they watched the hearings. Women, who seemed to feel they had the most at stake, said that listening to Professor Hill's account . . . stirred memories of their own unpleasant experiences in the workplace" (p. 8).

The *Times* did not worry about men as sexual prey. Indeed, reporters studiously avoided both Sen. Simpson's innuendos about Hill's sexual orientation and the larger issues about sexual orientation. But reporters did causally connect men's standpoints to their positions as actual, alleged, or potential "defendants." Several times, writers speculated that Sen. Kennedy's low profile during the hearings resulted from his reputation as a womanizer. Of course, journalists speculated about the emotional and cognitive impact of the controversy on Judge Thomas and the American public. Noting that several Justices had been changed by their confirmation experiences, for example, Neil Lewis (1991b) predicted the hearings would directly affect Thomas's standpoint, judicially and otherwise.

Meanwhile, *New York Times* reporters never explained their own histories with sexual harassment, as accused or accuser. Stories about corporate policies on sexual harassment never mentioned whether the *Times* had such policies (e.g., Strom, 1991).[11] As with gender per se, journalists disallowed any autobiographical reference to sexual habits. Nor did they address the potential impact of their own attitudes about sex and morality.

Ironically, accusations that columnist Juan Williams had sexually harassed several co-workers at the *Washington Post* emerged just when Williams was writing about the Thomas-Hill controversy. Williams (1991) had published a widely quoted column that trivialized Hill's allegations, defended Thomas, and criticized news media for exaggerating concerns about Thomas. But he claimed that he had knowingly harassed no one. Williams ridiculed the allegations as "nothing more than women taking a passing word in the wrong way" (p. 23). The *Post* acknowledged the allegations about Williams but provided no background about Williams beyond describing him as a family man and rising star. It neither outlined its policies on harassment nor indicated whether similar accusations had emerged before at the *Post*. Later, the *Post*'s ombudsman denounced the leaking of the allegations about Williams to other media; Richard Harwood (1991) condemned "the tainted practice of wounding reputations with the words of anonymous accusers" (p. C6). Without specifying any disciplinary actions by the *Post*, the ombudsman dismissed the allegations against Williams as "surprising" in view of the newsroom's "laid-back," "sexually tolerant" environment. More generally, at both the *Post* and the *Times*, male and female reporters refused to consider the possibility that workplace sexual relations had any impact. They presented themselves as desexualized as well as disembodied.

THE POWER OF RACE

Early accounts of the case mentioned the whiteness of the Judiciary Committee but otherwise downplayed race. For a couple of days, *Times* reporters did not mention that Hill was African American, although published photographs of her—typically in a jewel-collared blouse and pearls—revealed this. Not until Thomas accused the committee of "lynching" did accounts more openly discuss race. Then, reporters played off gender and race. "Taboo Issues of Sex and Race Explode in Glare of Hearing" analyzed how Thomas brought race to the fore, having initially kept it at bay (Dowd, 1991e). A story headlined "Thomas Hearings as Testimony to the Power of Race in American Politics" asserted that although the case was initially billed as watershed drama about sexual harassment, it ultimately turned on race and its "startling power" (Applebome, 1991). The agency of journalists in providing both "billings" was ignored. Instead, their point was that white television audiences were finally seeing conservative black professionals who disrupted stereotypes.

Lena Williams (1991) highlighted the determinative authority of race in "Blacks Say the Blood Spilled in the Thomas Case Stains All." She asserted: "While white Americans tend to view the case as a dispute over sexual harassment and the credibility of two believable witnesses, many blacks say it is much more: an embarrassment to their race. . . . And they are angered that two highly accomplished black people, in whom they might otherwise take pride, are at the center of such a nasty, lurid political soap opera" (p. 1). Ironically, polls betrayed no significant race-based differences in public opinion (Kolbert, 1991b). Even Williams, a reporter who is African American, reported a "split" between blacks who suspected that whites were using Hill to ruin a black man's life, and blacks offended that a black woman's claim was ignored.

The *Times* more gingerly hinted at blacks' fears that Hill's accusation would reinforce animalistic myths about black men's sexuality. Reporters tended to explain black men's particular support for Thomas as having little to do with Hill and much to do with presumably false accusations and distortions of their sexuality. The *Times* likewise mentioned fears that Hill's accusation would strain already fragile relations between black men and black women. Interestingly, the experts on black culture who were typically quoted in the *Times* were men who ignored the particular situation of black women and who criticized Hill. Essentially, following the leads of their sources, the reporters treated Hill in terms of gender and Thomas in terms of race. Thus, although, again, the *Times* visually and even linguistically acknowledged Hill's race, she was otherwise "whitened." The *Times* did not itself buy the claim that she was simply a pawn of liberals, whites, or feminists. But it never addressed what race might mean to Hill.

The *Times* also equivocated on whether it should identify the race of experts mentioned in stories, ordinary citizens interviewed on the streets, and others. Photographs sometimes clarified this, but more often readers were left to guess. One article quoted several Chicagoans who criticized Thomas for racializing the hearings and for calling himself black only when convenient; the sources were not identified as black, although savvy readers might have deduced this from the name of the neighborhood (Terry, 1991). Likewise, in the Juan Williams brouhaha discussed previously, the *Post* identified Williams as black, but the *Times* did not (Jones, 1991). Neither newspaper specified the complainants' race. Referring to other questions about Williams, the *New York Times* explained, "The huge impact the article had at a critical time raises questions about a news organization's sometimes conflicting obligations to be candid with readers and also to be fair to an employee under investigation" (Jones, 1991, p. 21). But the reporters never identified themselves by race or indicated how their own experiences might have been conditioned by the politics of skin color.

Most stories directly analyzing the relevance of race and racial stereotypes collapsed black professional women's problems into those of black men. They did not address whether racism might complicate gender issues. Ultimately, they presented gender as overriding race—perhaps because acknowledging divisions between black men and black women would compound the difficulty of neatly structuring stories around a polarized battle of the sexes. Notably, although they did not criticize the press, many black women commentators underscored their split loyalties and the way that this disadvantages African American women. Over 1,600 African American women signed a November 17, 1991, advertisement in the *Times* decrying the sexism *and* racism of the hearings. They were signalling their refusal to set racial oppression against gender oppression.

PARTY POLITICS AS A TRAP

Initially, the *Times* barely referenced party politics. After the hearings ended, however, reporters made political affiliation the dominant ingredient. This resulted in erasing Hill from the picture. Stories published after the confirmation vote barely mentioned Hill. Once they began to poll people about politics, journalists "found" that party affiliation predicted support for Thomas better than race or gender. Political fallout was eventually framed as an absolute, unavoidable trap. Washingtonians were categorized as either ever-powerful Republicans who had exploited a scorched earth strategy against Hill in order to win; or Democrats who, as white males linked with liberal advocacy groups, were too weak to fight (see Dowd, 1991b, 1991c). Stories framed the Senate vote as hanging on the search of senators (individually and as a group) for politically safe ground. Given the peculiar problems of southern Democrats, sometimes this dilemma had a regional twist (see Clymer, 1991b; Krauss, 1991; A. Rosenthal, 1991). "Senators Who Switched Tell of Political Torment" recounted competing pressures of eleventh hour lobbying from colleagues, interest groups, and President Bush (Berke, 1991b).

POLARIZED APPROACHES TO TRUTH AND SEX

Reporters were even more committed to the rhetoric of truth than Judiciary Committee members, who ritualistically recited lines about searching for facts but whose scripts included other characters and plot lines. Reporters maintained that a single, "crystal clear" truth was at stake. According to Suro (1991a), because both Thomas and Hill had been described as honorable and virtuous, "The Senate can only believe one of them" (p. 17). Dowd (1991d) sympathized with the "clearly confused" senators, "wondering how they would sift out the lies from truth in the diametrically opposed stories" (p. 1). One headline read, "Compelling Evidence on Both Sides, But Only One Can Be Telling Truth" (Wines, 1991b). A story on the highly detailed phone logs maintained by Thomas's staff was one of several to emphasize the "stark and seemingly irreconcilable conflict" between Thomas's and Hill's accounts (Wines, 1991a). Most of these news stories suggested that, unlike Hill,

Thomas had a clear motive to lie. But the point is this assumption that someone was delivering falsehood. Regarding a polygraph test taken by Hill (the results were eventually discredited because Hill herself had hired the tester), the *Times* dismissed the idea that Hill and Thomas might each have produced a separate, if partial, truth (Tolchin, 1991).[12]

As reporters framed the story, Hill was either a sociopath or a heroine. Conversely, Thomas was either wrongly maligned or despicable. One lead insisted: "The choices presented to the United States Senate by today's lurid, gut-wrenching proceedings on Capitol Hill could hardly have been much starker. . . . Either he said these wretched things to her—things that one associates with the seamiest of criminal cases or the raunchiest of locker rooms . . . or he did not. Yes or no. Up or down" (Apple, 1991b, p. 1). As the press noted, senators had resorted to the tradition of fetishizing body parts, forcing Thomas to agree that dirty talk represented slime at its slimiest. Journalists were not forced, however. Moreover, they hardly noticed that Hill herself carefully avoided this lexicon, despite ferocious Judiciary Committee harassment. They did not ask whether, in the late 20th century, references to pubic hair were really such toxins or merely disgusting weeds then enjoying hothouse treatment.

This equation of truth with moral virtue, and falsehood with evil, left reporters unable to account for some nagging paradoxes. Surveys and anecdotal evidence reported by the *Times* showed people believing Hill (believing that Hill accurately repeated what Thomas had said 10 years before) without believing "in" Hill. Evidence leaked into a few stories that Angela Wright, who had said Thomas's sexual harassment did not bother her, was not the only one who rejected journalists' assumption that all sexual talk is morally unacceptable. Many people apparently did not believe Thomas's verbiage was so terrible that it should disqualify him. For them, Hill's probity was irrelevant in the face of another larger truth, that Thomas was "essentially" innocent. For example, the 20 blue- and pink-collar women interviewed for one story resented sexual harassment but expressed little sympathy for Hill: "[W]hite and black women from the low-rent neighborhoods . . . look at Professor Hill as cowboys might look at a dude adrift in Dodge City, their incredulity spiced with contempt. The workplace they know is an untamed frontier where bad men roam and smart women learn how to take care of themselves or leave" (Barringer, 1991, p. 12). *Times* reporter Felicity Barringer could not explain why so many women simultaneously believed and rejected Hill. Likewise, the majority of 60 interviewees in Colorado believed Hill's story but supported Thomas (Johnson, 1991). With his wife apparently nodding yes, one Colorado man called Hill truthful but prudish. An older woman agreed: "But they're making too big a deal out of it. It's not like he's been raping women and beating children" (p. 16).

The *Times* staff was similarly surprised by the extent to which Europeans either discounted the controversy as a peculiarly American (i.e., silly) morality play, or ignored it altogether. One analysis quoted *Le Monde* as mocking the case as a mixture of "exacerbated moralism and inquisitorial passion, prudery and sordid confessions, outdated politics and an anxiety to denounce a practice—sexual harassment" (Riding, 1991, p. 16). Alan Riding added, "More surprising than the tone of some reactions was the remarkably low level of attention the Thomas case attracted outside the United States" (p. 16).[13] Riding's "surprise" at these reactions apparently derived from his assumption that everyone—save journalists—accepted an identical middle-class American paradigm. Reporters' failure to ask whether Thomas's behavior was so noxious left the *Times* unable to account for the many people who believed Hill but, notwithstanding, supported Thomas. Published histories of newspapers suggest that reporters have heard—and said—worse, not only in locker rooms but also in their own newsrooms. The pornographic language attributed to Thomas is also heard in television, film, and music. Nonetheless, having assumed their own uniqueness, reporters were amazed that "ordinary people" would tolerate such behavior in a judicial nominee, especially one who might, after all, have to rule on allegations of sexual harassment.

CONCLUSION

People quoted in the *Times* themselves testified to the formative impact of social location. They routinely referred to gender and race to explain or excuse their own responses. One woman said that "being a woman," she sided with Hill (Terry, 1991, p. 34). A black man said that, because he had once been falsely accused of "hitting on" a white cheerleader, "as a black American, it's been painful for me to watch this" (L.Williams, 1991, p. 16). Clearly, then, linking people's responses to sexual harassment with the material conditions of their lives, including the realities of sexism and racism, is valid.

What may be journalistically problematic is imposing a primitive sociology that sets different dimensions of identity (gender, race, sexual orientation, party affiliation, age, and so forth) against one other. Meanwhile, reporters assumed themselves to be immune from any personal influence. The press's version of objectivity forced a "masculinist," dichotomous thinking that was misleading with respect to complex issues like sexual harassment or complex people like Anita Hill. *Times* reporters obscured the historically contingent cultural processes involved. Those who defined themselves along multiple vectors were left homeless and nomadic. The press reduced the story to a series of conventional dimensions, each defined monolithically. Even when they confronted anomalous evidence, journalists read people's responses and judgments directly from their gender, politics, age, race, and sexual history. But other features were excluded, particularly religion, as well as cultural factors that cut across standard variables in complicated, ambiguous ways. They denied that people could be complex, much less unpredictable. Although Thomas may well have misread Hill, journalists most certainly misread much of what mattered to and about Hill.

Consistent with the journalistic norms of balance and "objectivity," the *Times* underscored the notion of dichotomy in several ways, not only in weighting the stories with an equal number of quotes and references to supporters and detractors, but also with its photographs. In one extreme, the *Times* juxtaposed nearly identical photographs of Hill and Thomas, each in profile, each with right hand raised to pledge truthtelling. The net effect, again, was to imply (wrongly) that the case involved two people of equal power and authority, and to imply (wrongly) that their stories were dichotomous versions of truth and falsehood. Just as importantly, such textual and visual images represented Hill and Thomas as opposites, which was reduced to sex. These images thereby denied the multiple, intersecting axes of race, religion, and class. This process, then, emptied Hill of complexity.

It may be noted that Women, Men and Media, a watchdog group founded by the feminist activist Betty Friedan, gave Dowd a "Breakthrough Award" for her coverage of the hearings; Friedan said Dowd deserved the Pulitzer Prize for her reporting. Conservatives apparently agreed that Dowd was partisan. A *Wall Street Journal* editorial published on October 17 ("Politically Correct Newsrooms") criticized Dowd, as did Media Watch, a conservative newsletter. Dowd continues to proclaim her neutrality and has denied that her stories on the confirmation hearings had a feminist bent (Kaufman, 1992).

In defense, it can be said that journalists have few models indicating how gender and race, in particular, are mutually embedded in hierarchical systems that unequally distribute status and power. Social scientists, from whom journalists have borrowed not only the conception of objectivity but theories about behavior, often treat race, gender (or sex), sexual preference, age, and class as static, global variables that per se describe people. Indeed, in this particular case, scholars often tended to privilege one variable over another, although not as stridently as the politicians. Many essayists (Morrison, 1992) read the Thomas hearings as reinforcing a long-standing American tradition of privileging the male story and erasing that of women, especially black women. But others connect Hill's difficulty in being heard and understood to her peculiar status at "the crossroads of gender and race hierarchies" (Crenshaw, 1992, p. 43). Crenshaw, who worked on Hill's legal team, notes that although many elements of the white feminist discourse about gender power and sexual domination applied to Hill, feminists' narrative about rape "de-raced" Hill and inadvertently enlarged the chasm between feminists and antiracists.

Some press critics highlight how the written structure of news stories and the reporting conventions of news gathering reinforce official viewpoints, thus bolstering institutional power (Sigal, 1973; Schiller, 1981). In this case, journalists legitimately went beyond the usual cast of elite experts and press colleagues. Yet, the ultimate mantle of authority remained wrapped tightly around journalists. As reporters construed it, all sources were equally tainted. Journalists retained a monopoly on the definition of reality and objective truth because, they suggested, only they are free of bias. They did not define themselves the way they defined others or answer the questions they asked of others.

Journalists may argue that they cannot afford to level with readers about their values, their assumptions, their personal histories. Credibility, their stock in trade, depends first on sincere attempts at objectivity and then on assertions that it has been achieved. This "strategic ritual" (Tuchman, 1972) may seem their only bulwark against accusations of bias. Claims to professional status and their economic viability require the appearance of neutrality and insulation from sources and subjects. The easiest way for organizations to present themselves as neutral is to round up the usual suspects and present the story as involving (exactly) two sides. Yet, the by-product is exaggerating and rigidifying differences and ignoring complexity and historical contingency. Reliance on the professional conventions of objectivity produces more confusion than clarity and obscures crucial themes.

Treating the story in terms of what happened yesterday ignores the larger context of sexual harassment. Apart from the problem of reducing Hill to a static product of gender politics, by personalizing the whole of the problem of sexual harassment in the "bodies" of Hill's and Thomas's evidence, reporters missed an opportunity to explain crucial power dimensions of workplace abuse of women. Likewise, simplifying everyone's responses as knee-jerk reactions to their own biographies overpowered more nuanced sociological explanations.

Hill was caught in a classic double-bind. Gloria Hull (1992) asks whether Hill's primness "emanated from her own nature or was adopted strategy" (p. 98). These two are not easily distinguished. The point is that black women in the United States are painfully aware of the difficulty of resisting racist assumptions about black women. Ironically, Hill's "nice girl" role—her calm, courteous obedience during the hearings—undermined her potential power. As Dowd said, the Senators refused in any event to listen to Hill. They stubbornly measured Hill against their ideas about hysterical female affect.

The event-centered newswriting paradigm may have seemed a relief to reporters who felt trapped between wanting to respect Anita Hill's steady insistence on privacy and detachment, no matter what the emotional impact, and to expose the inflamed diatribes of the senators and Thomas. It may be that what was most potentially explosive—an open discussion of sexuality in the context of both historically legitimate and illegitimate understandings of black women and black men—was simply too "hot" to handle. Nonetheless, nonracist and nonsexist accounts that treat people as fully human, repudiate the all-too-powerful stereotypes about black women, and present complex but useable definitions and explanations of sexual harassment remain to be written.

ENDNOTES

1. There have been some discussions of the rhetorical dimensions. For example, Lipari (1994) showed how journalists' use of the rhetoric of soap operas and melodrama depoliticized the Hill-Thomas hearings.
2. The legal foundation for objecting to harassment was embedded in the 1964 Civil Rights Act, but not until 1980 did the Equal Employment Opportunity Commission issue guidelines making it illegal, and those guidelines were not confirmed by the Supreme Court until 1986.
3. I also read all coverage in the Newark, NJ, *Star-Ledger* and in the *Washington Post*.
4. According to Goulden (1988), *New York Times* executive editor Abe Rosenthal was a notorious womanizer who had affairs with employees and employees' wives. Rosenthal once defended hiring another writer criticized as a womanizer by saying, "If that were a disqualification for working for the *New York Times* . . . this place would be empty!" (cited in Gates, 1996, p. 72). Now a semi-retired columnist, Rosenthal accused the press of harassing Thomas (A. M. Rosenthal, 1991).
5. Weaver and Wilhoit (1991) found that the religious backgrounds of American journalists almost perfectly match statistics for the overall population. They dispute earlier data that suggested that half the journalists working for elite papers, such as the *Times* and the *Washington Post*, claim no religious affiliation. But journalists working for elite national media may be more secular than journalists as a whole; furthermore, "background" cannot be equated with active practice and belief.

6. According to Goulden (1988, p. 377), Wicker was merely echoing
    policy when he once asserted, "No woman will ever be an editor of
    the *New York Times*."
7. No one has said who leaked Hill's story, which she had originally
    wanted to remain anonymous.
8. Burnham (1992) notes that because sexual harassment is seen as
    part of the white feminists' platform and because feminists rallied
    to Hill's defense, hostility to feminism was behind much of the sus-
    picion of Hill (see also Stansell, 1992).
9. Most of the quotes here are from a woman, but this is largely
    because, in providing analysis as opposed to transmitting informa-
    tion, Dowd used more interesting language than did other
    reporters. Fifteen minor stories, mostly under 10 inches, were not
    by-lined. Additionally, the *Times* devoted 1,135 inches to full or
    partial transcripts of testimony and speeches. One story was writ-
    ten by several men. Besides the nine unsigned editorials, the op-ed
    pages carried 33 columns, two-thirds by men, and a few by free-
    lancers. The length is approximate and does not count inches
    devoted to photographs, editorials, and op-ed pieces.

    For purposes of comparison, it may be noted that over the same
    period, the *Washington Post* carried 34 stories, taking up 1,110 inch-
    es, by individual women; 40 stories, taking up 940 inches, were
    attributed to individual men. Women jointly wrote eight *Post* sto-
    ries, taking up 317 inches; men jointly wrote six stories, for 216
    inches; and six stories, totalling 196 inches, involved a man and
    woman writing together.
10. Again, polling data were ambiguous and fluctuated over time. One
    story connected women lawyers' sympathy for Hill with evidence
    that 60% of them claimed to have been harassed (Kolbert, 1991a). But,
    according to Kolbert's poll, 38% of women respondents had been
    harassed at some point (with few of them reporting it); of these, 33%
    supported Thomas, whereas 26% opposed him. At that point, mean-
    while, one-third of all women supported him; 18% opposed him.
    Moreover, half the male respondents admitted they had engaged in
    workplace behaviors that might be construed as sexual harassment.
11. The Associated Press Managing Editors found in 1992 that 30% of
    the respondents to a survey said their newspaper had guidelines
    for complaints about harassment (Walsh-Childers et al., 1995).
12. In explaining to the press why his answers to Kenneth Starr's ques-
    tions about relationships with the White House intern might have
    been different from Monica Lewinsky's account, President Bill
    Clinton very specifically referred to the Hill-Thomas hearings.
    Clinton reminded the reporters that most people listening to the
    1991 hearings had assumed that only one party was telling the
    truth. In contrast, Clinton said that his own view was that both Hill
    and Thomas had tried to tell the truth and, indeed, had told the
    truth as they saw it. Anita Hill (1998) herself acknowledged that

Clinton and other people were drawing analogies between 1991 and 1998; in pointing out what she regarded as processual errors in how the two cases were investigated, however, Hill did not remark on the claim that in both cases, both parties could have been telling the truth.

13. Reporters, including those from the *Times*, were forced to concede similar surprise in the wake of responses to the Special Prosecutor's report to Congress on the relationship between President Clinton and Monica Lewinsky. Again, "ordinary" American people did not seem as uniformly outraged as reporters had apparently expected. Second, the foreign press did not seem to take seriously what was so scandalous to the Washington press corps.

REFERENCES

Apple, R. W., Jr. (1991a, October 9). Vote on Thomas is put off as Senate backing erodes over harassment charge. *New York Times*, pp. 1, 9.

Apple, R. W., Jr. (1991b, October 12). On Thomas: More questions, not fewer. *New York Times*, pp. 1, 9.

Applebome, P. (1991, October 18). Thomas hearings as testimony to the power of race in America. *New York Times*, p. 8.

Awkward, M. (1995). *Negotiating difference. Race, gender, and the politics of positionality.* Chicago: University of Chicago Press.

Barringer, F. (1991, October 18). Hill's case is divisive to women. *New York Times*, p. 12.

Berke, R. L. (1991b, October 16). Senators who switched tell of political torment. *New York Times*, pp. 1, 16.

Bogle, D. (1991). *Toms, coons, mulattoes, mammies and bucks: An interpretive history of blacks in American film.* New York: Continuum.

Burnham, M. A. (1992). The Supreme Court appointment process and the politics of race and sex. In T. Morrison (Ed.), *Race-ing justice, en-gendering power* (pp. 290-322). New York: Pantheon.

Chaudhary, A. (1980). Press portrayal of black officials. *Journalism Quarterly, 57*(4), 636-646.

Chrisman, R., & Allen, R. L. (Eds.). (1992). *Court of appeal.* New York: Ballantine Books.

Clymer, A. (1991a, October 11). Conflict emerges over a 2d witness. *New York Times*, pp. 1, 16.

Clymer, A. (1991b, October 16). Senate's futile search for safe ground. *New York Times*, pp. 1, 20.

Crenshaw, K. (1992). Whose story is it, anyway? Feminist and antiracist appropriations of Anita Hill. In T. Morrison (Ed.), *Race-ing justice, en-gendering power* (pp. 402-440). New York: Pantheon.

Darnton, R. (1975). Writing news and telling stories. *Daedalus, 104*(2), 175-194.

Dates, J. L., & Pease, E. C. (1994, Summer). Warping the world: Media's mangled images of race. *Media Studies Journal*, pp. 89-95.

Dowd, M. (1991a, October 8). The Senate and sexism. *New York Times*, pp. 1, 22.

Dowd, M. (1991b, October 9). 7 Congressmen march to Senate to demand delay in Thomas vote. *New York Times*, pp. 1, 19.

Dowd, M. (1991c, October 10). Facing issue of harassment, Washington slings the mud. *New York Times*, pp. 1, B15.

Dowd, M. (1991d, October 12). In an ugly atmosphere, the accusations fly. *New York Times*, pp. 1, 8.

Dowd, M. (1991e, October 13). Taboo issues of sex and race explode in glare of hearings. *New York Times*, pp. 1, 29.

Dowd, M. (1991f, October 15). Republicans gain in battle by getting nasty quickly. *New York Times*, pp. 1, 18.

Dowd, M. (1991g, October 16). Image more than reality became issue, losers say. *New York Times*, pp. 1, 20.

Entman, R. (1990). Modern racism and the images of blacks in local television news. *Critical Studies in Mass Communication, 7*(4), 332-345.

Entman, R. (1992). Blacks in the news: Television, modern racism and cultural change. *Journalism Quarterly, 69*(2), 341-361.

Fair, J. (1993). The women of South Africa weep: Explorations in race and gender. *Howard Journal of Communications, 4*(4), 283-294.

Fiske, J. (1993). *Power plays power works*. London: Verso.

Fiske, J. (1994). *Media matters*. Minneapolis: University of Minnesota Press.

Gans, H. (1979). *Deciding what's news*. New York: Vintage.

Gates, H. L., Jr. (1996, June 17). White like me. *The New Yorker*, pp. 66-81.

Goulden, J. C. (1988). *Fit to print*. Secaucus, NJ: Lyle Stuart.

Gross, J. (1991, October 12). Americans riveted by lesson in civics. *New York Times*, p. 8.

Harwood, R. (1991, October 27). Dirty talk. *Washington Post*, p. C6.

Hill, A. (1998, September 28). The Thomas lesson. *New York Times*, p. 17.

Hill, A. F., & Jordan, E. C. (Eds.). (1995). *Race, gender, and power in America*. New York: Oxford.

Hull, G. T. (1992). Girls will be girls, and boys will . . . flex their muscles. In R. Chrisman & R. L. Allen (Eds.), *Court of appeal* (pp. 96-98). New York: Ballantine Books.

Johnson, D. (1991, October 14). Puzzled and disgusted, but fixation on hearings. *New York Times*, p. 16.

Jones, A. (1991, October 16). Newspaper reveals editorial conflict. *New York Times*, p. 21.

Kaufman, L. (1992). Mo knows. *Washington Journalism Review, 14*(8), 16-20.

Kolbert, E. (1991a, October 11). Sexual harassment at work is pervasive, survey suggests. *New York Times*, pp. 1, 18.

Kolbert, E. (1991b, October 15). Most in national survey say judge is the more believable. *New York Times*, pp. 1, 20.

Krauss, C. (1991, October 15). On eve of vote on Thomas, a Senator grapples for answers. *New York Times*, p. 18.

Lewis, A. (1991, October 11). Wages of cynicism. *New York Times*, p. 31.

Lewis, N. (1991a, September 28). Judiciary panel deadlocks, 7-7, on Thomas nomination to Court. *New York Times*, pp. 1, 8.

Lewis, N. (1991b, October 18). After ordeal of Senate confirmation, views on Thomas's court opinions. *New York Times*, p. 8.

Lindsey, K. (1995). Race, sexuality and class in soapland. In G. Dines & J. M. Humez (Eds.), *Gender, race and class in media* (pp. 332-339). Thousand Oaks: Sage.

Lipari, L. (1994). As the word turns. *Political Communication, 11*(3), 299-308.

Lubiano, W. (1992). Black ladies, welfare queens, and state minstrels: Ideological war by narrative means. In T. Morrison, (Ed.), *Race-ing justice, en-gendering power* (pp. 323-363). New York: Pantheon.

Lule, J. (1995). The rape of Mike Tyson: Race, the press and symbolic types. *Critical Studies in Mass Communication, 12*(2), 176-195.

McAdams, K. C., & Beasley, M. H. (1994, August). Sexual harassment of Washington women journalists. *Newspaper Research Journal, 15*(1), 127-139.

Mapp, E. (1982). Black women in films. *The Black Scholar, 4*, 36-40.

Martindale, C. (1985). Coverage of black Americans in five newspapers since 1950. *Journalism Quarterly, 62*(2), 321-328, 438.

Martindale, C. (1986). *The white press and black America*. Westport, CT: Greenwood Press.

Martindale, C. (1990). Coverage of black Americans in four major newspapers, 1950-1989. *Newspaper Research Journal, 11*(3), 96-112.

Merritt, B. D. (1994). Illusive reflections: African American women on primetime television. In A. Gonzalez, M. Houston, & V. Chen (Eds.), *Our voices: Essays in culture, ethnicity, and communication* (pp. 48-53). Los Angeles: Roxbury.

Mills, K. (1988). *A place in the news*. New York: Dodd, Mead.

Morrison, T. (Ed.). (1992). *Race-ing justice, en-gendering power*. New York: Pantheon.

Noonan, P. (1991, October 15). A bum ride. *New York Times*, p. 25.

Painter, N. I. (1992). Hill, Thomas and the use of racial stereotype. In T. Morrison, (Ed.), *Race-ing justice, en-gendering power* (pp. 200-214). New York: Pantheon.

Patterson, O. (1991, October 20). *Race, gender and liberal fallacies*. New York Times, p. E15.

Phelps, T., & Winternitz, H. (1992). *Capitol games. Clarence Thomas, Anita Hill and the story of a Supreme Court nomination*. New York: Hyperion.

Rakow, L., & Kranich, K. (1991). Women as sign in television news. *Journal of Communication, 41*(1), 8-23.

Riding, A. (1991, October 14). Foreign press shrugs at latest U.S. morality play. *New York Times*, p. 16.

Robertson, N. (1992). *The girls in the balcony*. New York: Random House.

Rosenthal, A. (1991, October 15). Thomas's edge steady, vote due today. *New York Times*, pp. 1, 18.

Rosenthal, A. M. (1991, October 15). Harassment by the press. *New York Times*, p. 25.

Schiller, D. (1981). *Objectivity and the news*. Philadelphia: University of Pennsylvania Press.

Sentman, M.A. (1983). Black and white: Disparity in coverage by *Life* magazine from 1937 to 1972. *Journalism Quarterly, 60*(3), 501-508.

Sigal, L. V. (1973). *Reporters and officials*. Lexington, MA: D.C. Heath.

Stansell, C. (1992). White feminists and black realities: The politics of authenticity. In T. Morrison, (Ed.), *Race-ing justice, en-gendering power* (pp. 251-268). New York: Pantheon.

Stempel, G. (1971). Visibility of blacks in news and news-picture magazines. *Journalism Quarterly, 48*(2), 337-339.

Strom, S. (1991, October 20). Harassment cases can go unnoticed. *New York Times*, pp. 1, 22.

Suro, R. (1991a, October 8). A law professor defends integrity. *New York Times*, p. 22

Suro, R. (1991b, October 11). A private person in a storm: Anita Faye Hill. *New York Times*, pp. 1, 17.

Talese, G. (1970). *The kingdom and the power*. New York: Bantam.

Terry, D. (1991, October 13). On streets, confusion and talk of harassment. *New York Times*, p. 34.

Tolchin, M. (1991, October 14). Hill said to pass a polygraph test. *New York Times*, p. 10.

Tuchman, G. (1972). Objectivity as a strategic ritual: An examination of newsmen's notions of objectivity. *American Journal of Sociology 77*(4), 660-679.

Tuchman, G. (1978). *Making news*. New York: Free Press.

Turow, J. (1994). Hidden conflicts and journalistic norms: The case of self-coverage. *Journal of Communication, 44*(2), 29-46.

Tyler, P.E. (1991, October 11). New witness says she is willing to corroborate accusations by professor. *New York Times*, p. 17.

van Zoonen, L. (1994). *Feminist media studies*. London: Sage.

Wallace, M, (1992). Negative images: Toward a black feminist cultural criticism. In L. Grossberg, C. Nelson, & P. A. Treichler (Eds.), *Cultural studies* (pp. 654-671). New York: Routledge.

Walsh-Childers, K., Chance, J., & Herzog, K. (1995, August). *Outing sexual harassment of women journalists*. Paper presented at the Association for Education in Journalism and Mass Communication, Washington, DC.

Weaver, D., & Wilhoit, G. (1991). *The American journalist*. Bloomington: Indiana University Press.

Wicker, T. (1991, October 10). Blaming Anita Hill. *New York Times*, p. 27.

Williams, J. (1991, October 15). Open season on Clarence Thomas. *The Washington Post*, p. 23.

Williams, L. (1991, October 14). Blacks say the blood spilled in the Thomas case stains all. *New York Times*, pp. 1, 16.

Wilson, C. C., II, & Gutierrez, F. (1995). *Race, multiculturalism, and the media*. Thousand Oaks, CA: Sage.

Wines, M. (1991a, October 10). Stark conflict marks accounts given by Thomas and professor. *New York Times*, p. 22.

Wines, M. (1991b, October 15). Compelling evidence on both sides, but only one can be telling the truth. *New York Times*, p. 20.

IV

COMPLEXITIES AND CONTRADICTIONS

14

The Portrayal of Women in Television Advertising

Carolyn Lin

The controversy over the portrayal of gender roles in media is hardly new. For decades, social critics and scholars have discussed gender roles from feminist, humanistic, and social scientific perspectives, trying to gauge their impact on our sociocultural evolution. This evolutionary process is particularly intriguing now, as traditionally defined gender roles for men and women start to "overlap" or become less distinguishable. For instance, working women often double as single parents, taking on the duties of both a traditional breadwinner and homemaker.

With a little over half of the women in the United States now employed full-time, and about two-thirds of all women in the workforce, media portrayals of women's places in society remain outdated (Atkin, Moorman, & Lin, 1991). This outdated profile of existing social conditions reflects, for some, a hegemonic view based on conventional institutional bias (Gitlin, 1983). According to "cultural lag" theory (Ogburn, 1964), such bias is indicative of how the advertising industry lags behind in acknowledging or accepting certain social developments, relative to other segments of the society. When this institutional bias is found in advertising, due to its ubiquitous reach, the social consequences could assume critical importance.

In fact, few media issues have generated as much controversy as the portrayal of gender in advertising (e.g., Ferguson, Kreshel, &

Tinkham, 1990). Yet, despite efforts among feminists and others to raise consciousness levels among the viewing public, traditional gender and attractiveness stereotypes remain prevalent (Soley & Kurzbard, 1986; Soley & Reid, 1988). This study provides an updated examination of gender role portrayals of women in prime-time television commercials of the 1990s.

LITERATURE REVIEW

As most of the literature on gender and advertising involves magazines, which share certain visual themes with TV advertising, it is useful to review work addressing both media. Studies of women in print magazine ads suggest that a majority of ads "put them down" or "keep them in their place" (Pingree, Hawkins, Butler, & Paisley, 1976). Courtney and Whipple's (1983) review revealed that, from 1958 to 1978, print ads often showed both genders in a stereotypical fashion. In particular, typical portrayals reflect that a woman's place is in the home, as women are primarily concerned with household tasks and personal beauty. They are also more likely to be presented in a nonactive, decorative role, seemingly incapable of making a decision without the help of a man.

More recently, Ferguson, Kreshel, and Tinkham (1990) found that even *Ms.* magazine often depicted women as alluring sex objects, despite their stated policy to refuse advertising or products that are harmful or insulting to women. The authors concluded that the preponderance of men working in advertising encouraged such depictions.

Soley and Kurzbard's (1986) study of magazine ads from 1965-1984 found that females were more likely than males to be presented as partially clad or nude. Some of these practices may be attributable to more "revealing" women's fashion trends. The authors concluded that male advertising practitioners are more likely than their female counterparts to view "sex appeals" as socially acceptable and responsible.

Research addressing televised advertising provides an equally dour assessment of the portrayals of women. In both media, women have historically been shown as "stay-at-home" mothers, typically subservient to men and primarily concerned with raising a family (Courtney & Whipple, 1983; Whipple & Courtney, 1985). Because researchers have devoted relatively less attention to sexism expressed in television advertising, it is useful to explore the major themes concerning print media stereotypes (see, e.g., Courtney & Whipple, 1983). As Poe (1976) notes, this stereotype typically includes beliefs that:

(a) woman's place is in the home; (b) women do not make important decisions or do important things; (c) women are dependent upon men and are isolated from their own sex; and (d) men regard women as sex objects; they are not interested in women as people. (p. 186)

Many have protested this inequitable treatment of women in media, finding it symptomatic of a Western culture that remains strongly male-dominated (Barthel, 1988; Condra, 1992; Tuchman, 1979). Feminists (e.g., Brownmiller, 1984; Creedon, 1993; Dworkin, 1974; Millman, 1980) also decry the disembodiment of women's bodies apparent in the context of advertising. Others (Barthel, 1988; Schur, 1984) argue that men and women are both beginning to "objectify" the opposite sex, often drawing meaning from media images, although men are far more likely to treat women as sex objects.

Despite that, as modern feminism captured news headlines, particularly during the 1970s, advertising images were slow to reflect women's gains in the workplace (Schneider & Schneider, 1979). Subsequent research indicates that little has changed since that time, as female models are typically less independent or competent than their male counterparts (Caballero, Lumpkin, & Madden, 1989; Courtney & Whipple, 1983; Craig, 1992; Knill, Persch, Gilpin, & Perloff, 1981; Leigh, Rethans, & Whitney, 1987; Lovdal, 1989; Osborn, 1989; Sullivan & O'Connor, 1988).

Other work addressing voice-overs in televised commercials (e.g., Bretl & Cantor, 1988; Lovdal, 1989) generally reveals that males dominate the verbal portion of most commercials, including those ads featuring only female models. Women more regularly appear as the endorsers for products used in the home (such as food stuffs and laundry detergents), with the bulk of these ads aired during the afternoon.

This was confirmed by Scheibe (1979), who found that the portrayal of women has changed little through the late 1970s, with none shown outside of traditionally female occupations in the home. Knill et al. (1981) reached a similar conclusion, finding that males comprised 75% of the occupational roles in the evening, whereas females appeared in 69% of the family/home theme commercials.

Although others (Soley & Reid, 1988) find evidence of a decline in stereotyping after 1964, women still were more likely to be shown in physically alluring roles. Sexton and Haberman (1974) examined the role of women endorsers, from 1950 through 1971, in terms of their functional (or participative) relationship to the product endorsed. Their findings also revealed that, although women were primarily shown in a functional role (that is, using the product), the percentages of women depicted in nonfunctional roles have increased for certain products, such as cigarettes.

Although males and females now occur equally as primary characters in TV commercials (Bretl & Cantor, 1988), daypart differences also play a determining role in gender portrayals (Craig, 1992). Specifically, daytime ads—which are generally aimed at female home-makers—focused on traditional, stereotypical images of the American housewife. Products and settings were tied to family life and involved cooking, child care, and the like.

By comparison, women are more likely to be cast in positions of authority in ads aired during prime-time hours, particularly in relation to housekeeping or child-rearing situations. Even so, a good portion of women remain "boxed in" sexy "cheesecake"[1] caricatures and are much more likely to appear as sex objects than their male counterparts (Craig, 1992; Rak & McMullen, 1987; Sullivan & O'Connor, 1988).

Previous research has documented the effectiveness of physical attractiveness in eliciting positive emotional responses (Berscheid & Walster, 1974; Benoy, 1982; Debevec, Madden, & Kernan, 1986; Kahle & Homer, 1983; Patzer, 1985). The impetus for using sexy female carica-tures for their sales appeal also is firmly established among advertisers (LaTour, Pitts, & Snook-Luther, 1991). Hence, as Downs and Harrison (1985) conclude, "television commercials are a major repository of attractiveness stereotypes" (p. 10). Even so, recent study indicates that nonstereotypical roles can be just as effective as traditional ones in advertising (Whipple & Courtney, 1985).

Advertisers are continuing, however, to explore the bounds of sensuality/nudity for both genders (Soley & Kurzbard, 1986; Soley & Reid, 1988). For instance, Soley and Kurzbard (1986) reported an increase in the number of print ads showing near-nude female and paired male and female models from 1964 to 1984, as exemplified by two-gender paired ads portraying rather obvious sexual intimacy between the models. Reid and Soley (1983) also found that interest in the product type is more influential in getting males to read ad copy than the presence of an attention-getting, decorative female model in the ad.

Sexual portrayals are more muted in television than in print advertising as mass audience dynamics and government regulation may dictate a more conservative standard.

RESEARCH FRAMEWORK

Overall, the literature profiles a tradition of sex stereotyping, attractive-ness stereotypes, and gender-specific, product-model relations. To assess this form of sexism, this study adopted Pingree et al.'s (1976) five levels of media sexism as the basis for analysis. This scale was utilized to code the model's gender roles.

Level 1 applies to ads in which the model is a two-dimensional character. A typical example is when the model is nothing more than a sex symbol or decorative item in the ad. Level 2 is reflective of a "strictly traditional" portrayal, in which a woman's place is in the home or in womanly occupations. Such portrayals commonly include women performing household cleaning chores, housekeeping duties (such as buying toothpaste for the family), childcare tasks (such as being a doctor mom), or service jobs (such as waitressing, clerical work, etc.) while promoting a "relevant" product. Level 3 is indicative of a "chiefly traditional" depiction in which a woman may be a professional, but her first place is home. For instance, a recent campaign for Enjoli cologne featured a professional woman coming home to cook dinner, proclaiming that "I can bring home the bacon, and fry it up in a pan." Level 4 treats women as equal to men, without any sex-role types attached. The Level 4 measure is similar to the combination of Pingree et al.'s two highest levels. An example might include a couple contributing equally to the decision concerning an important automobile purchase or a gender-role-free ad featuring men and/or women adopting a particular brand of headache medicine. (For details of the full Pingree et al. scale, see Appendix I, adopted from Ferguson et al., 1990, and Pingree et al., 1976).

Applying this adapted scale, we can gauge the status of women in advertising. The previously mentioned literature suggests that women's images have moved beyond decorative or low status stereotypes, although they have not been fully emancipated from those caricatures. Given those countervailing influences, the following research questions are offered:

Research Question 1: Is there a difference in the proportions of women in traditional roles?

Research Question 2: Do the proportions of women shown in decorative and nondecorative portrayals differ?

Research Question 3: Do the proportions of women shown in alluring and nonalluring portrayals differ?

Research Question 4: Is the level of sexism reflected in the portrayal of a model associated with the model's relation to the product in the ad?

Research Question 5: Is the level of sexism reflected in the portrayal of a model associated with the model's physical appearance?

RESEARCH METHODS

The study sample was composed of a full week of network prime-time television commercials. The week was randomly selected from a randomly chosen month. All commercials aired from 8 to 11 p.m. on the three major broadcast networks (ABC, CBS, and NBC) during the second week of April 1993 were recorded. That time frame should reflect advertising patterns during a fairly "representative" month, when viewership or placement strategies are not influenced by special events such as the Superbowl.[2]

The final sample included 505 coded units, after excluding redundant commercials and commercials that did not feature adult models but instead used children, animals, animation, or no endorsers. All adult female models who appeared in a commercial as a unique character were individually coded. When a group of models appeared in a scene together, acting in a similar manner (as in a group activity such as walking down the beach), all models in the group were coded as a single unit.[3]

In addition to the levels of sexism, two conceptual items also were measured. Adapted from Sexton and Haberman's (1974) scales, the *model relation to product* was assessed by judging whether the model appears in: (a) a "functional role"—directly related to the product's use; (b) a "decorative role"—not related to the product's use or a verbal endorsement; or (c) "other"—direct verbal endorsement of the product without demonstrating the use of the product. An example of the "functional role" would be when Kathy Lee Gifford sings the praises of the Carnival Cruise Line on board the cruiser. By contrast, a "nonfunctional role" could be when actress Susan Sullivan talks in a library about how Tylenol is the best pain-relieving medicine, without demonstrating the use of the medicine. A decorative role often appears in Calvin Klein cologne ads such as "Eternity" or "Escape," which feature model Kate Moss walking on the beach or appearing in a mysterious dreamlike state; she neither demonstrates the use of the product nor verbally endorses it.

The *model physical appearance* was coded using two categories: (a) "obviously alluring," defined as the model's physical appearance (or sex appeal) being used to create viewer liking (or purchase intention) for the product; and (b) "other," a category that does not focus on the use of a model's physical appearance (or sex appeal) as part of the sales appeal.

RESEARCH RESULTS

All data analyses for the statistical association between variables were performed by applying the Chi-square (or χ^2) test of goodness-of-fit; significant chi-square values are denoted in the tables.[4] A statistically significant Chi-square value indicates that the differences or associations found in appearance frequencies (e.g., by gender) are valid within the tolerated probability of error. By contrast, a statistically insignificant Chi-square value indicates that the opposite is true; that is, the finding could be the result of error.

Table 14.1 details results addressing portrayals of sexism. To avoid interpretive bias with regard to the semantic meaning of different sexism categories, Levels 1 and 2 were combined to form the "traditional portrayal" category. Just over half (50.8%) of the female models were portrayed in the traditional roles of Levels 1 and 2, and slightly less than a quarter (23.1%) still were represented as primarily traditional (Level 3) in that they tended to be professionals second and homemakers first. Just over a quarter (26.1%) of the portrayals were of Level 4 models, who were represented as equal to men without being tied to gender-specific roles. In answering Research Question No. 1, the result indicates that traditional portrayals dominate over nontraditional portrayals.

Table 14.2 offers a more skewed distribution for the ways the model's role is portrayed in relation to the products endorsed. In particular, two-thirds (66%) of the models were portrayed in a decorative role, 10% in a functional role, and 24% in the catch-all "other" role in relation to the products they endorsed. Hence, the finding provides an affirmative answer for Research Question No. 2, as the prevailing trend favors decorative portrayals as opposed to the other two types of portrayals in relation to products endorsed. This suggests the following: (s) two-thirds of the models appeared in ads as irrelevant "window dressing"; (b) nearly a quarter of the models were presented as product users; and (c) the remaining one-tenth of the models were verbal endorsers of the product (who simply talked about the products).

Table 14.1. Portrayals of Models by Level of Sexism.

Level of Sexism	Models (%)
Traditional (Levels 1 & 2)	50.8
Chiefly Traditional (Level 3)	23.1
Gender Equality (Level 4)	26.1
Column χ^2 =	13.88*

*denotes statistical significance.

Table 14.2. Portrayals of Models by Their Relation to Product.

Relation to Product	Models (%)
Other	23.9
Decorative	66.0
Functional	10.1
Column χ^2 =	50.93*

*denotes statistical significance.

Table 14.3 details the physical appearance of the models, as out-lined in Research Question No. 3. Frequency distributions suggest that a slight majority of models (57.6%) fall under the "other" rather than "allur-ing" (42.4%) categories. However, the statistical test result indicates that the difference between these two types of portrayals is not significant. That is, the difference observed may be a result of chance error. Hence, a slightly larger number of models were not considered sexually appealing to a noticeable degree, and the rest did possess identifiable "sex appeal."

Research Question No. 4 is addressed in Table 14.4. Here, the level of sexism reflected in model portrayals is not significantly associat-ed with (or a function of) the roles the models perform in endorsing the product, and vice versa.[5]

Specifically, the column frequency breakdowns indicate rather small differences between the four levels of sexism reflected in the por-trayals of models in terms of the roles they perform in endorsing prod-ucts (i.e., "other," "functional," or decorative" roles). This suggests that sexism is not a factor associated with the way the model was portrayed in relation to the product endorsed. A two-dimensional portrayal of a model, for instance, was no more likely to be cast in a "decorative" or "window-dressing" role in product endorsement than was a gender-equality portrayal.

Row frequency breakdowns, however, tell a different story. Within the portrayals classified under each sexism level, the model was most likely to be performing a "functional" role than either the "other" or "decorative" roles. Hence, the model's relationship to the product endorsed was mostly a "functional" or "product user" role above all, regardless of the sexism level that might have been injected into the por-trayal of the model.

Contrastingly, in addressing Research Question No. 5, the results indicate that the model's physical appearance is associated with the level of sexism reflected in model portrayals. That is, the portrayal of the model's physical appearance—in terms of the degree of her allure—is found to be reflective of the level of sexism imbedded in a commercial.

Table 14.3. Portrayals of Models By Their Physical Appearance.

Physical Appearance	Models (%)
Other	57.6
Alluring	42.4
Column χ^2 =	2.34

Table 14.4. Sexist Portrayals of Models by Their Relation to Product.

	Model Relation to Product			
Level of Sexism	Other %	Functional %	Decorative %	Total %
Two-Dimensional (Level 1)	2.9	12.6	3.8	19.3
Strictly Traditional (Level 2)	9.2	18.9	3.4	31.5
Chiefly Traditional (Level 3)	5.9	15.6	1.7	23.1
Gender Equality (Level 4)	5.9	18.9	1.3	26.1
Overall χ^2 = 9.56. Total %:	23.9	66.0	10.1	100.0

As indicated by the column frequencies in Table 14.5, the sexism levels reflected in the portrayals of models classified under the "other" (or nonalluring) category appear to have a larger range of variations than the "alluring" (or sexy) category. Specifically, in the "other" (or nonalluring/sexy) category, the largest percentage (22.7%) of models were portrayed as "strictly traditional" (Level 2), followed by "gender equality" (15.1 %, Level 4) and "chiefly traditional" (14.7%, Level 3). The smallest percentage (5%) of models was presented as a "two-dimensional" character (Level 1).

In contrast, the patterns of sexism levels reflected in the portrayals of models categorized as "alluring" (or sexy) were somewhat different from those categorized as "nonalluring" (or unsexy). The largest percentage of these "alluring" models appeared as a two-dimensional character (14.3%), followed by "gender equality" portrayals (10.9%) and the "strictly traditional" (8.8%, Level 2) and "chiefly traditional" (8.4%, Level 3) categories.

As indicated by row frequency breakdowns, alluring portrayals account for just over 40% of model appearances. In the Level 1 category, in which alluring portrayals are most common, they are nearly three times more common than portrayals in the "other" category. Yet these alluring portrayals account for less than half of the "strictly traditional"

Table 14.5. Sexist Portrayals of Models by Their Physical Appearance.

	Model Physical Appearance		
Level of Sexism	Other	Alluring	Total
	%	%	%
Two-Dimensional (Level 1)	5.0	14.3	19.3
Strictly Traditional (Level 2)	22.7	8.8	31.5
Chiefly Traditional (Level 3)	14.7	8.4	23.1
Gender Equality (Level 4)	15.1	10.9	26.1
Overall χ^2 = 25.89* Total %:	57.6	42.4	100.0

*denotes statistical significance.

(Level 2) images, and just over half of those categorized as "chiefly tradi-tional" (Level 3). The gap in appearance frequencies between alluring (or sexy) and "other" (or unsexy) portrayals is narrowest for the Level 4 (gender equality) category, in which there are three "other" images for every two of an alluring nature.[6]

DISCUSSION

This study provided mixed results. With regard to the level of sexism, in the symbolic world of TV advertising, women were depicted largely in stereotypical "traditional" roles, which suggests that more traditional female roles are consistent with the gender perceptions held by the male-dominated corps of media gatekeepers.

That dynamic should also explain why women are more likely to appear in physically "alluring" portrayals than men, given that these images may coincide with male sexual fantasies concerning women. Such appeals are common in advertisements targeted to men, as they are often used to imply that the sexy female presented in the advertisement is the man's reward for using the product (see Courtney & Whipple, 1983).

Although study findings do not suggest that the "alluring" cate-gory dominates female model portrayals, a sizable 40% of the ads fell under that heading. This focus on women as sexy ornaments, however, extends to product-model relation stereotypes. That is, women (66%) were still likely to be presented in a nonfunctional, decorative role in relation to the product they endorsed in an ad.

These findings expand and complement past work (see, e.g., Sexton & Haberman, 1974) and suggest that product appeals have not been predominantly caged in female-dominated stereotypes. Nevertheless, sexism is found to have been associated with decorative stereotypes. Specifically, models portrayed in "two-dimensional" and "strictly traditional" roles are more likely to be decorative than those portrayed in "chiefly traditional" and "equal individual" roles. However, within each sexism level, the majority of the models were cast in "functional" rather than "decorative" or "other" categories. This is perhaps a result of the dominant use of women in household goods ads. Hence, the overall relationship between sexism and model relation to product is an ambiguous one at best, as it lacks an overarching direction.

By contrast, the findings concerning sexism and the use of alluring portrayals reinforces the need to carefully examine the context in which sexism might appear in advertising. For instance, we see that the ads in Levels 2 and 3 (strictly and chiefly traditional) are least likely to offer "alluring" images. Models are instead most likely to embody alluring portrayals in Level 1 (two-dimensional character) and Level 4 (gender equality) ads. This may be a reflection of the emerging images of independent females in advertising. Such images typically depict women as comfortable with themselves in their social and professional roles. In the meantime, they may also be sensuous sexual beings (e.g., Ally McBeal). Simply put, sexiness perhaps is not the exclusive domain of a select few male or female archetypes; being sexy could now be "respectable" in the symbolic world of advertising.

Level 1 or "two-dimensional" portrayals were least likely to occur with the "nonalluring" portrayal, whereas Level 2 or "strictly traditional" portrayals had the highest rate of occurrence in this "nonalluring" category. When exploring behavioral implications of the more sexist caricatures, it is important to consider the effects postulated by cultivation theory. Gerbner, Gross, Signorielli, and Morgan (1980) have argued that gender and other demographic factors learned from television become the basis for a broader worldview, making television a source of general values, ideologies, and perspectives. According to this view, then, advertising could be an important contributor to these gender conceptions. Morgan (1990), for instance, found a link between heavy viewership and beliefs that: (a) women are happiest at home raising children; and (b) household chores should be done by women. Such viewing also has been associated with sex-stereotyped beliefs (Morgan & Rothschild, 1983).

One of the implications of this study is in the effects of advertising's portrayals on women themselves. For instance, Richins (1991) found that subjects exposed to ads with highly physically attractive models were less satisfied with their own level of physical attractiveness. Thus, to the extent that gender images continue to favor attractiveness norms, a certain degree of social comparison may prove damaging to a woman's sense of self-identity and self-esteem.

This "attractiveness-oriented" advertising continues to be an "unreality industry," offering the public nothing more than pleasing visual images and unrealistic portrayals (Mitroff & Bennis 1993). If the gap continues to widen between what is reflected in advertising images and what is actually attainable for the public, consumers may be drawn to make more social comparisons or express greater cynicism (Richins, 1991).

The fact that nearly 42% of females appear in alluring contexts confirms past work (Reid & Soley, 1983), as sex appeals are still considered an important method in the advertiser's sales approach for a large number of product categories (Reid & Soley, 1983). This trend is evidenced by the continual typecasting of women in traditional domestic and cheesecake roles in television advertising. To the extent that advertisers use sexual stereotypes to promote their products, they demean both genders. This is especially true when women are downplayed or shown as deferring to men. With regard to audience perceptions, though, the impact of stereotypical portrayals may be more dysfunctional for the images of women. For, even though both genders face many gender-role stereotypes in ads, women do not command the sorts of countervailing "success" images that men do in general media news and entertainment fare (Gerbner et al., 1986). Gender portrayals in advertising are thus seen as a significant social issue because of their potential impact on audiences (Jeffres, 1994).

As these gender images in TV ads continue to evolve, we are also approaching the threshold of a "500 channel" digital multimedia environment, with its increased fragmentation of the mass audience (Lin, 1994). It is likely that advertisers will need to more carefully craft their selling appeals for targeted viewership. This "narrowcasting" may allow for a wider range of gender-related selling appeals, ranging from "liberated woman" appeals on a channel targeted predominantly to female audiences to more traditional roles for conservative outlets. In short, future electronic entertainment media will likely become highly formatted, emulating the specialized offerings that we associate with the magazine industry and online computer database services such as America On-Line and Prodigy.

Hence, the larger question remains concerning what the portrayals of women should be in this future advertising and marketing environment. Judging from the current social and cultural trend, it appears that more women will enter the workplace. Meanwhile, gender-specific occupational roles will also continue to diminish. This does not suggest that women will then refrain from the conventional "dutiful wife/mother" role. It does, however, point to the day when more women will play a major role in making purchase decisions that go beyond conventional household goods, as their share of economic power improves in the home and in society as a whole. Once this phenomenon is widely accepted, then marketers will perhaps start to portray women as what they are instead of what they should be in the eye of marketing and ad executives.

Would sexism then disappear from advertising? The answer is "probably not." However, sex-role portrayals in advertising should at least better reflect social reality. The familiar mass-appeal gender stereotypes need to be abandoned. Instead, scholars and practitioners alike should attempt to explore more fitting gender portrayals in relation to products in order to effectively utilize the ever-expanding multimedia narrowcasting modalities for advertising.

APPENDIX I: A CONSCIOUSNESS SCALE FOR MEDIA SEXISM (WOMEN)

Level 1: Woman is a two-dimensional, nonthinking decoration
Put her down and belittle her.
Dumb blonde, sex object, victim.
Focus on her body. She lets others think for her.

Level 2: Woman's place is in the home
Keep her in her place.
Woman shown in romantic situation.
Traditional role of wife, mother, secretary, nurse.
Unwomanly traits—a woman shown as a doctor,
    engineer, etc.
Seems to be doing something beyond her
    capabilities.

Level 3: Women may be professionals, but first place is home
Woman in two places.
May be a lawyer, but must still have dinner on the table.
Career is something extra after housework.

Level 4: Women and men must be equals
She is fully equal.
Woman treated as a professional.
Not necessary to mention home or mothering.
Men can do housework as well as the woman.

Level 5: Women as individuals
Nonstereotypic.
Women shown as superior to men in some cases, inferior
    in others.
People not judged by their sex.

(Pingree et al.'s [1976] "Scale of sexism" dimensions coded in study.)

ENDNOTES

1. The term *cheesecake* refers to classic stereotypes portraying women as sex objects, such as revealing portrayals of models in advertisements for cars or other products.
2. Because the study focuses on commercials broadcast to the general public, specialized cable channels were not included. Similarly, commercials aired during other timeslots were not addressed because they may target specific demographic segments. In addition, to standardize the basis for comparison, the Fox network was omitted because Fox did not have a full, prime-time schedule and lacked affiliation in several top markets at the time of this study.

   The recording schedule was determined by randomly assigning each evening's recording to a particular network. This randomization process generated the following recording schedule: NBC for Monday and Thursday; ABC for Friday and Saturday; and CBS for Tuesday, Wednesday, and Sunday evenings. By including all three major TV networks in this random assignment process, the sampling frame could include a wider variety of commercials than if only one network had been selected for recording purposes.
3. To avoid any potential gender bias in interpreting the coding scheme, two male and two female coders were trained together and then given a sample of 50 ads to code. The intercoder reliability was over 95% across all four coders. Then two coders, a male and a female, coded separately for the entire sample. The average intercoder reliability for the "sexism" scale, "model-relation-to-product," and "model physical appearance" was 95%, 97% and 92%, respectively, using Holsti's method of reliability calculation.
4. The statistical significance for all tests was set at the .05 level. This .05 significance level refers to a 5% error margin, a commonly accepted standard in social scientific research. It means that if the margin of error associated with a statistical result is less than or equal to 5%, then the statistical result is considered valid 95% of the time and is deemed significant.
5. The overall Chi-Square Value = 9.55536; DF= 6, P = .14467.
6. It should be noted that certain methodological limitations apply to this study. The sample was composed of a randomly selected composite week of prime-time commercials in April—a commonly accepted sampling practice for a content analysis study. Hence, the sample does not represent an accretion of continuous data nor reflect potential seasonal variability in advertising content. Although the intercoder reliability was very high, certain potential coder biases might have gone undetected.

REFERENCES

Atkin, D., Moorman, J., & Lin, C.L. (1991). Ready for prime time. *Sex Roles, 68,* 677-685.

Barthel, D. (1988). *Putting on appearances: Gender and advertising.* Philadelphia: Temple University Press.

Benoy, J. W. (1982). The credibility of physically attractive communicators: A review. *Journal of Advertising, 11*(3), 15-24.

Berscheid, E., & Walster, E. (1974). Physical attractiveness. In L. Berkowitz (Ed.), *Advances in experimental social psychology* (pp. 157-215). New York: Academic Press.

Bretl, D., & Cantor, J. (1988). The portrayal of men and women in U.S. television commercials: A recent content analysis and trends over 15 years. *Sex Roles, 18*(9/10), 595-609.

Brownmiller, S. (1984). *Femininity.* New York: Simon and Schuster.

Caballero, M.J., Lumpkin, J.R., & Madden, C.S. (1989). Using physical attractiveness as an advertising tool: An empirical test of the attraction phenomenon. *Journal of Advertising Research, 29,* 16-21.

Condra, M. (1992). Bare facts and naked truths: Gender, power and freedom of expression. *Free Speech Yearbook, 30,* 129-148.

Courtney, A. E., & Whipple, T.W. (1983). *Sex stereotyping in advertising.* Lexington, MA: Lexington Books, D. C. Heath.

Craig, S. R. (1992). The effect of television day part on gender portrayals in television commercials: A content analysis. *Sex Roles, 26*(5/6), 197-211.

Creedon, P.J. (1993). *Women in mass communication* (2nd ed.). Newbury Park, CA: Sage.

Debevec, K., Madden, T. J., & Kernan, J.B. (1986). Physical attractiveness, message evaluation and compliance: A structural examination. *Psychological Reports, 58*(2), 503-508.

Downs, A.C., & Harrison, S.K. (1985). Embarrassing age spots or just plain ugly? Physical attractiveness as an instrument on sexism on American television commercials. *Sex Roles, 13*(1/2), 9-19.

Dworkin, A. (1974). *Woman hating.* New York: E.P. Dutton.

Ferguson, J.H., Kreshel, P.J., & Tinkham, S.F. (1990). In the pages of *Ms.*: Sex role portrayals of women in advertising. *Journal of Advertising, 19*(1), 40-51.

Gerbner, G., Gross, L., Signorielli, N., & Morgan, M. (1980). Aging with television: Images on television drama and conceptions of social reality. *Journal of Communication, 30*(1), 37-47.

Gitlin, T. (1983). *Inside prime time.* New York: Pantheon.

Jeffres, L.W. (1994). *Mass media processes.* Prospect Heights, IL: Waveland Press.

Kahle, L. R., & Homer, P.M. (1983). Physical attractiveness of the celebrity endorser: A social adaptation perspective. *Journal of Consumer Research, 11*(4), 954-961.

Knill, B. J., Persch, M., Pursey, G., Gilpin, P., & Perloff, R. (1981). Still typecast after all these years? Sex role portrayals in television advertising. *International Journal of Women's Studies, 4,* 497-506.

LaTour, M. S., Pitts, R. E., & Snook-Luther, D. C. (1991). Female nudity, arousal, and ad response: An experimental investigation. *Journal of Advertising, 19*(4), 51-62.

Leigh, T. W., Rethans, A. J., & Whitney, T. R. (1987). Role portrayals of women in advertising: Cognitive responses and advertising effectiveness. *Journal of Advertising Research, 27*(5), 54-63.

Lin, C. A. (1994). Audience fragmentation in a competitive video marketplace. *Journal of Advertising Research, 34*(6), 30-38.

Lovdal, L. T. (1989). Sex role messages in television commercials: An update. *Sex Roles, 21*(11/12), 715-724.

Millman, M. (1980). *Such a pretty face: Being fat in America.* New York: W.W. Norton.

Mitroff, I. I., & Bennis, W. (1993). *The unreality industry.* London: Oxford.

Morgan, M. (1990). International cultivation analysis. In N. Signorielli & M. Morgan (Eds.), *Cultivation analysis: New directions in media effects research* (pp. 225-247). Newbury Park, CA: Sage.

Morgan, M., & Rothschild, N. (1983). Impact of the new television technology: Cable TV, peers, and sex-role cultivation in the electronic environment. *Youth & Society, 15,* 33-50.

Ogburn, W. F (1964). *On culture and social change* (O.D. Duncan, ed.). Chicago: University of Chicago Press.

Osborn, S. (1989, May). *Gender depictions in television advertisements: 1988.* Paper presented at the annual conference of the International Communication Association, San Francisco.

Patzer, G. L. (1985). *The physical attractiveness phenomena.* New York: Plenum Press.

Pingree, S., Hawkins, R., Butler, M., & Paisley, W. (1976). A scale for sexism. *Journal of Communication, 26,* 193-200.

Poe, A. (1976). Active women in ads. *Journal of Communication, 26*(3), 185-192.

Rak, D., & McMullen, L. M. (1987). Sex-role stereotyping in television commercials: A verbal response mode and content analysis. *Canadian Journal of Behavioral Science, 19*(1), 25-39.

Reid, L. N., & Soley, L. (1983). Decorative models and the readership of magazine ads. *Journal of Advertising Research, 23*(2), 27-32.

Richins, M. L. (1991). Social comparison and the idealized images of advertising. *Journal of Consumer Research, 18,* 71-83.

Scheibe, C. (1979). Sex roles in TV commercials. *Journal of Advertising Research, 19*(1), 23-27.

Schneider, K. C., & Schneider, S. B. (1979). Trends in sex roles in television commercials. *Journal of Marketing, 43,* 79-84.

Schur, E.M. (1984). *Labeling women deviant: Gender, stigma and social control.* New York: Random House.

Sexton, D. E., & Haberman, P. (1974). Women in magazine advertisements. *Journal of Advertising Research, 14,* 41-46.

Soley, L. C., & Kurzbard, G. (1986). Sex in advertising: A comparison of 1964 and 1984 magazine advertisements. *Journal of Advertising, 15*(3) 46-54, 64.

Soley, L. C., & Reid, L. N. (1988). Taking it off: Are models in magazine ads wearing less? *Journalism Quarterly, 65*(4) 960-966.

Sullivan, G. L., & O'Connor, P.J. (1988). Women's role portrayals in magazine advertising: 1958-1983. *Sex Roles, 18*(3/4), 181-188.

Tuchman, G. (1979). Women's depiction by the mass media: Review essay. *Signs: Journal of Women in Culture and Society, 4*(3), 528-542.

Whipple, T. W., & Courtney, A. E. (1985). Female role portrayals in advertising and communication effectiveness: A review. *Journal of Advertising, 14*(3), 4-8.

15

Gender, *Melrose Place,* and the Aaron Spelling Legacy
Elayne Rapping

By the mid-1990s, *Melrose Place*, the Aaron Spelling-produced "prime time soap opera" aired on the Fox network, had become something of a cult institution among young people. Every week across America—in bars, in dorm rooms and lounges, in living rooms—young people— mostly but not exclusively female—gather together on "Melrose Night" to share pizza, beer, and an hour of over-the-top, youth-oriented melo- drama of a particularly sexy, fast-paced, often highly sensational variety. But the rise of *Melrose Place* to such a position of popularity and cultural impact is not all that is noteworthy about this series. Its metamorphosis, since its first, largely unremarkable and low-rated season, is itself an interesting phenomenon, revealing important trends in television pro- gramming in recent years as the media, and the larger society in which it is produced, have gone through important changes.

Most important among those changes, and the major focus of this chapter, are the contradictory, often troubling ways in which media representations of women's lives and expectations have changed under conflicting pressures from feminists on the one hand, and the needs of a rapidly changing, postindustrial, corporate economic order on the other.

Melrose Place has been a trendsetter in this regard, on the cutting edge of
more widespread, if less dramatically blatant, changes in gender representation that are revealing of the tangled relations among media, society, and gender dynamics, and the directions in which they are leading.

Until recently—and *Melrose Place*, I argue, marks the dramatic
rupture in this always contradictory and difficult accommodation—TV
genres were aimed at a presumably homogeneous (implicitly white,
middle-class) audience assumed and meant to perceive themselves as
essentially "family" members, part of a clearly delineated structure in
which gender roles and relationships were hierarchical and clearly
defined. One's identity as a member of a family, and the gender norms
and roles that accompany that identity, have characterized the subject
position into which home television has, from the start, constructed and
positioned us all for economic as well as ideological reasons.

The master narratives of family, gender, and generation—the
sitcoms, soap operas, and dramatic series that television offers as staples
of cultural hegemony—have been the myths and rituals by which we all
have come to understand and relate—as men, women, and children—to
our common, if ever-changing, environment. From *Leave it to Beaver* to
The Cosby Show, television has, in its dominant, most-often-seen genres,
pushed an ideal of family life in which Dad worked, Mom—whatever
else she did—did most of the nurturing and caretaking, and the kids
pretty much followed their rules and planned to follow in their parents'
footsteps. *Father Knows Best* has always been the putative motto of home
television, even as Mother—the real center of the action—has done most
of the work of keeping things on track, cooking, car-pooling, caretaking,
and looking good. And the kids—whose troubles may have gotten more
complicated over the years—always came around to the wisdom of
these ways.

THE 1990S REVOLUTION: FOX, SPELLING AND THE POST-FAMILY ERA

Seen in this context, *Melrose Place* stands out as a radically aberrant kind
of "continuing drama" because of its departure from family norms generally and because—although this is not generally noted by commentators—of its absolute rejection of the notions of gender difference and
inequity, as well as the stereotypical gender images that have informed
classic TV genres. For until the 1990s and the rise of shows like *Melrose
Place* (which is not alone in this, but certainly is the most dramatic and
extreme in its departures), most TV genres, no matter how shaken by
social change and the influence of feminism and women's changing

lifestyles and attitudes, hung on for dear life to at least some semblance of traditional gender and family representation.

But in recent years, this model has been harder and harder to present credibly. Womens' lives and roles have been changing at a maddening pace, as divorce, single motherhood, and increasing emphasis on jobs (if not "careers") and economic survival made the *Leave it to Beaver* model obsolete. With the rise of industrialism and postindustrialism, and the breakdown of the family that followed—in real life if not on television—kids, too, have been moving more and more out of family life and its values and norms and into a peer-group culture centered on public, youth-oriented gathering places and rituals, and a sense of personal identity less and less constructed in terms of family roles. Amid all this, network television has, understandably, had its hands full trying to incorporate these social changes into its classic genres while maintaining the hegemonic norms that define them.

The changes in family and social life in recent years have run parallel to equally radical changes in the media industry itself, changes that are important to note if we are to understand the full meaning of *Melrose Places*'s radical approach to gender representation. On the business end, the TV industry itself has been expanding and reconstructing itself to fit new economic and social times. Network hegemony, as defined by the dominance of the three broadcast networks since the 1950s, has given way to the plethora of the increasingly narrowcast, special audience-targeted world of cable. The network's modernist worldview, in which a master narrative—battered and amended but still honored—of traditional patriarchal family life still reigned in virtually every format, gave way to a postmodernist structure in which a variety of cultural, ethnic, religious, age-based, and interest-based channels present an endless variety of alternatives.

Of course, these channels, tied to corporate sponsorship, still maintain allegiance to consumer values. But they no longer pay homage to the ideal of the putatively father-based, but mother-run, white, middle-class family that the original networks hawked for so long. And without the emphasis on keeping families together, cable—and the new Fox network which was able to challenge the three networks in this new, more competitive cable-driven market—reinvisioned the audience in ways which allowed for radical changes in the way the American consumer—especially the female consumer—was represented and addressed. For although the other networks had long targeted demographic segments for particular series, Fox, in its early years, focused almost exclusively on two segments of the demographic market—youth and African Americans. These two market segments had been largely ignored by the other networks which had, at best, half-heartedly attempted to address them within the constraints of traditional family genres[1] which were hard-pressed to adapt themselves to the cultural and social changes which marked the lives of most African Americans and young people.[2]

But in addressing a youth market, unmoored from traditional family goals, roles, and values, Fox also, inadvertently, confronted a truly problematic question: how to portray women characters, now that motherhood and caretaking were not, presumably, the point of life. For implicit in the idea of a "youth" market existing in its own cultural and economic environment and context and facing its own generation-specific problems, was a changed, or at least debatable, idea of gender norms. If not work and family, then what? Male genres, of course, have always portrayed men as heroic, adventuresome, saving the world for democracy, or whatever. But women have traditionally been—prominently or implicitly—kept at home, caring for and nurturing others (even when, as in the *Mary Tyler Moore* show, "home" is the workplace; Taylor, 1989). But in a youth culture unmoored from the economic and cultural demands of the traditional family, where were women to be positioned? How were they to behave? What were to be their goals and values?

On the network youth shows which, following Fox's success, came in great numbers—*Seinfeld, Friends, Ellen,* and so on—this problem is somewhat elided by the sheer silliness of the action. The "kids" on these shows do not really have lives and the implicit assumption, I think, is that life will eventually catch up with them and they will "grow up" and settle down. (The couple on *Mad About You* verges on this already.) But Fox, through Aaron Spelling, chose a different, more daring path. In *Beverly Hills 90210, Melrose Place,* and *Malibu Shores,* it presented series in which youth culture itself was the topic, and it was taken far more seriously than *Seinfeld* and *Friends* are made to take anything.

At first, this did not seem quite so obvious. *Beverly Hills 90210* presented a ground-breaking series in its focus on kids as relatively autonomous from adult society and authority. Although the kids confronted serious matters which their parents neither understood nor could help with, the show nonetheless maintained a shell of a "family" orientation that masked its often more radical implications. There was, after all, still one model, fully functional, traditional family on the series, transplanted from the Midwest and steeped in hegemonic gender assumptions that, even in Beverly Hills, seemed to work.

In its upscale, glamorous, soap opera-ish way, however, the series did tell certain truths about kids and parents—and by implication women and girls—that no network show had yet dared to do. Kids today, it admitted, were increasingly living lives dictated by their peer group's issues and agendas, lives in which parents' views and dictates played a smaller and smaller role. Nor were most women, as *90210* made shockingly clear, living out the traditional family-driven roles of wife and mother that classic genres still assumed. On the contrary, most *90210* mothers were so caught up in their own problems, or so strung out and dysfunctional, they could hardly manage their own lives, much less pay attention to or guide the lives of their kids. Indeed, parents on *90210* were a pretty sorry, dysfunctional lot. Divorce, drugs, financial problems, and other realistically portrayed matters plagued the lives of the mostly much-divorced and less-than-nurturing mothers on this show. (Fathers were often absent; one was even in jail.) Even if they had paid attention to their kids, their advice would not have been heeded. Why should it be? They no longer inhabited a work or social sphere in which their activities and concerns were likely to relate to those of their offspring. For kids in these shows inhabited a world in which their needs, their work skills, their very sense of identity and dreams for the future were no longer—as they certainly were on *Cosby* and even *Roseanne* and *Murphy Brown*—related to the models put forth by their parents.

As the Spelling ouevre developed into other series, the revision of family and gender norms went further. When *Melrose Place* aired in 1991, it took the suggested image of family and especially gender life put forth by *90210* and ran with it, allowing the implicit directions and assumptions of that series to be fully developed. Suddenly, television had a series in which young people were cut loose entirely from the assumptions and values of traditional family life and its images of masculinity and femininity as established under patriarchy and maintained, more or less intact, throughout the early years of industrialization and postindustrialization. And in this way, it blew the lid off the viability of not only traditional gender norms, but of the whole modernist, industrial model of progress and economic growth and success for all—of the very basis of the American Dream itself.

Melrose Place replaced the modernist narratives and structures of network fictional programming with a definitively postmodern worldview in which individual characters were set free—sometimes violently so—from traditional structures, identities, and assumptions. Instead, they existed in a world in which all values and assumptions—certainly about gender—were up for grabs, and each individual character might find her- or himself thrown into a chaotic, ever-changing series of relationships, workplaces, and situations to which she or he would be forced to adapt quickly.

Melrose presented a group of young people, on their own for the first time, living relatively marginal lives in a fairly downscale apartment complex in Los Angeles, where they pursued jobs and relationships which, more often than not, were dead end, temporary, and not gender specific. The apartment complex was endlessly reshuffled as new roommates emerged and disappeared, and new lovers appeared for overnight stays and breakfasts and then disappeared, only to be replaced by others in short order. In this social setting, traditional gender norms were largely overhauled as women and men—still young, unmarried, and independent—seemed to live very similar lifestyles and pursue similar goals. Mixed gender roommates were common, and housework and cooking patterns egalitarian and free-wheeling. All these young people—male and female alike—seemed to do similar work and inhabit a similar level of financial and social status. They drove cabs, they "temped," they worked at health clubs and low-rent social service agencies. They struggled to survive with absolutely no help or mention of parents, but turned instead to each other for advice and support.

Only one couple, Michael and Jane Mancini, in the first year of the series, had a stable marriage. The rest were endlessly in and out of relationships, all of which were plagued with contradiction and complexity. Traditional notions of female and male roles were in flux and far from rigid. Billy, the cab driver and would-be writer, dated a single mother, for example, and soon learned that love, in modern times, could not conquer the many problems in a relationship in which money was tight and another man's child was a key player. He soon opted out of the entanglement and returned to his shared apartment with his platonic roommate, Alison, where no family responsibilities were involved. Even the Mancini marriage underwent stress and strain as Jane—worried about money, concerned with her own career plans, and left much alone as her husband (the only obviously upwardly mobile member of the group) interned—toyed with the idea of an abortion, about which she only consulted her friends, not her husband.

So far was this show from the norms and assumptions of traditional family life and gender norms (no traditional sitcom would entertain the idea of abortion, and certainly not as casually as did this group) that it permitted a gay character, Matt Fielding, to be a part of the group and to have his relationships and personal problems taken as seriously as the others.[3] There was, generally, a sense of free-wheeling tolerance and open-mindedness about relationships and sexuality. Parents were mentioned in this series only when referred to as perpetrators of earlier sins and crimes, or as bad role models. Matt's parents, for example, were presented in a very bad light because they could not accept his gay sexuality. And Jake, who was then working as a car mechanic, was assumed to have been more or less abandoned by his hard-drinking mother.

Relationship problems, career problems, and a lifestyle and social environment that incorporated tolerant attitudes toward any number of unconventional attitudes and practices were the norm. And because jobs and relationships did not necessarily last, the group itself became a sort of surrogate family of siblings, in which parental roles were gone and the young people supported and helped each other emotionally and financially. Thus, the very values that television had relied upon—work and family and the symbiotic relation between the two spheres—were subverted and replaced by a much looser, less stable, and uncertain set of rituals and values that allowed for shifting identities and positions for all characters, and in which traditional sex and gender roles seemed not to figure.

There was something charming and real—if somewhat scary and dangerous—about this series in its first (now long forgotten) year. It dared to give voice to the truth that the old patterns were unworkable and to present a group of young people realistically facing the challenges and obstacles of sheer survival—material and emotional—in a postmodern world of identity and position shifting and of, implicitly, material expectations far less encouraging than those of their parents. The show's future in this form was cloudy from the start. But it was—interestingly and importantly—not the nontraditional sex and gender representation that was most problematic. Rather (and the changes actually made in the series bear this out), sponsors were not happy with the implicitly depressing view of the economic future the show projected. For it was a future in which not only were traditional values and assumptions disrupted, but—more problematically— the upscale lifestyles touted on commercials (lifestyles that traditional sitcoms and soaps almost always maintained) did not easily fit. Clearly, the series had to be overhauled or killed. For just as sitcoms like *The Honeymooners*, *The Goldbergs*, and *The Life of Riley*—which portrayed happy, working-class immigrant families in the 1950s—were soon dumped by sponsors who wanted shows in which upscale lifestyles and consumer values were valorized (Barnouw, 1975), so was *Melrose Place* soon in the precarious position of being made to shape up—for sponsors and network executives—or die.

Conventional wisdom credits the overhaul of *Melrose Place* to low ratings. But this, I would argue, is a bit disingenuous. After all, most new shows, especially those that break new generic ground, do poorly in their first seasons and must be allowed time to develop an audience and a following. Sometimes sponsors and networks allow this and sometimes not. Audience pressure may have something to do with it. If, for example, the demographically upscale "Quality Viewers" network protests the cancellation of a show, sponsors may take heed. But *Melrose Place* had bigger problems for Spelling and his colleagues. It was a youth-oriented show with little appeal to the lobbyists who generally

drive such campaigns. But even more importantly, its message to viewers was unlikely to appeal to advertisers either. For the low-rent
lifestyles and hand-to-mouth careers and relationships that the characters were seen to enjoy were hardly proper role models for an audience
supposedly being primed to consume. And because its characters had
no roots, no children to raise, no stable ties of any kind that would
insure their indentiture to stable jobs and lifestyles, there was no strong
message about a planned future of consumerism either.

MELROSE II: THE HORROR MOVIE VERSION

The answer to the problem of how to keep the show on the air, prof-
itable, and attractive to sponsors came with a dramatic flair. And its realization reveals much about the handy way in which gender values—
even ostensibly progressive, egalitarian, gender values—can be subverted in the name of commercial interests. Indeed, the significance of
Melrose Place I and *II* to feminists media analysts is in the way it dramatically reveals the slippages and contradictions between feminists'
demands for true equality for all women and the values of a free market
economy in which competition, individualism, and greed are the driving
forces.[4] The dropping of the original *Melrose Place* model, with its relatively progressive representation of both gender and economic issues, in
favor of a more upscale, less socially progressive model, allowed the
series—while ostensibly maintaining its portrayal of radically egalitarian
gender norms—to drop the depressing subtext of the series as a whole:
its projection of a downwardly mobile future for even middle-class, college-educated youth, whose careers and standards of living were likely
to be far less certain or predictable than their parents' had been.

To achieve this sleight of hand, the producers were forced to
alter the stylistic conventions of the series from a relatively realistic
show about urban youth to one based wholly and outrageously on
campy fantasy. Spelling and associates rapidly transformed the setting
and assumption of the show as quickly as was feasible while still maintaining the core cast of characters and the setting. With the introduction
of Heather Locklear, previously on Spelling's 1980s prime-time series
Dynasty, as a cutthroat, ambitious career woman of the corporate variety, the series suddenly became the site of a new kind of youth culture
lifestyle, one that played down sharing, support, and daily life struggles
in favor of the kind of corporate rat race world in which dog-eat-dog,
often violently vicious competition, individualism, and greed ruled. The
idea of gender equity was maintained, only now it existed in a world of
nightmarish competition and greed and often violent hostility.

In place of endlessly shifting McJobs and short-lived, socially unconventional relationships in which characters worked hard to maintain integrity and decency, the characters found themselves in a (still endlessly shifting) series of glamorous, upscale positions—as developers, doctors, lawyers, advertising executives, publishers, magazine editors, restauranteurs. The endless search for meaning and love gave way, or at least became subservient to, an endless search for profit and advantage, by any means necessary.

As before, gender roles and sexual orientations were presented as flexible, negotiable, and egalitarian. Indeed, I would argue that *Melrose Place* has been, and remains, the only series on television in which gender roles are actually equal, with men and women free to behave and thrive equally well and freely in both public and private spheres. But in presenting this idealized vision of gender equity, it updated the community and emotional themes of *Melrose I* with a disrupted, chaotic sense of personal life, in which relationships are endlessly changing and disintegrating, while career and work life—for men and women alike—take up much more time than domestic and personal life. The very meaning of gender equality took on a truly horrifying note of hysteria and danger. Women are seen on *Melrose II* as free to play in the big leagues, but at the cost of all values and ideals. The values of "interconnectedness . . . nurturance, responsibility, and mutual respect" which, in Gilligan's (1982, p. 273) construction are traditionally associated with the feminine sphere and are indispensable to the proper working of any decent, humane society, are nowhere to be found on *Melrose II*.

To examine the world of *Melrose Place* in its most recent incarnation is to see a genre—half horror movie, half high-camp melodrama—in which sexist gender roles and norms are indeed extinct. It is a world in which men and women compete equally, violence itself is no longer a strictly male prerogative in interpersonal conflicts, and marriage and child-rearing do not figure at all, making it possible for women to continue to devote almost all their time to careers and personally indulgent forms of pleasure and luxury.

Personal life, including romantic and sexual attachments, is now seen as temporary and volatile, not because of the pressures of a disintegrating social and economic world, but because human nature—male and female alike—is seen as endlessly aggressive, competitive, driven, and self-absorbed—the very traits which, in a globalized, transnational corporate universe will be most valued and most geared to success. No personal relationship, sexual or otherwise, is undertaken—or at least maintained for long—unless it fits well with the characters' personal ambitions and economic goals. Characters, male and female, are as likely to plot to do away with romantic partners because of financial dealings.

Nor are women—and this is perhaps the most politically disturbing aspect of the series—reluctant to do violence to men. Indeed, violence, like all else on this series, is an equal opportunity aspect of life, as likely to be done to or by men as women. A greedy business partner or jealous lover of either gender may decide to run her or his partner over with a car, contract to have her or him murdered, or drug or poison him or her in the interest of profit and power. Even sexual violence is generally portrayed as not qualitatively different from other forms of violence, in effect or consequence. Women do not suffer more or differently from such attacks than they or their male counterparts suffer from other forms of violence. A character raped by her angry ex-business partner/lover, for example, will suffer no greater trauma than a male character beaten by an opponent or even poisoned or tricked by a lover. And no sooner will she recover from the physical effects of the rape than she will be seen buying a gun, training to shoot, and exacting revenge on her attacker of a kind as damaging as the rape itself had been to her. Thus, even rape has been subtly transformed into merely one of many horrible atrocities that men and women perpetrate equally on each other. The score is kept even, with women and men doing equal damage to each other, emotionally and materially, on all fronts.

Because women and men alike are as often victims as victimizers, the very nature of all gender issues defined and articulated by feminists is subverted. Women do equal physical damage to men and exact as much emotional suffering and humiliation in relationships. Because power is equally distributed, there is no reason for one gender to be more prone to neediness or dependency than the other. All characters experience victory and rejection, humiliation and triumph, in love and war. Michael Mancini, now a ruthless, high-powered physician, for example, has brutally hurt and demeaned his ex-wife Jane. But he has been as hurt and bought low by his subsequent relationships with Locklear's character Amanda and his second wife Kimberly. With each shift in the emotional and material balance bar, characters seem to momentarily transform personalities as well, taking on the traditionally gendered characteristics of the role they temporarily must play in the love game. As a romantic sufferer, for example, Michael is a nurturing, caring, loving helpmate. But when he is on the hurting side of a relationship, he reverts immediately to traditional macho traits, behaving callously, insensitively, and with aggressive, unfeeling cruelty. But the women do the same flip-flops. Alison, the most decent woman in *Melrose I*, has gone through similar mind-boggling character changes, embodying the most ruthless, macho qualities in her career and love lives, then reverting to near-masochistic suffering and victimhood in both realms. Thus, gender traits are equally distributed to both sexes and all are equally defined by the most demeaning and oppressive qualities of masculinist society.

In such a world, of course, sexuality—unmoored from the family imperative of reproduction and child-rearing—is seen as liberated and tolerant. Women and men engage in sexual encounters for business and pleasure reasons only. Marriage is almost never an option, at least for long, because each relationship hangs on its usefulness to one's career. And because competition, greed, and selfishness define all business interests, each business alliance is short-lived and, when it goes, so does the sexual union. Even gay relationships are portrayed in this way. They are wholly accepted in the *Melrose* culture, and they are as brutal and painful as the heterosexual ones. Matt has had relationships with men who have seduced him in order to frame him for murder and with men whose response to gay bashing is to retaliate with equal, terrifying, violence. The points scored for sexual tolerance, even gay rights advocacy, are undermined by the nasty, brutish view of the gender-equal world and its inhabitants.

Appearance, of course, has always been crucial to the representation of women on television, and *Melrose* is no exception. But here again, men are seen every bit as dependent on glamorous, good looks—and health-defying thinness—to survive and succeed in the cut-throat world they inhabit. As the series has continued, the excessive thinness and sexually eroticized women's clothing styles—tiny miniskirts, low-cut jackets, and halters as standard office wear—have become even more extreme. But the men, too, are increasingly eroticized and displayed as sex objects. Youth, physique, and fashionable clothing are as central to the representation of masculinity as to femininity. And why not? For men are as often pursued, used, and humiliated by the women as vice versa. And they are as often in insecure jobs and careers in which the need to stay youthful and attractive is ever more important. What Wolf (1991, p. 27) has termed "the display professions"—acting, modeling, dancing, and so so—have, in *Melrose Place*, expanded to include all lucrative professions, as Wolf predicts will soon be the case generally. For in a world in which wheeling, dealing, and hustling define success, as downsizing and market shifts force us all to market ourselves on a permanent basis and no career is ever permanent or stable, this emphasis on personal appearance and fashionability, and the need to appear youthful and vital, is, like everything else about *Melrose Place*, only an exaggerated, over-the-top, campy version of what is the unsettling drift in social and gender trends.

It is worth commenting on the dramatic stylistic changes with which *Melrose Place* shifted from downscale, urban realism to this high-flying, upscale world of glamour and conniving. For whereas *Melrose I* was quite credible in its portrayal of Gen-X youth culture, there is little in the current series that approaches any sort of credibility, in plot or characterization. Characters behave in ways that have no psychological plausibility or consistency whatever. They rapidly transform themselves from vicious would-be killers to obsessively romantic lovers, and back again, within days. They may, one week, be fixing cars, the next tending bar, and the next entering a partnership in a trendy club or managing a rock group. Kimberly, a central character, began as a staff physician in a hospital. After suffering a breakdown—one which had her psychotically attempting mass murder—and hospitalization, she returned to the hospital, as a psychiatrist, only to take a briefly held job as a radio psychologist and then move on to a psychiatric clinic where she served as temporary director and even, at one point, was seen scrubbing up to perform a lobotomy. During all this, she was supposedly suffering from multiple personality disorder. But every character on the series could be described as suffering from such a disorder because no personality trait, gender-related or otherwise, is constant in any character.

Nor, as this example demonstrates, is there any attempt to provide plausible connections or background material explaining how characters gain the training or experience to move so rapidly and effortlessly from career to career, and how they can so easily switch from love to hate, from partner to partner, from good to evil, over and over again, in such short order. The series exists in a world of fantasy—part melodrama, part cartoon—and serves more as a metaphor for, than a realistic representation of, what life has become for those who manage to climb to the rarefied heights of glamour and power and money. It represents—indeed, is the vanguard in—a major trend that the media, through youth-oriented series and especially commercials, has been seductively putting forth as a model of "the good life," the newly overhauled American Dream, toward which young people are supposed to be aiming these days.

That the series is done in high camp style and attempts less and less to approximate any kind of reality is telling. For, like advertising itself, it is built on what Williams (1975) has called a "magic system," in which things—in this case, behaviors, goals, and values—with no ability whatever to bring happiness or self-esteem are represented as carrying the very keys to such fulfillment. Like advertising itself, *Melrose Place* is forced to use preposterous stylistic conventions because more realistic conventions would inevitably reveal the logical slippages, inconsistencies, and distortions on which the entire premise of the series is based. In reality, major changes in career paths or romantic partners are precipitated by great disappointments, traumas, rejections, and failures—or, at least, that is how they are experienced. One does not recover and move on quite so easily, nor—most obviously of all—does one simply retool and achieve the highest position in a new field of employment. Nonetheless, there is something metaphorically compelling about the way the characters on *Melrose Place* do these things. Indeed, the real-life experiences of young people today teach them that just such magical transformations and recoveries are required if one is truly to be resilient and flexible enough to succeed in the world of power, money, and even love. Anyone who attempts to imitate the high-wire acts of the *Melrose Place* heroes, however, will soon learn the hard way why so many of the other TV commercials tout over-the-counter remedies for headache, tension, heart-burn, and digestive disorder. We are a nation of strivers who live constantly in a state of emotional and physical distress. And *Melrose Place* intends to keep it that way.

THE FUTURE OF GENDER IN A POSTINDUSTRIAL, CORPORATE MEDIA MARKET

Did we ask for this, feminists may well be wondering, as we rub our eyes at the wild, but egalitarian, antics of the women and men on *Melrose Place*? Indeed not. But I think that the representational evolution of *Melrose Place* should serve as a metaphoric warning—exaggerated and distorted, but nonetheless symbolically telling—to feminists and progressive-minded people generally. For in its wildly off-kilter portrayal of a kind of personal viciousness and violence that goes beyond any real-world corporate arena,[5] it symbolically suggests the qualitative shifts in values and moral atmosphere that do, indeed, inflect the new economic and social order as the acceleration of the globalized, postindustrial, corporate order continues apace. To be sure, there is a place here for women to climb, to achieve, to compete with men in the fast-paced, grueling world of transnational capital and its collateral institutions. But only a relatively few, usually white, very privileged, and aggressively ambitious women need apply.

Where are the poor women, the women of color, the women whose interests and commitments involve public service? They are not relevant to the worldview put forth by those who sponsor and tout the new transnational, corporate capitalist world because they are destined to populate a permanent feminine underclass of low-paid service workers tending menial responsibilities and cleaning up the messes of the main characters as they pursue their all-consuming ambitions and passions. Their fates and their lifestyles are too depressing—as, indeed, were the lives of the characters in the first *Melrose* year—to present on commercial television. Only those who can compete in business and in physical appearance are likely to be living lives that sponsors want us to see and hear about—and try desperately to imitate. And that is a very small, very unusual group of women, indeed.

Will these women, freed of the bondage of family norms, have children? With no traditional family and no need for one, how will society reproduce itself? Not that the old ways were good for women—or men either, for that matter. But even though feminists have had good reason to attack and demand changes in the traditional female roles and norms put forth on classic television, that model did, at least, assume that childcare and meaningful work were essential to human life and happiness. The original feminist ideal was not only to overhaul the nuclear family, but to restructure and reorganize society generally, so that men, women, and children could share in a life in which caring, nurturing, and meaningful work were equally distributed. The idea was not to do away with social and personal values entirely, only to create a world that was fair and healthy for all. Back in the 1970s, Ehrenreich and English (1978) eloquently articulated this vision, in which the values and functions of families were not done away with, but integrated into all aspects of life. "There are no answers left but the most radical ones," they wrote.

> We cannot assimilate into a masculinist society without doing violence to our own nature, which is of course *human* nature. But neither can we retreat into domestic isolation, clinging to an archaic feminine ideal. Nor can we deny that the dilemma is a social one....
>
> The Woman Question in the end is not a question of *women*. It is not we who are the problem and it is not our needs which are the mystery. From our perspective (denied by centuries of masculinist "science" and analysis) the Woman Question becomes the question of how shall we all—women and children and men—organize our lives together. (p. 323)

Melrose Place's producers seem to disagree quite strongly. They suggest that women can, and should, assimilate into masculinist society—or die trying. And they have seductively packaged this anti-feminist message to appear not only glamorous but, on first glance, seemingly in compliance with feminist demands for equality in personal and professional life. It sounds good on paper. It even looks good—very good—on its glitzy surface. But it is, in reality, a nightmare vision from which women should be running for dear life.

ENDNOTES

1. *The Cosby Show* is the most obvious example.
2. It is interesting to note that, according to the *New York Times* (May 22, 1996, p. C12), the top 10 highest rated Nielsen programs for African American homes are almost wholly different from the ones watched by whites.
3. *Melrose* initially included an African American character in the group as well.
4. The recent works of Naomi Wolf, Katie Roiphe, Rene Denenfeld, and Camille Paglia, which tout "power feminism" and presume that women now have an even playing field on which to contend for success and power, are instructive here. For there is a trend within liberal, white, middle-class feminism—a trend much publicized and admired by the media—that seeks to redefine feminist goals and values in terms of the market and to argue implicitly or explicitly that feminist demands for equality have been met and the playing field is level. This is the very model of gender equity that informs *Melrose Place:* its race and class blindness also are apparent on that show. (See also Bauer & Maglin, 1996, for an interesting set of responses to this perspective from second wave and third wave feminists.)
5. However, it may well suggest, metaphorically, the very real disregard for human life and dignity that marks the plunder of the environment and the production and marketing practices of many corporations that employ workers, often small children, at slave wages and in subhuman working conditions, and sell inferior, often dangerous goods in areas where market regulation does not exist.

REFERENCES

Barnouw, E. (1978). *The sponsor: Notes on a modern potentate.* New York: Oxford University Press.

Bauer, N., & Perry, D. (1996). *Bad girls, good girls: Women, sex and power in the nineties.* New Brunswick: Rutgers University Press.

Ehrenreich, B., & English, D. (1978). *For her own good: 150 years of the experts' advice to women.* New York: Anchor.

Gilligan, C. (1982). *In another voice: Psychological theory and women's development.* Cambridge: Harvard University Press.

Taylor, E. (1989). *Prime time families: Television culture in postwar America.* Berkeley: University of California Press.

Williams, R. (1975). *Television: Technology and cultural form.* New York: Schocken Books.

Wolf, N. (1991). *The beauty myth: How images of beauty are used against women.* New York: Doubleday.

16

Film Noir, Feminism, and the Femme Fatale: The Hyper-Sexed Reality of *Basic Instinct*

Tom Reichert
Charlene Melcher

She would appear suddenly from behind a misty veil of fog, or late one night at the hero's dingy office. The camera, and the audience, would examine her slowly from spikey stiletto to coifed hairdo, concentrating in particular on a long, elegant leg thrust resolutely forward from the folds of her too-tight skirt. When the camera, and the hero's eyes, finally rested on her face—dramatically concealed behind a swooping curl cascading over one eye—the audience knew exactly who she was: the femme fatale.

    The femme fatale was a staple within *film noir*, that film genre dating to the 1930s and popular throughout the 1940s and 1950s, which was visually characterized by bleak settings, heavy shadows, sharp contrasts of light and dark (Konigsberg, 1987), and narratively structured as an investigative thriller with a male hero (often a police detective or private investigator) and a dangerous woman (the femme fatale) who is both the object of his investigation and sexual desire.

The femme fatale of *film noir* is still with us, but she has been updated to reflect the social and sexual concerns of the 1990s. What her representation says about female sexuality is the focus of this chapter. What we show is that the contemporary femme fatale is hypersexed and dangerous, an omnisexual, cunning, and graphically sexual predator whose sexuality and self must be contained by a "real" man to stave off disaster. Specifically, we examine a popular film in the *film noir* tradition—*Basic Instinct*, one of the most financially successful and controversial films to be released in 1992 (Lawrence, 1993). Prior to this, however, we discuss *film noir* as a generic convention and its traditional characterization of the femme fatale.

FILM NOIR AND THE FEMME FATALE

As Gledhill (1994) and others (Faludi, 1991; Mayne, 1994; Mulvey, 1975; Rich, 1994; Staiger, 1994) have noted, reality is constructed—not just reflected—through the devices a given medium employs. In the case of film, both the narrative and theatrical devices—the plots, characters, settings, framing, camera angles, and lighting—construct social meaning (Ditmar, Welsch, & Carson, 1994; Gledhill, 1994). Moreover, *film noir* is a particularly compelling film genre because it explicitly includes a characterization of women common to a number of texts: woman as danger.

The term *film noir*, which literally means "black (or dark) film," was applied by French film critics to a handful of American crime movies in the 1930s that were thought unusually despairing (Ewing, 1988). In the late 1950s, the term was retrospectively applied to a group of American movies that dominated the screen from the mid-1940s through the mid-1950s and were, like all films of this period, shot in black and white.[1]

Like more contemporary noir films, these films revealed the dark, seamy side of humanity and society. Konigsberg (1987) argued that films within this genre are grouped together by "common cynical attitudes about a corrupt and sordid human nature; a propensity for brutality and even sadism; a neurotic undertone in characters; [and] a pervasive mood of tension and impending violence" (p. 122). Konigsberg related these themes to the psychology of the country at the end of World War II when America's psyche was relatively pessimistic and nihilistic, due in part to loss of life during the war and the ensuing tensions and paranoia of the Cold War. These factors resulted in a general distrust of human nature and institutions. Other influences contributing to *film noir* include the English gothic novel of the 19th century, American horror and gangster films of the 1930s, and the American detective novels of Dashiell Hammett, Raymond Chandler, and others. German expressionism of the 1920s also is credited with affecting the film's style and mood (Stephens, 1995).

In addition to a predominantly dark mood, other conventions in *film noir* exist as well. For instance, there is a relatively stable cast of characters consisting of "private or police detectives, insurance sales-men, prostitutes, murderous housewives, two-time losers, ex-convicts, and gamblers" (Dick, 1990, p. 97). *Film noir* also is characterized by an investigative thriller narrative structure. According to Gledhill (1978), the narrative follows a typical pattern: A male hero searches for the truth regarding a recent event or one about to occur; the hero is introduced into a world of action where he encounters a woman (e.g., bar-fly, night-club singer, expensive mistress, etc.) with whom he must struggle dur-ing the course of the investigation. She frequently becomes the "object" of his investigation, and elements typical of solving the crime, such as clues and deductive reasoning, are immersed within the relationship between the hero and the woman. Ultimately, it is the twists and turns of this relationship that determine the plot. Thus, a critical staple of *film noir* is the femme fatale (literally, the fatal woman).

Allen (1983) defines the femme fatale as a woman who lures men into danger, destruction, or even death by means of her over-whelmingly seductive charm and "dishonest or disreputable motives" (p. 187). Moreover, a femme fatale is a woman who employs eroticism to recruit men for self-serving interests. Allen states that the femme fatale is a fairly recent construct, created in the 19th century but not labeled as such until the 20th century. Allen proposes that a significant social factor underlying the birth of the femme fatale was the threat to men inherent in the rise of feminism. In response to this threat, artists and poets creat-ed an iconic image of the femme fatale as an expression of what they saw in women who were beginning to declare their sexual as well as political freedom. The cinema is but one avenue where this icon is repre-sented, and she is especially presented in *film noir* (Doane, 1991).

The femme fatale in *film noir* is "unscrupulous" in her use of eroticism and sexual attractiveness to pursue her sexual prey and achieve her goals. It is her use of sex that frequently results in the male protagonist's loss of power and domination. But in the end, the femme fatale is frequently killed or severely punished. According to Doane (1991), "her textual eradication involves a desperate reassertion of con-trol on the part of the threatened male subject" (p. 2). Although the femme fatale is sexually manipulative, she is reprimanded for the effect this has on the male. More specifically, the femme fatale must be pun-ished for her dangerous and seductive nature. Seldom is she happy and alive once the mystery is solved.

Doane (1991) further notes that although the femme fatale in *film noir* is sexual, she also is sterile, barren, and "the antithesis of the maternal" (p. 2). For example, Barbara Stanwyck's character in *Double Indemnity* represents a woman who is "the ultimate in female independence: Total escape from control of her sexuality and conventional morality" (Allen, 1983, p. 194). Thus, the femme fatale's sensuality is in complete opposition to more traditional feminine attributes.

The femme fatale also is dangerous in part due to her changeability and treachery (Doane, 1991; Gledhill, 1978). Throughout the narrative, for instance, the hero (and often the audience) are never quite sure whether the heroine is friend or foe. Naremore (1988) described this uncertainty as performance-within-performance. Although the audience is asked to suspend disbelief and find the actions of the character truthful, they must also realize that the behavior of a character is only an act. For instance, in the movie *Double Indemnity* (1944), Barbara Stanwyck played a character who seduced an insurance salesman (Fred MacMurray) into killing her husband. It is not revealed until the end of the film (to the dismay of MacMurray and the audience) that her passion for MacMurray may have been a pretense. This changeability and uncertainty is an important, distinguishing characteristic of the *film noir* femme fatale.

Nuances of the femme fatale's sexuality also contribute to the plot. Questions about female sexuality and sexual relationships involving patterns of deception, seduction, and unrecognized revelations dominate. As Gledhill (1978) points out, *film noir* "probes the secrets of female sexuality and male desire within patterns of submission and dominance" (p. 15) so that the hero's emotional attachment to the femme fatale becomes a focus of the investigation.

A last distinguishing characteristic of *film noir* is the femme fatale as visual icon.[2] Unlike other characters, the femme fatale is filmed for her sexuality and eroticism. Gledhill (1978) illustrates this by pointing out that sexuality is often signaled by a "long, elegant leg," as in *The Postman Always Rings Twice, The Fatal Seduction,* and *Romeo is Bleeding* (p. 19). The femme fatale's style of dress is an important visual aspect of her character. Her clothing either emphasizes sexuality (in the form of long sequined dresses) or masculine independence and aggression (via square, padded shoulders and bold striped suits; Gledhill, 1978). This latter style of dress, exemplifying masculine characteristics, reinforces the androgynist attributes of the femme fatale.

In sum, the femme fatale in *film noir* is portrayed in opposition to traditional feminine attributes. She is reprimanded for being independent, dangerous, and sexually independent, while also being represented as a visual icon. This is certainly true in the film *Basic Instinct*.

BASIC INSTINCT

Basic Instinct, released in 1992, grossed over $385 million; $109 million of which was in the first 14 weeks of its release (Parish, 1993). It also was one of the highest grossing American films in Europe in 1992. *Basic Instinct* was controversial, both for its depiction of graphic sex and violence and for its homophobia (see Lawrence, 1993, for a detailed collection of reviews).

A contemporary example of *film noir*, *Basic Instinct* plunges head-first into its plot line with the opening scene. An unidentified woman writhes passionately astride ex-rock star Johnny Boz (Bill Cable) as they are having sex. She ties his hands to the bed with a white scarf. Just as Boz reaches climax, the woman arches back, grabs an ice pick, and repeatedly stabs Boz in the throat. In the next scene, San Francisco police detective Nick Curran (Michael Douglas) and his partner Gus (George Dzundza) are introduced. The prime suspect is Boz's "sometime" lover, Catherine Trammell (Sharon Stone): An orphaned million-dollar heiress who writes novels whose stories bear an uncanny resemblance to the real-life deaths of those close to her. Nick is the jaded and potentially out-of-control detective assigned to her case. Ultimately, Nick and Catherine become intertwined in each other's lives and bed-sheets. Also figuring in the twists and turns of the plot are Beth (Jeanne Tripplehorn), a police psychologist and Nick's former girlfriend; Roxy (Leilani Sarelle), Catherine's lesbian lover; and Hazel (Dorothy Malone), a friend of Catherine's who awoke one morning years earlier to kill her husband and children for no apparent reason. As is the case with most *film noir*, the narrative structure revolves around Nick's investigation of the murder and Catherine as the object of his desire. *Basic Instinct* follows the narrative structure of *film noir* in that it is driven by the erotic intensity of the femme fatale. Not only does Nick become obsessed with Catherine, but the nuances of their desire for each other contribute to the plot.

Catherine is also the consummate femme fatale. She fulfills the characterization of an "uncertain" heroine as Nick and the audience are never certain of "who-dun-it," nor are they certain of her motives or her sexuality, for that matter. In addition, Catherine truly exemplifies the erotic, seductive woman. Peter Travers (1992) of *Rolling Stone* described Stone's erotic performance in the movie: "[she] struts on with enough come-on carnality to singe the screen" (p. 114). Evidence of her sexual appetite is her sexual involvement with many of the characters in the film, including Nick, Roxy, Boz, and Beth.

Finally, Stone is filmed in such a way as to emphasize her body's sexuality. Stone is blond, tall, slender, and shapely. Not just one but both of her legs are "elegantly" displayed. In fact, her body is exposed throughout the film, leading one reviewer to describe Catherine as "the devil in a micro-skirt" (Johnson, 1992, p. 56). Catherine's clothing compliments her sexuality and serves as a visual representation of her eroticism.

In her embodiment of the modern femme fatale, Catherine addresses what it means to be female as well as sexual. Thus, the section to follow examines three issues: gender and sexual identity (which are not unrelated) and the shifting portrayal of sex in mainstream movies. The former produces a lesson about women, whereas the latter provides a cautionary tale of what the future may bring.

UNCOVERING FEMALE REPRESENTATION AND SEXUALITY

Catherine depicts what her creators believe it means to be female beyond the bounds of male domination in the 1990s. She rejects traditional female roles, cannot be controlled, and is overtly sexual. Catherine is highly intelligent, independent, and articulate; she also is manipulative and may be prone to murdering those she loves or desires, a slight variation on the theme that women and, more specifically, their sexuality, are dangerous and a threat to men. Catherine's sexual desirability and expertise appear to be her most important attributes: She is, as Nick says more than once, "the fuck of the century." Her ability to write best-selling novels is hardly her most valued trait.

Catherine is represented as a dangerous woman not only because she may be a murderer, but because she rejects traditional female roles. In fact, gender roles are conflicted from the moment the film begins. The first characters the audience encounters are the soon-to-be-murdered Boz and his female sex partner (the audience is never certain she is Catherine). The heterosexual paradigm dictates she be there for his pleasure, but, in this case, Boz is there for her pleasure: He lies passively beneath her while she controls the encounter by tying his hands to the bed, writhing and thrusting on top of him in pursuit of her own satisfaction. When Boz is brought to orgasm, she wildly stabs him with an ice pick. Thus, from the very beginning, women are represented as dominating and a threat to men.

Catherine further blurs the lines of gender identity by behaving mannishly. She is 30, unmarried, and apparently unconcerned about finding a husband. She is "one of the boys": Drinking Jack Daniels straight, driving recklessly in a sportscar, having recreational sex, and smoking without regard for her health. During her interrogation at police headquarters, Catherine is defiant and independent. She rejects having a lawyer present, clearly feeling capable of defending herself against the prying questions of several men. Once the interrogation begins, she sits center stage, talks frankly and graphically about sex, turns the table on her questioners, and toys with Nick repeatedly. Her posture is also mannish: She sprawls in the chair, arms dangling by her sides, her legs crossed ankle-to-knee, not demurely knee-to-knee as a "lady" would sit. Both through her dialogue and her nonverbal behavior, Catherine plays a "man's man," albeit one in a tight, white dress.

Catherine not only behaves mannishly, but she rejects the roles of the submissive female and motherhood: Catherine is often barefoot; never pregnant. When, after her interrogation, Catherine is driven home by Nick, she steps barefoot from the car into a rain-filled gutter, the camera lingering on the water rushing over her feet. Later in the film, she declares, "I hate rug-rats" when Nick suggests they "Fuck like minks, raise rug-rats and live happily ever after." It is Nick, not Catherine, who longs for family life, who says "I love you," who hopes for and desires a future together.

Catherine's inability to be controlled makes her dangerous. Like the biblical Eve, she leads men to disaster. Nick is goaded by Catherine to lose control: to smoke, to drink, to fuck, to drive too fast. When he is interrogated as a suspect in the murder of a co-worker, he follows her lead and appropriates her lines. When reminded there is no smoking in the building, he replies as Catherine had earlier during her interrogation: "You gonna charge me with smoking?" Later in the interrogation, he utilizes her alibi when asked if he killed Lieutenant Nielsen, who was shot at point blank range after a confrontation with Nick. Mimicking Catherine's retort, he replies, "No. Come on—I'm gonna storm into his office in front of everybody in the middle of the day and kill him that night? I'm not that dumb."

Catherine especially seems to delight in exerting control over Nick by sexually frustrating him. In one scene, Catherine slowly, seductively approaches Nick as she reveals what she knows about his past. As the conversation intensifies, she gets very close to him. She talks slowly and in a seductive whisper as their lips practically touch. When it is clear that Nick is aroused, she taunts him with her knowledge of his wife's suicide. After he angrily pushes her away, Catherine's female lover walks into the room. Catherine further teases Nick by greeting Roxy with a warm "Hi, hon" and wrapping one arm gracefully about Roxy's waist while brazenly fondling her breast.

Catherine's interrogation is undoubtedly the most talked about scene in *Basic Instinct*. Catherine's language is brash and explicit. Her remarks regarding her casual relationship with Boz, exemplified by "I liked fucking him," take the detectives by surprise. Finally, at one point during the interrogation, Catherine slowly uncrosses then recrosses her legs, revealing herself—and her lack of undergarments—to Nick and the others.[3] The detectives are visibly unprepared for and aroused by her behavior. Clearly, part of Catherine's dangerous nature is that not only can she not be controlled, but that she tempts men to lose control.

Of course, part of Catherine's danger stems from the possibility she is a murderer. The mystery of Boz's murder is apparently solved when Nick, having just found his partner murdered with an ice pick, shoots and kills Beth, who he believes is responsible. The murder of Nick's partner, Gus, is eerily similar to the ending of Catherine's just-finished novel based on Nick's life. The final twist to the plot comes in the film's concluding scene: After yet another vigorous sexual encounter between Nick and Catherine, an ice pick stashed under the bed is revealed, strongly implicating Catherine as the true murderer and Nick as her next victim.

Regardless of whether Beth or Catherine is the murderer, women who are sexually independent and refuse to be controlled or dominated by men are indicted. If Catherine really is the murderer and acting out the plots in her books, she has killed her wealthy parents (who died in a suspicious boating accident), stabbed two male lovers with ice picks (Boz and her former psychology professor), and contributed to the death of two female lovers (Roxy and Beth). Here, a woman has killed for money and sexual fulfillment. If Beth is the murderer, and the "evidence" at least convinces the police of this, she has killed her husband; two men (Boz and the professor) who slept with the one she presumably desired (Catherine); as well as Lieutenant Nilsen, presumably because he threatened someone she cared about; and, finally, Gus, who was simply in the way. In this scenario, a woman has killed to remove obstacles and competition.

However, Catherine and Beth are not the only women involved with murder. Roxy and Hazel have both confessed to murder. Roxy, at age 16, sliced up her younger brothers with her father's razor; Hazel stabbed to death her husband and children. Both women acted merely on impulse and were unable to explain why they had killed. Thus, a woman who goes against her "natural" instinct to nurture others (be they a lover, parent, husband, child, or sibling) appears to be pathologically insane, lacking in reason and self-control. Moreover, in an earlier meeting about Boz's murder, a consulting psychologist concludes that the police are dealing with someone very dangerous and very ill, while Gus describes the killer as "a once-in-a-lifetime looney tuney."

One of *Basic Instinct*'s underlying messages is that women who try to beat a man at a man's game, who are independent and refuse to be controlled, are at the least a little crazy, if not outright pathological. In addition, they will end up childless and husbandless. Women like Catherine can never be happy because they will kill all they desire. The lesson for women is to follow the traditional path leading to hearth and home, for only there can they find fulfillment and happiness. Anything else is deviant and potentially dangerous.

SEXUAL IDENTITY

Basic Instinct not only blurs gender roles, it also blurs sexual identity. Catherine is bisexual. As such, she represents the ultimate "other": Neither gay nor straight, she represents a group whose sexual identity is questioned by almost everyone. Bisexuals are too gay for straights, and not gay enough for gays (Leland, 1995). Whereas the femme fatale of the 1940s taunted the hero with her knowledge of information he was not privy to, Catherine, the 1990s' femme fatale, also taunts the hero with the unknowable. However, her knowledge is of sexual experience—specifically, sex between women—that the hero can never know.

Straayer (1994) has noted that film portrayal of "lesbian sexuality generates an identity that is not defined by an opposition to maleness" (p. 356). As such, lesbian sexuality rejects the "natural" male-female opposition as the defining principle of sexual identity. In a similar fashion, as a bisexual, it can be argued that Catherine both rejects sexuality defined opposite to maleness and embraces it. In fact, whereas the male-female relationship is normally one of conquest (Straayer, 1994), Catherine is both victor and prize. Not only can Catherine's sexuality not be defined opposite to maleness, neither can it be satisfied by males alone. Catherine is so sexually voracious that neither gender alone can satisfy her. *Basic Instinct* continues the stereotype that bisexuals will "sleep with anything" and are virtually incapable of monogamy.

Most damaging of all is that in the world according to *Basic Instinct*, lesbian and bisexual women are man-hating murderers: Nearly every female character has killed someone, and "the trigger for these murderous impulses is clearly identified as lesbian sex" (Ehrenstein, 1992, p. 87). Stuart (1993) noted that Catherine is:

> a sort of wise-cracking wild thing, so sexually self-sufficient (and therefore totally undemanding) that she can do it for herself—or maybe with just a little help from her (girl)friends. This . . . says a lot more about male angst and wish-fulfillment than it does about female sexuality. It tells us much about the unacknowledged crisis within heterosexuality, rather than reflecting a genuine concern with the lesbian community. (p. 32)

Gross (1991) has argued that minorities, including gays, share the common fate of relative invisibility in the media or portrayal via demeaning stereotypes. He noted that minorities are commonly cast as a "threat to the moral order which must be countered through ridicule or physical violence" (p. 30). This portrayal is of particular concern when considering that the mass media are primary sources of information about others. In particular, the mass media provide the bulk of information about people who are marginalized within society (Gerbner, Gross, Morgan, & Signorelli, 1986). Thus, those who interact the least with nonheterosexuals get most of their information and impressions about bisexuals, gays, lesbians, and transgenders from the mass media. Unfortunately, relatively few films have portrayed such individuals as multifaceted characters or role models. For example, gays are portrayed in a way that is likely to foster negative stereotypes: They are effeminate, cross-dressers, or murderers (Parish, 1993). When a film such as *Basic Instinct* portrays lesbian and bisexual women as murdering manhaters, there is likely to be a segment of the audience that will assume such a characterization is realistic if not typical.

Basic Instinct also presents the stereotype that lesbianism and bisexuality are mere stages. For example, when Beth confesses that she had slept with Catherine in college, she states, "I slept with her. Once. I was just a kid. I was experimenting." In an encounter at Boz's club, Nick first watches Roxy and Catherine kissing in a stall of the men's room (which, by the way, showcases a host of "deviant" behavior, from homosexual encounters to drug abuse). Later he watches the lovers pulsating suggestively against each other on the dance floor. Catherine, continuing to gyrate with Roxy, then turns to face Nick. At this point, Roxy, in frustration, turns away to dance with another man. Catherine then approaches Nick and dances with him. Finally, Nick pulls Catherine to him and she is instantly reduced to a heterosex-starved creature. The camera then cuts to Nick and Catherine engaged in their first sexual encounter. Scenes such as these suggest that sexual encounters between women are really just experimental or temporary measures until a real man can be found.

The film also perpetuates the stereotype that nonheterosexuals merely need to be "cured" through heterosexual sex, just as, ultimately, Catherine is cured by Nick. Although Catherine's sexuality can be read as defiance, this reading is ultimately inaccurate. In the end, the status quo of heterosexuality is left securely in place. In fact, Catherine's "outrageous" behavior may have been only temporary because she ends up in the arms of Nick. As well stated by Ehrenstein (1992), the film exists in a testosterone-crazed never-never land in which women, groomed to Cosmo-girl perfection, bark obscenities, smirk defiantly, and strike Valkyrie-like poses, only to meld into a puddle of feminine submissiveness when placed in the arms of a "real man". The film warns, "lesbians may be a threat . . . but when push comes to shove, they just can't take the straight male competition." (p. 87)

Moreover, if the "lesson" of *Fatal Attraction* (1987)—an earlier film in which the male lead (also played by Michael Douglas) has an affair that leads to obsession and murder (and which was also penned by *Basic Instinct*'s writer, Joe Eszterhas)—was to be faithful in marriage, the lesson of *Basic Instinct* is to be faithful to the heterosexual ideal. It seems not coincidental that a caveat against exploring sexual identity occurred at a time of rising concern about AIDS "crossing over" to the straight community. It is bisexuals, after all, who are argued to be the primary vector for such transmission (Leland, 1995). As a result, *Basic Instinct* reinforces monogamous heterosexuality as the cultural ideal as it infers that bisexuals are unknowable, uncontainable, and will ultimately be the death of all heterosexuals.

PORNOGRAPHIC OBJECTIFICATION

Much of *Basic Instinct*'s success may be attributable to its sensationalistic depiction of sex, and the subsequent magnification of this by the mass media. In many respects, the inclusion of graphic sex scenes allowed a mainstream audience to flirt with pornography while not actually going to a pornographic film house. In this way, *Basic Instinct* exemplifies a trend toward increasingly graphic depictions of sex within mainstream cinema (Dowell, 1988; Greenberg et al., 1993). The film also illustrates the blurred distinction between sexual depiction within mainstream cinema and that of pornography. As Goldberg (1995) so aptly stated, sex is coming out from beneath the covers.[4]

The evidence in support of this uncovering is strong. In 1992, half of the top box-office movies were rated R. In fact, 45% of major studio films were rated R, as were 75% of independent productions (Valenti, 1993). This trend is not limited to adult-oriented films. One recent study found that R-rated films targeted toward adolescents featured intercourse between unmarried partners an average of eight times per film (Greenberg et al., 1993). Goldberg (1995) noted that "the media have probably broken more visual taboos in the last two decades than were overturned in the previous half century" (p. H40). Although filmmakers are willing to break visual taboos, they are still unwilling to break through the ceiling of an R rating. As Griffin (1992) noted about *Basic Instinct*, "Not since Last Tango in Paris has a mainstream film busted open America's coy sexual screen conventions with such uninhibited love scenes" (p. 86). However, to avoid an NC-17 rating, *Basic Instinct*'s director, Paul Verhoeven, cut out some of the most explicit segments.

Nonetheless, the explicit sex scenes not cut from the film more closely parallel pornographic depictions than erotica. Although both pornography and erotica have sexual arousal as a goal, there is an important distinction between the two. Erotica traditionally depicts sexual behavior and desire as linked to or derived from love (Williams, 1989). In this tradition, suggestive and moderately explicit (i.e., soft-core) acts of sex are commonplace, and such depictions are used to advance narrative elaboration, plot, and character development. Pornography, however, presents sex for its own sake, without need for advancing the plot or developing characters. According to Cline (1994), pornography is a lay term simply defined as graphic and explicit depictions of sexual activity. Williams (1989) further described it as a genre unto itself that highlights the "visual representation of living, moving bodies engaged in explicit . . . unfaked, sexual acts" (p. 30). Williams argued that the use of graphic depictions of sex acts within narratives is an unprecedented mass commercialization of sex as both a visual pleasure and spectator sport. What makes these acts so powerful is the cinema's ability to transport each viewer, by the magic of close-ups and editing, to the ideal position for their witnessing.

The sex in *Basic Instinct* clearly rejects the representation of sexual desire as created or driven by love. Given the length of the sex scenes in the film—especially those featured on the videotape of *Basic Instinct* released as the "director's cut"—one must question whether the sex is more "useful" for plot advancement or merely for voyeurism. More troubling, however, is that *Basic Instinct* presents sex as violent or potentially violent. One explicit example of this occurs in the opening scene with Boz's murder. In a later scene, Nick and Beth have sex in her apartment. Nick disregards foreplay, slams Beth into a wall, rips open her blouse, pushes off her bra, grabs at her breasts, and, against her protestations, forces her over a chair so he can enter her from behind. This latter scene was described as so "violent and sadomasochistic that it looks like dramatized rape" (Welsh, 1992, p. 187).

The sex scenes between Nick and Catherine do not feature such overt acts of violence, although violence is always looming as an all-too-near possibility. Not surprisingly, these scenes also employ technical conventions common to pornography. For one, women are available for men's visual pleasure. Beyond mere visual representation, however, Catherine's voice—or, more specifically, her moaning during sexual acts—is recorded in a pornographic fashion that highlights the higher vocal register of females. Nick, however, is virtually silent, but nonetheless depicted as capable of reducing Catherine to a whimpering, sex-starved creature. Depictions of women in such a manner are unsettlingly similar within pornography: Women are submissive, sexually eager, and objects of desire. Weaver (1991) described the women in pornography as promiscuous and sexually hyperactive. Catherine represents dangerous, out-of-control female sexuality that must be "tamed" by a real man.

The shift in mainstream cinema toward presenting sexual behavior in pornographic ways as illustrated by *Basic Instinct*, constitutes a new, "lite-porn" (Goldberg, 1995), which spotlights the sexual desires and prowess of men while consistently and persistently portraying women as sexually willing and available (Brosius, Weaver, & Staab, 1993). Mainstream films as a result may become increasingly "projectile" (Rich, 1994), representing men's fantasies about women's lives rather than the reality of women's lives. This is no surprise: pornography is a genre typically produced by men for men. According to Williams (1989), "pornography [has] long been a myth of sexual pleasure told from the point of view of men with the power to exploit and objectify the sexuality of women" (p. 22). This is especially disturbing given recent empirical evidence regarding the effects of pornography.

Although there has been considerable debate regarding the censorship of pornography (see Bullough, 1994; van Zoonen, 1994; Williams, 1989), recent research suggests that exposure to pornography affects attitudes and behaviors, fostering both inappropriate perceptions of and abusive behavior toward women (see Harris, 1994; Lyons, Anderson, & Larson, 1994; Weaver, 1991). Studies have found that exposure to pornography contributes to calloused attitudes and negative orientations toward women. For example, Weaver (1994) concluded that the effects of pornography include "the trivialization of rape as a criminal offense, exaggerated perceptions of the prevalence of most sexual practices, increased callousness toward female sexuality and concerns, dissatisfaction with sexual relationships, and diminished caring for and trust in intimate partners" (p. 219). Zillmann and Weaver (1989) also found that men exposed to sexual media depictions, whether violent or not, perceived women as more sexually receptive and permissive and were more lenient regarding the sentencing of a convicted rapist. Other research has found a strong relationship between the incidence of rape and the availability of sexually explicit material (Scott & Schwalm, 1988). A comprehensive review of 81 pornography studies similarly concluded that exposure to aggressive pornography contributed to an increase in the perceived likelihood to rape (Lyons et al., 1994). The evidence from these studies strongly suggests that exposure to sexually explicit material has a deleterious impact on attitudes, perceptions, and behaviors toward women.

CONCLUSION

This chapter has discussed the modern femme fatale within the genre of *film noir* as represented within *Basic Instinct*. Catherine represents a modernized femme fatale in her explicit sexuality, a characterization shaped by the times and an increasingly pornographic standard within mainstream cinema. As femme fatale, Catherine presents the age-old view of woman's sexuality as dangerous and uncontrollable; her only options are to be reigned in by a "real" man or punished for her social deviance. Thus, the increasingly blurred distinction between mainstream cinema and both violent and nonviolent pornography, as exemplified in *Basic Instinct*, represents a "mainstreaming" of misogynist sexual representations.

In this way, *Basic Instinct* presents a hyper-sexed view of reality that thrusts the viewer into the role of voyeur. Even though sexual and gender identity are blurred in *Basic Instinct*, that identity is graphically sexual and largely tied to sexual behavior. In this view, sexually independent women are dangerous, pathological, and need to be dominated and made dependent on a man for their own salvation, as well as to prevent them from harming men.

Basic Instinct also implies that women are not just deviant when they want sexual independence, but when they want sexual independence from men. This deviance extends beyond the bedroom and into all areas of their lives, for the lesbian and bisexual women of *Basic Instinct* appear to be murdering maniacs, pathological killers bent on destroying (mostly male) lives.[5] *Basic Instinct* cautions the audience that when heterosexuality is circumvented, murder and destruction are the inevitable outcomes.

Last, the hyper-sexuality of *Basic Instinct* illustrates the continued blurring of mainstream cinema with pornography. *Basic Instinct* moves beyond mere plot development in its hyper-emphasis on sexual activity. Catherine is a vision of woman constructed by men: The sex scenes are filmed from a male perspective, with Nick and other men in the film frequently taking on the role of voyeur. In this sense, *Basic Instinct* parallels pornographic films. The explicit portrayal of sex, whether it is violent or not, contributes to the objectification of women, as well as leading to callous attitudes and subsequently abusive behavior toward women. Thus, *Basic Instinct* contributes to the continuing misogynistic focus of contemporary American society.

In sum, *Basic Instinct* is concurrently modern and archaic—modern in that women strive for independence, and archaic in that they are punished for it. The hyper-sexed nature of this film tells us much about women, society at large, and women's and men's places in such a society. Ironically, *Basic Instinct* can fool the viewer into thinking that women are liberated: At the very least they can choose and discard their sexual partners at will. Yet, at its core, *Basic Instinct* presents the most archaic of all views of women: They are dangerous, wild things whose uncontrollable sexuality is a threat not only to themselves, but to men and society at large. Ultimately, the film suggests that murder is women's basic instinct. Additionally, it suggests that women's submission to the controlling and stabilizing influence of men *should be* their basic instinct.

ENDNOTES

1. Most films were not shot in color until 1959. In fact, some purists claim that real *film noir* can only be filmed in black and white (Dick, 1990).
2. Particular patterns of visual imagery are expected in a given genre. Monsters are expected in horror films, and guns, suits, and hats are staples of gangster films (Williams, 1989).
3. It is interesting to note that although Catherine was manipulating the detectives, the director, Paul Verhoeven, was manipulating the actress: Stone had been told before filming the scene that the lighting and camera angle would guarantee that "nothing" would be seen.
4. An important historical factor that contributed to the relaxation of sexual restrictions in mainstream cinema was the overturning of the Hays Production Code in the 1950s (Valenti, 1993). The Code forbade kisses longer than 30 seconds and the showing of underwear, women's breasts, and illicit affairs (Goldberg, 1995). It was not until 1968 that the Motion Picture Association of America instituted a voluntary rating code for films based on the accumulation and degree to which language, violence, sensuality, or drugs are presented (Valenti, 1993).
5. It seems worth noting that the film is set in San Francisco, which has one of the nation's largest homosexual populations.

REFERENCES

Allen, V. (1983). *The femme fatale erotic icon.* Oxford: Oxford University Press.

Brosius, H., Weaver, J. B., & Staab, J. F. (1993). Exploring the social and sexual "reality" of contemporary pornography. *The Journal of Sex Research, 30,* 161-170.

Bullough, V. L. (1994). *Science in the bedroom: A history of sex research.* New York: Basic Books.

Cline, V. B. (1994). Pornography effects: Empirical and clinical evidence. In D. Zillmann, J. Bryant, & A. Huston (Eds.), *Media, children, and the family: Social scientific, psychodynamic, and clinical perspectives* (pp. 229-247). Hillsdale, NJ: Erlbaum.

Dick, B. F. (1990). *Anatomy of film* (2nd ed.). New York: St. Martin's Press.

Dittmar, L., Welsch, J. R., & Carson, D. (1994). Introduction. In D. Carson, L. Dittmar, & J. R. Welsch (Eds.), *Multiple voices in feminist film criticism* (pp. 1-23). Minneapolis: University of Minnesota Press.

Doane, M. A. (1991). *Femme fatales: Feminism, film theory, psychoanalysis.* New York: Routledge, Chapman and Hall.

Dowell, P. (1988, September). Sex makes a comeback. *Psychology Today,* pp. 64-65.

Ehrenstein, D. (1992, April 21). *Basic Instinct*: This is a smart, hot, sexy commercial film? *The Advocate,* p. 87.

Ewing, D. E. (1988). Film noir: Style and content. *Journal of Popular Film and Television, 16,* 60-69.

Faludi, S. (1991). *Backlash: The undeclared war against American women.* New York: Doubleday.

Gerbner, G., Gross, L., Morgan, M., & Signorelli, N. (1986). Living with television: The dynamics of the cultivation process. In J. Bryant & D. Zillmann (Eds.), *Perspectives in media effects* (pp. 17-40). Hillsdale, NJ: Erlbaum.

Gledhill, C. (1978). Klute part 1: A contemporary film noire and feminist criticism. In E. A. Kaplan (Ed.), *Women in film noire* (pp. 14-20). London: British Film Institute.

Gledhill, C. (1994). Image and voice: Approaches to Marxist-feminist criticism. In D. Carson, L. Dittmar, & J. R. Welsch (Eds.), *Multiple voices in feminist film criticism* (pp. 109-123). Minneapolis: University of Minnesota Press.

Goldberg, V. (1995, October 29). Testing the limits. *New York Times,* p. H1, H40.

Greenberg, B. S., Siemicki, M., Dorfman, S., Heeter, C., Soderman, A., & Linsangan, R. (1993). Sex content in R-rated films viewed by adolescents. In B. S. Greenberg, J. D. Brown, & N. L. Buerkel-Rothfuss (Eds.), *Media, sex and the adolescent* (pp. 45-58). Cresskill, NJ: Hampton Press.

Griffin, N. (1992, April). The sympathetic sinner [Review of *Basic Instinct*]. *Premiere*, pp. 84-96.

Gross, L. (1991). Out of the mainstream: Sexual minorities and the mass media. *Journal of Homosexuality, 21*, 19-46.

Harris, R. J. (1994). The impact of sexually explicit media. In J. Bryant & D. Zillmann (Eds.), *Media effects: Advances in theory and research* (pp. 247-272). Hillsdale, NJ: Erlbaum.

Johnson, B. E. (1992, March 30). Killer movies: *Basic Instinct* pushes the boundaries of the Hollywood mainstream [Review of *Basic Instinct*]. *Maclean's*, pp. 48-51.

Konigsberg, I. (1987). *The complete film dictionary*. New York: NAL Books.

Lawrence, C. M. (1993, February). *Ambiguity and controversy in Basic Instinct: A feminist response*. Paper presented at the Western States Communication Association Convention, Albuquerque, NM.

Leland, J. (1995, July 17). Bisexuality emerges as a new sexual identity. *Newsweek*, pp. 44-50.

Lyons, J. S., Anderson, R. L., & Larson, D. B. (1994). A systematic review of the effects of aggressive and nonaggressive pornography. In D. Zillmann, J. Bryant, & A. Huston (Eds.), *Media, children, and the family: Social scientific, psychodynamic, and clinical perspectives* (pp. 271-310). Hillsdale, NJ: Erlbaum.

Mayne, J. (1994). Feminist film theory and criticism. In D. Carson, L. Dittmar, & J. R. Welsch (Eds.), *Multiple voices in feminist film criticism* (pp. 48-64). Minneapolis: University of Minnesota Press.

Mulvey, L. (1975). Visual pleasure and visual cinema. *Screen, 16*, 6-18.

Naremore, J. (1988). *Acting in the cinema*. Berkeley: University of California Press.

Parish, J. R. (1993). *Gays and lesbians in mainstream cinema: Plots, critiques, casts and credits for 272 theatrical and made-for-television Hollywood releases*. Jefferson, NC: McFarland.

Rich, B. R. (1994). In the name of feminist film criticism. In D. Carson, L. Dittmar, & J. R. Welsch (Eds.), *Multiple voices in feminist film criticism* (pp. 27-47). Minneapolis: University of Minnesota Press.

Scott, J. E., & Schwalm, L. A. (1988). Rape rates and the circulation of adult magazines. *Journal of Sex Research, 24*, 241-250.

Staiger, J. (1994). The politics of film canons. In D. Carson, L. Dittmar, & J. R. Welsch (Eds.), *Multiple voices in feminist film criticism* (pp. 191-209). Minneapolis: University of Minnesota Press.

Stephens, M. L. (1995). *Film noir: A comprehensive illustrated reference to movies, terms and persons*. Jefferson, NC: McFarland.

Straayer, C. (1994). The hypothetical lesbian heroine in narrative feature film. In D. Carson, L. Dittmar, & J. R. Welsch (Eds.), *Multiple voices in feminist film criticism* (pp. 343-357). Minneapolis: University of Minnesota Press.

Stuart, A. (1993, August 13). A touch of taboo. *New Statesman & Society*, pp. 32-33.

Travers, P. (1992, April 16). *Jagged Edge* meets *Fatal Attraction* [Review of *Basic Instinct*]. *Rolling Stone*, pp. 89-90.

Valenti, J. (1993, September). Hollywood, the rating system, and the movie-going public. *USA Today*, pp. 87-89.

van Zoonen, L. (1994). *Feminist media studies*. London: Sage.

Weaver, J. B. (1991). Responding to erotica: Perceptual processes and dispositional implications. In J. Bryant & D. Zillmann (Eds.), *Responding to the screen: Reception and reaction processes* (pp. 329-354). Hillsdale, NJ: Erlbaum

Weaver, J. B. (1994). Pornography and sexual callousness: The perceptual and behavioral consequences of exposure to pornography. In D. Zillmann, J. Bryant, & A. Huston (Eds.), *Media, children, and the family: Social scientific, psychodynamic, and clinical perspectives* (pp. 215-228). Hillsdale, NJ: Erlbaum.

Welsh, J.M. (1992, June). *Basic Instinct* [Review of *Basic Instinct*]. *Films in Review*, 43, 186-187.

Williams, L. (1989). *Hard core: Power, pleasure, and the "frenzy of the visible."* Berkeley: University of California Press.

Zillmann, D., & Weaver, J. B. (1989). Pornography and men's sexual callousness toward women. In D. Zillmann & J. Bryant (Eds.), *Pornography: Research advances and policy considerations* (pp. 95-125). Hillsdale, NJ: Erlbaum

17

"Who Talks Like That?" Foregrounding Stereotypes on *The Nanny*

Barbara Wilinsky

Sitting with her mother and grandmother in her boss's upscale New York City brownstone, Fran Fine—the central character of the sitcom *The Nanny*—remarks that she loves the *Saturday Night Live* skit they are watching: Mike Myers playing a stereotypical Jewish woman hosting a cable-access program. Myers, wearing tacky clothing and too much make-up, produces a steady barrage of Yiddish words in a thick, New York accent. Fran's grandmother, Yetta, responds in her own heavy New York accent (shared by Fran): "Oh, please, who talks like that?" Fran's mother, Sylvia, chewing a wad of gum, adds: "And that big hair. I think it's very stereotypical." Sylvia, Fran, and Yetta then each put a hand to their styled and teased hair to poof it up just a bit more.

The humor in watching these three women—all heavily made-up and wearing brightly colored, almost garish clothing—lies in the obvious fact that they personify the stereotype in Myers's character, which they themselves find "very stereotypical." Herein lies the contradictions within and the fascination of *The Nanny*—a formulaic yet curious television program that both offers another stereotyped vision of Jewish women at the same time it foregrounds and calls into question those stereotypes.

Televised images of Jewish women exist at the intersection of stereotyped representations of women and stereotyped representations of Jews. This examination of *The Nanny*, which premiered on CBS in 1993, illustrates that the strain resulting from this double inscription of Jewish female characters allows *The Nanny* to draw on various stereotypes of Jews to counter existing stereotyped representations of women. When the depiction of *Jewish* female characters becomes a strategy for reconceptualizing the stereotypes of women on television, however, we must question what is gained and what is lost for these characters as Jews. The purpose here is not to label certain representations positive and others negative, but to consider how images utilize existing stereotypes, and the possible meanings that emerge from these portrayals.

THE JEWISH FLAVOR: JEWISH CHARACTERS ON TELEVISION

Several differences exist in the depiction of Jewish men and Jewish women. Although the ethnicity of Jewish men marks them as "other" in relation to white, nonethnic, male society, the mark is generally weak because Jewish males, who are often considered "white," can "pass" as non-Jews.[1] However, Jewish women are doubly coded as "other." They may be able to "pass" as non-Jews, but they cannot escape the mark of femininity. Jewish women, therefore, rarely are seen and heard on television.[2] Furthermore, as Kray (1993) notes, the rare Jewish female characters on television are frequently portrayed by non-Jewish actresses, thus decreasing the Jewish flavor of the characters. For example, the non-Jewish actresses Valerie Harper, Theresa Saldana, and Marion Ross portrayed Jewish women on the programs *Rhoda*, *The Commish*, and *Brooklyn Bridge* respectively. What the viewer sees, then, is only an illusion of a Jewish woman without the authenticity of a Jewish actress behind the character.

Alleviating the Threat: The Jewish Stereotype

Despite the involvement of many Jewish people in creating television images of Jews, these representations grow out of contemporary stereotypes and their antecedents perpetuated by societies—both in America and Europe—in which fear of those who are different results in scapegoating and hostility. Indeed, many of the qualities which form the Jewish stereotype serve to explain and alleviate the "threat" of the Jews emerging from their religious differences and supposed economic success.

Whereas ethnicity is frequently associated with the working class (Gans, 1979), Jews' "relative economic success" (Kaye/Kantrowitz, 1992, p. 6), their (predominantly) white skin, and their values (which include education, ambition and delay of gratification) link Jews to the white, privileged classes (Erens, 1984; Wernick, 1992). Commenting on the image of Jews as "wise men," Whitfield (1993) writes that the non-Jew "tended to associate Jewish figures with wealth" (p. 20). Altman (1971) suggests humor about Jews, often in the form of anti-Semitic jokes, sometimes doubles for humor about the middle and upper classes. Altman writes, "The Jew himself, supposedly the target of the attack, remains a 'front' for the American middle class ethos" (p. 58). The uneasiness caused by the "difference" of Jews combined with this ability to "stand in" for the upper classes—and thereby absorb and deflect criticism of these classes—uniquely positions Jews in popular culture.

Gilman (1991) suggests that one of the main characteristics attributed to Jews is a unique relationship to language. To the non-Jew, according to Gilman, European Jews seem to possess a "hidden" language—Yiddish—that others cannot understand and that may be used in subversive ways. At the same time, however, Jews may be viewed as unable to master the national language of the country in which they live (Gilman, 1991). Therefore, attempts by Jews to use these national languages appear nonauthentic and false (Gilman, 1991). Jews, then, have a problematic relationship with language: they appear deceptive through their use of a "hidden" language that others do not understand and also dishonest in their use of national languages to which they do not have complete access.

Stereotypes also generally portray Jews as sensitive and weak. This image evolved from several myths historically associated with Jews, such as the myth of the Jews' physical inability to serve in the military, a fiction that facilitated a clear differentiation between Jews and "true" citizens who served their countries (Gilman, 1991). Jewish males, according to Gilman, also became associated with hysteria, generally considered a "women's" illness. Gilman observes, "The Jew is the hysteric; the Jew is the feminized Other; the Jew is seen as different, as diseased" (p. 76). This association of Jewish men and hysteria connected the Jews with observable emotional states. Their depictions as physically weak and emotionally sensitive work to feminize all Jews.

Although the representation of today's Jew is less overtly anti-Semitic, remnants of these conceptualizations emerge in today's popular culture. The image of Jews as weak, emotional, and deceptive helps to limit their threat to nonethnic society, particularly in a field such as television, which they are suspected of dominating.

The ways in which television limits the threat of Jewish men strongly impacts the representations of Jewish women—often rendering them invisible. The incorporation of Jewish men (as well as other so-called "minority" groups) into the pursuit of the American dream weakens their power through the suggestion that what all "different" people really want is to be like WASP, middle-class Americans. Daniel Lipman, the co-creator and an executive producer of *Sisters*, explains that Jews seek to attain "this image, which I guess television perpetuates, of the blond goddess, the beautiful house in the suburbs, the two-car garage, whatever the American ideal is" (cited in Lovece, 1992, p. 18). A relationship with a non-Jewish woman is a mark of the Jewish man's incorporation into this American dream. As a result, television programs often couple Jewish male characters with non-Jewish female characters.[3] Kray (1993) notes that television programs naturalize the invisibility of Jewish women by ignoring their absence in romantic relationships with Jewish men.

Embodying the Excess: Jewish Women on Television

When Jewish women are depicted, they are painted within the confines of Jewish stereotypes and set in contrast to the images of television's WASP women. For the depiction of Jewish women, the problem becomes how to represent the already feminized as feminine. The Jewish woman, doubly coded as feminine, is made to display "over the top" feminine qualities. Her sensitivity becomes emotional excess, the "hidden" language becomes one of overt manipulation, and lack of access to the national language becomes deceptive use of this language in order to control men.

Television's difficulty with the vocalization and demonstration of feelings results in television being, according to Mellencamp (1990), "a training manual for controlling and repressing emotions" (p. 233). The aggressive, emotional openness of Jewish women places them in opposition to the dominant conceptions of women on television, who may be more active than they were in the past yet still seem to mainly function to quietly support their husbands or laugh at their jokes. Thus, the depiction of Jewish women potentially offers alternative images of femininity.

The contradictions within the images of Jewish women result in two predominant cultural stereotypes which, of course, predate their representation on television: the manipulative Jewish mother and the neurotic, single, Jewish woman.[4] Both of these stereotypes involve the manipulation of language and emotion on the part of Jewish women in order to control men. Erens (1984) charts the evolution of the Jewish mother in U.S. cinema into the "Suffocating Mother" who "threatens the well-being of her daughters and especially her sons" (p. 257). Through control of the "hidden" language (of guilt and whining), the Jewish mother emotionally manipulates her children.

Explaining the myth of the single Jewish woman, Ron Cowan, the co-creator of *Sisters*, suggests she is "somewhat aggressive, somewhat insecure about herself, always hunting for a man" (cited in Lovece, 1992, p. 18). The related stereotype of the Jewish American Princess also makes Jewish women less threatening by making them appear foolish. Rubel (1992) describes a Jewish American Princess as a "loud, overweight, pushy, capitalistic, materialistic, undeserving, New York, greedy, sexually frigid or promiscuous, selfish, calculating, vulgar, ugly Jewish woman" (p. 43).

SHE HAD STYLE, SHE HAD FLAIR, SHE WAS THERE . . . THE NANNY

As part of the recent spate of situation comedies featuring stand-up comedians, *The Nanny* not only offers the two most prominent stereotypes of Jewish women but embodies them within one character. This examination, focusing on the central character, Fran Fine, considers how *The Nanny* mobilizes different stereotypes to both reconfigure and reinforce traditional representations of Jews and women.

The Nanny offers an example of a Jewish female character actually portrayed by a Jewish woman. Although *The Nanny* did not prove to be an immediate ratings success, its audience improved. Airing at 8 p.m. (EST) as the lead-in program to CBS's Wednesday night line-up, in its first few seasons *The Nanny* consistently had the highest ratings and the largest share of the audience during its time slot. As with many programs that feature Jewish characters, Jews created *The Nanny*: the show's star Fran Drescher and her husband Peter Marc Jacobson (from whom Drescher is now separated).

Without Restraint: The Nanny as a Jewish Woman

As the series begins, Fran Drescher plays Fran Fine, a single, Jewish woman from Queens, New York, hired by widower Maxwell Sheffield, a British Broadway theatrical producer, as the nanny for his three children. In effect, Fran is the Jewish mother to non-Jewish children. Not only does her job put her in charge of the children, but at times she overtly slips into the role of mother, such as when she hosts a mother-daughter tea for the oldest child and enters a mother-daughter beauty pageant with the youngest. Although Fran may not be the typical Jewish suffocating mother, in many ways she embodies the stereotype. She certainly uses language to control Mr. Sheffield and the children. For example, Fran manipulates Mr. Sheffield into allowing her sister Nadine to stay in his home for a few days by asking him questions leading him to suggest that Nadine visit. Unlike the typical Jewish mother (who is visible in the recurring character of Fran's mother, Sylvia Fine), however, Fran often has the children's—not her own—best interests at heart.

Fran's character can be more closely aligned with the stereotypical Jewish American Princess. Though not overweight or ugly, Fran can certainly be loud, pushy, materialistic, self-absorbed, and vulgar. Fran's image includes what the program often itself refers to as her "big hair and too much make-up." One instance (of many) illustrating Fran's obsession with her looks occurs when Fran believes that Mr. Sheffield is dying and she and the children will be sent to live with his sister in England. Fran's friend, Val, points out that the weather in England will cause Fran's hair to frizz and Fran replies, "Now you know how upset I am. I didn't even think about my hair." Fran's materialistic leanings are seen in an episode in which, after being mugged, Fran is able to identify the type of stocking her assailant wore over his face, down to the brand name.

Until Fran and Mr. Sheffield marry at the end of the show's fifth season, Fran is also a single, Jewish woman in search of a man. The reason she works as a nanny is that her boyfriend, whom she worked for, fired her when he began to date another woman. Fran frequently makes comments about dating and men. She generally wears very bright and tight-fitting clothing that establish her as a spectacle for men. Holding up the skimpy bathing suit she bought for a family vacation, Fran says, "If we're going to Gilligan's island, I want to be Ginger."

As noted earlier, Fran actually dates and marries Mr. Sheffield during the fifth season. It will be interesting to see how this dynamic changes the program. This chapter, however, is based on the first seasons of *The Nanny*, before the relationship between Mr. Sheffield and Fran is firmly established and while Fran is still searching for romance.

It is worth noting that in earlier episodes, Fran was not depicted as desperate for a man. When her ex-boyfriend returns with a marriage proposal, Fran actually refuses to marry him because he expects her to leave the Sheffield family to work with him. Later episodes, though, center around Fran's desire for a love life (a device that sets up romantic situations for Fran and Mr. Sheffield). Taken in by a con man pretending to love her, Fran is told by a police officer that "he usually preys on women over 30. You know—single, desperate, lonely." In another episode Fran is assumed to be gay because she is over 30, has never been married, and doesn't have a man in her life. Fran comments, "I'm not gay. I'm just pathetic." This later depiction of Fran as "desperate," "lonely," and "pathetic" weakens the potential image of Fran as a strong and self-determining woman—even when she gets her meddling, pushy-yet-caring mother to admit that "you don't have to be married to have a full life." Remarks about her inability to find a husband, which poke fun at Fran, limit the narrative and discursive power granted her.

Fran, like other female, Jewish characters, has a unique relationship with both emotions and language. A *Variety* review of the program observes, "Based on evidence in 'The Nanny,' Fran Drescher has many talents, but restraint isn't one of them" (Gray, 1993, p. 32). This lack of restraint helps Fran fulfill her functions within the program's narrative, which include encouraging the family members to express *their* emotions. This same lack of restraint also offers viewers an emotionally expressive woman within a medium given to "repressing emotions." When the oldest daughter gets angry at Fran, Mr. Sheffield tells his daughter to calm down. Fran tells him to "let her vent. It'll make her feel better. It'll make us all feel better." Here, Fran points out the importance of expressing emotions. In a Mother's Day episode, Fran suggests it is not healthy that the family does not talk about the deceased mother but instead tries to ignore Mother's Day. Fran wants the children to remember their mother and talk about their loss.

Fran's emotional expressiveness also is emphasized by setting her in contrast to both the program's British characters and Mr. Sheffield's American, female business partner, C.C. Babcock. The British characters are stereotypically unemotional. The lack of emotion displayed by Mr. Sheffield's sister before her wedding amazes Fran. In this episode, Fran asks, "How are you supposed to know what you British are feeling? What do you all wear—mood rings?" Fran's close connection to emotions becomes clear when she is the only character to recognize that the sister actually loves her chauffeur, not the duke she plans to marry. When Fran confronts the chauffeur, he asks if his feelings are that obvious. Fran replies that they are apparent to "a trained eye." Fran is established as a professional when it comes to reading emotions.

C.C. Babcock, the program's representative of American WASP culture, embodies all the outward signs of the "blond goddess" but does not represent the "American ideal." Rather, she is depicted as desperate and pathetic; a successful yet unfulfilled, repressed, self-centered woman. In contrast, Fran is nurturing and emotional. C.C. wants to be romantically involved with Mr. Sheffield, but he is not interested in her. A romantic relationship is established, though, for Mr. Sheffield and Fran. The program's opening song reinforces this conflict with the lines: "The father finds her [Fran] beguiling. Watch out C.C." Even C.C.'s dog prefers Fran to its owner. C.C.'s attempts to exploit people always fail because they are based on self-interest, whereas Fran, who frequently tries to manipulate people to help others, usually gets her way.

Fran's means of manipulating people almost always involve talking them into things. Like the "typical" Jewish mother, Fran uses language to control. The reliance on the stereotype of the Jew's relation to language—like Fran's emotional expressiveness—stretches the boundaries of what is generally allowed women on television. That Fran's use of language is "different" is constantly marked by Fran Drescher's heavily New York-accented, nasal voice. She also frequently uses Yiddish words such as "plotz" and "nuch schlep" which she must explain to the family,[5] indicating her knowledge of the "hidden" language. A conversation between Mr. Sheffield and his butler Niles illustrates the mysteries that Fran's language holds for these British men:

> Niles: She's [Fran's] upstairs getting all fapitzed.
> Maxwell: What does that mean?
> Niles: You know, dressed.
> Maxwell: I thought that was flubunged.
> Niles: No, sir, that means confused.
> Maxwell: No, man, that's fechachda.
> Niles: Well, then, what's flishimeld?
> Maxwell: I think that's her uncle.

As this conversation demonstrates, Niles and Mr. Sheffield cannot grasp Fran's "hidden" language. However, Fran differs somewhat from the Jewish stereotype because, in many ways, she does not lack access to the national language. In fact, Fran comprehends the language of U.S. popular culture better than the upperclass, British Mr. Sheffield, having to explain to him, for example, the premise of *Gilligan's Island*.

However, Fran does resemble earlier representations of Jewish women in her depiction as someone who talks too much. Fran's access to language appears comic and stereotypically excessive. When Fran asks Mr. Sheffield if she can speak with him for "just one minute," he replies, "I doubt it." Fran's excessive talking occasionally causes problems within the family. She talks Mr. Sheffield into letting her participate in a Mother's Day mother-daughter beauty pageant with the youngest daughter. The daughter is eventually forced to blurt out that she is participating in the event with her nanny because her mother is dead. As Mr. Sheffield feared, the daughter is hurt by the experience. Fran tells the daughter, "Your father didn't want us to enter, but I didn't listen. I was just too busy talking. I do that sometimes. I just talk and talk and talk. . . ." When Mr. Sheffield points out that she is doing that just now, Fran continues, "I'm gunna stop now. The talking, not the listening. The listening I'm gunna keep doing. It's the talking I'm gunna stop. Okay . . . I've stopped."

Fran's control also is limited by the narrative because her plans—which she has talked someone into—usually backfire in some way. In the Mother's Day episode, as Mr. Sheffield anticipated, his daughter is upset by the contest. In another episode, when the Sheffields (and Fran) go on vacation at Fran's suggestion that the family spend some time together, she insists that they take a short-cut to the airport. The family ends up stranded at Fran's parents' cramped apartment for a night.

Although there are always problematic consequences to Fran's schemes (the situations of this situation comedy), Fran's authority is often reinstated by the end. As Fran recognized, the youngest daughter really needed to talk about her mother. The Sheffields also actually enjoyed their "family" time in Fran's parents' apartment. The program repeatedly upholds Fran's basic values—particularly the importance of family and emotional honesty—and reinforces her dominance within the show.

"The Front:" The Nanny as Working Class?

Clearly, *The Nanny* is not the first or only program to offer women on television a strong and authoritative voice. Recently, *Roseanne*—as well as *Grace Under Fire* and perhaps even *Married . . . with Children*—illustrated television's tentative willingness to present *blue collar* women who (loudly) question male hegemony. However, because Jews are traditionally associated with the upper classes, *The Nanny*'s depiction of a working class Jewish woman needs further consideration.

Importantly, *The Nanny* foregrounds class distinctions between the Jewish-American characters and the British and American WASP characters. According to Fran Drescher, the show was consciously developed with the nanny as a member of the lower class and the Sheffields as upper class in order to ease some of the tension created by her ethnicity ("In the Spotlight," 1993, p. 6).

Although *The Nanny* does suggest a working-class background for Fran, this representation is ambiguous. Fran is a woman who can tell if an episode of *Wheel of Fortune* is a rerun based on what Vanna White is wearing; she shops at discount stores with names like Blouse House and Slack Shack; and she grew up in a home with plastic covering on the couch. Her knowledge of popular and mass culture, which at times allows Fran to appear more knowledgeable than the Sheffields, also associates her with the lower classes and often makes her appear unintelligent. Preparing to audition for the television game show *Jeopardy*, Fran responds to "The oldest body orbiting the sun?" with the properly phrased-in-the-form-of-a-question response, "Who is William Shatner." Fran knows the rules of popular culture; however, she does not have access to the more intellectual or high-class "right answers."

Fran's coding as working class is further associated with her language. Mr. Sheffield often uses words, frequently French, that Fran does not understand. In response to Mr. Sheffield's announcement that he has pulled a major coup, Fran tells him not to worry—it will heal itself. As Drescher expected, this confusion of language based on class disperses some of the tension surrounding Fran's ethnicity by emphasizing and finding comedy in her lack of "culture" rather than her Jewishness.

This connection between Fran and the lower classes is limited, though, by both the stereotype she embodies and her placement within the luxurious Sheffield home. Although Fran's family might be working class, she seems to represent the stereotype of the "Jewish princess"—generally associated with the middle and upper classes. Fran is narratively placed within the Sheffield's beautiful, New York brownstone, in which she enjoys all the pleasures of the wealthy. In one episode, Fran champions the working class by refusing to cross a busboys' picket line to attend the opening night party for one of Mr. Sheffield's plays. But, at the end of the episode, when Fran learns how much the busboys earn ($8 an hour), she becomes outraged: "What? Just for bringing you water that you have to ask 16 times for?" Fran suggests to the butler, Niles, that they are being exploited and the two domestic workers intersperse remarks about the need to organize with comments about having eaten too much caviar. They then sit at the kitchen table drinking champagne and rummaging through baskets of gourmet food while humming the tune that urged consumers to "look for the union label."

In the end, the narrative reinstates the Jewish character of Fran Fine to the upper classes, allowing her the potential to raise contradictions within these supposedly homogenous groups. *The Nanny* illustrates, as Altman (1971) suggests, how Jews can be used as a front for the middle and upper classes. Whereas Roseanne's female voice came from her working-class, decorated-by-Sears home, Fran's voice emanates from an elegant, upper class home in which it is sometimes forgotten that she is *only* a nanny.

"Very Stereotypical:" The Nanny as a Jew

Through the use of Jewish stereotypes, Fran Fine adds a complex and ambiguous image of femininity to television by depicting a woman who encourages emotional expressivity and speaks her mind with confidence. On television, women are expected to remain silent, but Fran speaks loudly and often; women are expected to control their emotions and repress their fears, but Fran expresses her feelings and concerns. On the other hand, Fran is, after all, a loud, pushy, vulgar, and materialistic New Yorker; she is a manipulative "mother" and, until this season, a neurotic single. In other words, Fran is a stereotypical Jewish woman. It is necessary to ask if, in the attempt to use emotions and language to liberate the television woman, *The Nanny* only reinforces existing (and insulting) stereotypes about Jews.

It must be remembered that through Fran Drescher and her character Fran Fine, *The Nanny* offers viewers a depiction of a Jewish woman by a Jewish woman. Additionally, as a woman with keen business and promotional skills, Drescher successfully brought the image of a Jewish woman into many different areas of popular culture. The marketing of *The Nanny* includes a "Nanny" doll and a book based on the series (*The Wit and Wisdom of "The Nanny,"* 1995). Drescher also appeared in character, with the program's children, on the cover of *Newsweek*'s special issue, "Computers and the Family" (1995). Outside of her television persona, Drescher has appeared on many television talk shows and on the covers of women's magazines. Drescher also hosted the 1996 Women in Film Crystal Awards (broadcast on the Lifetime Network), appeared in a couple of major motion pictures (*Jack*, 1996; *Beautician and the Beast*, 1997), and wrote an autobiography, *Enter Whining* (1996). Therefore, even though *The Nanny* may present a stereotypical image of a Jewish woman, Drescher has managed to introduce a Jewish woman into mainstream culture without hiding her ethnic identity.

The meaning of Fran Drescher's and *The Nanny*'s success for Jews must also take into account the attitude that *The Nanny* takes toward the stereotypes it deploys. As described in the scene opening this chapter, the program frequently draws attention to the stereotype of Jewish women embodied by Fran Fine. This scene (in which the show's Jewish women comment on the stereotypical nature of another television program) illustrates the self-conscious stylization and reflexivity of the program while emphasizing the artifice of the stereotype and opening up the possibility of viewers questioning these depictions. *The Nanny* repeatedly highlights the construction of Fran's image, overemphasizing elements of her character associated with the Jewish stereotype—such as her extreme materialism, her self-involvement, her sometimes unrefined fashion sense, her New York accent, and her use of language. In a sense, the comic excessiveness that limits Fran's strength as a woman also draws attention to and questions the "naturalness" and "reality" behind the stereotypes of Jewish women.

The program's tendency toward exaggeration and overstatement foregrounds the artificiality of Fran's character and the stereotype she embodies. *The Nanny*'s opening sequence, a musical retelling of how Fran came to work at the Sheffield home (reenacted with animated versions of the show's characters), underscores the sense of fabrication and artificiality which surround *The Nanny* ("She had style, she had flair, she was there. . . . That's how she became the nanny").

Additionally, the show frequently includes self-reflexive references to accentuate the process of its construction. For example, guest star Tyne Daly (playing a retiring nanny fearful of her future) tries to convince Fran not to worry that her life will turn out the same as Daly's. Daly explains that she never chose to be a nanny but just fell into the job: "I was working at a bridal shop in Flushing, Queens, when my boyfriend threw me out in one of those crushing scenes." Here, Daly echoes the opening line of the show's theme song about Fran's start at the Sheffields, thereby highlighting the fictionality of *The Nanny*.

The artificiality of Fran's representations is further reinforced by the program's overemphasis on certain characteristics of Fran's style. Frequent comments are made about Fran's tight-fitting and brightly colored, high-fashion outfits. When Mr. Sheffield expresses surprise on learning that fashion designer Todd Oldham is Fran's cousin, Fran responds: "How do you think a nanny could afford to dress the way I do?" *The Nanny* concedes the improbability of a nanny dressing like Fran and reminds viewers that this program is only make-believe.

Like Fran's style of dressing, her acting and voice are exaggerated,[6] and attention is drawn to their artificiality. Although this tactic of exaggerating stereotypical qualities is undoubtedly a means of poking fun at Jewish women, it also underscores the ridiculousness of the stereotype. The "over-the-top" qualities found within *The Nanny* allow viewers—instead of laughing *at* Jewish women—to laugh at the absurdity of the stereotype of Jewish women.

Behind the simple conception of this program, then, lies the possibility of alternative readings that bring to mind the notion of camp, which involves a "love of the exaggerated, the 'off,' of things-being-what-they-are-not" (Sontag, 1966, p. 279). As Sontag (1966) explains, the foregrounding of the artificial in camp allows "a private zany experience of the thing" (p. 281). *The Nanny*, by offering the opportunity to look beyond the formulaic sitcom to a camp performance of the stereotype of Jewish women, reveals the superficial and contrived silliness of this representation.[7]

Notably, Dyer (1992) emphasizes that viewing something as camp is dependent on the viewer: camp exists potentially, not inevitably. Camp, Dyer writes, "is far more a question of how you respond to things rather than qualities actually inherent in those things" (p. 138). To refer back to the scene which opens this chapter, although Fran's mother Sylvia found Mike Myers' spoof of Jewish women "very stereotypical," Fran enjoyed the skit and found humor in it. Similarly, although some people may see *The Nanny* as camp, for others it may simply reinforce stereotypes. However, the potential of *The Nanny* to allow viewers to see an alternative image of a woman on television and to question existing ethnic stereotypes offers hope that television someday will present a more diverse range of Jewish female characters: characters who do not rely on stereotypes for their humor but represent the disparate and contradictory Jewish voices of Jewish actresses involved with but not limited to their ethnic and gender identities.

ACKNOWLEDGMENTS

I would like to thank Marian Meyers, Mimi White, and Karla Fuller for their valuable assistance at various stages in the development of this chapter.

ENDNOTES

1. Both Judd Hirsch on *Taxi* and Hal Linden on *Barney Miller*, for example, portrayed characters coded as Jewish but never explicitly described as Jewish.
2. A list of Jewish female characters in current or recently canceled television shows includes: *Ned and Stacey*'s Stacey Dorcey, *Beverly Hills 90210*'s Andrea Zuckerman, *Sisters'* Frankie (who converted to Judaism), *The Commish*'s wife Rachel, the sarcastic daughter-in-law Alex on *The Five Mrs Buchanans*, the female members of the Silver family on *Brooklyn Bridge*, *thirtysomething*'s Melissa Stedman, and *Reasonable Doubts'* Tess Kaufman.
3. For example, consider Paul and Jamie Buckman on *Mad About You*, Stewart Markowitz and Ann Kelsey on *LA. Law*, Miles Silverberg and Corky Sherwood on *Murphy Brown*, Michael and Hope Stedman on *thirtysomething*, and Joel Fleischman and Maggie O'Connell on *Northern Exposure*.
4. These two caricatures of Jewish women have appeared on television programs such as *The Goldbergs*, the 1950s program that centered around matriarch Molly Goldberg, and *Rhoda*, which returned *The Mary Tyler Moore Show*'s Jewish, single woman, Rhoda, to her hometown of New York and set her against her mother, Ida, effectively bringing together the two images of the Jewish woman: the manipulating mother and the neurotic single. Gertrude Berg wrote for *The Goldbergs* and portrayed Molly Goldberg, on radio, television, and film. Berg, herself a Jewish woman, had a great deal of creative control over the program, offering an example of the ways in which Jews, while opening doors for Jewish talent, also perpetuated Jewish stereotypes. As noted earlier, Rhoda Morgenstern was played by Valerie Harper, a non-Jewish woman with enough of a New York accent to play a Jewish woman. Nancy Walker—by all indications also a non-Jew—played Rhoda's mother, Ida.

5. Plotz means to burst with emotion ("I'm so happy I could plotz")
    and a nuch schlep is a tag-along, someone unwanted.
6. Though Fran Drescher does use her "natural" voice on the program,
    she appears to magnify it by frequently whining and speaking loud-
    ly to find the comic possibilities in her accent and intonations.
7. It is important to note that I am not referring to Sontag's (1966) cat-
    egory of pure camp, which is not self-consciously trying to attain
    the level of camp, but to the "less pure" form of camp which is con-
    scious of its focus on surface style and artificiality. Clearly a more
    detailed discussion of camp is required to fully flesh out the poten-
    tial connections between *The Nanny* and the camp aesthetic.

REFERENCES

Altman, S. (1971). *The comic image of the Jew: Explorations of a popular cul-
    ture phenomenon*. Rutherford: Fairleigh Dickinson University Press.
Computers and the family [Special Issue]. (1995, Fall/Winter). *Newsweek*.
Dyer, R. (1992). It's being so camp as keeps us going. In *Only entertain-
    ment* (pp. 135-147). London: Routledge.
Erens, P. (1984). *The Jew in American cinema*. Bloomington: Indiana
    University Press.
Gans, H. (1979). Symbolic ethnicity: The future of ethnic groups and cul-
    tures in America. In H. Gans (Ed.), *On the making of Americans* (pp.
    193-220). Philadelphia: University of Pennsylvania Press.
Gilman, S. (1991). *The Jew's body*. New York: Routledge.
Gray, T.M. (1993, November 8). Review of the television program *The
    Nanny*. *Variety*, p. 32.
In the spotlight: Fran Drescher. (1993, November). *Jewish Televimages
    Report*, pp. 5-8.
Kaye/Kantrowitz, M. (1992). Is focusing on anti-semitism a diversion from
    working against racism? Relationship between Jews, race and class.
    New Jewish Agenda: Carrying it on (pp. 4-7). Conference program.
Kray, S. (1993). Orientalization of an "almost white" woman: The inter-
    locking effects of race, class, gender, and ethnicity in American
    mass media. *Critical Studies in Mass Communication, 10,* 349-366.
Lovece, F. (1992, December 13). Deck the halls with boughs of challah.
    Newsday, p. 18.
Mellencamp, P. (1990). *High anxiety: Catastrophe, scandal, age and comedy*.
    Bloomington: Indiana University Press.
Rubel, L. (1992). "The Jewish American Princess" on campus. *New Jewish
    Agenda: Carrying it on* (pp. 43-44). Conference program.
Sontag, S. (1966). Notes on "camp." In *Against interpretation* (pp. 275-
    292). New York: Dell Publishing.
Wernick, L. (1992). Jewish and white: Issues of passing. *New Jewish
    Agenda: Carrying it on* (pp. 39-40). Conference program.
The wit and wisdom of The Nanny. (1995). New York: Avon Books.
Whitfield, S. (1993). The Jew as wisdom figure. *Modern Judaism, 13,* 1-24.

V

REPRESENTING
PROGRESS

18

And She Lived Happily Every After . . . The Disney Myth in the Video Age

Jill Birnie Henke
Diane Zimmerman Umble

> There may be something there that wasn't there before . . .
> —Mrs. Potts and Cogsworth in Beauty and the Beast.

Americans swim in a sea of Disney images and merchandise. Children can watch Disney videos before they brush their teeth with a Disney character toothbrush, go to sleep in their *Beauty and the Beast* pajamas, rest their heads on *The Little Mermaid* pillow cases, check the time on *Sleeping Beauty* watches, tuck their Pocahontas doll in next to them, and drift off to sleep listening to a cassette tape of Cinderella singing "No matter how your heart is grieving, if you keep on believing, the dream that you wish will come true." American children can watch Disney stories over and over again, memorizing each lyric and line via home videos. And the entire family can see Disney's fairy tales in the theatre because Disney systematically re-releases its films to theaters on a rotation of approximately every seven years.[1]

In the face of the ubiquity of the images, sounds, and stories of Disney's interpretations of classic fairy tales, we began our study with the question: How do Disney animated features construct gender roles of heroines in the most recent animated films: *The Little Mermaid* (1989), *Beauty and the Beast* (1991) and *Pocahontas* (1995)?[2]

Our approach has been to conduct a narrative analysis of these three films from a feminist perspective that examines: (a) how women's roles are defined in the films; (b) how power is structured; (c) the degree to which women are agents of narrative action; and (d) the degree to which females shape their own destinies.[3]

The analysis shows that even though Disney's fairy tale heroines have become more assertive over time, the social worlds that shape their choices and identities remained unchanged until *Pocahontas*. Although Disney writers took creative license with Pocahontas' story in the film, the female heroine occupies the majority of the screen time, acts on her own, rejects marriage to both the warrior Kocoum and the explorer John Smith, and follows her own instincts and beliefs.

This chapter begins with a discussion of scholarly analyses of three animated Disney features. Then we analyze the films chronologically, exploring their constructions of gender.

THE WORLD OF DISNEY ANALYZED

Many scholars see the "World of Disney" as a fundamental vision of contemporary mythology. In the past, scholarly analyses of Disney productions have taken a variety of approaches, applying psychoanalytical theory, critiquing gender stereotyping, and applying Marxist feminist analysis.[4] Recent scholarship has extended earlier critical analysis of Disney productions to map "the ideological contours of economics, politics, and pedagogy by drawing Disney films as vehicles of cultural production" (Bell, Haas, & Sells, 1995, p. 7). Zipes (1995) concludes that Disney characterizations remain one-dimensional "stereotypes arranged according to a credo of domestication of the imagination" (p. 40). He argues that Disney fairy tales are neither those of the original folk tellers nor the original writers, such as Perrault (1976) or Andersen (1974); instead they are the "pale and pathetic" versions of Disney screen writers (p. 37). Murphy (1995) adopts an ecofeminist template to analyze *The Little Mermaid* and *Beauty and the Beast*, among other films, and concludes that Disney films link the exploitation of women with the exploitation of nature. Sells (1995) takes a Marxist-feminist approach to *The Little Mermaid* to examine patriarchal language, evil female characters, and the loss of voice and innocence in the film.

Earlier Disney heroines, such as *Cinderella* and *Sleeping Beauty*, were portrayed as beautiful, obedient, and essentially powerless to control their own destinies. They are thwarted by evil, jealous, female villainesses. In the end, they find safety and happiness in marriage to a prince while essentially having no narrative action of their own. The heroine is happy to accept a more comfortable life with a male controlling her new station.

Our analysis focuses on what Disney communicates about love, evil, beauty, dreams and power in its three most recent films with female heroines: *The Little Mermaid* (1989), *Beauty and the Beast* (1991), and *Pocahontas* (1995). These stories are part of the cultural repertoire for the ongoing performance and reproduction of gender roles for children. Are they really any different from what went before?

THE LITTLE MERMAID (1989)

The Little Mermaid's heroine is a sea princess named Ariel who has a beautiful singing voice. Her father is a very powerful and good sea king named Triton. Triton's nemesis is, as in other Disney tales, an evil female, Ursula the sea witch. Ursula, angry because Triton banished her from the kingdom, seeks revenge by manipulating his favorite and most beautiful daughter, Ariel. Ursula covets power—she wants to usurp Triton's position and become ruler of all the oceans. We find a theme of good versus evil, with evil personified as female.

Ariel, even though she has six sisters, has no real female community.[5] Her friends (all Disney creations) are male sea animals—Flounder, a fish; Sebastian, a crab and the royal court composer; and Scuttle, a sea gull. Scuttle substitutes for the role of the grandmother in the original Hans Christian Andersen (1974) tale. However, Scuttle is inept and gives Ariel much misinformation, whereas Andersen's grandmother gives the little mermaid accurate information about the world up above and the plight of the mermaids below.

Ariel's Dreams

From the beginning of the film Ariel is portrayed as disobedient and willful. She misses her debut concert and regularly disobeys her father's rule that "contact between the human world and the mer-world is strictly forbidden." In her song, "Part Of Your World," Ariel sings that she wants more.

> I wanna be where the people are. I wanna see—wanna see 'em dancin', walkin' around on those, what-d-ya call-'em, oh feet. Up where they walk, up where they run, up where they stay all day in the sun. Wanderin' free. . . . Betcha on land they understand. Bet they don't reprimand their daughters. Bright young women, sick of swimmin', ready to stand. . . . When's it my turn? Wouldn't I love, love to explore that shore up above, out of the sea. Wish I could be part of THAT world. (Menken & Ashman, 1990, pp. 14-21)

Ariel sings of freedom, of questioning, and of exploring new worlds. She willingly disobeys her father and Sebastian, who Triton charges with chaperoning his daughter "to protect her from herself." And Ariel acts for herself and others. She acts bravely as she rescues Eric (a human prince) from the sea as his ship explodes. Ariel also acts as she strikes a bargain with Ursula so she can become human, sacrificing her own voice in the process. She acts to stop Eric from marrying Ursula, the sea witch. And she acts when she stops Ursula from killing Eric near the end of the film. Her motivation in her quest to be human is to be with "her Prince"—which is different from the Andersen version, in which the mermaid acts to attain a human soul.

Ariel's dream changes after she rescues Eric. As Ariel lies beside the unconscious Eric on shore, she sings different lyrics to the original tune's reprise:

> What would I give to live where YOU are. What would I pay to stay here beside you? What would I do to see you smiling at me? Where would WE talk? Where would WE run if WE could stay all day in the sun, Just YOU and ME and I could be part of YOUR world. (Menken & Ashman, 1990, pp. 34-35)

Love At First Sight

Ariel instantly falls in love with Prince Eric. Her actions to win her prince cause her great personal sacrifice—she is rendered mute in the process. After Ursula turns Ariel into a human, Sebastian and Flounder must help her to shore. Later, it is Scuttle who informs Ariel that Eric is really marrying the sea witch in disguise. Ariel, who cannot swim as a human, is again taken to the ship by Flounder, while Scuttle and his sea animal friends stall the wedding. In the end, the male characters resolve the conflicts; Eric kills Ursula and Triton enables Ariel to become human again in order to marry Prince Eric. By authorizing the male characters to act on Ariel's behalf, Disney maintains a chauvinistic, patriarchal message about unempowered females and powerful males who act on their behalf.

In *The Little Mermaid*, we find a heroine who dreams of standing on her own and exploring the world up above, who questions authority and does things her way, even to the point of relinquishing her own voice. Yet by the film's close, she chooses to align herself with a powerful male to live "happily ever after in HIS world." In this, she is aided by her father, who grants her human form because now she will be under another man's rule. Power over her life merely changes from her father's rule to the prince's rule.

Tolerance

In addition to granting greater narrative agency to a female heroine, Disney presented new themes, such as tolerance, in *The Little Mermaid* (to be developed more fully in *Beauty and the Beast*). Although a patriarchal system prevails, and the males attempt to control the young heroine's life, their attempts to do so present young viewers with a lesson in tolerance. Sebastian tells Ariel that "looking leads to wanting and wanting leads to trouble;" Triton angrily tells Ariel that humans are "all spineless, savage, harpooning fish-eaters." Triton says that had Ariel let Eric drown, it would be just "one less human to worry about." Triton also tells Ariel that he does not need to know Eric because "they're all alike."

Triton uses stereotypes to describe humans, whereas Ariel tries to explain to him that Eric is different. Ariel tells her friend, Flounder, that she wishes she could "make her father understand" and "listen" to her. The film presents a male power figure representing the status quo who is unwilling to explore or even consider alternatives, especially those ideas espoused by a young mermaid.

Ariel is a "misunderstood teenager" who wants to expand her horizons. She looks at the artifacts she has collected and wonders how a people who can create such beautiful things can be "all bad." But it is the male power figure who defines what is good or bad, what is beautiful or ugly, and who sets limits for Ariel. Eric also is open in his acceptance of Ariel, even though she is mute. After Ariel turns back into a mermaid, Eric determines he "lost her once, I'm not going to do it again."

Our heroine is constantly constrained by either a jealous, power-hungry female (Ursula) or by males—Triton, Sebastian, Flounder and Scuttle, and even Eric. In the end, Ariel denies her own identity as a mermaid and looks longingly at Eric, who is washed onto the shore. Her father enables Ariel to be human once more by using the power of his magic scepter to transform her. Although Triton had the power to transform Ariel all along, he withheld his action until he saw Ariel under another man's power. As Ariel walks ashore and kisses Eric, the scene dissolves into them kissing on their wedding ship. Ariel waves good-bye to Triton and the sea world as Triton waves his scepter, placing a rainbow in the sky to symbolize peace between the two different worlds. Although their worlds are at peace, Ariel must forsake her world to live in Eric's human domain.

BEAUTY AND THE BEAST (1991)

Disney's rendition of *Beauty and the Beast* represents the incremental development of Disney heroines as narrative agents. Based on a story published in France in 1756 by Madame Le Prince de Beaumont, the animated version is the first to be written for Disney by a female scriptwriter.[6] Belle is portrayed as smart, strong, and courageous.

Belle's Dreams

Indeed, Belle is no damsel in distress, and she takes far more action than Ariel in *The Little Mermaid*. Neither is she a helpless witness to the action or removed from it. Belle occupies double the screen time of any other character in the film (Thomas, 1991, p. 181). She acts for herself, reads (novels about meeting Prince Charming), and dreams of "more than this provincial life." She wants adventure: "for once it might be grand, to have someone understand, I want so much more than they've got planned" (Menken & Ashman, 1991, pp. 21-22).

Belle helps her father with his experiments. She rejects the uninvited advances of Gaston, the most attractive and powerful man in the village, and she leaves the village to find and rescue her father, offering herself as the Beast's prisoner in his place. She refuses the Beast's demands to dine with him; she explores the castle, despite warnings to avoid the west wing; and she uses her charm to disarm the servants. She flees the castle in the face of the Beast's burst of temper, and she takes the injured Beast back to the castle to dress his wounds instead of taking the opportunity to run away. She scolds him for his behavior, standing up to his verbal abuse. She leaves the castle again to rescue her father and nurses him back to health. She argues with Gaston and the villagers in an attempt to head off the mob, and she returns to the castle to warn the Beast of the impending attack. Near the end, she saves the Beast again. And in the end, her love is the agent of his liberation. Her confession of love releases the prince from his bestial form. Here is a heroine who is at the center of the action.

Missing from this Disney tale is the evil villainess. Disney's adaptation of the story eliminates the two jealous, materialistic, plotting sisters from the original story. The father is translated from a failed merchant who steals a rose from the Beast's garden into a bumbling inventor. In the Disney version, the rose functions to mark the passage of the time the Beast has left to win the love of another. The standard Disney animal helpers become enchanted objects in *Beauty and the Beast*: a candle stick, a clock, a teapot, a cup, a wardrobe, and a feather duster.

A Different Version of Love

Here, too, we find a different version of love. Love is not activated at first sight or even with the first kiss—it is much more complex. Gaston defines love in terms of physical appearance, when he sings "Belle," in the opening number of the film:

Right from the moment when I met her, saw her, I said she's gorgeous and I fell. Here in town there's only she who is beautiful as me, so I'm making plans to woo and marry Belle. (Menken & Ashman, 1991, pp. 14-15)

In contrast, Belle, by her actions, defines love not by physical appearance, but by sacrifice. She offers herself in her father's place and risks physical danger to protect him from the elements.

The film also proposes that love involves struggle, discovery, and compromise. In the song entitled "Beauty and the Beast," Mrs. Potts, the teapot, sings:

Barely even friends, then somebody bends unexpectedly. Just a little change. Small to say the least. Both a little scared, neither one prepared, Beauty and the Beast. (Menken & Ashman, 1991, pp. 74-78)

Nevertheless, in the same song she also sings about the growth of love as inevitable: "tale as old as time, true as it can be," and, later in the song, "Certain as the sun, rising in the East" (Menken & Ashman, 1991, pp. 74-78). In the song, "Something There," Belle admits that the Beast is "no Prince Charming," yet she sings, "but there's something in him that I simply didn't see" (Menken & Ashman, 1991, pp. 57, 59). Like Ariel, Belle finds love after struggle, great personal risk, and sacrifice.

Beauty Within

At the beginning of the film, the narrator recounts how the spell came to be cast on the Beast, warning us that we should not be "deceived by appearances; beauty is within." On the surface, this notion of "beauty within" seems to be the theme of the film. As elaborated, however, the contrast between ugliness and beauty is enmeshed in a debate over what is human and beastly and what is civilized and uncivilized. During the narrator's voice-over, we see the tattered ruins of the Beast's lair. It is dark and foreboding. Signs of civilization—tapestries and portraits—are in ruin. Immediately after the prologue, we are introduced to both Belle and Gaston in the village. The villagers sing about how different Belle is: a beauty, but rather odd, her nose stuck in a book, strange but special. Gaston, we are told, also is gorgeous, the greatest hunter in the world, and a tall, dark, strong, and handsome brute. His side-kick, Le Fou, tells him, "No beast alive stands a chance against you, and no girl for that matter."

Although a respected and admired member of the community, Gaston is portrayed as less than civilized. Belle calls him "primeval," and he takes it as a compliment. Later she describes him as "boorish" and "brainless." He stomps on Belle's books, covering them with mud, and tells her that "it's not right for a woman to read—it puts ideas in their heads." Later he is consigned to the mud with the pigs after he proposes to Belle. Gaston is large, he shoots beasts, uses antlers in all of his decorating, and is especially good at expectorating. Ultimately, he resorts to force in his efforts to "win" Belle.[7] Gaston incites the mob to attack the Beast by appealing to their fears. In "The Mob Song," the villagers sing:

> We don't like what we don't understand; in fact, it scares us and this monster is mysterious at least. Bring your guns, bring your knives, save your children and your wives. We'll save our village and our lives. We'll kill the Beast! (Menken & Ashman, 1991, pp. 68-69)

Gaston leads the mob in the plunder of the castle, and he stabs the Beast in the back. He taunts the Beast into defending himself, but after the Beast sets him free, Gaston attacks him from the rear. Gaston fights without honor. His quest for Belle brings out the beast in him.

The Beast, on the other hand, has the physical attributes of an animal. And he has an explosive temper that leads to verbal abuse. His displays of ferocity are manifested first when he is confronted by Belle's father, Maurice. Maurice is an intruder who threatens the Beast's privacy, and the Beast throws him in the dungeon and then throws him out of the castle. The Beast roars again when Belle reaches out to touch the rose, an object he must protect to keep his hope alive. He frightens her away, and then rescues her by fighting off the wolves. He gives Belle the gigantic library (symbolic of civilized life) in his possession and encourages her reading. In her presence, he straightens his bearing, polishes his manners, and learns to control his temper. In the battle scene at the end of the film, the Beast does not defend himself until Belle reappears. He submits to Belle's pleas and releases Gaston, instead of killing him. In the case of the Beast, Belle brings out the human in him.

Belle, An Agent of Transformation

In the film, the theme of beauty is elaborated onto a conflict over what it means to be human or beastly, civilized or uncivilized. Belle is the central figure in the animation of this conflict, and she is the agent of transformation. In his quest to have her, Gaston becomes beastly and pays with his life. Through the Beast's love for her, the Beast becomes human. Belle is repelled by Gaston and learns to love the Beast. Her role as agent of transformation serves to preserve civilized life.[8]

Nevertheless, Belle's happiness "forever after" is defined in exactly the same way as it is for her counterparts. Belle's happiness, in the end, is found in her submission to a Prince. Her dreams for "something more" come true in the form of marriage to a prince and a life in his world.

POCAHONTAS (1995)

Pocahontas extends the development of Disney heroines as narrative agents, and she is the first non-Caucasian human princess to have a film of her own.[9] Pocahontas is a princess story based loosely in history, rather than a fairy tale. Disney makes a concerted attempt to portray Native Americans in a positive light, as opposed to their former portrayals as caricatures in films such as *Peter Pan* (1953). *Pocahontas* also presents the first image of a father who is not bumbling, but instead is sensitive to his daughter's dreams and encourages her to find her destiny.

Pocahontas is the first Disney heroine to have her own female friends and mentors. Although Pocahontas is motherless, the film portrays her mother as a strong, guiding spirit. Pocahontas feels the presence of her mother at every defining moment of the film through the physical manifestation of the wind that sweeps around her and her people. The spirit mother is alive in the memory and the temporal experience of the people of the tribe. Pocahontas also receives guidance and insight from Grandmother Willow, a 400-year-old willow tree that is Pocahontas's spiritual mentor. Grandmother Willow encourages Pocahontas in her quest to find the meaning of her dreams by assuring her that her mother asked the same questions.

Pocahontas's Dreams

Like other Disney heroines, Pocahontas has dreams. Her search for the meaning of her dreams becomes a narrative theme throughout the story. Pocahontas's dreams, unlike those of the previous Disney heroines, were not immediately personified. Pocahontas dreams of a spinning arrow and white clouds, of change, of something coming. Pocahontas begins a journey in search of an interpretation of her dreams, whereas the earlier heroines saw their dreams fulfilled by a man. Pocahontas talks about her dreams with her friend, Nakoma, Grandmother Willow, and her father, Chief Powhatan. Even though Pocahontas's father would like her to marry the warrior Kocoum, she seems to have an intuitive sense that marriage is not the end of her quest. In the song, "Just Around The River Bend," she asks:

> Should I choose the smoothest course, steady as the beating drum? Should I marry Kocoum? Is all my dreaming at an end? Or do you still wait for me, Dream Giver, just around the river bend? (Menken & Schwartz, 1995, pp. 23-23)

Unlike the other Disney heroines, Pocahontas recognizes risks and acts to make deliberate choices, rather than simply reacting to circumstances as they occur. In her first song in the film, "Just Around The River Bend," she sings:

> The water's always changing, always flowing. But people, I guess, can't live like that; we all must pay a price: to be safe, we lose our chance of ever knowing what's around the river bend. (Menken & Schwartz, 1995, pp. 18-19)

Grandmother Willow, too, recognizes that the journey may be hard and advises Pocahontas to continue her quest, reminding her that the "right path isn't always the easiest." Unlike the dreams of other Disney heroines, Pocahontas's dreams must be interpreted through testing and experience. Her dreams force her to make difficult choices and place her in danger. The fulfillment of Pocahontas's dream is more important than a relationship with a man. Fulfillment represents her destiny, not only as an individual, but as the leader of her people. Her destiny is not defined by marriage and a future family, as in previous films which perpetuate the status quo. By assuming the spiritual, political, and cultural leadership of her people, Pocahontas represents an alternative to conventional notions of women's roles. The affirmation of her cultural heritage and Pocahontas's leadership in her community are unique developments in the progression of the heroine in Disney animated features.

Spiritual Love

Love, as in *Beauty and the Beast*, is not at first sight. However, love in *Pocahontas* is different, too, from *Beauty and the Beast*. John Smith first lays eyes on Pocahontas as she appears almost ephemeral, rising from the mist of a waterfall. Pocahontas seems larger than life. John Smith, who holds a gun, seems awestruck and lays down his weapon. Pocahontas peers at him, then runs away. She runs like the wind, an illusion to the spirits who guide her. Even though Pocahontas is portrayed as more beautiful and shapely than the other female members of her own community, the film does not suggest that Smith is smitten by her beauty alone. It is her larger than life presence that strikes him. She becomes his teacher, for he believes all Indians are ignorant savages. Pocahontas chides him as she sings "The Colors of the Wind":

> You think I'm an ignorant savage, and you've been so many places, I guess it must be so. But still I cannot see, if the savage one is me, how can there be so much that you don't know? . . . I know ev'ry rock and tree and creature has a life, has a spirit, has a name. You think the only people who are people are the people who look and think like you, but if you walk the footsteps of a stranger you'll learn things you never knew, you never knew. (Menken & Schwartz, 1995, pp. 43-45)

She wins Smith's respect through her knowledge and wisdom. She advocates that neither culture is better than the other, only different. Late in the film, Pocahontas declares her love for John Smith as she saves his life. She goes on to say, "Look around you—look where this path of hatred has brought us, this is the path I choose—[as she cradles Smith]—what will yours be?" Her father announces to the warriors and the approaching Englishmen: "My daughter speaks with wisdom beyond her years. She comes with courage and understanding." And he proclaims that his people will not be the first ones to take a life. In this film, love is not at first sight. It is not based on physical attraction, and it is not happily ever after. Love can be shared without lodging it in a marriage relationship. Love, in *Pocahontas*, is built on appreciation of difference and mutual respect for another's knowledge, wisdom, and culture.

Tolerance With a Twist

Although Pocahontas teaches John Smith to appreciate and value her culture, the members of their respective communities find these same lessons more difficult to learn. The climax of the film places the English and Indian communities on the edge of armed conflict. As they each prepare for battle, they display their respective prejudices about the other. In the chorus, from the song entitled "Savages," they all call: "Destroy their evil race, until there's not a trace left. We will sound the drums of war" (Menken & Schwartz, 1995, p. 54). Despite their shared convictions of the other's savagery, Disney's portrayal of the Englishmen is predominantly negative. They are portrayed as inept and greedy, displaying blatant disrespect for the land they seek to "own." While the Englishmen dig for gold, the Native Americans cultivate their golden corn—the key to survival for both communities in the end. Cultural conflict in the other Disney films analyzed was framed by the dominant culture. The heroine in those films consistently conformed to the culture of her new husband. Pocahontas twists this convention around by its positive portrayal of Native peoples and its affirmation of their contributions. At the end, Chief Powhatan tells Smith that "you are always welcome among my people" and calls him "brother."[10] The English leave without riches, but the film suggests they are rich in the knowledge that some things are more valuable than gold.

Disney's previous film conventions are further challenged when Pocahontas refuses to leave her homeland to go with Smith. When Smith asks her to go with him, Chief Powhatan says, "You must choose your own path." And Pocahontas responds, "I'm needed here." When Smith declares, "I cannot leave you," she replies, "You never will—no matter what happens, I'll always be with you, forever." As Pocahontas runs to the cliff to watch Smith's ship sail away, Smith signs the Native American sign for good-bye that she taught him, as the spirit of the wind surrounds them both from her place atop the cliff to his place on the ship. The closing images of the film show Pocahontas encircled by the swirling wind, symbolically portraying her as the spirit of the wind and the leader of her people.

CONCLUSION

Until 1995, the Disney animated feature remained much the same as it was in the 1950s. Even though Disney heroines Ariel and Belle are allowed greater narrative action than their predecessors, the majority of female heroines are perennially under the control of a male. Furthermore, most females with power, such as Ursula, are portrayed as evil. The films are filled with absent mothers and inept fathers. Minor female characters are portrayed as servants—ugly, ill-tempered, and less powerful than their evil counterparts or the males in the story. Female communities are, for the most part, nonexistent, even when they are a part of the original story, as in Andersen's *The Little Mermaid.*

Until *Pocahontas,* Disney females who showed spirit, intellectual curiosity, or disregard for authority always suffered and inevitably accepted male control, as did both Ariel and Belle by the end of their films. Males who could help the female heroines achieve their goals are either bumbling or powerless (Maurice), jealous (Gaston), or refuse to help (Triton). The heroines' friends are nonexistent for the most part and are cast in the Disney versions as animals or household objects. These friends also are usually male.

Prior to 1995, Disney's heroines were fundamentally alone and vulnerable outside a nurturing female community.[11] Even though Ariel and Belle advocate exploration and acceptance of other cultures and what it means to be civilized, they, too, in the end, give up their dreams to become part of their true love's world. And in the indomitable Disney way, they "live happily ever after."

Pocahontas represents a significant shift in the construction of a Disney heroine. She is portrayed as a strong, young woman who pursues her destiny in the context of a loving, supportive community that encourages her to follow her dreams. Happiness is not equated with love and marriage, but by an affirmation of her destiny as a leader. Critics may say this is Disney's means of avoiding the portrayal of interracial marriage. Nevertheless, Pocahontas is portrayed as a person of value on her own terms, a theme unique to Disney heroines.

What do these films communicate to children about love, dreams, and happiness—and how to achieve them? How is gender constructed and performed in the world of Disney? In a world where women are struggling to be heard, it is disconcerting to see a heroine relinquish her voice in order to pursue her dreams. In a world where women are trying to expand their social and intellectual horizons, it is troubling to note the messages that physical attractiveness is paramount and girls who are inquisitive are disobedient and peculiar.[12] Most Disney heroines suffer for challenging conventional expectations, and, in the end, they submit to the patriarchal system. It is equally disquieting to witness an adventurous role model define her future happiness solely in terms of marriage to a handsome prince. It seems that Disney's heroines have only been "sowing their oats," and with maturity come to understand that the prescription for happiness "ever after" is not their individuality or their accomplishments, but who they marry.

Admittedly, a heroine who reads and explores is an improvement over one who sleeps through most of her own story, as does Sleeping Beauty. Furthermore, Pocahontas does break the conventional norms for a Disney heroine by providing a model of self-actualization. However, the film itself denies the facts of her experience as a person of historical record. The "real" Pocahontas did not live "happily ever after" as a leader of her people, as the film proposes. She was held captive in an English stockade, married one of her English captors, and later died of small pox in England, far from her native home.

Finally, although Pocahontas provides a sign of hope for a broader construction of female roles, she does not supersede the previous heroines. Earlier Disney female characters, including Cinderella, Sleeping Beauty's Aurora, Ariel, and Belle, continue to coexist in the cultural repertoire, available for repetition the next time we watch a Disney video. Pocahontas is but one voice among the others, competing for space, waiting to be heard:

> I don't know what I can do, still I know I've got to try. Eagle, help my feet to fly. Mountain help my heart be great. Spirits of the earth and sky, please don't let it be too late. (Menken & Schwartz, 1995, pp. 58-59)

ENDNOTES

1. In 1991, *Beauty and the Beast* became Disney's all time box office favorite, earning $144.8 million. Second of the top five favorites is *The Little Mermaid* (1989), which earned $84.3 million ("A wish," 1992). In addition, 8 million video cassettes of *The Little Mermaid* and 21 million copies of *Beauty and the Beast* were sold (Landis, 1994). And although *Aladdin* and *Lion King* grossed more money than *Pocahontas* at the box office, *Pocahontas* still grossed $125 million for Disney—quite respectable given the fact that "one of Hollywood's truisms is that both sexes go to boys' movies, but boys don't go to girls' movies" (Shapiro, 1995, p. 57).
2. We excluded an analysis of Aladdin because it is Aladdin's story; Jasmine is only a secondary character in that film.
3. Disney films also would be fertile ground for an analysis of the construction of social class. Many of Disney heroines either are royalty or become royalty through marriage.

4. Brody (1976) describes the success of Disney fairy tales from a psychoanalytic perspective. Trites (1991) contrasts from a Freudian perspective Disney's version of *The Little Mermaid* with the original Hans Christian Andersen tale. Others (May, 1981; Stone, 1975) critique the way in which Disney selectively appropriated classics of children's literature. Sex-role stereotyping has been the focus of Levinson (1975) and Holmlund (1979) extends concerns about stereotyping using a Marxist feminist approach to the sexual politics of Disney films. Some work has celebrated Disney films for their connection to the oral tradition (Allan, 1988) and their artistic accomplishments (Morrow, 1978).

5. We see the sisters only three times during the film—once to introduce Ariel, next when they reveal to Triton that Ariel is in love, and, finally, to wave good-bye to her as she marries the human prince, Eric. This lack of female community is in direct contrast to the original Andersen version of the tale, in which her grandmother, whom Disney omits from the story altogether, and Ariel's sisters figure prominently.

6. Linda Woolverton, the screenwriter, writes:

> It's very difficult to take the originals and convert them into a story that works for the Nineties. You have to consider what kids are like now in terms of sophistication, you have to make sure that your themes are strong, that people can relate to the characters, that the story isn't sexist. Belle is a strong, smart, courageous woman. She sacrifices herself for her father. There are great themes. She's a Disney heroine who reads books. It excites me. We've never seen that before. (cited in Thomas, 1991, p. 43)

7. Belle is unwilling to submit to Gaston's offer of marriage in exchange for her father's freedom.

8. Belle's role as the agent of the Beast's transformation is not unproblematic. Disney portrays her in stereotypical roles as teacher, caregiver, and nurturer, which could lead some children to assume these roles are the only ones acceptable for females.

9. Princess Jasmine also is a non-Caucasian beauty, but she appears as only a secondary character to Aladdin in the film of the same name.

10. Russell Means, who lends his voice to the character of Chief Powhatan, says: "Pocahontas tells children that pigmentation and skin color have no place in relationships between human beings. If Disney can tell the truth to children, then adults can take it" (Wloszczyna, 1995, p. 5D).

11. Friends of the heroine also are nonexistent for the most part and are cast in the Disney version as animals or household objects who also usually are male. Sebastian, Flounder, and Scuttle are male sea creatures in *The Little Mermaid*; and Cogsworth, Lumiere, and Chip in *Beauty and the Beast* are male household objects. Although Mrs.

Potts, the feather duster, and the wardrobe are female objects, they play lesser roles. In *Pocahontas*, two animal friends, Meeko and Flit, are neither gendered nor do they speak.

12. The Disney heroine is portrayed as virginal, shapely and physically attractive, an approach that perpetuates a limited cultural vision of beauty and acceptance.

REFERENCES

A wish for Aladdin. (1992, November 4) *USA Today*, p. 10.

Allan, R. (1988). 50 years of Snow White. *Journal of Popular Film and Television, 15*(4), 156-163.

Andersen, H. C. (1974). *The complete fairy tales and stories* (E. Christian Haugaard, trans.). Garden City, NY: Doubleday.

Bell, E., Haas, L., & Sells, L. (Eds.). (1995). *From mouse to mermaid: The politics of film, gender, and culture.* Bloomington and Indianapolis: Indiana University Press.

Beaumont, M. L. P. (1990). *Beauty and the Beast* (R. Howard, trans.). New York: Simon and Schuster.

Brody, M. (1976). The wonderful world of Disney—its psychological appeal. *American Imago, 33*(4), 350-360.

Holmlund, C. (1979, Summer). Tots to tanks: Walk Disney presents feminism for the family. *Social Text, 2*, 122-132.

Landis, D. (1994, February 23). Heigh-ho, heigh-ho, it's off to video. *USA Today*, p. 10.

Levinson, R. M. (1975). From Olive Oyl to Sweet Polly Purebread: Sex role stereotypes and televised cartoons. *Journal of Popular Culture, 9*, 561-572.

May, J. (1981). Walt Disney's interpretation of children's literature. *Language Arts, 58*(4), 463-472.

Menken, A., & Ashman, H. (1990). *The Little Mermaid songs for piano.* Milwaukee, WI: Hal Leonard Publishing.

Menken, A., & Ashman, H. (1991). *Beauty and the Beast songs for piano.* Milwaukee, WI: Hal Leonard Publishing.

Menken, A, & Schwartz, S. (1995). *Pocahontas.* Milwaukee, WI: Hal Leonard Publishing.

Morrow, J. (1978). In defense of Disney. *Media and Methods, 14*(8), 28-34.

Murphy, P. (1995). The whole wide world was scrubbed clean: The androcentric animation of denatured Disney. In E. Bell, L. Haas, & L. Sells (Eds.), *From mouse to mermaid: The politics of film, gender, and culture* (pp. 125-136). Bloomington and Indianapolis: Indiana University Press.

Perrault, C. (1976). *The sleeping beauty* (D. Walker, trans.). New York: Crowell Publishers.

Sells, L. (1995). "Where do the mermaids stand?": Voice and body in *The Little Mermaid*. In E. Bell, L. Haas, & L. Sells, (Eds.), *From mouse to mermaid: The politics of film, gender, and culture* (pp. 175-192). Bloomington and Indianapolis: Indiana University Press.

Shapiro, L. (with Chang, Y.). (1995, May 22). The girls of summer. *Newsweek*, pp. 56-57.

Stone, K. (1975). Things Walt Disney never told us. *Journal of American Folklore, 88*(347), 42-50.

Thomas, B. (1991). *Disney's art of animation*. New York: Hyperion.

Trites, R. (1991). Disney's sub-version of Andersen's "The Little Mermaid." *Journal of Popular Film and Television, 18*(4), 145-152.

Wloszczyna, S. (1995, June 16). Bringing "Pocahontas" to animated life: Russel Means hails portrayal of the chief. *USA Today*, p. 5D.

Zipes, J. (1995). Breaking the Disney spell. In E. Bell, L. Haas, & L. Sells (Eds.), *From mouse to mermaid: The politics of film, gender, and culture* (pp. 21-42). Bloomington and Indianapolis: Indiana University Press.

19

Las Familias y Las Latinas: Mediated Representations of Gender Roles

Lisa A. Flores
Michelle A. Holling

Beginning in 1987, films that centered on Latinas/os became more common in U.S. mainstream film culture. With films such as *The Milagro Beanfield War, Stand and Deliver, La Bamba,* and *Born in East L.A.,* all released in 1987 and 1988, "Hispanic Hollywood" drew America's eyes toward Latino/a culture. Since that time a few more films have gained box office exposure across the United States.[1] Following this recent growth of Latina/o films has been increased critical attention to the characterization of Latinos/as in mass media (see Fregosa, 1993; Fregosa & Chabram, 1990; Noriega, 1992; Noriega & López, 1996). Although much development has occurred in Latina/o cinema, few studies have explored in detail the characterization of Latinas/os in U.S. mainstream mass media.

This chapter seeks to further the dialogue on Latinas in film by examining two recent productions: *The Perez Family* and *Mi Familia/My Family.* These two films, both in theaters in 1994/95, mark the current moment in Latinas/os of film and offer two possible visions for Latina representation. As both movie titles suggest, family is a predominant theme in the representations of Latinas/os.

The concept of *la familia* [the family] among Mexican Americans serves as a means through which cultural values, attitudes, and assumptions are taught (Gangotena, 1994). Gangotena (1994) discusses several rhetorical devices in the discourse of Mexican Americans (i.e., harmony/silence; rationality/emotionalism; the concept of personhood; respect for hierarchy, age and gender; and solidarity and a sense of community). These devices create a rhetorical vision that provides for a fuller understanding of family, specifically women's roles, among Mexican Americans. Gangotena (1994) concludes her article by stating: "As the Euro-American community becomes more aware of the rhetorical vision of *la familia* and comes to respect it, Mexican Americans will be granted a more distinguished place in American life" (p. 79). With such a position, viewing audiences will gain alternative ways of understanding and coming to know the Latina/o population that challenge traditional representations.

Historically, depictions of Latinas/os in mass media have been one-dimensional and, largely, negative. Latinas/os are commonly depicted as being lecherous, thieving, dirty, violent, and cowardly (Limón, 1992; Pettit, 1980). Often emphasized in representations of Latinas/os is sexuality. In early films, the attention to the Latin lover signaled a move away from criminal depictions and toward a new standard of beauty (Rios Bustamante, 1992). However, as Rios Bustamante (1992) explains, often within the Latin lover character was an element of danger and a "dark and primitive sexuality," or a "'greaser girl of easy virtue'" (p. 24). Thus, the Latin lover image, although broadening conceptions of beauty to include darker features, was a double-edged sword, promising a new Latin character type, but still falling into the original trap of a tainted character.

For Latinas, the attention to attractiveness turned quickly to a heightened representation of sexuality. According to Cortés (1985), the most common depiction of the Latina is as a whore. Pettit (1980) agrees and notes that "the most obvious . . . female stereotype . . . is the half-breed harlot. Her primary function is . . . to provide as much sexual titillation as current censorship standards will permit" (p. 61). Within this equation of Latinas and sexuality are the notions of the Latina Spit Fire, or the embodiment of the sexual and sensual woman or the "hot" woman, and the Chiquita Banana, which exoticizes and naturalizes the "primitive" Latina who is equated with jungle themes (Fregoso & Chabram, 1990). This depiction of Latinas as sexual bodies is not limited to Anglo productions, but extends into those from within Latino/a communities, which often relegate women in film to secondary and gender stereotypical roles (Broyles González, 1990; Cotto-Escalera, 1990; Fregoso, 1993).

Motherhood is also a central theme in media representations of Latinas, with Latina mothers often falling into the category of good mother, defined as the self-sacrificing and/or virginal mother, and coded as the *Madre Sufrida or La Virgen* (Garcia, 1990; Herrera-Sobek, 1985; Mirandé & Enríquez, 1979). Opposite of and as common in media representations as the good mother is the evil mother, who abandons or mistreats her children and often is sexually promiscuous (Anaya, 1984; Herrera-Sobek, 1982). In Chicano/a and Mexican culture, the evil mother has taken the form of *La Malinche*, the traitor/whore who was deemed responsible for the downfall of Mexico, and *La Llorona*, the paramount evil mother who killed her children and is destined to walk the earth grieving for them (Anaya, 1984; Herrera-Sobek, 1982; Paz, 1961).

The limitations placed on the concept of motherhood result in a denigration of mothers, for, in much Latino/a and Western popular discourse, women become bad mothers. From fairy tales such as Cinderella and Snow White in the West to legendary Mexican women such as *La Malinche* and *La Llorona*, the stereotype of the evil mother is perpetuated. Within Latino/a discourse, the evil mother often is also a traitor, betraying her people for selfish gain.

However, the performance of such roles, constituted in the private sphere, need not be constrained by such traditional and problematic stereotypic depictions of viewing women solely as mothers, wives, and daughters. Rather, these roles can be developed such that the role does not *define* the woman. The emphasis can be shifted from the role itself (i.e., wife, mother) to the woman in the role. Although familial roles for women are often stereotypic, they are not inherently problematic. Female characters can maintain individuality within their roles as wives and mothers, and by doing so, can challenge the stereotypic boundaries of those roles.

ANALYSIS OF FEMALE REPRESENTATIONS: *THE PEREZ FAMILY*

The representation of Latinas in mass media today remains a central question. In the case of the 1995 film *The Perez Family*, the answer to how Latinas/os are positioned in film is much the same as it has been. The film records the voyage of marielitos[2] escaping Castro's Cuba and searching for freedom in the United States, and Cuban Americans who have already made new homes in the United States. The women in the film fall into the virgin/whore dichotomy. Added to the dilemma of the categorical positioning is the question of legality. In *The Perez Family*, the undesirable elements of Cuba, found in the sexuality and criminality of the characters, make their way to the United States.

The two main female characters in *The Perez Family* function as opposites, with Dottie (Marisa Tomei) representing Cuban culture encapsulated in sexuality and Carmela (Anjelica Huston) portraying assimilated Cuban American culture depicted in purity. With this dichotomy, *The Perez Family* continues to use sexuality as the dominant lens through which mainstream America understands Latina populations. The most prominent depiction of sexuality comes in the character of Dottie Perez, who yearns for the United States and the chance to meet and sleep with John Wayne. With her black high heels, bright clothing, and swinging hips, Dottie embodies the Latina whore. The viewers learn early in their introduction to Dottie that the only jobs she has held are cutting sugar cane and whoring.

Dottie's goal throughout the film is to become a U.S. citizen. In her quest, she is willing to buy legitimacy through the bed. The selling of Dottie is accomplished in the film through the various interactions she has with America, usually white America. Sitting astride her "white hero" with her skirt up around her waist, she hopes for an escape from the refugee camp. On the street corner selling flowers and dressed scantily and flamboyantly, Dottie plans on buying her way to the freedom she desires. Within the "respectable" job of selling flowers on the street is the reference to the parallel street whore, who also approaches drivers flaunting her wares.

In stark contrast to the images of Dottie dancing her way through life in bra and panties is Carmela Perez, the long-suffering wife and mother. Carmela has devoted the past 20 years to raising her daughter in a respectable and sterile Anglo suburb and waiting faithfully and patiently for the arrival of her husband, Juan Raul Perez (Alfred Molina), from Cuba, where he has been imprisoned for 20 years for refusing to bow to Castro's regime. Carmela, clad in soft pastels and whites, embodies the virginal and pure image of Latinas. The virginal allusions in Carmela are magnified when viewers learn she has repressed her sexuality for 20 years in faithfulness to her husband.

Through her purity, Carmela gains access and acceptance into Anglo American culture. Carmela's movement into Anglo American culture is signaled in the film through her home life. Carmela is typically positioned throughout the film in her suburban home and engaged in such activities as making lemonade, enjoying a bubble bath, and talking with her daughter, Teresa (Trini Alvarado). Her home life is absent of the cultural signs of Cuba that surround Dottie, and the contrast between Dottie's obvious Cuban culture and street home and the absence of that Cubanness in Carmela's life moves Carmela into an acultural and, hence, Anglo identity position.

Implied in Carmela's character is also a helplessness and dependence on men. In the absence of her husband, Carmela is cared for and protected by her domineering and macho brother, Angel, who buys her a gun and installs a complex security system in her house that she invariably, through technological ignorance, sets off. When she comes to understand that her husband will not return, Carmela replaces him and her brother with a third male protector, Officer Pirelli (Chazz Palminteri), who responds to the frequent triggering of the alarm system. As she moves from one male guardian to another, Carmela remains demure and sweet. In Carmela's attraction to Officer Pirelli, the audience is reminded of her purity, for their romance moves slowly with intimacy indicated in light touches of hands, glances, and finally a kiss. The juxtaposition between Carmela's innocent romance with Dottie's interest in more sensual play highlights Carmela's purity and Dottie's promiscuity.

The two Perez women, who represent the good and the bad, the pure and the tainted, are connected to each other through the character of Juan Raul Perez, Carmela's legal husband and Dottie's adopted husband. With Juan Raul, the recognized head of the Perez family, the film continues the tradition of diminishing the importance of female characters, for Juan fills neither the good nor the bad role. Instead, he is awarded a more complex and multidimensional role that eventually centers him in the film. Faithful to his wife and daughter, Carmela and Teresa, Juan resists Dottie's proposal that they form a Perez family and thus escape the refugee camp. Although Juan is torn between two families, he ultimately legitimates both, freeing Carmela and joining with Dottie. It is only with Juan's "permission" that Carmela feels able to be with Pirelli, and it is again Juan who makes Dottie's plan for freedom work. Thus, by the end of the film, Juan becomes the mainstay of the Perez family, and Dottie's and Carmela's actions and wishes are made possible through Juan.

Although early in the film Juan resists Dottie's attempts to position him as the head of their family, he assumes this role once it is clear that neither Dottie nor Carmela can manage it. As the center of the family, Juan is able to merge his first family with his second. Through Juan's character, the film pushes at traditional definitions of family, moving beyond family as necessarily based in biology and marriage to family as a union of people joined by need. In this constructed family, we recognize the extended family as defining family, which is common in Latina/o cultures.

The play on the extended family continues throughout the film, beginning with the title *The Perez Family*, which implies a single family. Although the film shows us two seemingly separate families, or perhaps only the one "true" family comprised of separated husband and wife Juan and Carmela, daughter Teresa, and in-law Angel, *The Perez Family* also asks viewers to envision a larger family. In this broadening of the boundaries of the extended family to include those who share a need and a name, *The Perez Family* bridges the contrasts between the Cuban culture, as seen in Dottie, and the Cuban American culture, contained in Carmela.

In this challenge to limiting definitions of family, *The Perez Family* offers a version of family pieced together in necessity and name. Dottie, desperate for freedom and devoid of inhibitions, builds a family for herself. She learns upon arriving in the United States that single adults are a low priority in getting sponsors, whereas families of three or more are the top priority. Her response to this knowledge is to find a husband, Juan Raul Perez, a son, Felipe Perez, and a father-in-law, Papi Perez. Though she must convince each of the three that they want to become a family, they do join forces and find a sponsor.

As Dottie finagles her way to a family and thus to legitimacy in the United States a displacement occurs. Fregoso (1993) explains that Latina representation in mass media often suffers from displacement in which (usually female) characters become carriers of meaning, standing in for larger cultural and societal images. In *The Perez Family*, Dottie embodies the Cuban opportunist who threatens the integrity of American culture by taking what she can get without earning it, in contrast to Juan, who prefers to follow a more traditional path to family and legitimacy. Dottie's lack of social conscience is evident in her willingness to coopt the place of the real Mrs. Perez, as well as in Dottie's flamboyant sexuality. Anglo Floridians, and to some degree the larger national culture, have expressed concern with a Cuban "takeover," and the film *The Perez Family* provides a scenario in which viewers can visualize the "Cuban threat." Dottie, with her flagrant abuses of the sponsorship system for Cuban refugees, becomes representative of the dangers of immigration, especially from Latin America. The threat Dottie brings to her "family" conjures images of declining "family values," and the chaos that seems to follow Dottie has the potential to invade the rest of the country.

Even though Dottie's newly constructed family does not meet standard definitions, it begins to show itself as a Latino/a family. Family relations among Latinas/os have been described as intimate, with parents and children freely and frequently expressing their love through physical and verbal expressions of affection (Gangotena, 1994). Such intimacy is evident in Dottie's family. Almost immediately Dottie refers to her "husband" Juan as *mi amor*. Although Juan, still hoping for a reunion with Carmela, remains more distant, he and Dottie sleep curled in each other's arms. The affection that Gangotena (1994) notes as common between mother and child is also evident in the interactions between Dottie and Felipe, who use the terms of affection *mi'jo* and *Mami* respectively. When Felipe dies only days after the family has come together, Dottie's grief is real, and it is Juan who comforts her, holding her in his arms.

However, even as the film offers a positive portrayal of a loving family, it simultaneously implicates that loving family by imbuing it with gender stereotypes. Most problematic is the construction of Dottie as wife and mother, which perpetuates a limiting representation of sexual woman. Free with her body, she interacts with all of her family in sensual ways that violate U.S. puritanical standards. In Dottie as sexual woman, we witness the latent danger in the sexuality of Latinas/os (Rios Bustamante, 1992) that lurks beneath the surface. Although "mother" and "child" are close, there are suggestions that their intimacy is not always purely maternal. Dottie's penchant for skimpy attire is not affected by her new position as mother. Mother and child embrace while Dottie again wears nothing but bra and panties. Moreover, it is with her family that she is positioned on the street corner using her body to earn money. Thus, Dottie entangles her family in her promiscuity. In much traditional Latino culture, the promiscuous woman, especially the promiscuous wife and mother, is responsible for the destruction of her family (Anaya, 1984; Paz, 1961). In *The Perez Family*, Dottie's son, Felipe, dies while running free in the city; a good mother would be responsible for her child, keeping the child home with her, but Dottie does not. Thus, in the beginning of the film when Dottie is placed in the role of the head of the family, a role she claimed through her bringing together of the family, the family is at risk. It is not until later in the film, when she forfeits this role to Juan, that he brings stability to the family. Dottie's inability to function successfully as head of the family contrasts sharply with Juan's finesse in managing the family, illustrating again that patriarchal norms are effective.

Like Dottie's family, Carmela's family, also lacking an effective patriarch, experiences trouble. Her brother Angel attempts to fill the role of family patriarch by taking responsibility for the family's safety. However, he ultimately fails in his move to position himself as the head of the family. He is shot with the gun he bought, his girlfriend conspires to reunite Carmela and Juan, and Carmela replaces him as protector with Officer Pirelli. Angel's inability to shed the "greaser" elements of his Cuban heritage result in his unsuccessful adaptation to the Anglo world where Carmela lives. Thus, Carmela's family, although meeting a more traditional definition of family, also is constrained by imposed gender stereotypes. Carmela, like Dottie, must move between men in order to find stability and happiness. Unable to care for and protect herself, Carmela must wait for her male savior.

In another essentialist move in *The Perez Family*, both families are made safe when they are united under the one true patriarch, Juan.

Juan's reunion with Carmela and Teresa restores balance to both Carmela and Juan, linking them forever through their shared history and affection and freeing them to follow their now separating paths in life. Juan and Teresa share the joy of their reunion and look forward to their new relationship as father and daughter. And Juan and Dottie come together in love, rather than in need, signaling their birth as a true family. The members of the Perez family, then, find the answers to their dreams through Juan.

The film, *The Perez Family*, is ultimately able to bridge cultures, biology, and need into one family with two branches. This creation of the complete Perez family is made possible through Juan's joining with his first family and his commitment to his new family. With this combination of all into one family, the film promises a successful integration of Cuba into America through assimilation.

MI FAMILIA/MY FAMILY

Analyzing female character representations in the film *Mi Familia* provides another level of understanding of the construction of *family* and its importance to Mexican Americans. *The Perez Family* portrays Latinas stereotypically, keeping wives and mothers in the private sphere, which demarcates women in relation to men. However, *Mi Familia* resists this depiction because its female characters not only maintain their role in the private sphere, but use their roles as wives, mothers, and daughters to challenge cultural expectations of women. In *Mi Familia*, the central female characters can be seen as falling into the stereotypic roles for women; they are, in fact, wives and mothers. And yet, these characters *challenge* role-defined prescriptions in the performance of their roles. Unlike Carmela and Dottie, the women in *Mi Familia* amend traditional definitions of wives and mothers through subtle and overt challenges to role restrictions.

The construction of *la familia* and the role of women (especially in relation to maintaining *la familia*) are analyzed in *Mi Familia*. The purpose is not to diminish what the movie seeks to accomplish—to provide a contemporary portrayal of Mexican Americans. It is important to bear in mind, as Ríos (1994) writes, that an "audience function" focuses not on what the media "does *to* a person" but rather what a "person does *with* a media form" (p. 111; emphasis in original). Although the movie offers a culturally and ethnically validating and affirming portrayal of Latinos/as, it can also be used to perpetuate stereotypes. Thus, a review and critique by Mexican Americans and, likewise, all viewers, is necessary.

Mi Familia chronicles the experiences of the Sanchez family: the parents, María and José, and their six children, Paco, Irene, Chucho, Toni, Memo, and Jimmy. Through the Sanchez family, the viewing audience learns about generational differences, class, race, and gender issues. Also, via the family's interactions and the roles of the women, a sense of community is established and multiple values—*respeto* [respect], *dignidad* [dignity], *trabajar* [work], *hijos* [children], and *matrimonio* [marriage]—are espoused, reinforced, and held in high regard.

The concept of *la familia* is highly valued among Mexican Americans because of the sense of security, community, and safety that it offers. Within the movie, we see the female characters greatly contribute to instilling a sense of home and maintaining *la familia*. The importance of family is emphasized when José Sanchez toasts them at his daughter's wedding as being "the greatest riches" a person can have. Furthermore, *la familia* also moves beyond immediate family members to include extended members by virtue of blood ties. Among extended family members there is an automatic acceptance and offering of all that one has—food, clothing, shelter, money, and so on. Any sacrifice or debt that is endured is cast aside because it is understood that no repayment is necessary among *la familia*.

Within the movie, an example of this is when María Sanchez (Jennifer Lopez) is deported from California to Mexico, where she stays with an aunt. The aunt provides María with food and shelter until she is ready to leave a year later. We witness the care, concern, and trust demonstrated and offered by an extended family member. Furthermore, this exemplifies what Gangotena (1994) argues is the maintenance of harmonious relationships—the sacrifice made by the aunt to care for María until she is able to return to California. Specifically, the aunt acts as a support network (Gangotena, 1994) for María who provides emotional, psychological, and practical support. For example, when María tells her aunt she plans to return to California as soon as her child is born because that is what *La Virgen* (similar to the Virgin Mary) would want for María's family, the aunt supports María's decision and encourages her to maintain faith in *La Virgen*.

A sense of family is introduced initially through Paco's oral narration of the family history. Through the family's experiences, we begin to understand how "family" is constructed, and specifically, how women's roles serve in this construction. Paco (Edward James Olmos) begins his narration by detailing his father's (José's) journey from Mexico to California. Once settled in California, José obtains a job on the west side of Los Angeles (a privileged, middle-class Anglo suburb), working as a laborer/gardener. Soon after this, we are introduced to the first female character, María.[3]

While working at one of the Anglo homes, José (Jacob Vargas) is attracted to a Mexican American woman, María, who works as the family's caregiver. Soon after, they are married and have two children, Paco and Irene. María stops working to stay home to maintain and care for her own family and realizes she is pregnant with her third child. While out shopping one day, María is picked up by *la migra* [immigration], who deport her to Mexico,[4] and it is at this point wherein we witness a change in María's character. Thus far, she has been depicted stereotypically as "bare foot and pregnant." However, once María is deported to Mexico, she struggles to return to her husband, José, and the depiction of María changes. María exudes strength and determination to reunite with José because she feels her place is with her family.

María's determination and strength is demonstrated by her two-year journey back to California. More than this, though, she needs to cross a dangerous river with her son, Chucho. In doing so, she nearly drowns striving to maintain her and her son's safety. This scene reveals two things about María: first, she is a survivor who is maintained by her strength and determination to reunite with her family; second, she is a spiritual and religious person who maintains faith in *La Virgen de Guadalupe* (considered the patron saint of Mexican Americans; see Wolf, 1958). The first trait of being a survivor challenges the notion that Mexican American women are docile, submissive, weak, and passive (Gangotena, 1994). Instead, the river scene reveals how important it is to María to return to her family—so much so that she is willing to risk the dangers of trying to cross a river and to ignore the pleadings of a man (who takes her across the river) to wait a year until the river is calmer. María is not passive, but active in choosing to maintain agency; she is strong (both physically and emotionally) and able to swim to shore with her baby. Through her actions, María moves beyond the stereotype of the *Madre Sufrida;* she is not a helpless and passive mother.

María's second trait of being a spiritual and religious person demonstrates her belief in a higher power, which supports her during the journey. María's strong belief in La Virgen sustains her until she reunites with her family. María's spirituality is illustrated when she takes her son Chucho to *curanderas* [healers] because he has fallen ill due to the journey. The *curanderas* tell María that she must maintain her faith in *La Virgen*. Through a combination of María's faith in *La Virgen* and in indigenous/homeopathic medicine, Chucho does get well. Throughout the movie, María's religious faith in the Catholic church and her spirituality are constants that assist her in maintaining la familia.

Throughout the movie, we see how both parents are committed and dedicated to raising their children in the best way and with the means that they have available—and in maintaining the cohesiveness of *la familia*.

However, a closer examination of María, as wife and mother, reveals other things about her character and her role in constructing the family. We see María's determination to reunite with her family because she believes this is where she belongs. Once united with her family, María's role is as the primary caregiver. As José's wife, we see that she is cherished through the affection demonstrated to her by her husband and the name he calls her, *mi vida* ["my life"]. This title of affection illustrates more than if José called her "honey" or "dear"; it demonstrates how much María means to both José and to the family. Specifically, María is the person who physically gave life to her children and who metaphorically maintains "life" in her family.

María (played in her later years by Jenny Gago) is the family's caregiver: she cooks and cleans, she nurtures both her children and her grandchildren, she mediates between her husband and her children. María's role in the private sphere aids in constructing the notion of "home." Through María's work, a house develops into a home filled with the aroma of fresh food, family pictures, and a loving and supportive atmosphere. Her nurturing is illustrated through the loving and affectionate ways she refers to her children (e.g., *mi'ja* or *mi'jo* [my daughter/son]) which, Gangotena (1994) argues, assists in maintaining family relations. María also encourages and is proud of her children's accomplishments—a son who is in the Navy, a son who is a lawyer, a daughter who is married with children, and another daughter who becomes a nun. Beyond caring for her children, María also cares for one of her grandchildren by raising him—in effect, serving as a mother to him by feeding, clothing, and teaching him Spanish—until his father is ready to take over care for the child. As a grandmother, she participates, along with José, in passing on family traditions and stories.

María also fulfills her roles as mother and wife by mediating family conflicts. She tries to intervene between any conflicts that occur in the family and to relay information between José and the children. María is the one with whom the children share information. One example is when José (played in later years by Eduardo Lopez Rojas) and Chucho (Esai Morales) get into an argument over how Chucho earns money, which is by selling marijuana. The two begin to argue, which leads to José hitting Chucho. At this point María tries to stop the violence by separating the two in an effort to talk with them. We see the anti-violence message throughout the family; the parents are never shown hitting their children when they do something that José and María disapprove of. Both examples support Gangotena's (1994) argument that within Mexican American families, physical violence and/or verbal conflicts are eschewed in an effort to maintain the harmony of the family.

Finally, María's role as the primary caregiver is balanced and/or reconciled with the title given to her by her children—*jefita*, which refers to María's status as "boss" in the home. Similarly, the children refer to José as *jefito*. Rather than only one parent being referred to as the boss, both parents hold this title, illustrating the respect bestowed on them by their children as "heads of the household." The title also represents the power that both parents retain in the home. Within the movie, the construction of "family" is maintained on the basis of the family's interactions and acceptance of who has power and how power is enacted. This challenges the notion that within a family there is one parent who is in control and holds power, making the family either patriarchal or matriarchal. The Sanchez family is neither patriarchal or matriarchal; instead the children view each parent with respect, trust, and dignity, which serves to maintain the stability of *la familia*.

María and José's six children also play roles that affect the idea of family. As previously mentioned, there are four sons and two daughters; hence, the two daughters along with the wife of one of the sons is discussed. By focusing on the daughters and the daughter-in-law, we are able to see how they assist, as well, in constructing a sense of family and home.

In the movie, both daughters are characterized as vocal and outspoken but in different ways. Irene's outspokenness is based on her being the oldest; she is granted *respeto* as a woman and as the eldest daughter. Irene (Lupe Ontiveros) is portrayed as making her parents proud of her—she is the first, and, especially, the first daughter to marry. Thus, she also is granted *respeto* by the family in upholding the sacredness of marriage. Furthermore, she supports the value placed on *hijos* because she is the first child to have her own children. Irene and her husband, Geraldo, own a restaurant together, which further secures her a place in maintaining the family's value based on *trabajar* [work]. In family discussions, she may be deferred to because she is the eldest daughter with a family of her own. With Geraldo her role is now in relation to her own family and the need to provide and care for them.

Irene's role balances multiple responsibilities. Moraga (1983) explains that Chicanas and Mexicanas must juggle their feminism: "the Chicana . . . must keep the cultural home-fires burning while going out and making a living" (p. 107). Thus, Irene's commitment to her family's emotional and financial well-being enlarges cultural and stereotypic definitions of motherhood. Within traditional Mexican culture, mothers are expected to remain in the private sphere, whereas fathers are typically held responsible for providing for the family. Irene's actions represent a divergence from the expected separation of public and private realms.

However, in Paco's narration about Irene and her restaurant traditional gender images resurface, for he indicates that Irene grew in size just as her business grew. This mocking of Irene's weight gain also occurs when she is getting married and trying to fit into her wedding gown.

This emphasis on Irene's weight diminishes her accomplishments—owning a successful, family-operated restaurant—and reinforces traditional notions of beauty and appropriate female form.

The second daughter, Toni (Constance Marie), is vocal in familial issues and is represented as "bossy and beautiful." Throughout the movie, Toni, who became a nun, is depicted as always bossing around her siblings. The movie equates being a nun with being bossy when Paco narrates that nunnery life fits Toni because she is bossy. Likewise, being beautiful and bossy become linked in the character of Toni. One potential implication of linking beauty and bossiness is that they become inseparable, and beautiful Mexican American women are ridiculed in their inevitable bossiness.

The characterization of Toni is different yet similar to that of her sister Irene in that both are "married"—Toni decides "to marry our Lord Jesus," as her mother says. Her decision to become a nun surprises some family members because of her potential to become a "beauty queen." But Toni's parents admire and respect Toni's decision. In becoming a nun, Toni becomes visually "plain," and no longer requires the material elements that make her physically beautiful—thus challenging and resisting her representation as being "beautiful and bossy." Later in life, Toni decides to leave her order because she has fallen in love with and decides to marry a priest with whom she was doing missionary work. When Toni tells her parents, her mother faints. Toni's actions can be construed as disrespectful of the church—which, in terms of Sanchez family values, is to be revered. Nevertheless, Toni maintains her sense of compassion and continues to help others in need.

The depiction of Toni is one that diverges dramatically in two respects from that of both her sister and her sister-in-law. First, the characterization of Toni changes from one of being physically or cosmetically beautiful, bossy, overbearing, boisterous, and vocal, to being demure, passive, and outspoken. Second, because Toni's character is more complex she avoids being caught in the virgin/whore dichotomy. The role of Toni melds a sexually and physically attractive teenager with an asexual and selfless nun. Toni develops into a woman comfortable with her physical beauty but not consumed with it. Instead, she becomes a competent woman committed to assisting displaced individuals. Consequently, Toni avoids easy stereotyping and creates a new subject position for herself.

The final female character to be discussed is Isabel (Elpidia Carillo), the wife of Jimmy, the youngest son. Isabel's character is introduced through Toni, who is trying to prevent Isabel from being deported back to El Salvador by finding her a husband. Toni convinces her brother Jimmy (Jimmy Smits) to marry Isabel, but they both understand and agree that the marriage is a facade and one in name only. Early in the marriage,

Jimmy tells Isabel she cannot live with him. However, for Isabel, the marriage is not a facade, but something that she holds as sacred. She refuses to move out of her home with Jimmy.

Isabel represents the traditional wife who cooks and cleans; yet she also challenges this role by refusing to submit to what her husband tells her. In being both the "good wife" and the assertive woman, Isabel, like Toni, is neither the pure virgin nor the promiscuous whore. By returning to Jimmy's house and continuing to fulfill her role as wife, Isabel accomplishes three things. First, Isabel reinforces and greatly assists in establishing a sense of "home" and *familia* for Jimmy, who becomes the "outcast" of the family because he is in and out of jail for crimes that he commits. Isabel is able to transform Jimmy's house from a "bachelor pad" into a home in some of the ways María established a sense of home among her family—livening up the house, filling it with the aromas of freshly cooked food, and so on. When Isabel becomes pregnant, Jimmy begins to think about the future for the first time. The idea of having his own family and needing to provide for it pushes him to turn his life around. In addition, Isabel is vocal (as are the other Sanchez women) in expressing her needs and emotions. She wants to be happy and to have family, and she shares her personal experiences with Jimmy who, like her, has witnessed a family member being murdered. She is able to connect with Jimmy by getting him to open up to her and express his feelings. Thus, in wanting to be a wife to Jimmy, and managing to establish a sense of home, intimacy, and family for him, Isabel reinforces the values maintained by the Sanchez family.

The portrayals of all of the Sanchez women challenge traditional and stereotypical images of Latinas in media. The mother, María, although stereotypically depicted as fulfilling her duties as "the good wife and mother," defies these roles by not remaining passive and submissive. Instead, María represents a strong and determined woman who is outspoken over issues concerning *la familia*.

Likewise, the two daughters challenge preconceived ideas of young Mexican American women as sexualized beings. Through Irene's character, we witness a successful woman who manages her own business and takes care of her own family, as well as attending to the needs of her larger family. Toni's character represents a woman who has decided to devote herself to God. Even though she later leaves her order, Toni remains dedicated to assisting individuals in need. And although her decision to leave the order distresses her family, it underscores her independence and individuality. Finally, the daughter-in-law, Isabel, illustrates a refusal to adhere to and be submissive to her husband with whom she becomes an equal. Furthermore, she demonstrates her power in assisting her husband to use his voice as well.

CONCLUSION

The Perez Family and *Mi Familia* offer two sometimes overlapping, often distinct rhetorical visions through which viewers can gain some understanding of the lives of Latinas. By understanding the importance of *la familia* to Latinas, we should challenge ourselves to see beyond the stereotypical representations of Latinas—the devoted mother, the promiscuous woman, or the illegal immigrant. Whereas *The Perez Family* perpetuates simplistic, essentialistic, and dualistic portrayals of Latinas as good or evil, *Mi Familia* resists such depictions and instead attempts to provide more nuanced characters. And although those portrayals may appear tied to the stereotypic roles of dutiful daughter or supportive wife, they nevertheless expand those roles to reveal a complexity of character that transcends the stereotype while remaining true to the historical, social, and cultural reality of *la familia*.

ENDNOTES

1. Films such as *American Me* (1992), *Mi Familia/My Family* (1994), *The Perez Family* (1995), and *A Walk in the Clouds* (1995) have recently been released.
2. After the Cuban revolution which led to the Castro regime, Cubans who wished to leave were allowed to do so from the port of Mariel, thereby earning them the name "marielitos." Unlike many of the previous immigrants from Cuba to the United States who were professionals, most of the marielitos were unskilled and uneducated. United States society had little interest in these immigrants. Upon arriving in the U.S., many marielitos were detained in refugee camps until they could find sponsors to help them find housing and jobs.
3. Within this chapter and as in the movie, the main female characters are María, Irene, Toni, and Isabel.
4. Maria's deportation takes place during the Great Depression of the 1930s. The deportation of "Mexican looking" people was initiated by the U.S. government, which entered into an agreement with Southern Pacific Railroad. The company, by deporting Mexican Americans, would be paid approximately $14 per person.

REFERENCES

Anaya, R. A. (1984). *The legend of la llorona*. Berkeley, CA: Tonatiuh-Quinto Sol International.

Broyles-González, Y. (1990). What price "mainstream"?: Luis Valdez' *Corridos* on stage and film. *Cultural Studies, 4,* 281-293.

Cortés, C. (1985). Chicanas in film: History of an image. In G. D. Keller (Ed.), *Chicano cinema: Research, reviews, and resources* (pp. 94-108). Binghamton, NY: Bilingual Review.

Cotto-Escalera, B. L. (1990). *Chicana characters in Mexican American drama.* Unpublished master's thesis, University of Texas, Austin.

Fregoso, R. L. (1993). *The bronze screen: Chicana and Chicano film culture.* Minneapolis: University of Minnesota Press.

Fregoso, R. L., & Chabram, A. (1990). Chicana/o cultural representations: Reframing alternative critical discourses. *Cultural Studies, 4,* 203-212.

Gangotena, M. (1994). The rhetoric of La Familia among Mexican Americans. In A. González, M. Houston, & V. Chen (Eds.), *Our voices: Essays in culture, ethnicity, and communication* (pp. 69-80). Los Angeles: Roxbury Press.

Garcia, A. M. (1990). The development of Chicana feminist discourse, 1970-1980. In E. C. DuBois & V. L. Ruiz (Eds.), *Unequal sisters: A multicultural reader in U.S. women's history* (pp. 418-431). New York: Routledge.

Herrera-Sobek, M. (1982). The treacherous woman archetype: A structuring agent in the corrido. *Aztlán, 13,* 135-148.

Herrera-Sobek, M. (1985). Introduction. In M. Herrera-Sobek (Ed.), *Beyond stereotypes: The critical analysis of Chicana literature* (pp. 9-28). Binghamton, NY: Bilingual Review.

Limón, J. E. (1992). Stereotyping and Chicano resistance: An historical dimension. In C. A. Noriega (Ed.), *Chicanos and film: Representation and resistance* (pp. 3-17). Minneapolis: University of Minnesota Press.

Mirandé, A., & Enríquez, E. (1979). *La Chicana: The Mexican-American woman.* Chicago: University of Chicago Press.

Moraga, C. (1983). *Loving in the war years: Lo que nunca pasó por sus labios.* Boston: South End Press.

Noriega, C. (Ed.). (1992). *Chicanos and film: Representation and resistance.* Minneapolis: University of Minnesota Press.

Noriega, C. A., & López, A. M. (Eds.). (1996). *The ethnic eye: Latino media arts.* Minneapolis: University of Minnesota Press.

Paz, O. (1961). *The labyrinth of solitude: Life and thought in Mexico* (L. Kemp, trans.). New York: Grove Press.

Pettit, A. G. (1980). *Images of the Mexican American in fiction and film.* College Station: Texas A&M University Press.

Ríos, D. I. (1994). Mexican American cultural experiences with mass-mediated communication. In A. González, M. Houston, & V. Chen (Eds.), *Our voices: Essays in culture, ethnicity, and communication* (pp. 110-116). Los Angeles: Roxbury Press.

Rios Bustamante, A. (1992). Latino participation in the Hollywood film industry. In C. A. Noriega (Ed.), *Chicanos and film: Representation and resistance* (pp. 18-28). Minneapolis: University of Minnesota Press.

Wolf, E. R. (1958). The virgin of Guadalupe: A Mexican national symbol. *Journal of American Folklore, 71,* 34-39.

20

Immigrant Inscriptions: Redefining Race and Gender in *Mississippi Masala*

Anjali Ram

When Mira Nair approached Hollywood looking for someone to finance her film *Mississippi Masala*, a producer asked her whether she could make room for a white protagonist. Her retort was that all the waiters in the film would be white. Needless to say, she was turned down by Hollywood, but went on to make her film, financed by private sources (Mehta, 1992). Nair's determination is testimony to a small but growing trend of films being made by, about, and for women of color. Unfortunately, and not surprisingly, most of these films remain on the fringe, attracting select audiences. However, *Mississippi Masala* managed to break away from the margins of invisibility and make an impact on mainstream audiences in the West. Virtually every major video store in the United States keeps the film, and it was reviewed in major newspapers and magazines across the country.

Disrupting the familiar orientalist depiction of the South Asian woman[1] as the silent subaltern and/or the exotic Other, *Mississippi Masala* offers an alternative to dominant western film representations with regard to race and gender. The term *subaltern* was prevalent mainly during British colonialism and refers to those in subordinate positions. In its current usage, subaltern has been recuperated as a theoretical concept by both feminist and postcolonial scholars[2] to examine the positions, the politics, and the practices of women belonging to societies that have witnessed the brutalities of colonialist expansion. Initiated partly by the work of Gayatri Chakravarty Spivak (1985), several feminists argue that one of the ways nonwestern women are denied a voice and access to power is by representing them as the "other" to the western self and viewing them as exotic objects. Nair's film provides several textual instances that attempt to dislodge South Asian women from such traditionally marginal, passive representations of the exotic, the elusive, and the ethereal, and redefine them as protagonists, principal causal agents, and desiring subjects.

   Mississippi Masala essentially portrays the life of an immigrant South Asian woman. Living between "a lost past" and a "non-integrated present," immigrant lives exemplify postmodernity (Chambers, 1994, p. 27). Postmodernity challenges the cardinal principles of modernity such as a stable sense of identity, absolute truths, a sense of the center, and cultural homogeneity (Chambers, 1994). Such a condition very aptly defines migrant lives. Displaced and uprooted from their homeland, immigrants are forced to adapt to a new world. To do so, they develop a hybrid identity that conflates past and present, east and west, tradition and modernity, old and new, so that their experience is one full of blurred boundaries and fragmented narratives. Asian Indian immigrant women are doubly vulnerable to the ordeals of dislocation as they are compelled to negotiate with the brutalities of patriarchy and racial prejudice simultaneously (Ganguly, 1992). Film provides a powerful political space to contest the oppressive practices that are endured by groups marginalized because of their gender, race, and/or class. According to Gibson-Hudson (1994), cinematic representations have the potential to transform audiences into "proactive, socially-conscious viewers" (p. 26).

   I have chosen to examine *Mississippi Masala* for several reasons: First, it was successful at the box office, received popular and critical acclaim, and is better known than other films made by South Asian women; second, it highlights the themes of hybrid consciousness and cultural collision that are increasingly becoming an integral part of the western metropolitan landscape; and third, and most importantly, it is among the first full-length films made by an Asian Indian woman and has an Asian Indian woman protagonist.

   A study done by Oshana (1985) found that between 1930 and 1983, only 19 films produced in the United States had Asian Indian women characters. Most of these women characters had supporting roles and/or were played by Caucasian women. In the last decade, emerging South Asian directors have tried to fill this gap. However, reaching a mainstream audience either has proven difficult or has not been attempted at all. *Mississippi Masala* is thus a first of its kind in reaching a mainstream audience, aided perhaps in no small part by the inclusion of Denzel Washington as the African American lover of Mina, an Asian Indian immigrant living with her family in a small southern town.

Some critics have argued that *Mississippi Masala* glides rather too glibly over the uncomfortable area of racism (Jiwani, 1992; Radhakrishnan, 1994). They contend that Nair has failed to deal with the theme of racial prejudice adequately and provides easy solutions for what is a very complex and many-layered problem. For instance, Radhakrishnan (1994) acerbically remarks that *Mississippi Masala* uncritically commodifies hybridity and presents the young lovers as "walking into the rain in a Hollywood resolution of the agonies of history" (p. 225).

Although I agree that *Mississippi Masala* offers an unsatisfactory resolution to the race issue in the form of an uncomplicated, idyllic heterosexual union, I believe that there are several aspects of this film that do warrant merit. *Mississippi Masala* sketches the lives of Asian Indian immigrant women in bold strokes and provides valuable redefinitions of race and gender in film. As Gammon and Marshment (1989) point out, it is important not to dismiss popular culture when it offers some valid feminist interventions.

In what follows I foreground these aspects and demonstrate that *Mississippi Masala* does allow spaces for the inscription of the female gaze and the construction of a feminine subjectivity. First, I provide a summary of the film. Second, I lay out some of the theoretical concepts that guide my analysis. Third, I undertake an analysis of the film that focuses on representation. Finally, I conclude with some of the issues involved in ethnic and gendered film practices and politics.

SUMMARY: *MISSISSIPPI MASALA* (MIRA NAIR, 1991, USA)

Mississippi Masala is a film primarily of diaspora,[3] cultural disjunctions, and the uncomfortable jostling of plural ethnic identities. *Masala* serves as a metaphor for this theme of cultural potpourri and is the Hindi word for a blend of hot spices. Described as a brave idea, a witty and fresh romantic comedy, and a welcome relief from Hollywood's white bread diet, *Mississippi Masala* was received by and large favorably by the popular press in America (Anderson, 1993; Ansen, 1992; Rozen, 1992). The film is set in two locations—Uganda under the reign of the dictator Idi Amin and the racially divided Greenwood, Mississippi. The opening scenes are shot in Uganda and document in swift scenes the trials of an Indian family faced with the grim reality of forced migration. Jay (played by Roshan Seth) and his wife Kinu (played by Sharmila Tagore) are both descendants of Indian laborers brought by the British in the 1800s to Uganda. Jay is a lawyer and considers Uganda his home. He is forced to give up that home when Uganda is declared a nation exclusively for "Africans—black Africans," as his closest friend, Okelo, an African Ugandan, points out. Along with hundreds of other Indians, Jay, Kinu, and his daughter, the seven-year-old Mina, immigrate to the United States. However, Jay is never comfortable in the United States and nurses a quixotic quest of returning back to Uganda and reclaiming his property and his life there. Kinu, with the help of some Indian relatives, opens up a liquor shop, and the family lives ensconced by the local Indian immigrant community.

Mina (played by Sarita Choudhury) grows up as a young woman of the 1990s in Greenwood, Mississippi, where the lines of race are deeply etched, separating communities by the color of their skin. Mina's first encounter with Demetrius (played by Denzil Washington) occurs when her car collides into his truck. Demetrius is an industrious young African American male who has struggled with the white-dominated institutions of the Deep South to develop his carpet cleaning business. Mina and Demetrius fall in love. Their affair raises a hornet's nest of racial prejudice in both their communities. Mina's family prohibit her continuing the relationship. Demetrius' reputation as a reliable worker is jeopardized and his business suffers. In a climatic scene, he confronts Jay in disgust and scathingly accuses him of acting white, when in fact Jay is only a shade lighter than his own color.

Mina and Demetrius finally escape from Greenwood in a bid to start a life together. Jay returns to Uganda only to recognize that "home is where the heart is" and reconciles himself to life as an immigrant with his wife Kinu. The film closes with scenes of Jay in Uganda mingling with the local Africans and watching an Ugandan woman dancing in the street. As the credits roll, Jay's smiling face, along with the dancing woman, are spliced with Demetrius and Mina embracing each other in romantic bliss. In addition to the central narrative theme, the film is filled with cameo scenes of both communities that demonstrate with humor and irony the stereotypes and assumptions that each have about the other.

A NOTE ON FEMINIST FILM THEORY

Most accounts of feminist film theory take as their starting point the essay *Visual Pleasure and Narrative Cinema*, by Laura Mulvey, published first in 1975 and republished several times since then. Mulvey used psychoanalytic theory to argue that the visual pleasures afforded by cinema are scopophilic and narcissistic. Scopophilia arises from "pleasure in using another person as an object of sexual stimulation through sight" (Mulvey, 1988, p. 61). Narcissism, on the other hand, is present when the spectator of a film recognizes *himself* and identifies with the screen image.

The pronoun "himself" is key here because Mulvey argues that the "spectator" of mainstream cinema is essentially male. In other words, films are made for the male viewer who derives pleasure by looking at the female figure on the screen and by identifying with the male hero. Cinema is structured to inscribe the male spectator, with the woman serving as spectacle. The possession of the gaze, Mulvey pointed out, clearly privileges the male in most popular film texts.

Several feminist analyses of film have used Mulvey's framework. Kaplan (1983) elaborated on it by referring to three "looks" described by Mulvey that are built into the cinema. The first is within the text itself, in which the male character gazes at the female character with the effect of turning her into the object of his gaze. The second is the spectator's gaze, which is made to identify with this male gaze and similarly objectifies the women on the screen. The third is the camera's original "gaze," which occurs in the very act of filming (Kaplan, 1983, p. 15). Williams (1984) similarly notes that "to see is to desire" and "the good girl" of classical narrative cinema fails to return the gaze of the male who desires her. This objectification of women in popular cinema denies them a subject-position. In other words, the rendering of women as objects for male consumption precludes them from being represented as individual social subjects, capable of leading lives without being mere appendages to a male figure.

However, Mulvey's theory of the male gaze could not account for women spectators and the pleasure they derive from viewing film. Moreover, as Walker (1994) points out, Mulvey's psychoanalytical model is overly monolithic and does not allow for: "the spaces of female resistance that give rise, for example, to classical film texts that depart from the model, to radically other sorts of pleasurable filmic representations" (p. 84). In response to Mulvey's article, feminist scholars started asking questions: Is the gaze always male? (Kaplan, 1983); How do women look at women? (Stacey, 1989); Can the male body be the spectacle? Can there be a female gaze? (Moore, 1989). Finally, what about the woman of color as both spectacle and spectator? (Gaines, 1988; Roach & Felix, 1989).

If the cinematic world privileges the male's viewing pleasure, the issue becomes further compounded when race is considered along with gender. Women of color in film are "othered" both by gender and race. One rarely encounters a successful, mainstream film that attempts to situate women of color as speaking subjects and principle agents in a film. In *Mississippi Masala*, however, Mina not only returns the gaze but very often possesses it and initiates the action to finally attain the object of her desire. By removing the Asian woman from her stereotypical role of submissiveness and relocating her as spunky, self-assured, and spirited, Nair attempts to make "her" speak.

FEMALE GAZE IN *MISSISSIPPI MASALA*

To understand the inscription of the female gaze in *Mississippi Masala*, I focus on four aspects of the film narrative: (a) the female protagonist as prime mover of the narrative; (b) the female as desiring subject and the coding of the masculine as erotic spectacle; (c) the mother-daughter plot; and (d) the emasculation of the Indian male.

Female Protagonist As Prime Mover Of The Narrative

Mina wrests control of the narrative through her constant questioning and initiation of the action. The opening scenes in Uganda determine that the gaze in the film is primarily located in the character of Mina. We are made to witness the ordeal of the family primarily through her eyes as a child. The camera lingers on her peeping through the curtain, looking wistfully through the rear window as the car pulls away from her home, and watching wide-eyed at the chaotic events of forced exile. Later on in the film, when Mina recalls her childhood in Uganda, we again see her eyes dark with anxiety as the adult voices in the background discuss the situation.

At 24, confined to a tacky motel cleaning bathrooms, Mina is portrayed as a self-assured young woman with an independent spirit. The episode in a bar in the beginning of the film sets the tone, indicating Mina's role in promoting the action. Mina is invited by Harry Patel, the most eligible bachelor of the Indian community, to a bar. Serendipitously, Demetrius also happens to be there, and they encounter each other on the dance floor. Earlier that morning, Mina had collided into his truck. As the following dialogue demonstrates, she remembers him, but he does not recall her:

Mina:	(enthusiastically) Hi!
Demetrius:	(smiles, pauses) Hey . . . how're you doin?
Mina:	We met this afternoon—the accident.
Demetrius:	(pauses) Oh, yeah, yeah, yeah!

Mina attempts to keep up the conversation, but Demetrius is distracted as his ex-girlfriend Alishia enters the bar with her latest beau. Although the next move is made by Demetrius, his focus is on Alishia and his sole aim is to save his wounded pride by dancing with Mina. When Harry Patel wants to leave, angry about being upstaged, Mina *chooses* to stay. On the ride home, Mina again attempts to initiate conversation as Demetrius continues to be distracted and not very interested. Again, it is Mina who makes the first phone call to Demetrius. Demetrius follows along and invites her to his house for dinner, his motivation still primarily to snub Alishia rather than to court Mina. Demetrius soon succumbs to her charms and invites her for an overnight trip to a beach resort, but it is Mina who makes the trip possible by telling her parents that she is visiting a girlfriend.

Mina's role in impelling the plot has been noted by critics. Anderson (1993) refers to her as an "active female character" (p. 24), unusual for most commercial film. The final scene confirms Mina's assertive, dynamic role. In an effort to bring a peaceful resolution to her relationship, Mina takes the family car and races across Greenwood in search of Demetrius. This car chase is complete with screeching maneuvers, racy music, and a fast pace. Such scenes are normally restricted to the male action hero in popular film. By deliberately transposing such a familiar Hollywood masculine/heroic/action routine, Nair manages to reinforce her portrayal of Mina as the major architect of the narrative. The representation is complete when Mina takes the final decision to leave Greenwood and proposes, "Demetrius can I come with you . . . wherever you are going. . . . I could be your partner . . . its crazy to stay here" (*Mississippi Masala*).

Mina, a woman of color, is thus positioned as the central character. The plot is propelled by her desire, her will to grow and break free from both the racial and patriarchal categories that constrain her as an immigrant woman in Mississippi. As her mother explains tearfully at the end, "she has a mind of her own; she can't grow here anymore."

Female As Desiring Subject And Coding: The Male As Erotic Spectacle

Denzil Washington's representation of eroticized masculinity was noted by the popular press. In *People's Weekly*, Rosen (1992) commented:

Washington's performance in *Masala* will make a believer out of
anyone who ever doubted that he is an A-list movie star and a sex
symbol. This man is debonair. And magnetic. And he has an innate
sweetness like Henry Fonda's but with even more steel. (Rozen,
1992, p. 17)

Similarly, in *Maclean's*, Johnson (1993) declared, " Washington reveals a
quality of tenderness that he has never shown before: the camera adores
him" (p. 52). The eye behind the camera that "adores" Washington is
that of a woman of color. And by positioning a male "sex symbol," the
film provides a space for a spectator other than the dominant white, heterosexual male in Mulvey's (1988) model. But most importantly, within
the text itself it is the woman protagonist who largely possesses the
gaze, with the male served up as erotic spectacle.

The male gaze carries with it the "power of action and possession" (Kaplan, 1983, p. 31). In the bar scene, Mina appropriates this gaze
as she pointedly glances around the dance floor. She barely pays attention to Harry Patel as she scans the bar and her gaze picks up Demetrius
dancing in abandon. In renegotiating the space reserved traditionally for
the male protagonist, Mina's gaze redraws and restructures the power
dynamics associated with female/male difference. However, we need to
be careful not to assume that the gaze as seized by Mina is a simple
reversal of the male gaze.

A reversal would simply keep the dualistic ideological positions
of the powerful/powerless, active/passive, male/female,
spectator/spectacle in place. Instead, these dichotomies dissolve as the
subject/object positions are constantly shifted and redrawn. By locating
herself as desiring subject and coding masculinity as erotic spectacle,
Mina does not deny the male his subjectivity. Demetrius shares her gaze
as the narrative develops, thus resisting being simply the fetishized
Other. The sharing of the site of desire is illustrated pointedly in the
scene in which Mina and Demetrius talk to each other over the phone.
Both are shown lying in their respective beds, their separate spheres.
The scene is shot with the camera overhead. Their minimal clothing, the
ruffled bedsheets, Mina's hair wildly flung across the pillow, and their
low voices make up a mosaic of erotic, sensual signifiers transforming
both into desiring subjects. Nair is careful to portray both the male and
female characters similarly, in terms of exposure and camera position.
Thus, the site of erotic desire as a masculine domain is interrupted as
spaces open up in the text that allow for the female to be an equally
desiring subject.

In the climatic scene of sexual intimacy, the camera again pans
on both their bodies. However, it is Mina's face in frontal shot that we
are shown continuously. We see only her face lit up with desire and we

only hear *her* voice sighing with pleasure. *Mississippi Masala* invites a reading of the female gaze. Although it is not as aggressive or dominant as the classic Hollywood male gaze, it nevertheless subtly reinforces the centrality of the woman of color in the film.

Mother-Daughter Plot

One of the strategies in popular mainstream cinema to challenge sexist representations of gender has been the depiction of women as strong and successful in positions of wealth and power (Marshment, 1991). But representing women in positions in which they have access to the signifiers of masculine monopoly merely reinforces patriarchal binary oppositions.

Mississippi Masala contests this equation of wealth/power/liberation by locating the female gaze in a South Asian immigrant woman who cleans bathrooms in a tacky motel. Kinu, like her daughter, Mina, resists a passive object position. Both Mina and Kinu are shown in occupations that are divested of any glamour, status, or allure. Kinu runs a liquor store. The significance of their occupations needs to be understood in the context of the notion of caste and class in India. Cleaning bathrooms transgresses all the upper caste codes of purity and pollution as it was (and still is, for the most part) an occupation deemed fit only for the *bhangis*, one of the lowest castes in the hierarchy. Similarly, a woman working in a liquor store defies Indian middle-class moralities and would be considered taboo in the middle class/upper caste Indian mileau to which Mina and Kinu obviously belong. As a woman gossiping at an Indian wedding remarks to a friend: "That's the mother, owns a liquor shop. Can you imagine!" By being positioned in such occupations, both mother and daughter resist the constraining, hierarchal class norms imposed within their own community. Their occupations are signifiers of their marginalization within their own community and their dogged resistance to its norms.

At the level of feminine sexual subjectivity, Mina is connected implicitly to her mother. There is a strong suggestion in the film that Kinu had an intimate liaison with Okelo, Jay's close friend in Uganda. In the last encounter with Okelo, Kinu turns toward him; no words are exchanged, just a long embrace and a longer look. Okelo's picture with the child Mina is kept constantly in the liquor shop where Kinu spends most of her time. As Anderson (1993) observes, Mina's skin is a shade darker than her parents, and she refers to herself as a "darkie," hinting unconsciously at her possible interracial heritage. Mina not only traverses the two cultures, "she is the embodiment of the traversal itself" (Anderson, 1993, p. 25). Mina thus can be seen as carrying on her mother's tale, and her relationship with Demetrius as the unconscious fulfill-ment of her mother's desires. When Mina announces tearfully over the phone that she is leaving, it is her mother who finally understands and explains the situation to Jay. She tells Jay that Mina has a mind of her own and that, after all, she is his daughter. The repressed, unsaid impli-cation is that it is not Jay that Mina takes after, but her mother, Kinu.

The mother figure as a strong role model is echoed in the char-acter of Grace, Demetrius's aunt and surrogate mother. She is the only one who supports his relationship with Mina and acerbically points out the internalized racism in the African American community. When Demetrius father, Willie Ben, bemoans the loss of his reputation due to his son's relationship with Mina, Grace chastises him and says, "All you and the rest of them want is that he know his place and stay in it . . . the days of slavery—they over, Willie Ben."

Mina is thus provided with two stalwart women predecessors. Both Kinu and Grace serve as maternal prisms refracting strength, courage, endurance, and wisdom, casting light on Mina's quest to free herself from and grow beyond the parameters of both patriarchy and racism.

The Emasculation Of The Indian Male

If, by inscribing a non-Western erotic feminine subjectivity, Nair chal-lenges colonial and racist stereotyping, then by emasculating the Indian male, she challenges the patriarchal coding within her own community. By denying the Indian male his sexuality and providing the Asian Indian woman with an African American consort, she contests both the patriarchal discourses that shackle the Indian woman in her own com-munity and the colonial/racialist discourses that marginalize her into the exotic Other in the west.

The younger Indian males are caricatured portraits, the main thrust of which is their utter and complete castration and emasculation. The two scenes of the newly wed Indian couple illustrate the point. On their wedding night, Anil, a young Indian male, sits upright in bed not knowing what move to make, as his bride sleeps by his side. As he con-templates his next move, she delivers a swift slap on his face, apparently swatting a fly that was annoying her. The next night is worse as Anil hastily jumps on top of his wife in an attempt to initiate sexual inter-course. She pushes him off, as though he were the fly of the previous night, and in an exasperated voice tells him that he was hurting her.

Even Jay, who is portrayed with dignity in every other aspect, is not spared from this castration. The implication that Mina was born of the liaison between Kinu and Okelo, coupled with the fact that Mina is an only child, suggests at least metaphorically, if not literally, Jay's sexual inability. In contrast, both Demetrius, as the eroticized male, and his narrative precursor, Okelo, stride across the screen in all their flamboyant masculinity. Using an African American male as the erotic, the vital, the sexualized and sensualized masculine image opens up larger spaces for the intervention of a non-Western female gaze. The Indian male through caricature and the white male through absence is exiled from the sites of desire and subjectivity in the text.

Although the castration of the Indian male is designed to challenge the patriarchal underpinnings of the Asian Indian community, it has the unfortunate effect of perpetuating spurious stereotypes of the Indian community. By portraying Indian men as asexual and greedy business men, Nair plays into racist clichés and presents a monolithic, distorted view of the Indian community. One wonders if it was necessary for Nair to depict the Indian woman as positive at the cost of lampooning the Indian man.

CONCLUSION: THE CONTEXT OF PRODUCTION

This chapter has attempted to locate the inscription of the female gaze and the activation of a feminine subjectivity in *Mississippi Masala*, a film made by and about an Asian Indian woman in the diaspora. By the textual analysis presented so far, I do not intend to suggest that this film is an uncontested territory of feminist intervention. Rather, I have attempted to draw attention to those aspects of the text that invite subjectivities and representations usually repressed in mainstream cinema. By incorporating textual instances that position an immigrant woman of color as the prime mover of the narrative and the desiring subject, *Mississippi Masala* ruptures dominant Western representations of gender and race.

However, *Mississippi Masala* has also drawn considerable ire from several fronts. Apart from the scholar-critics such as Jiwani (1992) and Radhakrishnan (1994), some members of the Indian community reacted negatively to the film. A number were offended by the stereotyping (Rasiah, 1993), and others denied the possibility of an underprivileged Indian woman marrying an African American male (Snyder, 1992).

Although the film maker must always consider her audience, this can become a particularly complex undertaking when she sets out to make a film about the marginalized community to which she belongs. On the one hand, subtle, cultural nuances will be lost on viewers unfamiliar with the community. On the other hand, the film might be viewed as offensive to the community it is portraying if it uses parody and presents generalizations, as did *Mississippi Masala*. The film maker thus walks a tightrope as she attempts to negotiate with multiple audiences.

Despite the odds weighed against her, and some of the serious omissions in the film, Mira Nair made us a film that defies the stereotypical representation of the muted, passive Asian Indian women and redefines race and gender in some important ways. By centering communities of color and marginalizing the white community, Nair's film echoes Rushdie's (1989) words:

> African, Caribbean, Indian, Pakistani, Bangladesh, Cypriot, Chinese, we are other than what we would have been if we had not crossed the oceans, . . . we have been made again: but I say we shall also be the ones to remake this society, to shape it from the bottom to the top. (pp. 413-414)

As we move into the next millennium, the geopolitical architecture of Euro-American society is being altered by immigrant communities and other marginalized groups. Films such as *Mississippi Masala* are important indicators of such change and need to be recognized for their attempts to refute imperialist and patriarchal representations.

ENDNOTES

1. South Asian refers to people originally from the Indian subcontinent which includes India, Pakistan, Bangladesh, Nepal, and Sri Lanka. For the purposes of this chapter I use the word South Asian, Asian-Indian, and Indian interchangeably.
2. Postcolonial scholarship is devoted to critically examining colonial representations and discourses. See, for example, Bhabha (1990), Fanon (1952/1968), Mohanty, Russo, & Lourdes (1991), Said (1978), Suleri (1992), and Trinh T. Minh-ha (1989).
3. The term *diaspora*, a Greek word meaning "dispersion," originally described ancient Jewish communities living outside Palestine. It is currently employed to refer to communities composed of exiles, refugees, and immigrants.

REFERENCES

Anderson, E. S. (1993). Review: *Mississippi Masala. Film Quarterly, 46*(4), 26-27.

Ansen, D. (1992, February). Combustible mixture. *Newsweek, 119*(7), p. 65.

Bhabha, H. (Ed.). (1990). *Nation and narration*. London: Routledge.

Chambers, I. (1994). *Migrancy, culture, and identity*. London: Routledge.

Fanon, F. (1968). *Black skins, white masks* (C. L. Markmann, trans.). London: MacGibbon and Kee. (Original work published in 1952)

Ganguly, K. (1992). Migrant identities: Personal memory and the construction of selfhood. *Cultural Studies, 6*(1), 27-50.

Gaines, J. (1988). White privilege and looking relations: Race and gender in feminist film theory, *Screen, 29*(4), 13-27.

Gammon L., & Marshment M. (1989). Introduction. In L. Gammon & M. Marshment (Eds.), *The female gaze—Women as viewers of popular cinema* (pp. 1-7). Seattle: Real Comet Press.

Gibson-Hudson, G. J. (1994). The ties that bind: Cinematic representations by black women filmmakers. *Quarterly Review of Film and Video, 15*(2), 25-44.

Jiwani, Y. (1992). The exotic, the erotic: South Asian women. *Canadian Woman Studies, 13*(1), 42-46.

Johnson, B. (1993, March). The spice of life. *Maclean's, 105*(10), 52.

Kaplan, E. A. (1983). *Women and film: Both sides of the camera*. New York: Metheun.

Marshment, M. (1991). Substantial woman. In L. Gammon & M. Marshment (Eds.), *The female gaze—Women as viewers of popular cinema* (pp. 27-43). Seattle: Real Comet Press.

Mehta, G. (1992, February) Vogue arts. *Vogue, 182*(2), 114-118.

Mohanty, C. T., Russo, A., & Lourdes, T. (Eds.). (1991). *Third world women and the politics of feminism*. Bloomington: Indiana University Press.

Moore, S. (1989). Here's looking at you, kid! In L. Gammon & M. Marshment (Eds.), *The female gaze—Women as viewers of popular cinema* (pp. 44-59). Seattle: Real Comet Press.

Mulvey, L. (1988). Visual pleasure and narrative cinema. In C. Penley (Ed.), *Feminism and film theory* (pp. 46-57). New York: Routledge.

Oshana, M. (1985). *Women of color: A filmography of minority and third world women*. New York: Garland.

Radhakrishnan, R. (1994). Is the ethnic "authentic" in the diaspora?. In K. Aguilar-San Juan (Ed.), *State of Asian-America: Activism and resistance in the 1990s* (pp. 219-234). Boston, MA: South End Press.

Rasiah, D. (1993). *Mississippi Masala* and *Khush*: Redefining community. In The South Asian Women Descent Collective (Eds.) *Our feet walk the sky: Women of the South Asian diaspora* (pp. 267-273). San Francisco: Aunt Lute Press.

Roach, J., & Felix, P. (1989). Black looks. In L. Gammon & M. Marshment (Eds.), *The female gaze—Women as viewers of popular cinema* (pp. 130-142). Seattle: Real Comet Press.

Rozen, L. (1992, February). *Mississippi Masala*. *People's Weekly, 37*(6), 17-18.

Rushdie, S. (1989). *The satanic verses*. New York: Viking Penguin.

Said, E. (1978). *Orientalism*. London: Routledge.

Snyder, D. (1992, February 28). Indians say "Masala" plot unlikely. *Times-Picayune*, p. A1.

Spivak, G. (1985) Can the subaltern speak? *Wedge, 7*(8), 120-130.

Stacey, J. (1989). Desperately seeking difference. In L. Gammon & M. Marshment (Eds.), *The female gaze—Women as viewers of popular cinema* (pp. 112-129). Seattle: Real Comet Press.

Suleri, S. (1992). *The rhetoric of English India.* University of Chicago Press.

Trinh T. Minh-ha. (1989). *Woman, native, other.* Bloomington: Indiana University Press.

Walker, J. (1994). Psychoanalysis and feminist film theory: The problem of sexual difference and identity. In D. Carson, L. Dittmar, & J. R. Welsch (Eds.), *Multiple voices in feminist film criticism* (pp. 82-92). Minneapolis: University of Minnesota Press.

Williams, L. (1984) When the woman looks. In M. A. Doanne, P. Mellenchamp, & L. Williams (Eds.), *Re-vision: Essays in feminist film criticism* (pp. 742-775). Frederick, MD: University Publications of America.

21

Gettin' Real Love: *Waiting to Exhale* and Film Representations of Womanist Identity

Meta G. Carstarphen

With rented limousines and lively house parties, African American women celebrated the 1995 film, *Waiting To Exhale*, directed by actor Forest Whitaker. This movie's surge to the top of the box office was not difficult to predict; after all, the 1993 novel by Terry McMillan had already shown its staying power by carving an enviable spot on the *New York Times* bestsellers list for 37 weeks in 1992 and 1993 ("Beauty of black art," 1994).

African American women embraced the cinematic version of *Waiting To Exhale* for its ability to cast a representational eye on the nuances of being young, single, black, and female in contemporary America. But women of all hues identified with the struggles and triumphs of the movie's four heroines: Savannah (Whitney Houston), Bernadine (Angela Bassett), Robin (Lela Rochon), and Gloria (Loretta Devine). The film connected viewers with each other, to a slice of women's society, and with the world "out there," through its skillfully dramatized fiction. Embodying many symbolic and realistic aspects of

369

the African American experience, *Waiting To Exhale* is an example of womanist expression.

DIFFERING PERCEPTIONS

Waiting To Exhale opened to a storm of controversy in spite of, or maybe because of, its enthusiastic reception by many African American women who felt the movie somehow reflected real life. Certainly, not all viewers found this realism comforting or positive. For instance, educator Beverly Guy-Sheftall found fault with the film's selective exclusion of details accented in the book on which it was based, such as the main characters' community activism through a service group called "Black Women On The Move." ("Exhaling and inhaling," 1996, p. 122). However, the groundswell of controversy centered more often on the film's images and messages. As a symbolic depiction of contemporary African American women and, to an extent, the men in their lives, did the movie overstate the issues or underplay the problems?

That the film and its images resounded so strongly with women placed it also within the context of women-centered expression and heightened the tension about what the film "really meant." Therapist Audrey B. Chapman, in an *Ebony* magazine round-up discussion about the film, said she wished that the main characters had been shown "making better choices for themselves." Nevertheless, she applauded the film for being a "woman's movie with a woman's point of view" ("Exhaling and inhaling," 1996, p. 118). Similarly, film reviewer Linda Lopez McAlister (1995) celebrated what she saw as the long-awaited arrival of "a Hollywood film that reflected black women's experiences of friendship." As such, McAlister declared *Waiting To Exhale* to be "certainly a womanist film—though such words as womanist or feminist are never uttered."

Alice Walker (1983, p. xi), one of the earliest proponents of supplanting feminist philosophy with a "womanist" ideology, defined *womanism* as celebrating things womanly, both singly and in a group. Thus, her definition, in part, says that a womanist "loves other women" as well as men, and appreciates and "prefers women's culture," but is "traditionally universalist" in her appreciation for all ethnicities and both genders. For some, the distinction between a feminist and womanist point of view may seem to turn on semantics, although some early feminists of color, such as bell hooks (1981), saw the need to treat feminism as "an ideology in the making" (p. 194). However, the divergence between feminism and womanism has, in fact, everything to do with the collision of sexual and racial politics in the 20th century.

SURFACE VIEWS AND SYMBOLIC MEANINGS

On the surface, *Waiting to Exhale* has a simple enough storyline: four middle-class friends, with varying degrees of professional and personal achievements, share mutual tribulations in their discovery that the route to "true love" can be paved with uncertainty, deceit, and heartache. In the process of negotiating their way through these relationships, the four women confront their own fears and fantasies about what it means to be in love. Savannah (Whitney Houston), the newest resident to Phoenix, has opted for a salary cut to pursue a new career in television production, but has real problems cutting ties with a married lover. Bernadine (Angela Bassett), ensconced in luxury as the wife of a millionaire, faces the collapse of her picture-perfect marriage and her long-repressed desire to succeed on her own.

Robin (Lela Rochon), a mid-level manager at an insurance company, fixates on pretty looks, both her own and her suitors, often to the exclusion of common sense. Finally, Gloria (Loretta Devine) has a successful hairstyling salon and a teenaged son she has shepherded, as a single parent, to young manhood. With his inevitable autonomy, she has to decide whether to continue to avoid new relationships and stay trapped by her longings for food and her former husband.

Beneath the surface, *Waiting To Exhale* is a display of self-determinant imagery. Every key aspect of *Waiting To Exhale* is defined by African American sensibilities: the original text on which it was based, its director, and the ensemble of actresses. Within the long-standing Hollywood tradition of filmmaking, such a concerted collaboration among African Americans has been rare indeed.

Taken as a whole, the film derives its most comprehensive symbolic value from the black experiences it evokes and simulates. It symbolized by its presence the absence of what Hollywood had ignored for decades: a rendition of life in communities of color. Paradoxically, such symbol making was inherently fraught with tension, for it placed an inordinate amount of representational power on one single film. And, in the absence of a plethora of movies depicting relationships within the African American community, *Waiting to Exhale* stirred both men and women to passionate views about how well or how poorly it showed the "truth."

BARELY VISIBLE, NEVER PLAUSIBLE

Ossie Davis, a veteran of film and stage roles, has pointed out that the absence of African Americans from film and theater is long-standing:

> We were the only group that, for a long time, was not allowed to
> represent itself on the stage. In the early days, blacks were represent-
> ed on the stage by whites who put black on their faces. Actors of
> great note did that. We were the only ones who had to go through
> that, and we knew that the stereotypes which we saw and became
> familiar with were often derogatory. (cited in Jones, 1991, p. 7)

The transition in American popular arts from stage to film during the first two decades of the 20th century amplified this demeaning
imagery to mass audiences. In a society that remained rigidly segregated
along color lines for nearly 60 years, such images became truth for millions of viewers who lacked personal experiences to counter the celluloid representations.

But if the presence of African Americans in film was minimal
during those years, the impact of sepia females was further diminished
by the limitations of their portrayals whenever they did appear on-
screen. Segregated not only by ethnicity but by gender from choice roles
and complex scripts, women of color were all but invisible, prompting
one film scholar to observe that of "all the film characters, the black
woman had consistently been the one most ignored" (Bogle, 1988).

Even further complicating the full representation of the African
American woman in film has been the manipulation of her sexuality.
Frequent portrayals of women as domestics or poverty-stricken mothers
have fairly stripped them of any overt sexual intention. In this tradition,
actress Hattie McDaniel won the first Oscar given to an African
American for her selfless—and sexless—rendition of Scarlett O'Hara's
faithful servant in the 1939 popular epic, *Gone With The Wind*.

Noting the recurrence of African American women as either
"domestic servants" or "welfare mothers," film scholar Jacqueline Bobo
(1991) identified three dominant characterizations that over time have
transcended particular roles: "the sexually promiscuous Black woman,
the overbearing Black matriarch, and the strident, domineering black
woman known as 'Sapphire'" (p. 73).

Theatrically vivid, not one of these images is complimentary, and
collectively they form a disturbing pattern. Isolated from healthy family,
friendship, or community relationships, each stereotype projects a woman
unable to change her life for the better. If cast as sexual siren, her libido
eventually becomes her downfall, as portrayed by Dorothy Dandridge in
Carmen Jones (1954). Playing a romantic foil to Harry Belafonte's portrayal
of an idealistic young soldier, Dandridge's Carmen is a sexual predator
whom women envy and men desire. Although an adaptation of Bizet's
Italian opera, *Carmen*, the black film finds easy cultural translation in its
depiction of a street-wise, brown-skinned vamp, who loves jazz, drink,
and good times with the same abandon that she loves men.

In the 1934 film, *Imitation of Life*, Louise Beavers portrayed a strong matriarch who loses the family she loves despite the sacrifices she makes to keep her family. Beavers perfectly fit the physical characterization that had become standard for African American mothers: she was heavy, big-bosomed, and dark. In contrast with other characters on-screen, she held viewers' attention with her commanding size and claimed authority virtually on sight. However, Beavers' matriarch exudes a hollow strength, as she silently sanctions her fair-skinned daughter's decision to "pass" as a white woman, though this decision necessarily cuts her off from giving and receiving her daughter's love. And anywhere a shrill, carping incarnation of "Sapphire" appears, she is still designed, as was the original, to offer comic relief through her complaining, proving that for all her "sound and fury," her presence signifies nothing.

WOMANISM: A NEW SENSIBILITY EMERGES

Despite the surge in African American film portrayals after the 1970s, as Hollywood discovered economic gold among black audience films, women still largely remained trapped by powerless stereotypes. Among black independent filmmakers, however, Mark A. Reid (1991) observes a different trend, a willingness to cast women in what he calls a "black womanist" sensibility. Into this category, he assigns all films that "dramatize the shared experiences of black women" (p. 376).

This concept of sharing alludes to a mutual understanding between audience and viewer that transcends many levels. To be sure, on a fundamental level, women characters operating within this construct can be seen "sharing" with other characters in ways reflecting their intrinsic abilities to form intimate partnerships. More abstractly but equally profound is the "sharing" such films anticipate for their primary viewership—other African American women. Thus, as Reid explains, black womanist film must have a story or "narrative content" true to a world view that "real" women share. Second, the film itself must incorporate cinematic devices designed to allow for a participatory experience, or "spectatorial space," for its audience.

When Walker (1983) explored the womanist concept in a collection of essays that embraced shared experiences as necessary ingredients to empower the individual, she wrote, "And so our mothers and grandmothers have, more often than not anonymously, handed on the creative spark, the seed of the flower they themselves never hoped to see: or like a sealed letter they could not plainly read" (p. 240). She analogizes that "womanist is to feminist as purple to lavender" (p. xii). That purple is the darker shade is an obvious reference to her definition of a womanist as "a black feminist or feminist of color." However, Walker also says that a womanist is a "traditional universalist, as in: 'Mama, why are we brown, pink, yellow, and our cousins are white, beige, and black?'" (p. xi). In placing the womanist sensibility outside rigid ethnic boundaries, a womanist is characterized as flexible, intercultural, and self-defined.

FEMINIST VERSUS WOMANIST IDENTITY

In her comprehensive and insightful history of the impact of black women on the women's movements of the 19th and 20th century, Paula Giddings (1984) notes that efforts promoting women's rights emerged from the involvement of white women in the racial movements of their eras. Thus, feminist leaders often found their voice in movements for gender-based improvements as a result of sensibilities stirred by the blatant racial injustices of their times. Post-antislavery and post-Civil Rights movements for women provided fertile opportunities, according to Giddings, for white women to springboard their own legitimate causes for equity and fairness.

However, the African American woman, literally caught between the imperatives of two movements relevant to her experiences, felt ambivalent. Called on to participate in both movements (as their numbers were needed), African American women have been loathe to forsake racial goals for those defined strictly by gender. This dichotomy may not have been the intention of the feminist movement, but often has been the result. Thus, feminism as articulated by white spokeswomen has often set an agenda in opposition to the power, authority, and control exercised by white men. But for women of color who knew that their men, on the whole, did not participate in the power elite, taking up the feminist agenda against patriarchy seemed to be a bittersweet battle indeed. As Giddings concludes, "both the past and present tell us it is not a question of race versus sex, but race *and* sex" (p. 352; emphasis in original). These aspects of collectivism and struggle are reflected in the sensibilities of African American women.

WOMANIST THEORY: PAVING THE WAY FOR SELF-IDENTITY IN *WAITING TO EXHALE*

Womanism allows for self-definition and empowerment, but it does not force conformity to social movements. In their exploration of how black women use gender ideology to achieve or maintain mental health, researchers Robert T. Carter and Elizabeth E. Parks (1996) found in their study of 218 female college students that womanism can have social and individual benefits. On the whole, they found that to the extent a student had developed an internally defined sense of womanhood (womanist), as opposed to an external, ideologically defined concept, she was healthier. Adapting the model the Carter-Parks study uses, the evolution of a womanist identity progresses through four stages, with the final and highest stage representing internalization. Significantly, this final stage is preceded by one in which "women typically seek out intense interpersonal relationships with other women" (p. 2).

Waiting To Exhale dramatizes this "womanist" sensibility. At the time the movie debuted, dating and establishing relationships was an infrequent topic in films featuring African Americans. At the same time, for many sisters, the refrain, "a good man is hard to find," was not just a string of entertaining words from a blues song, but a fact of life. This reality was reflected in *Waiting to Exhale*. Savannah, Bernadine, Robin, and Gloria—the story's main protagonists—are successful women who wonder if finding their own power must come at the expense of the romantic relationships about which they fantasize.

Interestingly, although the film itself represents a reality consistent with experiences shared by many African American women, its very construct imposes a context in which discerning fantasy from reality in relationships becomes the film's object lesson. This distinction is most keenly apparent in the film's sociopolitical use of color, its merger of voice-over and song juxtaposed against visual images for ironic effect, and the staging of its female ensemble around "womanist" principles.

Of Color and Identity in Film

Waiting To Exhale's camera becomes the eye through which viewers enter its world, and it is a colorful one indeed. The four actresses, when shot together, do not simply look like four nondescript "brown" people. Instead, they reveal subtle shifts in skin hues, from light ginger to a rich-coffee-with-light-cream tint, that African Americans have always accepted as being true to their experiences. And those variations are intentional, made visible through the manipulation of traditional movie lighting techniques.

High key, or high contrast, lighting, which calls for the use of bright, full lighting, is the expected approach for directors who are shooting dramas, comedies, or action films. On color film, such lighting brings out sharper details and "bluer" tones. Consequently, low key, or more darkly lit films are representative of choices made by directors shooting thrillers or mysteries. But in *Waiting to Exhale*, low-key lighting dominates, despite the clearly dramatic, and occasionally comic, thrust of this movie. Coupled with colored filters that accentuate the "yellow" and orange tints in the color film, a traditional paradigm—one that has made Anglo flesh tones the "standard" for lighting and film color formulas—is quietly reversed.

That such technical choices are "an ideological expression of culture" is illustrated by Brian Winston (1985, p. 106) in his historical analysis of the development of color film technology. He notes that far from registering the natural world in an objective, nonjudgmental fashion, color film technology exercises a range of choices and combinations of its three primary color tints: blue, red, and yellow. Lighting decisions are driven by the need to forge a relationship between the chemistry involved in shooting and developing film, and the desired effect of reproducing pleasing "flesh tones." When Caucasian flesh becomes the standard for such choices, other skin variations must, in effect, be sacrificed.

Citing research conducted during the 1950s by scientists working for the Kodak film company, Winston shows how such decisions evolved. The researchers' experimentation with the photograph of a young Anglo woman led to considerable investigation into what balance of colors would actually compensate for the perceived defects in her skin color, which when reproduced exactly was thought to be "too beefy" (p. 120). The subsequent distortion lightened her skin to what was believed to be a more preferred tone, "a whiter shade of white," underscoring that reality as reflected through technology is not without bias: "Exact reproduction, a supposed goal of the photographic and cinematographic project, takes second place to inexact, culturally determined, 'optimum' reproduction" (p. 121).

In *Waiting to Exhale*, director Whitaker subverts this tradition to make the flesh of his subjects more pleasing, to create a visual reality African Americans would find comforting and true to their own experiences, and to establish part of a "spectatorial space" for these viewers.

Telling the Story in Voice and Song

In addition, the combination of the musical soundtrack and the voice-over segments were used to create irony and intimacy. A movie fundamentally about romance, *Waiting to Exhale* highlighted love songs. The selective use of the main characters' voices talking over the action offered effective, often ironic insights into the characters' lives. Moreover, the voice-over segments invited audiences to eavesdrop as another way to enhance intimacy between viewers and screen characters. As film scholar Eric Smoodin (1983) explains it, once the voice-over is established, it serves to unite the action and subsequent dialogue in the entire film "as a sort of linguistic event, as the narrator's speech even when there is none" (p. 19).

At the film's opening, the sound of a velvet-voiced radio announcer sets the stage. It is New Year's Eve, and everyone—including Savannah, Bernadine, Robin, and Gloria—is preoccupied with romance. Savannah, new in town, primps before going to meet a blind date. Bernadine prepares to accompany her husband to a business affair she does not want to attend. Robin and Gloria are alone in their respective homes, with Robin resolved to see the new year in with her dog, while Gloria uses food to escape her loneliness.

Savannah's voice-over sets the tone for the rest of the film and, in many ways, sets up its essential irony: how should these accomplished women balance their need for independence with their desire to be romantically linked to a man? In a wary and accusatory statement, Savannah dismisses men's abilities to understand women and concludes, "What they're best at is convincing us we should feel desperate. Thank God I don't fall for that shit." But, in fact, the audience knows that Savannah is preparing carefully for a date with a stranger because she does not want to be alone in a town new to her, and the audience begins to sense her desperation.

Later that evening, when Savannah meets Lionel, her prearranged date, she slow dances with him and fantasizes that he is the one she has "been waiting for all her life." The ballad playing in the background features a male singing group crooning the lyrics, "I'm going to make you my wife/'cause you're my everything." The couple are filmed in slow motion, and as the camera circles them at this speed, accentuating every gesture and embrace they share, Savannah exhales, letting loose a symbolic sigh of relief and contentment. Once more, Savannah's "hidden" thoughts are given expression in a voice-over that also invites participatory support from the viewers. Therefore, not only do women see her in a highly romanticized situation, they hear her thoughts celebrating the exhilaration of the moment: *"Thank you, Jesus! And then I did it. I closed my eyes and I . . . exhaled . . . and pretended this man was mine. That he was everything I ever dreamed of . . . that he was the one I'd been waiting for all my life."*

Savannah's imagined joy is short-lived, however, as a woman's voice off-screen calls Lionel's name, forcing her back into a reality that does not include Lionel. Back in the safety of her home, the dateless Savannah has discovered that the fantasy of her dream for companionship has yielded to the reality of her loneliness.

An important counterpoint to Savannah's experience is that of her friend, Bernadine. Unlike her career-successful friend, Bernadine chose to invest her time in nurturing family over career. The wife of a prosperous businessman, Bernadine has a fabulous house, two children, and a much-deferred dream of starting her own catering business. On the same New Year's Eve that Savannah tries to find true love in a blind date, Bernadine is shown in an over-the-shoulder shot that reveals her reflected image in a mirror as she applies make-up in preparation for an evening out with her husband. Bernadine's voice-over mutes the celebratory aura of New Year's Eve as the audience hears her thinking aloud: *"I do not feel like going to another one of these boring affairs."*

When her husband suddenly appears, reflected in her mirror, and offers them the chance to skip the party, Bernadine mistakes his offer as evidence that he shares her desire for a more intimate celebration. Instead, he declares his love for another woman and announces he is leaving her. A little later in the film, in a scene literally and metaphorically representative of Bernadine's explosive anger, the audience witnesses her fury and newly found personal resolve.

Shot frenetically, with lots of movement and tilted angles, Bernadine's furious rampage through her husband's closet to rid it of his clothes and shoes reflects her fiery rage. Declaring him, in her interior voice, to be "psychotic," Bernadine then expresses out loud the disappointments of her marriage and her recognition of her husband's controlling ways. Her angry trek from the bedroom closet to a car in the garage, into which she stuffs his belongings, culminates in her calmly driving the expensive car to the front of her house, where she puts a lighted match to its contents, and then resolutely walks back to her house as the enflamed car burns brightly in the background.

In the next scene, a fireman calls her to the door. "Ma'am," he asks, "are you aware your car was on fire?" As she acknowledges that not only was she aware, but intimates that she was responsible, the fireman admonishes her about the city ordinance regarding the burning of trash and warns her against future infractions. However, when Bernadine tells the fireman that the expensive belongings were "trash" and that "It won't happen again," the audience knows the double meanings inherent in her statements. The trash she was expunging was the debris of a marriage gone wrong. Also, we understand that because she has resolved not to repeat the mistakes of her marriage, she will not leave herself so vulnerable to domination by another.

Fantasy Versus Reality

The last two women of this ensemble, Gloria and Robin, also have their defining cinematic moments. In pivotal scenes, each character reveals her special vulnerabilities. Once more, a combination of voice-over monologues and dialogue is used to communicate their dilemmas to the audience, inviting viewers into an empathic view of these women's situations.

During the opening New Year's Eve sequence, Robin experiences what she calls "a first"—the prospect of spending one of the most romantic nights of the year alone and at home. Speaking to her Shiatsu dog, she obsessively thinks about her last love, Russell, revealing her fantasy about this absent lover through wistful hyperbole. "Russell was so fine," she says. "Probably every woman in America wanted to be with him." Despite those formidable odds, Robin convinces herself that Russell had been equally enamored of her, although evidence of his devotion is less than convincing. "I just knew he was mine," she says, "until I found that half-slip in his gym bag." During this scene, the audience sees that Robin has created more out of her own longing for a relationship than is justified by Russell's behaviors. Her fantasy romance is reinforced by her aloneness on New Year's Eve.

Later, in a bedroom adventure notable for its bawdiness and humor, Robin seduces a co-worker named Michael. Although the camera shows a smiling and apparently willing temptress, the voice-over expresses Robin's grave doubts. Silently calling her approaching lover a "human submarine sandwich," Robin displays her willingness, nonetheless, to create a fantasy love experience as a substitute for a reality she is not willing to face. While pining for Russell, she is still willing to engage in other relationships in a rebellion against Russell's inattentiveness. Thus, Robin's encounter with Michael, doomed before it starts, leads to a disastrous lovemaking session. Out of the pain of that failure, however, the determined Michael asks Robin to tell him her "fantasy," asking her for details about what she really wants out of life. In this self-revelatory moment, Robin does not discuss good looks or a great physique. Rather, she confides to Michael that her fantasy is for a man who would marry her, buy her a suburban house, raise children with her, and allow her to eat out three times a week. Underscoring the "ordinariness" of her fantasy, Michael answers pointedly, "You don't want much. I can give you that and a whole lot more."

Gloria, the fourth friend, spends New Year's Eve alone as the silky voice of the deejay on her radio admonishes his listeners that "love might be waiting right there at home." These words prove prophetic for Gloria. The heaviest of the four, Gloria blames her weight for keeping men at bay, yet she uses food as solace for her loneliness. Unsuccessful in convincing her 17-year-old son to spend New Year's Eve with her instead of with his friends, she settles in at home with fresh groceries and anticipation of her ex-husband's visit in a few days. By the time she encounters her ex, David, Gloria's interior voice has already told the audience what her expectations are. "*When David was here last time,*" she says, "*he did me a favor by spending the night. Lord let him be merciful tonight.*"

However, the audience watches Gloria's fantasy reunion shattered by David's revelation that he is gay. Gloria retreats into activities
that have habitually shielded her from romance: preparing food, caring
for her son, and managing her hair salon. Later in the film, Gloria's
friends converge at her house for a birthday party in her honor.

ON THE WAY TO REAL LOVE: INTERNALIZATION AND THE WOMANIST PERSPECTIVE

This celebration brings all four women together in a rare instance in
which their lives intersect. Unlike a brief bar scene earlier in the film in
which the friends gather to hunt for romance, this grown-up sleep-over
party features giddy moments in which the women laugh, drink, and
dance, as well as somber moments when they argue, cry, and complain.
In one particularly telling moment, Savannah expresses their common
frustration in trying to sort out what is real and what is not in the world
of romance. As they listen to a romantic ballad, she complains aloud,
"Why do they write these damn songs? To make you think and dream,
and believe you can really feel like this?" None of her friends has an
answer, as each nods in mute agreement.

However, this silent exchange spotlights what has up to this
point been an undercurrent—the distance between expectation and experience. The audience is told explicitly what it has been implicitly shown
throughout the film—that what these women expect to feel in romantic
relationships contradicts their actual experiences with the men in their
lives. Yet, within their common friendship, these four women demonstrate their ability and willingness to endure myriad ups and downs with
each other, negotiating places within their relationships where all can fit,
in ways they do not quite emulate with men. In womanist terms, they
show their appreciation and preference for "women's culture," noting
especially an affinity for women's "emotional flexibility" and "strength"
(Walker, 1983, p. xi). Through it all, each woman, by the film's conclusion, grows to experience a final tenet of the womanist creed, that she can
learn to "love herself. Regardless" (Walker, 1983, p. xii).

This womanist transition does not, of course, translate automatically into successful romantic liaisons. It is not that the womanist experience excludes males or an appreciation of them; rather, it celebrates
femaleness first. So it is for Savannah, Robin, Gloria, and Bernadine: their
paths to finding satisfying male-female romantic relationships seems
marked by a journey first through positive female-centered, self-love.

Although all four of the film's heroines have used their group
relationship to emerge after a year in a wiser, better place, none has

defined "success" in exactly the same way. In fact, of the four, only Gloria and Bernadine seem destined for successful romantic relationships, despite this being a stated objective for all.

Gloria, who bonds with a new neighbor named Marvin, and Bernadine, who befriends an out-of-town businessman named James, share the common experience of friendship, not sex, with these men. By contrast, Robin and Savannah are shown to be most alike, for although their approaches differ, they both use physical cues—good looks, good sex—as pathways to creating the relationship of their dreams. They repeat this pattern until the very end of the movie, when they finally come to terms with the fantasy of their relationships with the men in their lives. At that point, they are able to reject these men and their promises, even if it means being alone, or—in Robin's case—raising a child on her own.

As if to highlight the experiences of Gloria and Bernadine separately from the disastrous, more physically based relationships of Savannah and Robin, director Whitaker frames them differently, crafting scenes involving Bernadine and James, as well as Gloria and Marvin, which are conversation-driven and notably devoid of a soundtrack filled with romantic songs and wistful lyrics. The friendships Bernadine and Gloria have developed with James and Marvin exist because the women used a womanist sensibility to build meaningful connections from their friends, to themselves, to men.

By the end of the film, the four friends celebrate another New Year's Eve. This time, they are together and, in womanist fashion, celebrate themselves and the occasion as a group.

Waiting to Exhale inevitably leaves open many unresolved and controversial issues by inviting viewers into the private thoughts and experiences of four independent women and their sexual/romantic dilemmas. And, as Beverly Guy-Sheftall asserts, *Waiting to Exhale* is not perfect in its representations of African American women, nor in its attempt to "capture the complexity of our lives" ("Exhaling and inhaling," 1996, p. 122). In truth, one single film—any single film—would find the responsibility to accurately reflect collective experiences a daunting—if not impossible—one. However, in a celluloid world starved for inventive images of African American women, *Waiting to Exhale* offers a breath of fresh air.

REFERENCES

Bobo, J. (1991). Black women in fiction and nonfiction: Images of power and powerlessness. *Wide Angle, 13*(3) , 72-81.

Bogle, D. (1988). *Blacks in American film and television: An encyclopedia.*
New York: Simon & Schuster.

Carter, R.T, & Parks, E.E. (1996). Womanist identity and mental health.
Journal of Counseling & Development [online], 74. (Available: Electric
Library [1996, December 19])

Giddings, P. (1984) *When and where I enter . . . the impact of black women on
race and sex in America.* New York: William Morrow.

The beauty of black art. (1994, October 10). *Time*, p. 66.

Exhaling and inhaling: A symposium—was the film fair to black men
and black women? (1996, April). *Ebony, 51,* 116-127.

hooks, b. (1981) *Ain't I a woman: Black women and feminism.* Boston: South
End Press.

Jones, G. W. (1991) *Black cinema treasures: Lost and found.* [Foreword by
Ossie Davis]. Denton: University of North Texas Press.

McAlister, L. L. (1995). Review of the film *Waiting To Exhale.* "The
Women's Show," WMNF-FM (88.5). Tampa, FL. (Available: The
Electric Library [1996, December 19])

Reid, M. A. (1991). Dialogic modes of representing Africa(s): Womanist
film. *Black American Literature Forum, 25*(2), 375-388.

Smoodin, E. (1983). The image and the voice in the film with spoken narration. *Quarterly Review of Film Studies, 8*(4), 19-32.

Walker, A. (1983). *In search of our mothers' gardens: Womanist prose by Alice
Walker.* New York: Harcourt Brace Jovanovich.

Winston, B. (1985). A whole technology of dyeing: A note on ideology
and the apparatus of the chromatic moving image. *Daedalus, 114,*
105-123.

22

News, Feminism and the Dialectics of Gender Relations

Carolyn M. Byerly

Information, we have often been told, is power. The question today is, as it was a century ago: How can women ensure that the information, images and pictures of the world received through the mass media serve their needs and interests. (Gallagher, 1987, p. 11)

The news and entertainment media remain men's domains, even after a quarter century of feminist activism—much of which has focused on making the media more egalitarian in both representing and employing women. My purpose here is not to argue with the fact that men control the media, because it is amply demonstrated by empirical data and a significant body of critical literature. Rather, I point out why I believe feminist analysis should move beyond the limitations imposed by what might be called the paradigm of the misogynist media. This paradigm has dominated feminist communication research for two decades and manifested itself most recently in the theory of a media backlash against feminism. In addition, I seek to show how research that analyzes discrete aspects of media process and content can reveal how feminism, over time, has deeply imbedded itself in the fabric of media messages and the industries that produce them. My concern is particularly with news, which has the power to define serious topics for public debate and to identify major players in political, economic, and social processes.

In this chapter, I argue that media research concerned mainly with how and why the media neglect, misrepresent, and trivialize women's ideas and experiences fails to give an accurate and complete account of how feminism has influenced today's news agendas, content, and professional standards. I follow Rapping's (1994) reasoning that we simply are not at the same point that we were two and three decades ago, in terms of women's relationship to the news industries, and that changing times require changing research agendas.

Since the late 1960s, feminists have fought for and won an end to segregated job advertisements in newspapers, an end to the use of "Miss" and "Mrs." in news stories, changes with respect to gender in Associated Press and other news styles, the right to be hired and promoted within media professions, and entree to increasing numbers of stories, both as news sources and as news subjects, among other things. Though still underrepresented in both news content and journalistic professions, women play a more vital role in defining and developing news stories today than ever before in history. Many reporters, both men and women, today consider themselves feminists and admit to taking an active role in trying to bring feminist principles to newsroom policies and the news they write (Byerly & Warren, 1996). Some recent feminist research on content has shown that news routinely contains feminist language, ideas and perspectives, particularly in years when the feminist movement is making gains and perceived to be strong (Bridge, 1994; Cancian & Ross, 1981; Rapping, 1994).

These developments suggest a research agenda in which feminism is explored not as a failed or even a defensive force but, as Rapping (1994) insists, "a militant force which, since the late 1960s, has forced its way into the major channels of discourse and representation in both subtle and dramatic ways" (p. 7). Much of the current popular feminist discourse, as well as much feminist academic scholarship, seems to have lost sight of the ways that enduring social movements like feminism transform social institutions, including the media, over time, through a dialectical process that engages women in struggle at every level of production and consumption.[1] Feminism and its impact on the news media can only be understood within this larger historical context.

A word about terminology. I use the term *feminism* to refer to the broad, collective efforts by women of varying philosophies to expand women's rights and to reformulate social norms in terms of women's experiences. I engage the notion of a *dialectical process*, one in which certain forces and conditions produce changes in relations of power over a period of time, to analyze women's long-term struggle to assert greater authority within media industries and the messages and images they produce. I use the concept of *consciousness* in its traditional sense to refer to awareness of one's position in relation to social, political, and economic forces. Women's consciousness-raising has figured prominently in the modern feminist movement's strategy for social change, particularly in its organizing stage during the late 1960s. *Violence against women* means all forms of sexual and physical assault (battering) that women experience, mostly from male assailants, both strangers and acquaintances. Many of my examples are drawn from news coverage of violence against women, which has been a major part of feminist media agendas, as well as the focus of my own activist work for more than 20 years.

BACKLASH AMNESIA

Few books have captured the imagination of women these last few years—both those who call themselves feminists and those who do not—as Susan Faludi's book *Backlash: The Undeclared War Against American Women*. Published in 1991 by Crown Books, a trade press that guaranteed a wide audience, the book built extensively on a series of articles that Faludi wrote while working for the *Wall Street Journal*. In those articles, Faludi had carefully dismantled and debunked several studies that purported to show how feminism had produced new problems for women, including "the man shortage," "the biological clock," and the "mommy track," all of which supposedly threatened the personal happiness and careers many women had chosen instead of traditional home and motherhood. Faludi also criticized the notion of "postfeminism," which embodies the belief that the women's liberation movement, which many nonfeminists alleged had made women miserable by opening up new opportunities, was over (Faludi, 1991, p. 77).

Faludi's articles won a Pulitzer Prize for explanatory journalism in 1991, lending mainstream credibility to her claims and giving her a high profile in the very media she had criticized. Faludi had used extensive government data and anecdotal and other evidence to build her case against the news and entertainment media, which, she said, had trivialized, pathologized, and marginalized feminism and its followers during Reagan's and Bush's presidential terms, thereby providing a conservative context for antifeminism to take hold. Although the backlash was not orchestrated from a central place, it had a central mission, and it engaged the media in what she called a "relentless whittling-down process—much of it amounting to outright propaganda—that served to stir women's private anxieties and break their political wills" (Faludi, 1991, p. xvii). The media had shown a particular disposition toward "trend journalism,"[2] according to Faludi, by publishing and broadcasting a steady stream of studies and social commentaries emanating from universities, government agencies, and other sources. These replaced the "pro-family" diatribes of fundamentalist preachers with sympathetic and even progressive-sounding rhetoric. It cosmeticized the scowling face of antifeminism while blackening the feminist eye. In the process, it popularized the backlash beyond the New Right's wildest dreams.

Faludi's case against the media found considerable currency among many feminist communication scholars, some of whom had seen obstacles to feminist ideas and research surface in their own academic departments and institutions.[3] Faludi's explication of the media's participation in the backlash also resonated with feminist scholars who had embraced the research paradigm of media misogyny. That paradigm traces its roots most strongly to Tuchman, Daniel, and Benet's *Hearth and Home: Images of Women in the Media* (1978), the definitive collection of early theoretical and empirical research on the media's neglect and stereotypical portrayal of women. Tuchman's introduction to the book chastised the media for their "symbolic annihilation of women" through trivialization and absence, an indictment that has endured and inspired nearly two decades of feminist media research intent on revealing when, how and why the mass media have discriminated against women and feminism.

Hearth and Home provided the essential baseline data at a particular moment in time. In the 1970s, feminists in the United States and other nations were in the process of amassing evidence of their secondary status, formulating critiques, and setting their political and cultural agendas in order to challenge the gendered social systems that oppressed them. Feminists wanted to overhaul the media, just as they did laws, public policies, and other standards for gender relations. A particular goal regarding mainstream news was to reverse the stunning omission of women's achievements and concerns. Research of the period found that less than 10% of U.S. news was about women (Butler & Paisley, 1978), and even the small percentage that did exist concerned mainly white women (Window Dressing, 1977). Less than 3% of the international news in the 1970s was about women (Gallagher, 1981), and news that did concern women was likely to cast them in their traditional identities as caretakers, sex objects, or men's complements rather than in the increasingly varied roles that women actually filled in society (Ceulemans & Fauconnier, 1979; Window Dressing, 1977).

Much has happened in the way of feminist intervention since these years, and for this reason, the backlash discourse has always seemed oddly uninformed and ahistorical to me. Backlash theory loses sight of the many ways that feminists have found to communicate ideas about women's liberation among each other, as well as with women in more general audiences who might not identify with the feminist label. Second, feminism's profound impact on legal and other social policy has helped to circulate both feminist language and the ideas it contains in the news media and other forums. Third, feminism is at work on the inside of news organizations through new generations of reporters and managers who understand and identify with feminism for a variety of reasons. The following discussion takes up these points.

FEMINIST INTERVENTION IN NEWS

Feminism is by nature interventionist, seeking to interrupt social practices that lead to women's oppression and to replace them with new ones that better ensure women's full participation. Women's media action goals were first spelled out at the international level when, in 1975, delegates at the first United Nations Decade for Women conference, held in Mexico City, adopted the *World Plan of Action*. Among other things, the *Plan* called on the world's news media to remove prejudices and stereotypes and to promote women's full integration into their societies (Byerly, 1995). Feminists next succeeded in getting U.N. agencies to fund five women's news feature services, whose mission it was to expand news coverage of women in developing nations. Two of these services—Women's Feature Service, based in New Delhi, India, and Depthnews Women's News, based in Manila, Philippines—continue to operate, circulating news about women and society internationally to both specialized and mainstream news media, government offices, and nongovernmental organizations (Byerly, 1995).

Throughout the Decade for Women (1975-1985), the U.N. agencies underwrote dozens of studies on the media's portrayal of women and women's employment in media industries, and they funded training for women journalists and others in development occupations. In addition, women around the world, both in developed and developing nations, established their own newsletters, newspapers, magazines, book publishing houses, film and video production companies, and other media.

Closer to home, the U.S. National Commission on the Observance of International Women's Year wrote guidelines in 1976 calling for the definition of news to be expanded to "include more coverage of women's activities locally, nationally and internationally" and for general news stories to "show their effect on women" (cited in Butler &

Paisley, 1978, p. 186). Grassroots U.S. feminist publications like *Quest* (1976) called both for increasing feminists' access to mainstream news and creating alternative media.

Since then, delegates to the Fourth U.N. Conference on Women, held in Beijing in September 1995, again recognized in their summary document, *Platform for Action,* "Section J: Women and the Media," that the role women play in the media and the media's representation of women are keys to implementing all other proposals in the document (cited in Empowering Women, 1996). In response, the U.S.-based non-governmental organization International Women's Media Foundation, adopted an action plan to encourage women's advancement into media management, workplace policies aimed at retaining women, education for journalists about discrimination and other issues related to women, and stronger networks to foster women's professional mentoring and other support (Empowering Women, 1996).

These events coincided with feminist activities in political, educational, and other areas of society, which the news media covered with greater frequency after the early 1970s.

FEMINISM'S AGENDA-SETTING EFFECT

The term *agenda setting* has been used since the early 1970s by mass media and public opinion researchers to identify the media's ability to tell the public what to think *about*, but not necessarily what to think (McQuail, 1983). Researchers have given much less attention to the possibility of a reverse phenomenon—the power of organized groups to tell the media which events, issues, and ideas to move onto news agendas, but not necessarily how to cover them. Social movements, like feminism, which begin outside of the mainstream, have found varied ways of getting news coverage of their goals and activities for at least a century because they needed the visibility in the early stages both to build legitimacy and membership and, in the later stages, to maintain momentum (Kielbowicz & Scherer, 1986). We can discern the power of social movements to place issues within routine news by examining when, why, and how many of those movements' issues surfaced as news stories.

Both *pseudo events* organized specifically for media coverage (such as press conferences or mass demonstrations), and *real events* that occur without specific staging, are especially likely to capture media attention when they coincide with other compelling events and issues of the moment, or when they somehow threaten the status quo. The civil rights movement for racial equality and the women's rights movement for sexual equality, both with roots in the 19th century, reemerged in the mid-20th century through compelling political events that moved their central concerns onto news agendas.

Race relations became newsworthy in 1954 with *Brown v. Board of Education*, in which the U.S. Supreme Court barred segregation in public schools. The case against the Topeka, Kansas, school board was argued by the National Association for the Advancement of Colored People (NAACP), which had systematically moved cases challenging segregation through the lower courts for years. The Brown case helped mobilize the modern civil rights movement, which had its roots in a longer historical struggle for racial justice. That case and the movement it represented compelled the news media to cover race relations more routinely because it signaled that the old order (legal segregation and inequality) had given way to the new (an interracial, multicultural society with greater equality).

In a similar vein, modern feminism, in its earliest stages in the 1960s, was largely overlooked by the news media—in part because its emphasis was on rather hard-to-cover events like grassroots organizing and raising women's political consciousness (Tuchman, 1978b). Feminism became more newsworthy as a political movement when it succeeded in mobilizing women to challenge the structures of gender oppression, and when it laid out a media strategy for coverage. The *New York Times*, the nation's premiere agenda-setting newspaper, had been primed to follow feminists' efforts to legalize abortion in the face of organized opposition in New York State as early as 1965. Thirty-eight abortion-related stories appeared that year, along with another five on equal rights for women. In 1966, the year that the National Organization for Women was established, 37 stories were listed under the entry "Women-U.S." Within five years, 155 stories were listed—more than a 400% increase. That figure nearly doubled in another year, with 270 stories. Additionally, by 1972, the *Times Index* had added the word "feminist" to its index categories, thereby recognizing that movement as a continuing and significant news category.

Feminism's agenda-setting effect was first examined by Cancian and Ross (1981), who demonstrated that news coverage of women had been highest when the feminist movement this century was strong and voiced specific goals rather than general concerns. News content, they said, also was most likely to have a feminist-orientation, focusing on women's changing roles and new demands, during the movement's strong periods. The reverse was true—that is, the news focused on women's traditional roles of mother and caretaker—when the movement waned. Feminism made its first organized news intervention in the summer and fall of 1970 when the National Organization for Women and its allies conducted a media blitz of information about their political activities. This coalition of feminist groups was preparing its legislative agendas on abortion rights, rape law reform, equal employment, and other issues at the time, and the news media flocked to interview feminist leaders in response (Carden, cited in Cancian & Ross, 1981).

Feminism has continued to set news agendas by creating the social climate and historical conditions within which many events related to women's status could emerge, become newsworthy, and enter public discourse. For instance, Anita Hill could not have sat before a U.S. Senate judiciary committee in 1991, detailing the alleged sexual harassment against her by Supreme Court nominee Clarence Thomas, without a feminist movement that named the problem and lobbied for legislation in the 1980s to make sexual harassment illegal. Thomas was finally confirmed, but predictions that this would put a chilling effect on women's willingness to make sexual harassment complaints never came to pass. A year later, 90 female Naval officers complained about being sexually assaulted and harassed at the annual Tailhook convention for naval aviators held in Las Vegas. Lt. Paula Coughlin, the first victim to go public, gave interviews to ABC-TV and other media. The publicity forced the Navy to take unprecedented steps to address widespread discrimination against women at all levels and caused Admiral Frank B. Kelso (who ultimately resigned over mishandling of the case) to tell the media: "Tailhook was clear evidence that we were confronting broad cultural problems. . . . It was not the first evidence. . . . No one regrets that more than I that it took an incident of this magnitude to force changes" ("Chief admits," 1992).

Soon after, female soldiers who had served in the Persian Gulf war also came forward to complain about sexual assaults by their male colleagues during the war. On July 6, 1992, CNN call-in host Larry King dedicated his program to the issue, with military personnel on hand to answer viewers' questions. King provided a respectful forum for victims to speak first-hand about being assaulted. This media event could not have occurred without the feminist antiviolence movement two decades before.

Feminists also kept their other political agendas in the news through the 1980s and 1990s by regularly holding public demonstrations in support of the Equal Rights Amendment (which failed finally in 1984), abortion rights, and other issues; continuing to challenge sex discrimination in the workplace; lobbying for custody and other family-related legislative issues; publishing an unprecedented number of books; and generating feminist-inspired films and television programs. The news and entertainment media continued to regard feminism as newsworthy, and the ideas about women's worth and equality that feminism put into circulation shaped or framed much of the media content in the decades of the 1980s and 1990s. The following discussion, which explores feminist framing in news stories and programs about violence against women, also explains how the media's more specific representation of feminist ideas has been uneven through the years, sometimes favorable and sometimes not.

NEWS FRAMES

Tuchman (1978b) and Gitlin (1981) were among the earliest news sociologists to show that news stories are structured or "framed" in ways that convey value-laden messages about issues central to news events. Framing analysis allows one to locate the underlying meanings in stories by identifying which facts are included or omitted, which persons are used for sources, and how information is arranged. In this way, one can trace the ways that news stories adopt, negotiate, or reject philosophies and meanings about women that the feminist movement has sought to institutionalize. As a result, one can see that the news media are neither monolithic or static, but widely variable in their ability to incorporate feminism (Rapping, 1994, p. 13). One also can discern, as Entman (1993) says, the significant power of reporters to "promote a particular problem, definition, causal interpretation, moral evaluation, and/or treatment recommendation" (p. 52).

Butler and Paisley's (1978) important early study of mainstream popular magazines considered the subtle ways that news reports of the Equal Rights Amendment had framed stories by emphasizing one of two positions: (a) that the ERA *would strengthen* women's legal protections, or (b) that the ERA *would not weaken* existing protections for women. The second emphasis, the authors believed, gave readers the assurance that the ERA would leave intact traditional arrangements between men and women. Butler and Paisley concluded that articles about the ERA regarding economic and legal issues tended to be framed using the first position by showing that "the ERA will strengthen your protections," whereas ERA stories on marriage and family issues used the second position.

News stories about violence against women—rape, incest, sexual harassment, battering, and so forth—can be considered to have a feminist frame when they place feminist language and analyses about women's victimization central to the story, and when victims are allowed to talk about their experiences in their own words. Feminists had placed antiviolence campaigns at the top of their political agendas after large numbers of women revealed in consciousness-raising groups in the late 1960s that they had been raped or battered and that these experiences had seriously impaired their self-esteem, confidence, and otherwise held them back.[4] Brownmiller (1975), Medea and Thompson (1974), Russell (1975), and other feminist authors placed men's victimization of women central to a new analysis of women's secondary position in society, a theoretical breakthrough that generated rape law reform, the establishment of women's shelters and rape crisis centers, and volumes of new academic research. Through the years, feminists working in rape crisis centers and battered women's shelters became increasingly adept at bringing news attention to their antiviolence campaigns, and at educating reporters working for both local and national news media to understand the causes of violence, its effects on victims, and the importance of women being able to tell their stories publicly.[5]

These activities helped to increase both the amount of news about violence against women, as well as the likelihood that news frames would reflect a feminist philosophy. Benedict's (1992) historical analysis of how the media have covered sex crimes found that before the civil rights and feminist movements, the U.S. media typically reported on cases in which black assailants allegedly violated white women. However, "after 1971, rape stories not only discussed racial prejudice but, for the first time, examined prejudice against victims, too" (p. 42).

Statistical analysis of the nation's top agenda-setting newspaper, the *New York Times*, shows that coverage of sexual assault issues increased more than 250% between 1972 and 1974. Rape speakouts, debates over rape reform legislation in the New York Assembly, and the publication of Brownmiller's book *Against Our Will* (1975), the first historical examination of rape from the victim's perspective, all challenged traditional thinking about women's secondary status.

Analysis of the early news coverage of violence against women reveals several trends. First, the news tended to improve as reporters became better informed about the facts surrounding sexual assault and domestic violence. Benedict (1992) found that most reporters who covered the John and Greta Rideout marital rape case in Oregon in 1979 knew little or nothing about domestic violence. Many stories (carried by the major newspapers she analyzed) published Greta's trial testimony detailing John's abuse of her, thereby letting the victim tell her story. However, stories after John's acquittal and the Rideouts' brief reconciliation stressed John's innocence and Greta's lies and promiscuity, thereby damning her as a "woman who likes rape" (Benedict, 1992, p. 86). According to Benedict, few papers reported the couple's divorce, John's jail time for violating his probation, or Greta's eviction from her apartment after the trial. Most important, nearly all reporters missed the big story, that Greta was a battered woman and that the couple was locked into a classic cycle of domestic violence in which violent episodes and reconciliation follow each other repeatedly until someone is killed or the relationship ends. More than a decade later, when Benedict interviewed reporters who had covered the Rideout case, several acknowledged that they knew little of battering at the time and that they allowed prosecuting and defense attorneys to shape their ideas about the case rather than seek a wider range of experts. All said they would have done it differently had they understood more about sexual and domestic violence.

By contrast, Byerly (1994) noted the surge in public support for a marital rape bill before the Washington state legislature a few years later, in 1982, after a savvy female reporter from a major Seattle television station included in her evening newscast footage a veteran state senator standing on the Senate floor asking, "Well, if you can't rape your own wife, who can you rape?" (p. 60). The story foregrounded the reasonableness of lifting the marital rape exclusion from state law and, conversely, the unreasonableness of the mostly male legislators who opposed it. These events were bolstered by interviews in the Seattle area media with sociologist Diana E. H. Russell, who had just published her groundbreaking study, *Rape in Marriage* (1982). Russell had been brought to Washington State by feminists to testify on the proposed marital rape legislation and to give public lectures on her research. The outrageousness of the bill's opponents contrasted sharply with the evidence offered by Russell and other feminist leaders, and reporters followed the debates for several weeks before the bill's passage.

A major indication of feminism's enduring impact on news reporting of sexual violence can be seen in today's newsroom policies on identifying victims. Most newsrooms during the 1980s and 1990s continued the practice of not naming or otherwise identifying victims, and many newsrooms have adopted written policies for handling sex crime stories. Some also do not name the accused assailant to protect the identities of his victims. There have been other feminist-inspired advances. Both general assignment and sports journalists have been increasingly likely in the last few years to report on sexual assaults and battering by athletes. The O.J. Simpson case in 1995, in which the former pro-football player was charged with the murder of his ex-wife Nicole and her friend Ron Goldman, inspired many of these, including stories in major agenda-setting newspapers like the *Washington Post, Los Angeles Times,* and *Nashville Tennessean,* which explored football players' off-the-field violence against women and the National Football League's program in violence prevention and counseling with athletes. Bill Brubaker's (1995a, 1995b, 1995c) three stories in the *Washington Post* presented a feminist frame by foregrounding the players' responsibility for the violence and the harm to victims. Extensive interviews with victims, their advocates, and psychologists; profiles of abusive men; and data on the arrest and conviction rates of NFL players helped to develop the series, which got front page and inside front-section play.

However, even though feminist ideas are adopted into news frames, those ideas are sometimes negotiated or distorted to reach mainstream audiences. This practice can be seen in several prime-time television programs of the 1980s, such as "Something About Amelia" (about childhood incest), "He's Not a Stranger" (about date rape), and "The Burning Bed" (about a battered woman who is acquitted of killing her abusive husband) (Rapping, 1994, p. 12). Some of these made-for-TV stories about women's victimization, like Francine Hughes's in "The Burning Bed," drew their characters and facts from real-life stories that had been in the news. All these programs negotiated feminism's analysis of women's victimization in various ways to make controversial issues "accessible to people of all ages, classes and educational levels" (Rapping, 1994, pp. 138-139). "Something About Amelia," for instance, tied up the story with a happy ending, complete with contrite father and a supportive mother (two elements often missing in real-life incest cases). "The Burning Bed" kept a feminist analysis of Francine Hughes's growing awareness of her danger, her need to get away, and her final desperate escape by killing her battering husband Mickey. But the end, in which she retreated into middle-class security, by no means reflected her real-life difficulties to reestablish a life for herself and her children.

The negotiation of the feminist analysis of rape can also be seen in Jane Schorer's Pulitzer Prize winning series on Nancy Ziegenmeyer's rape case, which was published in the *Des Moines Register* in 1990. The series initially drew national attention because it demonstrated a rape victim's willingness to be publicly identified in the news. Schorer's series foregrounded Ziegenmeyer's efforts to stand up for herself and fight back in court (two strong feminist antiviolence themes), as well as her frustrations with an indifferent criminal justice system that revictimized women and their families with repeated delays. However, from the beginning, Ziegenmeyer's case was atypical: her rapist was a stranger (most are acquaintances), African American (most are the same race as the victim, who in this case was white), and brutal—he both battered and sexually assaulted Ziegenmeyer (most rapists do not physically injure their victims). Although placing many feminist meanings central to the series, the stories also reinforced old rape mythology about dangerous strangers and the victimization of white women by men of color. For these reasons, the Ziegenmeyer series also contains elements of distortion, which is discussed next.

News about particular events may consistently fall back onto old myths about victims, perpetrators, and violence against women, thereby reflecting antifeminist philosophies in its framing. As demonstrated by Schorer's series on Nancy Ziegenmeyer, rape stories today are not always free of outdated, incorrect assumptions about violence against women. Some news coverage also sustains blame-the-victim framing, thereby rejecting feminism's messages. Cuklanz's (1992) analysis of the news about the Gary Dotson-Cathleen Crowell Webb case is one example. In the late 1980s, in Illinois, the press avidly followed legal developments after Webb recanted her key testimony charging Dotson had raped her. Cuklanz found that most news stories had favored Dotson for his likable personality and unlikely profile as a rapist and emphasized Webb's unbelievability. By framing stories to favor Dotson, Cuklanz concluded, the news media had probably contributed to Dotson's pardon for a crime for which he had already been convicted.

Similarly, news coverage of a New Bedford, Massachusetts, case in 1983, in which six men were accused of gang raping a young woman on a pool table at Big Dan's pool hall while onlookers jeered and cheered, generally failed to explore the causes of rape and gang rape, who was responsible, or how complex factors of gender, race, and class figured into the crime and its handling by the criminal justice system. Many stories were supportive of the victim, Cuklanz (1995) found, owing to substantial eye-witness corroboration, medical evidence, and the fact that the victim was a mother of two young children. However, news accounts from major newspapers that Cuklanz examined had overall reinforced the notion that women provoke rape, that they are raped by strangers, and that socially marginal, ethnic minority men (in this case, Portuguese Americans) are the assailants. Absent also were Portuguese feminist voices, who might have articulated a more complex analysis of victimization and ethnicity. (The victim was also of Portuguese descent, although few news accounts mentioned this.) Instead, the news media focused on conflict between feminists in rape crisis centers and members of the Portuguese community, and on the lurid descriptions of the rape crime (Cuklanz, 1995).

FEMINISM IN NEWSROOMS

Feminists have made much about the media's failure to hire and promote women on a par with men, particularly within newsrooms, even after 20 years of feminist activism. The underlying assumption is that more women will better assure attention to women's and feminists' views and concerns in news content. There is much here to contemplate. Women in the United States entered journalism fields in larger and larger numbers after feminism expanded women's opportunities in the 1970s. Women made up only about 20% of the U.S. journalistic workforce in 1971; that increased to 34% a decade later, and, in 1992, women were closer to a par with men, with numbers ranging somewhere between 39% and 45%, depending on the source (Empowering Women, 1996; Lafky, 1993).

Although small percentages of those women hold supervisory positions at their newspapers and broadcast stations, there is evidence that they have brought feminist principles squarely into many newsrooms by vying for personnel policies, news assignments, and stories that reflect women's experiences, needs, and interests. Women journalists achieved these gains in part by establishing caucuses or other support groups in U.S. newsrooms to advocate for women's advancement in the profession, beginning in the 1970s. After Congress passed Title VII (of the Civil Rights Act of 1964) in 1972, extending employment discrimination to cover sex, women's groups supported their members in filing successful sex-discrimination suits over hiring, pay, and promotion issues. Feminist journalists recognized the importance of keeping their organizations alive during the conservative 1980s, when women's status was under attack (Byerly & Warren, 1996). Claims that women's advancement within the profession generally has been "a long, slow journey" (Lafky, 1993, p. 87) are accurate. However, Bridge (1994) found that by the end of the 1980s, women journalists accounted for 29% of the bylines in major U.S. dailies and 40 percent of those in minor markets; about a fourth of all major news sources quoted in print journalism are female. Bridge also argues that since about 1989, women's representation in the news overall has been more "positive"—that is, descriptors increasingly refer to women as winners, leaders, or talented in some way, rather than as victims, criminals, sex objects, wrongdoers, or connected to newsworthy men as wives or mothers (Bridge, 1994, p. 7).

Feminist presence in newsrooms is a fact of life today. Byerly and Warren (1996) found most of their female respondents from 18 major U.S. daily newspapers considered themselves feminists and had participated in newsroom activities aimed at changing personnel policies and news coverage with respect to gender, race, and sexual orientation during the 1980s and early 1990s. Feminists remobilized women's groups in many newsrooms in the early 1990s, outraged over two particular events: (a) an all-male Senate Judiciary Committee's confirmation of U.S. Supreme Court nominee Clarence Thomas, in spite of testimony by law professor Anita Hill that he had sexually harassed her years earlier when she was his assistant; and (b) news media treatment of Patricia Bowman, whom several media named as the victim in the William Kennedy Smith rape case, and then used her background to imply she was an unstable person with loose sexual morals (Byerly & Warren, 1996).

Women journalists who wrote about these and other feminist-oriented events gained steady recognition for their excellence in journalism during the backlash years. The number of Pulitzer Prizes awarded to women for stories broadly construed as "women's issues" increased from only one in the 1970s, to four in the 1980s, and six in the years 1990-1993. In this last group were Schorer's public service award for the Ziegenmeyer rape case, and Faludi's own prize for explanatory journalism for her expose of the backlash in the prestigious *Wall Street Journal*.

REPORTER CONSCIOUSNESS

Former *Los Angeles Times* columnist Kay Mills (1988) has theorized that the feminist movement has had a major impact on the thinking of today's reporters and editors, and, in turn, on the way that news is defined, selected, written, and edited. In *A Place in the News*, a history of women's increased participation in the profession, Mills notes:

> There is a clear and current interaction between the women's movement, the presence of women on American newspapers, and coverage of women by American newspapers. No one planned such interaction. It was not a conscious act. It is one segment of a massive social evolution. (p. 3)

Mills is taken to task for this assertion by journalism historians Beasley and Gibbons (1993), who conclude that feminism has had little impact on news definitions, news gathering routines, and operations in mainstream daily news organizations in the last two-plus decades. There are numerous inconsistencies in these authors' analysis of feminism and journalism. On the one hand, they acknowledge more women are employed at daily newspapers today than in the mid-1970s, that newsrooms are largely pro-abortion because of feminist journalists' presence, and that it is feminist journalists who have insisted on shining the news spotlight on the extramarital affairs of male politicians. Still, they insist on a limited effects model of feminism in shaping news and editorial content in metropolitan newsrooms, saying that feminist ideas remain largely the stuff of columnists and editorial writers (Beasley & Gibbons, 1993). Like Faludi, these authors miss the chance to interpret women's participation from the longer view of women's struggle for liberation and equality at every level of society.

There is a growing chorus of feminist journalists who struggled in a male-dominated profession during the 1960s, while feminism arose around them, and who continue to work within mainstream industries. This generation of women in newspapers and television was at the forefront of bringing new ideas about women into the news. Sanders and Rock (1988) have described at length how they and other women in broadcasting convinced their male supervisors in the late 1960s to let them put a human face on feminism, from the movement's perspective. Dorothy Gilliam, an African American journalist who found employment in mainstream newspapers in the 1960s, believes she was able to get many of her stories because she could empathize with and speak for the poor rural and inner-city black people she was sent out to interview (cited in Mills, 1988). Gilliam, now a columnist at the *Washington Post* and a former chairperson of the National Association of Black Journalists, insists that a "lack of diversity in newsrooms can create warped news judgment" (cited in Colon, 1994, p. B1). Today she devotes her columns to issues of race and gender.

Many female feminist reporters have brought their male colleagues along with them to feminism. As a result, many women and men journalists today write insightfully about a range of human concerns—war, poverty, violence, and other issues—in ways that reflect they have learned and adopted much from feminism. Though by no means complete, newsroom evolutions in thinking are abundantly clear in examples like the *Dallas Morning News* series in Spring 1993 on violence against women in nations around the world, in which both female and male journalists brought solid research and substantial knowledge to bear on stories that covered forms of violence from nation to nation, cultural and religious factors, changes in laws and behavioral standards in recent years, and recent global feminist efforts to make violence against women a human rights issue. All stories asked the questions that feminism raised with regard to the effect of violence on women's overall status, and in all stories women's voices and feminist analysis shaped the dominant narrative.

Similarly, Lardner's (1996a, 1996b) excellent commentaries in the *Washington Post* about the U.S. justice system's failure to prosecute violent men reveal a feminist analysis of violence against women. Lardner (1995), who wrote a book about the 1992 stalking and killing of his own daughter, Kristin, criticizes judges and prosecutors for their gender bias in court, and conservative senators for their refusal to fund provisions of the federal Violence Against Women Act of 1994 earmarked for gender studies in the court system.

The increasing likelihood that stories embodying feminist ideas and principles are written both by men and women reporters gives a journalism teacher like myself great hope. Each semester, young men and women sit in my classroom, preparing to take their place in the profession, and I try to find appropriate ways of exposing all of them to the social movements that have so much to do with the issues and events they will report on, both as student and professional journalists. Feminist readings and issues have always had a place in my journalism curricula, as have issues of race, sexual orientation, the environment, and other burning social concerns. Although my commitment to teach social issues from the perspectives of groups that led major movements has seemed the responsible thing to do, this approach has not always been smooth sailing. Students have sometimes resisted writing stories about diversity, which I typically require as part of reporting classes, because they believe it is being imposed on them as "political correctness." And, once on an interview for an academic position at a major midwestern university, I was asked point blank by a senior faculty member if my research and teaching didn't have a political agenda. These instances of opposition to feminist and other progressive ideas in journalism education signal the need for continued efforts to make a place for feminist and other social movements.

Critical communication scholars have long argued the inevitability of ideology and subjectivity in newsmaking. However, on the whole, the critical literature is limited concerning research about how journalistic consciousness is formed and acted on in the newsmaking enterprise. Hall (1980) theorized that "frameworks of knowledge" enter into media professionals' formulation of story content. Fishman (1990) extends Tuchman's (1978b) work by showing how bureaucratic routines help to define what will become news and how news issues will be imbued with dominant values. Similarly, Herman and Chomsky (1988) focus on structural and ideological factors that filter information about news events and issues. All stop short of a deeper questioning of what motivates journalists to perpetuate dominant (mainstream) values and ideas in their stories, or, conversely, what motivates them to adopt new ideas that challenge and oppose dominant values.

Meyers's (1992) study of how reporters covered the midwestern farm crisis in the 1980s, however, makes some progress in this regard. In following several reporters' stories at a major daily newspaper for a one-year period, Meyers found that two female reporters at the newspaper had opposed management's pro-business interpretation of the crisis in their reporting. Looking to Gilligan's (1982) research on women's ability to speak "in a different voice," Meyers raised the possibility that the female reporters' life experiences as women may have caused them to ask questions about the human consequences of economic problems that did not occur to their male colleagues. Meyers argues that researchers should take care not to lump reporters into a single category but that each "must be regarded as a complex totality" formed by experience as much as the reporting job's requirements. She looked to Morley's (1985) conceptualization of internal "codes" in surmising that reporters look to their own knowledge as a way of understanding, or "decoding" what they gather in preparation to write their news; but she cautions that "reporters are no more likely to be aware of their decoding strategies than viewers or readers are likely to be aware of their decoding techniques" (Meyers, 1992, p. 85).[6]

CONCLUSION

Social change often occurs by fits and starts, with periods of backsliding and sudden lurches forward. Women's struggle to advance socially, economically, and politically has indeed followed this course for more than 150 years. For this reason, feminist social transformation has all the hallmarks of what Mitchell (1992) called the longest revolution. Feminist scholars who want to reveal the movement's real impact on media structures and messages must look at a larger window of time than a few short years to make their analyses, and we must seek signs of feminism's embeddedness within all aspects of the media. Thirty years—the length of time for our modern feminist movement—is not very long in the scheme of things. Put into its proper historical perspective, the backlash and the media's part in it must eventually be understood as a part of the longer, ongoing struggle in gender relations.

ENDNOTES

1. Though feminism's roots are centuries old, the modern movement in the United States is usually dated from 1963, with publication of Betty Friedan's *Feminine Mystique*, or from 1966, with the formation of the National Organization for Women. Global feminism also dates its modern movement from the 1960s, when women of diverse nations began to lobby for United Nations support for women's rights, a process that produced the U.N. Decade for Women, 1975-1985.
2. Faludi (1991) observes that "trend journalism attains authority not through actual reporting but through the power of repetition. . . . A trend declared in one publication sets off a chain reaction, so the rest of the media scramble to get the story, too" (p. 79).
3. Soon after Faludi's book was published, backlash issues surfaced in many feminist scholarship circles, organizations, and publications. Since 1992, research papers, panels and roundtable discussions on backlash issues have been on the programs of the International Communication Association, the Association for Education in Journalism and Mass Communication, and the National Communication Association.
4. What became the "anti-rape movement," for instance, began as private talk that went public. For a well-developed discussion of the

way public talk contributes to egalitarianism in social process, see Fraser (1993).

5. These activities often involved the help of feminists working in media professions. For example, as a former newswriter and public relations practitioner, I have trained personnel in women's shelters and rape crisis centers to write press releases, hold press conferences, and give interviews. I also have advised victims and survivors of their rights as news sources and worked closely with reporters in their coverage of violence against women.

6. This suggests the importance of journalism education in introducing students to feminist ideas so that they can see the relationship between these ideas and the stories they cover. Journalism educators have a crucial role to play in assuring that reporters, in Benedict's (1992) words, are not afraid of feminism, feminist sources, or the issues that feminism has raised with regard to women's status and roles in society.

REFERENCES

Beasley, M. H., & Gibbons, S. J. (1993). *Taking their place: A documentary history of women and journalism.* Washington, DC: American University Press.

Benedict, H. (1992). *Virgin or vamp: How the press covers sex crimes.* New York: Oxford University Press.

Bridge, J. (1994). Arriving on the scene: Women's growing presence in the newsroom. In *Women, men and the media.* Washington, DC: Unabridged Communication.

Brownmiller, S. (1975). *Against our will: Men, women and rape.* New York: Simon & Schuster.

Brubaker, B. (1995, November 13). Violence follows some in football off field. *Washington Post,* pp. A1, A24.

Brubaker, B. (1995, November 13). NFL teams support Perry despite past. *Washington Post,* p. A24.

Brubaker, B. (1995, November 13). NCAA intensifying educational effort. *Washington Post,* p. A25.

Butler, M., & Paisley, W. (1978). Magazine coverage of women's rights. *Journal of Communication, 28*(1), 183-186.

Byerly, C. M. (1994, Spring). An agenda for teaching news coverage of rape. *Journalism Educator, 49*(1), 59-69.

Byerly, C.M. (1995). News, consciousness and social participation: The role of women's feature service in world news. In A. Valdivia (Ed.), *Feminism, multiculturalism and the media: Global diversities* (pp. 105-122). Thousand Oaks, CA: Sage.

Byerly, C.M., & Warren, C. A. (1996, March). At the margins of center: Organized protest in the newsroom. *Critical Studies in Mass Communication, 13*(1), 1-23.

Cancian, F. M., & Ross, B. L. (1981). Mass media and the women's movement: 1900-1977. *The Journal of Applied Behavioral Science, 17*(1), 9-26.

Ceulemans, M., & Fauconnier, G. (1979). *Mass media: The image, role and social conditions of women.* Paris: UNESCO.

Chief admits Navy moved too slowly on harassment. (1992, July 31). Associated Press story published in *Roanoke Times & World-News.*

Colon, A. (1994, July 24). Minorities in media seek unity at meeting. *Seattle Times,* p. B1.

Cuklanz, L. (1992, August). *Media coverage of the Webb-Dotson rape recanting case.* Paper presented at the Association for Education in Journalism and Mass Communication, Montreal, Canada.

Cuklanz, L. (1995). News coverage of ethnic and gender issues in the Big Dan's rape case. In A.Valdivia's (Ed.), *Feminism, multiculturalism and the media: Global diversities* (pp. 145-162). Thousand Oaks, CA: Sage.

Empowering Women in the Media: A Call to Action (Report). (1996, July). Washington DC: International Women's Media Foundation.

Entman, R. M. (1993, Autumn). Framing: Toward clarification of a fractured paradigm. *Journal of Communication, 43*(4), 51-58.

Faludi, S. (1991). *Backlash: The undeclared war against American women.* New York: Crown Books.

Fishman, M. (1990). *Manufacturing the news.* Austin: University of Texas Press.

Fraser, N. (1993). Rethinking public sphere: A contribution to the critique of actually existing democracy. In C. Calhoun (Ed.), *Habermas and the public sphere* (pp. 109-142). Cambridge, MA: MIT Press.

Gallagher, M. (1981). *Unequal opportunities: The case of women and the media.* Paris: UNESCO.

Gilligan, C. (1982). *In a different voice.* Cambridge, MA: Harvard University Press.

Gallagher, M. (1987). Introduction. In *Women and media decision-making* (pp. 11-16). Paris: UNESCO.

Gitlin, T. (1981). *The whole world is watching: Mass media in the making and unmaking of the new left.* Berkeley: University of California Press.

Hall, S. (1980). *Encoding/decoding.* In *culture, media, language.* London: Hutchinson.

Herman, E. S., & Chomsky, N. (1988). *Manufacturing consent: The political economy of the mass media.* New York: Pantheon Books.

Kielbowicz, R. B., & Scherer, C. (1986). The role of the press in the dynamics of social movements. *Research in Social Movements, Conflicts and Change, 9,* 71-96.

Lafky, S. A. (1993). The progress of women and people of color in the U.S. journalistic workforce: A long, slow journey. In P. Creedon (Ed.), *Women and mass communication* (2nd ed., pp. 87-103). Thousand Oaks, CA: Sage.

Lardner, G., Jr. (1996, June 2). The stalking game. *Washington Post,* p. C3.

Lardner, G., Jr. (1996, June 2). The law stops at the state line. *Washington Post,* p. C3.

Lardner, G., Jr. (1995). *The stalking of Kristen*. New York: Atlantic Monthly Press.

McQuail, D. (1983). *Mass communication theory: An introduction*. Beverly Hills: Sage.

Medea, A., & Thompson, K. (1974). *Against rape*. New York: Farrar, Straus & Giroux.

Meyers, M. (1992). Reporters and beats: The making of oppositional news. *Critical Studies in Mass Communication, 9,* 75-90.

Mills, K. (1988). *A place in the news*. New York: Dodd, Mead & Co.

Mitchell, J. (1992). Women: The longest revolution. In K.V. Hansen & I. J. Philipson (Eds.), *Women, class and the feminist imagination* (pp. 43-73). Philadelphia: Temple University Press.

Morley, D. (1985). Cultural transformations: The politics of resistance. In M. Gureritch & M. Levy (Eds.), *Mass communication review yearbook* (pp. 237-250). Beverly Hills, CA: Sage.

Quest: A Feminist Quarterly. (1976). Special issue on Communication and Control, *III*(2).

Rapping, E. (1994). *Media-tions: Forays into the culture and gender wars*. Boston: South End Press.

Russell, D. E. H. (1975). *The politics of rape*. New York: Stein & Day.

Russell, D. E. H. (1982). *Rape in marriage*. Bloomington: Indiana University Press.

Sanders, M., & Rock, M. (1988). *Waiting for prime time: The women of television news*. New York: Harper & Row.

Schorer, J. (1990). It couldn't happen to me [pullout composite of published stories on Nancy Ziegenmeyer case]. *Des Moines Register*.

Tuchman, G. (1978a). The symbolic annihilation of women by the mass media. In G. Tuchman, A. Daniels, & S. Benet (Eds.), *Hearth and home: Images of women in mass media*. (pp. 5-38) New York: Oxford University Press.

Tuchman, G. (1978b). *Making news: A study in the construction of reality*. New York: The Free Press.

Tuchman, G., Daniels, A., & Benet, S. (1978.) *Hearth and home: Images of women in mass media*. New York: Oxford University Press.

Window Dressing on the Set: Women and Minorities on Television. (1977). Washington DC: U.S. Civil Rights Commission.

Author Index

Subject Index

413